Presented by
the author.

THE GHOSTS
OF PEACE

THE GHOSTS
OF PEACE

1935 – 1945

Richard Lamb

Presented to Oratory School Library
by Richard Lamb Febuary 1992

MICHAEL RUSSELL

© Richard Lamb 1987

First published in Great Britain 1987
by Michael Russell (Publishing) Ltd,
The Chantry, Wilton, Salisbury, Wiltshire

Typeset by The Spartan Press Ltd, Lymington
Printed and bound in Great Britain
by Biddles Ltd, Guildford and King's Lynn

ISBN 0 85955 140 7

Contents

Acknowledgements

I am most grateful to the following who have been generous with their time in helping me with this book:

The Hon. David Astor; Professor Michael Balfour; Professor F. Bandini; Walter Bargatzky; Peter and Christabel Bielenberg; Michael Bloch; Andrea del Bosco; Tom Braun; Martin Brett; Axel van der Busch; Sir Hugh Carleton Greene; Avvocato Lucio Ceva; Sir John Colville; Charles Cruickshank; Sir William Deakin; Captain Henry Denham; Professor David Dilks; Nicholas Elliott; Gordon Etherington-Smith; Professor Frediani; Martin Gilbert; Lord Gladwyn; Professor Giulio Guderzo; His Royal Highness Archduke Otto von Hapsburg; Ludwig von Hammerstein; Sir Geoffrey Harrison; Professor Peter Hoffman; Dr Visser't Hooft; Otto John; Andrew King; Philip Knightley; Judith, Countess of Listowel; Brian MacDermot; Professor Denis Mack Smith; Sir Ivo Mallet; John McCaffery; Hon. Sir Con O'Neill; the Rt. Hon. David Owen, MP; the Duke of Portland; Robert Rhodes James, MP; Sir Frank Roberts; James Rusbridger; H. E. Sadler; Professor A. Santoni; Christopher Seton Watson; Lord Sherfield; the Rt. Hon. Lord Strauss; Sir Peter Tennant; Gina Thomas; Professor A. Varsori; Erich Vermehren; Air Commodore Freddie West; Brigadier Sir Edgar Williams; Sir Geoffrey Wilson.

I feel privileged to have had the help of survivors of the German conspiracy against Hitler – Clarita von Trott zu Solz; Peter and Christabel Bielenberg; Axel van der Busch; Walter Bargatzky; Ludwig von Hammerstein; Otto John; and Erich Vermehren. I thank Clarita von Trott and Christabel Bielenberg also for the loan of photographs and documents.

I am most grateful to Sir William Deakin, Christopher Seton Watson and Giulio Guderzo for reading parts of the manuscript on Italy, and to David Astor, Michael Balfour, the late Sir Hugh Carleton Greene and Gordon Etherington-Smith for reading parts on the German Resistance.

My thanks are due to Messrs Weidenfeld & Nicolson for permission to quote from *Maurice Bowra: Memories 1898-1939*; to Messrs Macmillan for permission to quote from Balfour and Frisby, *Helmuth von Moltke*; to Mrs McCaffery for the loan of her late husband's (John McCaffery, OBE) unpublished autobiography 'No Pipes or Drums' and for permission to quote from it.

I am indebted to the staff of the London Library; the Public Record Office, Kew; the Library of the University of Birmingham; Churchill College, Cambridge; the Hoover Institute; Institut fur Zeitgeschichte; St Antony's College, Oxford; the Nordic Ecumenical Institute, Sigtuna, Sweden; and to C. M. Woods of the Colonial and Foreign Office (for help over the SOE archives).

Transcripts of Crown Copyright material in the Public Record Office appear by kind permission of the Controller, Her Majesty's Stationery Office.

Finally I give warm thanks to Mrs Joan Moore and to John Mark for their secretarial help.

RICHARD LAMB

Introduction

This is the sad story of the collapse of the high hopes for permanent peace raised by the League of Nations, and by the unity of Britain, France and Italy up to 1935. Until then it seemed that working together they would have no difficulty in thwarting the designs of the German Nazi Government.

Postwar efforts at a definitive history of the Government's actions during the period were handicapped because prior to the replacement of the sixty-year rule by the thirty-year rule there was no access to key State papers, although some documents were published in the series *Documents on British Foreign Policy* and in the *Official History of British Foreign Policy in World War Two*. As A. J. P. Taylor wrote about the first volume of *DBFP*, the editing 'is shoddy, sycophantic in tone, no minutes introduced, and altogether a cover up for the Foreign Office'.

I was one of the generation of Oxford undergraduates who passed the Union motion that under no circumstances would they fight for King and Country; at the time I was bitterly opposed to the Hoare-Laval Pact and was one of my college organizers for the Peace Ballot. With hindsight I am convinced that the Hoare-Laval pact was good diplomacy and could have kept the two dictators apart.

During my youth I witnessed how from the accord at Stresa in 1935 Britain slid down the slippery slope to war in 1939 by driving Mussolini into the arms of Hitler, acquiescing in the remilitarization of the Rhineland, the Anschluss, the rape of Czechoslovakia, and the offer to Hitler of Danzig and the Polish Corridor.

The archives disclose it is a myth Eden resigned because he opposed Chamberlain's policy of appeasement of Hitler. In 1938 Eden was sacked by the Prime Minister because he was driving the Italian dictator into Hitler's camp, and Britain and France desperately needed Mussolini's aid if they were to stop Hitler. Britain only declared war on Germany in September 1939 because Chamberlain's hands were tied by his ill-considered guarantee to Poland the previous March. The Poles, not the British, called Hitler's bluff, and triggered off the war by refusing to send at the eleventh hour a plenipotentiary to Berlin to negotiate the immediate surrender of Danzig and the Polish Corridor to Hitler. Then Goering established contact with Downing Street and made strenuous efforts to preserve peace. Even after Hitler had invaded Poland, Chamberlain and the Foreign Secretary, Halifax, were anxious to make terms with Hitler provided the remainder of Poland was left intact; but the Commons overruled them.

Britain was close to peace during the Phoney War of 1939 and early 1940. War Cabinet minutes reveal that at the time of Dunkirk Halifax and Chamberlain wanted to ask for terms, and for one brief moment Churchill faltered.

After Dunkirk, with Churchill firmly in the saddle, there was no chance of a negotiated peace with Hitler; the Prime Minister issued the edict that there was to be 'absolute silence' and no parley through neutral countries even with well-known *bona fide* anti-Nazis. He was later equally rigid about 'unconditional surrender'. Thus Whitehall cold-shouldered those democratic Germans who had been on the brink of overthrowing Hitler in 1938 before Munich and who continued to risk their lives until nearly all of them were killed when the Stauffenberg bomb plot failed in July 1944.

The archives show that even in 1944, after Stauffenberg had exploded his bomb, Whitehall failed to recognize the nature of the conspiracy and would not consider offering any peace terms to anti-Nazi democrats. The hitherto unpublished Wheeler-Bennett memorandum to the Foreign Office advising that the Allies were 'better off with Hitler alive than dead' and that were no 'good' Germans may seem shocking. Unfortunately his view was accepted by Churchill, Eden and the Foreign Office.

In 1944 Whitehall refused to believe in the existence of a band of well-organized and influential anti-Nazis; instead it claimed the only serious opposition came from dissident German generals whose sole motivation was fear of losing the war in the field. Evidence of the conspirators' intention to assassinate Hitler and seize power was ignored by the Foreign Office. Anti-Nazi exiles in London and the United States were treated with scorn, and embassies in neutral countries were instructed that negotiations with any German resistance movement were taboo.

The Government's aim was to crush the German army in the field so that the myth of German invincibility could never be revived.

What is certain is that if the war had been brought to an end by negotiations with the 'good' Germans in 1944, vast numbers of lives would have been saved both in the Allied forces and among civilians in the German-occupied countries. The Allied Governments were by then well aware of the extermination of the Jews and the wholesale deportations of slave labour. A swift end to hostilities would have stopped it. The British Government's policy, however, was that it was better to continue the war than seek peace with 'good' Germans. As a result the Goerdeler-Beck-Stauffenberg conspirators failed to win over enough German generals in key posts to their side. If Britain and the USA had abandoned the unconditional surrender formula and promised reasonable treatment to a Germany rid of Hitler and the Nazis, the conspirators could probably have persuaded German generals in the field to abandon Hitler and the war would have ended in 1944.

Once the horrific slaughter was over it would have been up to the Russians, Americans, French and British to take joint measures to prevent Germany from ever rearming again without 'dismemberment', and we should have been able to profit from our mistakes of the twenties and thirties. I cannot accept that this would have been impossible.

It is widely held that Britain did not negotiate with the German Resistance because the Government believed if they did so Hitler and Stalin might make peace behind their backs. This argument is refuted by documents which show that Churchill was prepared to back an anti-Nazi movement in Austria or Hungary led by Otto Hapsburg. To the Russians a monarchist revival would presumably have been more distasteful than negotiations with the Beck-Goerdeler-Stauffenberg movement.

In 1941 Churchill was ready to go to great lengths to encourage the anti-Fascists in Italy to end the war – including bribing the Italian fleet to surrender, and offering a non-Fascist Italy a colony in Cyrenaica. Yet in 1943, when Italy was down and out, no gesture was made by the Allies to the anti-Fascists and monarchists plotting to overthrow Mussolini, and thus was missed a chance to occupy Italy with Allied forces before the Germans poured over the Brenner Pass. This extraordinary and illogical *volte-face* towards the Italian Resistance inside Italy was extremely costly.

This is the story of my own time. During the war I felt strongly that unconditional surrender and indiscriminate bombing were grave errors, but it was almost impossible for serving soldiers to protest effectively. The archives tell a tale both of missed opportunities of preventing the war and of bringing it to an earlier end. Readers may consider the evidence and judge for themselves.

I

Hitler, Stresa and Abyssinia
1935

Italy, France and Britain – victors of the First World War – met in unity for the last time in the spring of 1935 at Stresa in the Italian Alps. They were considering Hitler's threats to Austria, one of the two black clouds over Europe that in 1935 increasingly menaced the peace agreed at Versailles. The other was Mussolini's intention to attack Abyssinia; and it was because the British leaders completely underestimated the Abyssinian crisis that mistakes were made that drove Mussolini into the arms of Hitler. Within weeks Britain was sliding down the slope towards the Second World War.

Much of the so-called Abyssinian empire was not legally a state. In 1891 Anglo-Italian protocols had assigned almost all of this part of North-East Africa, apart from French and Italian Somaliland, to Italy. Immediately there was friction between the Italian Government and the Emperor of Abyssinia, Menelik. Fighting followed, and in the Battle of Adowa in 1896 the Italians were defeated, with the Abyssinians castrating and slaughtering their prisoners. At that time the recently united Italy was not in favour of acquiring colonies and in 1906 the French-Italian-British agreement gave the disputed area to Menelik, apart from coastal strips in Italian Eritrea and Somaliland. Menelik conquered and occupied all the tribal territories up to this thin coastal strip, but the frontiers were never properly drawn. The ruling Amharas were settled on the land at the expense of the existing inhabitants and each Amharic family was allotted one or more families of the departed tribe in servitude. If these escaped they were subject to barbarous penalties.

The total population of the area was between five and ten million, but the ruling Amharas under Menelik occupied less than one-third of the land – in the central nucleus surrounding the capital, Addis Ababa – and were less than one third of the total population. In 1935 around two thirds consisted of the conquered races, who differed from the Amharas in almost every respect.

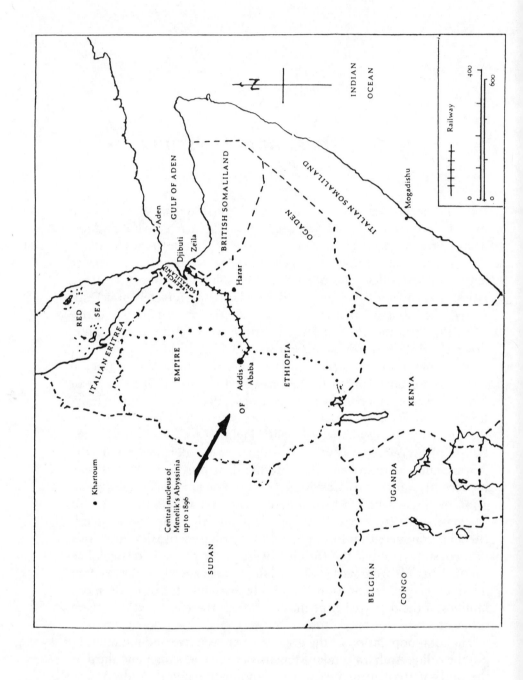

The Amharas were nominally Christian in religion and they all understood the same language. The conquered races were pagan or Moslem and spoke seventy languages. A feudal system existed throughout and the whole social-economic structure was dependent on slavery which was supported and practised by the Church, even in the capital. Abyssinia was not only a source of supply of slaves for the Arab market but also a trade route connecting the source of supply in the Sudan with the Red Sea. In the conquered territories during the forty years of Abyssinian rule from 1896 to 1936 there was severe depopulation owing to slave raiding, and as a result great areas of cultivated land reverted to scrub and forest.

There was scope for improved agriculture in many parts, especially on the cool and wet mountain sides which rise out of the parched deserts. Yet the system of farming had not changed for centuries and nothing was done to improve the farming methods. Under the feudal slavery and serf system foreigners were not allowed to own land or invest capital.

Abyssinia continuously attacked her neighbours over the ill-defined borders – not only Kenya and the Sudan, but Italian Eritrea and Italian Somaliland. To protect her colonies against Abyssinia, Italy needed to keep an army there.

In the international climate of the thirties Mussolini had a good case for claiming a mandate over the backward Abyssinian empire with its appalling record of slavery and economic neglect. In the secret London Treaty of 1915 Italy had been promised a share of German African colonies, and Italy as one of the victors of the First World War had a claim for colonies as an outlet for her increasing population of peasant cultivators. It was reasonable for her to assume that the European powers would agree to Abyssinia being the Italian sphere of influence in Africa, because Italy held Italian Somaliland and Eritrea, narrow strips of barren steeps on the perimeter north and south of the Abyssinian empire.

The dilemma was Abyssinia's full membership of the League of Nations. The majority view of enlightened people was that the peace of the world would be endangered if the League did not act automatically to prevent any infringement of the sovereignty of any member state. Here was a quicksand which had to be avoided by the French and British if they were to preserve the essential Italian cooperation against renewed German aggression which was sought at Stresa. Laval, the French Prime Minister, understood this, but the British Government faced the problem too late.

Abyssinia should never have been admitted to the League of Nations. France proposed her admission in 1923 in a move which Conservative Member of Parliament Christopher Hollis described as 'an outrage against any true principles upon which the League of Nations professed to be built'.[1] The Italians blundered and supported France. Mussolini and his Foreign Office calculated that the Abyssinian empire under Haile Selassie was in the process of disintegration and that it was merely a matter of time before the League of Nations would hand it over to Italy.

The British opposed Abyssinian admission on the grounds that she was not a state and in particular because the slavery and serf system breached Article 23 of the League of Nations Covenant which outlawed forced labour. Haile Selassie accordingly told the League he would stamp out the slave trade, but in his enormous country with non-existent communications he was impotent to do so. Eventually Britain agreed to Abyssinia's entry, but the best comment comes again from Hollis who says that Britain should have left the League 'sooner than assent to this chicanery'.

In April 1933 the German Parliament had committed suicide by passing an enabling Act which authorized the Cabinet to govern by decree. This gave Hitler absolute power; all political parties except the Nazis were suppressed; all important organizations were nazified, and there was complete control of the press and radio by Josef Goebbels. The next year the German President Hindenburg died and Hitler made himself 'Fuehrer and Reich Chancellor and supreme commander of the armed forces' – in short, the dictator he remained until his death.

The Nazis now began infiltrating into Austria and on 25 July 1934 they murdered Dollfuss, the Austrian Chancellor, in an attempted *coup d'état*. Mussolini was angry and alarmed. He had been very friendly with Dollfuss (whose wife was staying with him at the time of the murder),[a] and he immediately moved troops to the Italian frontier on the Brenner Pass, with the result that Hitler was obliged to stop his attempted Austrian revolution.

The Fuehrer was determined, however, to widen Germany's frontiers. He knew this would make him personally popular as it would give the German nation a sense of purpose and achievement

[a]Count Giusti, former Italian Ambassador to Japan, told the author that as a young diplomat on duty with Mussolini on the Adriatic it fell to him to break the news of the murder to the Duce and Dollfuss's widow. Mussolini was apparently furious with Hitler. At the time it seemed to Giusti impossible that anything like the Rome-Berlin axis could be established within a few years.

and put an end to the frustrations of Versailles. Within a few months of coming to power he had begun to build military aircraft and formed unofficial military organizations in defiance of the Treaty of Versailles. At that time Britain was in an acute pacifist phrase, the majority of the nation believing the League of Nations could keep peace, and ready for a drastic revision of the Treaty of Versailles in favour of Germany as long as British colonial interests did not suffer. Hitler cynically told the British Ambassador, Sir Eric Phipps, that his new SS and SA military formations might be compared with the British Salvation Army. For his part Phipps warned the Foreign Office in January 1935 that the new regime believed 'neither in the League nor in negotiations' and that Hitler wanted chunks of Poland, Czechoslovakia, and the return of her colonies.[2]

Sir Robert Vansittart, head of the Foreign Office, was sure that if Germany continued to rearm there would be no way of controlling her territorial ambitions without fighting. It was too late to re-create the successful military alliance which had defeated the Kaiser's Germany in 1918: the French and British armies were weak, and the Americans had no intention of sending another expeditionary force to Europe.

Yet even Vansittart thought that Hitler might agree to arms limitation if we could satisfy him over the colonial question, but he was always positive that Germany would before long break out to the east.

His warnings aroused no spark within the British Cabinet – national in name, with the Socialist Ramsay MacDonald as Prime Minister but with Baldwin, the Conservative ex-Prime Minister, really in control. Indeed there was a strong feeling in the Conservative Party and in the City of London that Germany would suffer an economic collapse. In the City gloomy prognostications were made that Germany might repudiate her trade debts.

On 4 March 1935 the Prime Minister signed a White Paper drawing attention to German rearmament, which might 'produce a situation where peace will be in peril'.[3] It announced the Government had abandoned all hope of international disarmament and intended itself to start rearming. The Opposition under Attlee jibbed on the grounds that British rearmament would imperil the Disarmament Conference and was contrary to the spirit of the League of Nations under whose Covenant we were pledged to preserve peace by collective security, not by piling up arms.

Following the White Paper, the British Cabinet proposed to send Sir John Simon, Foreign Secretary, and Anthony Eden, Lord Privy Seal, on a tour to Berlin, Moscow, Warsaw and Prague. Simon was to visit Berlin and Eden was to go on alone. Then, on 9 March, Goering disclosed the existence of a new German air force, and on 16 March Hitler decreed German conscription and an army of thirty-six divisions in peacetime. Both the French and Italians, with reason, claimed that the British trip to Berlin should be cancelled as a rebuke to Hitler, but the British Government refused and this temporarily soured relations between Britain and France and Italy.

Eden wanted to cancel the visit as a counter to Hitler's breach of the Treaty of Versailles, but he was not in the Cabinet and was overruled by Simon. Without waiting for the French or the Italians, Britain sent a stiff formal protest to Berlin but the effect was spoilt because it also asked if the German Government still wanted Simon and Eden to come. Hitler and von Neurath, German Foreign Minister, had already told Phipps that they did.

It was a grave diplomatic mistake not to draw up the British note in concert with the French and Italians, and the French press commented that the British were 'the dupes of Hitler'. Simon and Vansittart erroneously thought the note would 'not be unsatisfactory' to the French and Italian Governments, but were soon disillusioned by despatches from the British Ambassadors in Rome and Paris stating the French and Italian Governments were expressing themselves forcibly and interpreting the British note as dividing Britain from France and Italy. According to Phipps, Berlin took the note as evidence that France was unable to form a common front against Germany.[4]

The damage done by the note and the British failure to cancel the visit to Berlin marked the beginning of appeasement. The German nation received the announcement of conscription with evident satisfaction and Hitler's popularity increased sharply. Hitler told the British Ambassador he was introducing conscription because France had increased the length of compulsory service to two years and because of the reference to Germany in the British White Paper. He must have parity with France on land, sea and air.[5]

With the Simon and Eden visit to Hitler so close, neither the French nor the Italians could take a really strong line without destroying the common front. In Rome the British Ambassador, Sir Eric Drummond, was so alarmed at the damage done to Anglo-French and Anglo-Italian relations that on 20 March he proposed a three-power meeting in North Italy with Mussolini as host in order to undo the damage and re-create the common front which Mussolini had just told him 'no longer existed'. This was accepted by

Simon on 22 March, and thus it was agreed with France and Italy that the Stresa conference should take place in April.

Meanwhile Simon, in Berlin with Hitler, raised futile legal arguments about colonies and the Covenant of the League of Nations which Hitler probably did not even take in. Eden noted in his diary: 'Results bad . . . Prussian spirit very much in evidence.' Eden was closer to the ball than Simon, writing en route for Moscow a despatch to the Cabinet that there was no basis for agreement with Germany in view of her demands on land and sea.[6] Phipps, too, warned from Berlin of the German delight at the breaking up of the common front against them, and on 22 March reported that Hitler looked on Czechoslovakia as 'a regrettable smudge on the map of Europe' and that the German minorities must be restored to the Reich when Austria joins Germany. Vansittart commented: 'This is everybody's secret.'[7]

Both Mussolini and the French were realistic about Germany and wanted at Stresa to re-create a united front and convince Hitler that the Locarno pact, which guaranteed the Versailles frontiers, still stood. France, Britain and Italy would not only stand firm against German aggression in Austria, but would try to persuade all the European powers in the League to fight if necessary against Hitler if he attacked any member state of the League.[8]

Eden was not well enough to go to Stresa after a bad air journey from Prague, so he is absolved of responsibility for this diplomatic disaster. In his absence Ramsay MacDonald offered to accompany Simon, and insisted – against protocol – that Vansittart went also. Normally the permanent head of the Foreign Office is never abroad at the same time as the Foreign Secretary.

The Foreign Office brief for Stresa stressed the main issues were the risk of a German violation of the demilitarized zone in the Rhineland; the German threat to Austria; German plans for expansion in the east together with German rearmament; the proposal for an air pact; Germany's return to the League.

Eden noted in his memoirs that before Stresa he was much worried about Italy's intentions in Abyssinia and felt sure the 'mounting dangers' must be discussed at Stresa, and that from his bed he told the Prime Minister and Simon so. If this is so, Eden's warning fell on deaf ears although in his autobiography he wrote: 'Both agreed that Mussolini must be confronted on this subject.' Mussolini brought his Abyssinian experts to Stresa but the subject was never raised by the heads of state.

On 7 January 1935 France and Italy had made an agreement over ratifications of the French-Italian frontier in Somaliland, and at the same time Laval[b] gave Mussolini a secret understanding that France would condone Italian aggression in Abyssinia. At Stresa, therefore, the Duce knew Laval was on his side; just as he also knew Britain felt that Abyssinia should never have been admitted to the League. Britain had not taken sanctions against Japan because of her attack on Manchuria four years before; and Britain's attitude had been for fifty years that the sooner Italy took over Abyssinia, the better. Further, the British Foreign Secretary and his wife were not only heads of the well-publicized British pressure group against slavery, but also consistently cited Abyssinia as the worst offender. Can one therefore blame Mussolini for believing that when Abyssinia was not placed on the Stresa agenda he was being given the green light to go ahead with his colonial plans?

Yet in a few weeks this firm Italian-French-British front against Hitler was destroyed by British opposition to Italian expansion in Abyssinia. The main responsibility lies with Simon, who knew at Stresa all about the Italian preparations for a coup in Abyssinia and the desperate Foreign Office negotiations to solve the dispute without breaching the Covenant of the League of Nations. It was foolish to ignore the problem when face to face with the Duce. At Stresa Simon and MacDonald, who was past his best, threw away the chance of stopping Hitler before he had gathered military strength.

The Abyssinian crisis had first erupted in December 1934 with the Walwal incident when Italian troops fought Haile Selassie's troops for the possession of wells on the undefined border between Italian Somaliland and Ethiopia. Mussolini had begun to fear that the British and French would appease Hitler by offering Germany colonies in Africa, and that Abyssinia as the only independent state left in Africa would be a strong candidate to satisfy German claims. He wanted to get in first and secure the Ethiopian part of Abyssinia as a colony for Fascist Italy. Abyssinia was landlocked and had no exit to the sea except through Italian Somaliland, and it was obvious the best prospects for her economic expansion lay in an Italian mandate for colonization. Mussolini was very conscious both of the mandate in Egypt which the British held, and of the French mandate in Morocco. He felt that Italy as a victor should have been given a similar mandate under the Treaty of Versailles. There was sympathy with his viewpoint

---

[b]Laval was then French Foreign Minister. He became Prime Minister on 4 July 1935.

in the British Foreign Office and after the Walwal incident they urged a solution which would not involve a complaint by Abyssinia to the League. The Emperor was even persuaded by Sir Sydney Barton, the British Ambassador, to pay compensation to Italy.

Before Stresa Simon was well aware of the Abyssinian problem. He had signalled to Drummond, on 16 January 1935:

We must make last attempt to prevent matter going before the Council of the League. The Italian attitude as you forecast it may provoke a lamentable crisis at Geneva in which the blame would not be put on Ethiopia . . . This appears to be the last contribution that we can make to assist in bringing about the amicable settlement which Italy desires; and if Signor Mussolini rejects it there will be nothing further that I personally, or this country individually, can do to avert a crisis which may be disastrous for the League.[10]

Geoffrey Thompson, the Foreign Office expert on Abyssinia, has recalled that Simon said to him at Geneva in January 1935: 'You realize, don't you, that the Italians intend to take Abyssinia.' This makes Simon's conduct at Stresa surprising. Thompson wrote a Foreign Office minute on 27 March stating that the Italian Foreign Office had let it be known that they considered Stresa an opportunity for informal talks [on Abyssinia] 'between Italian, French and British statesmen which should not be missed'.[11]

Mussolini brought his Abyssinian experts Signori Vitetti and Guareschelli to Stresa. Simon brought Thompson. These officials talked, but the British Prime Minister and Foreign Secretary ignored the problem in the conversations with Mussolini, who not unreasonably concluded the silence of the British delegates at Stresa gave him a free hand in Abyssinia.

At Stresa the heads of state discussed the European situation, and particularly German rearmament and the threat by Germany to Austria. They set up what became known as the Stresa Front against German expansion. Mussolini was delighted: he was frightened of Hitler's intentions in Austria and he did not dare to attempt aggression in Africa without security against Germany to his north. At that time Germany was stirring up trouble in Abyssinia and supplying arms to the Emperor.

Thompson had three cordial talks with Guareschelli and Vitetti. Guareschelli told Thompson that the Duce regarded a settlement of the Abyssinian question as urgent, and that he did not consider it could be settled by the Conciliation Committee of the League as Britain wanted. Abyssinia, according to the Italians, was a fourteenth-century state with a continuing tradition of slavery and cruelty. She failed to develop her resources and Italy was denied the opportunity for constructive work in her colonies because they consisted only of arid stretches of coastline.[12]

Thompson warned the Italians of the dangers of a 'forward' military policy in Abyssinia, the consequences of which would be impossible to foresee. The Italians countered by expanding on Italy's need for more colonies – especially as Germany now wanted overseas possessions in Africa. Thompson evaded this point, but when Guareschelli suggested that Britain should aid Italy in her Abyssinian adventure he told the Italians it was useless to expect it. He had no authority to warn the Italians that Britain would treat an attack on Ethopia as a breach of the Covenant of the League of Nations, with its attendant dire consequences, but he was left in no doubt that the Duce would take a great deal of satisfying. All that was agreed was that the Italians and French would exchange views in Geneva with Jese, the French legal adviser to the Emperor.[13]

Thompson's talks with the Italian diplomats took place on 12, 13 and 14 April. He wrote four long memoranda in his hotel bedroom and handed them to Vansittart. Thompson was deeply concerned at the danger of an Italian attack on Ethiopia with the resultant menace to the League and collective security. So he was very pleased when he got an invitation to breakfast with Simon on 14 April to discuss the problem. For five minutes they discussed Thompson's papers; then the Foreign Secretary's private secretary came in and interrupted the tête-à-tête. Simon did not refer to Abyssinia again, and immediately after breakfast said it was time to go to the island on the lake for the main conference. Thompson described it as 'a sad anti-climax'.[14] It was surely stupidity to let Mussolini leave Stresa without discussing Abyssinia personally with him, and Simon's conduct then was a major cause of the Second World War. Thompson thought that if Eden had been well enough to go he would have insisted on raising the Abyssinian problem.

MacDonald held a press conference at the end of the Stresa talks and said Locarno was reaffirmed and the policies of the three countries aligned. He said nothing about Abyssinia. When Alexander Werth of the Manchester Guardian asked whether Abyssinia had been discussed, the Prime Minister replied: 'My friend, your question is irrelevant.'[15] This was widely reported, and Mussolini thought it another nod to go ahead.

To the world it seemed that a united front against Hitler had been formed at Stresa. Simon and Laval went on from Stresa to Geneva; on the way Simon was applauded at the opera in Milan. It would not be long, however, before Mussolini realized that he had been misled and the Italian press became violently anti-British. Yet, as Phipps wrote to Sir Maurice Hankey, the Secretary to the Cabinet: 'How could MacDonald, Simon and Vansittart have gaily omitted even to mention Abyssinia? . . . all the Ethiopian imbroglio sprang from that hideous error . . . Naturally Mussolini thought he could go safely ahead despite what Drummond and Grandi may have told him.'[16]

On 21 May Drummond had an alarming talk in Rome with the Duce. Mussolini told him he did not want to damage the League, but if it became hostile and supported Abyssinia against Italy, he would leave. On his own responsibility Drummond tried to find out if the Duce would be satisfied with an Italian mandate for Abyssinia such as Britain had in Egypt. The Duce replied that Abyssinia might come under Italian influence as Morocco was under French and Egypt under British influence. He cited Egypt as a country with a king who was more or less independent, but who would not be allowed to do anything to endanger the Suez Canal or other British vital interests while Britain had there a High Commissioner, the head of the Army, the Chief of Police, and various advisers. Vansittart on 22 May minuted on Drummond's report:

There is one ray of hope in this; the analogy of Egypt with her 'King and political independence'. We ought to bear this in mind and explore it further. It is probably the least that the League (and the peace of Europe) will get away with. We ought to think of this seriously and in advance.

Simon initialled this minute, but did not comment.[17]

By a mandate putting Abyssinia under Italian control lay the best chance of both satisfying Mussolini and preserving the ever so much more important Stresa Front. On this point, however, Vansittart quickly changed his mind, and a defeatist minute by him dated 12 June said:

I also at one time had played with the idea of the Egyptian analogy. I have now abandoned it. If therefore we cannot satisfy Italy at Abyssinia's expense we are as before confronted with the choice of satisfying her at our own (plus some eventual Abyssinian frontier rectification) or letting things drift on their present disastrous course.

On 8 June Vansittart had minuted for the Foreign Secretary:

Italy will have to be bought off – let us use and face ugly words – in some form or other, or Abyssinia will eventually perish. That might in itself matter less if it did not mean that the League would also perish (and that Italy would simultaneously perform *another volte face* into the arms of Germany) . . . we cannot trade Abyssinia. The price that would now satisfy Italy would be too high for Abyssinia even to contemplate . . . either there has got to be a disastrous explosion that will wreck the League and very possibly His Majesty's Government, or else *we* have got to pay the price with British Somaliland. Personally I opt unhesitatingly for the latter . . . We are grossly overlanded (and British Somaliland is a real debit).[18]

Vansittart's realistic suggestion might have appealed to Mussolini and nipped the crisis in the bud. However, the British Government would not have it, and Eden did not agree with Vansittart about appeasing Mussolini. Owen O'Malley, of the Italian Department, in a minute on 3 June, wrote: 'We must stick to League principles and stand the racket and the sooner that this is made plain beyond all possibility of doubt to Signor Mussolini, the better.'[19] Eden commented on the O'Malley minute: 'I agree.' Unlike Vansittart, he was ready to let Britain and Italy set out on a collision course.

On 7 June – much to the disappointment of Eden, who nearly got the post – Samuel Hoare replaced Simon as Foreign Secretary. Eden was elevated to the Cabinet with Special Responsibility for League affairs. Hoare was to be a short stay tenant. Eden commented on Simon's shortcomings: 'He found it difficult to devise and hold on to a policy . . . too penetrating a discernment and too frail a conviction encouraged confusion where there should have been a fixed intent.'

He was also uncomplimentary about Hoare. Privately he called Hoare 'Aunt Tabitha'.[20]

Hoare spent the first few days in his new office largely in consultation with Vansittart and Eden on the Italian problem, and he endorsed in principle giving Mussolini part of British Somaliland.

Ronald Campbell[c] wrote a minute on 12 June suggesting that Mussolini's colonial ambitions might be satisfied by 'an international conference' which would redistribute colonies as part of 'a readjustment of the colonial and mandatory settlements' after the 1914–18 war. Vansittart commented the next day: 'I don't think we can follow this. In any case it would be too indefinite to produce any effect on Signor Mussolini.'[21] Here was a possible escape route, but instead Hoare, Eden and Vansittart decided to pacify Mussolini by offering

[c]Sir Ronald Ian Campbell, Bt, later Ambassador to Egypt – not to be confused with Sir Ronald Hugh Campbell, Ambassador in Paris and Lisbon.

Abyssinia a port and British territory in Somaliland if Haile Selassie in return would concede sovereignty over part of his empire to Italy.

When Vansittart briefed Hoare for the Cabinet meeting on 19 June 1935, he told him Italy might take military action against Abyssinia at the end of July, at which point there would be such an outbreak of criticism that Italy 'will leave the League and thereby throw herself into the arms of Germany . . . The League and the Stresa front will thereby both be simultaneously broken and all our past policy shattered, and our national future will be in clear danger!' He went on to suggest giving Mussolini 'definite and concrete inducement. Therefore we should cede Zeila [in British Somaliland] to Abyssinia and in return ask her to cede territory in the Ogaden to Mussolini.'

This was approved by the Cabinet after Hoare cabled Drummond in Rome to ask him if, in his opinion, Mussolini would be pacified by ceding the port of Zeila to Abyssinia together with a corridor leading to it, and in return Abyssinia should cede territory in the Ogaden to Italy. Hoare added that this might pave the way for economic concessions by Abyssinia in favour of Italy. Drummond wired back: 'The proposition is assuredly worth trying.' The Cabinet authorized Eden to go to Rome to see Mussolini with the suggestion. Drummond was wrong. Hoare's signal to Drummond with details of the proposal had been leaked to Mussolini by the doorman at the British Embassy. The Duce was contemptuous of the Zeila offer and immediately said so to his Foreign Secretary, Suvich.

Drummond saw Suvich on 19 June. Just before midnight he signalled Hoare that he feared the cession of Zeila would seem to Mussolini like 'the strengthening of Abyssinia and may render acceptance difficult'. This time he was right and Suvich had warned him correctly of the Duce's reaction to the latest leaked British signal.[22]

The Ogaden suggestion was dead before Eden left London. He saw Mussolini at the Palazzo Chigi in Rome on the morning of 24 June. The visit was a disaster; from then on Eden was an implacable opponent of Italy. Professor Frediani was working at the Italian Foreign Office at the time and told the author that within minutes of the end of the interview news ran round the Palazzo like wildfire that Mussolini and Eden had quarrelled bitterly ('hanno litigato in mode spaventoso'). The same rumour was current in all the Rome seminaries and embassies. Yet Eden always denied that he had taken offence,[23] though in a signal to the Foreign Secretary he wrote that 'there was a gloomy fatality about his temper which I fear may be beyond the power of reasoning to modify'.

In his autobiography Eden recorded that at the following luncheon, Mussolini made an imperious gesture and marched in alone as soon as the meal was announced, while Eden hung back, to let the ladies go first. The next day there was an official lunch arranged for Eden. Mussolini absented himself, and when Eden with the Ambassador went to Ostia in the afternoon they saw him dashing over the waves in a speedboat standing in the stern with his chin thrust out.

According to the Italian diplomatic historian Mario Toscano[24] Eden became in Italy after this visit 'the symbol of blind opposition to Italy's legitimate right to win her place in the sun' in Africa, and the Italian public thought of him as Enemy Number One. Toscano wrote: 'The dictator was said to have used violent language.' According to Samuel Hoare, 'He [Mussolini] and Eden did not conceal the extent of the differences that separated them or the personal dislike that they felt for each other'.[25]

Camillo Pellizi, Professor of Italian at London University, a strong supporter of Mussolini, told Tower, the diplomatic correspondent of the *Manchester Guardian*, that he had heard on good authority from Rome that at the luncheon on 24 June Mussolini had maintained 'a glum silence' while sitting next to Eden, and that the general view inside the Italian Foreign Office was that Eden felt personally insulted and had since adopted an almost vindictive attitude to Italy. Tower told the Foreign Office of Pellizi's comments and Eden minuted:

Pure balderdash. There was nothing in my reception at which I could have been offended even if I were an Italian and therefore susceptible to such feelings at the dinner table. Mussolini was definitely cordial throughout – our final interview was, of course, gloomy – it had to be – but sad rather than bad and there was no personal feeling whatever.

Eden's reference to not being an Italian is strange and strengthens the author's conviction that he took offence, feeling that Mussolini had humiliated him.[26]

The Italian diplomat Guariglia wrote: 'Mussolini managed to keep his calm in face of this show of British obtuseness, impudence or absolute disdain of Italian policy and people, Fascist or non Fascist, of whose intelligence the British took no account.' He told Mussolini that evening he could not conceal his indignation over a gesture which was in effect almost offensive to Italy.[27]

Mussolini had rejected out of hand the Zeila proposal, much to Eden's annoyance. He said it would shift most Abyssinian trade towards Zeila, taking away from the Italians in Eritrea and

Somaliland an important commercial resource. He then pointed out to Eden that although he foresaw a crisis both with the League of Nations and with Britain he was determined to go ahead with the annexation of Ethiopia. Either there would be a peaceful solution with outright cession of the territories surrounding Abyssinia to Italy, plus Italian control over Addis Ababa and the central nucleus, or a war which 'would wipe Ethiopia off the map'. Clearly Mussolini had in mind the parallel of the British mandate in Egypt. Eden replied that 'the difficulty of the situation was Abyssinia being, through no fault of England's, a member of the League of Nations'.

When the Duce told Eden that Laval had promised him a free hand in his adventure, the row started. Eden interjected that Laval had only said France gave Italy a free hand in economic matters. At this 'Mussolini flung himself back in the chair with a gesture of incredulous astonishment'.[28]

Eden saw the Duce again at 5 p.m. on 25 June at the Palazzo Venezia and Mussolini showed him on a map the parts of Abyssinia where he insisted on direct dominion and where he would allow the Negus nominal sovereignty subject to Italian control. Eden did not even return to the Zeila proposal. According to Guariglia he 'received another cold douche'. The next day Guariglia told Eden that Abyssinia looked on Britain as a protectress.[29]

Eden returned to London fully aware that his visit had been a failure. Nothing but control over Abyssinia either by surrender of sovereignty or an Italian mandate would satisfy Mussolini, and France would not back Britain in encouraging Abyssinia to resist. Eden also knew that the Maffey Report,[d] circulated by the Foreign Office on June 18 and showing Britain had negligible interests in Abyssinia, had been leaked to the Duce.[30] He made a statement in the House of Commons on 1 July, describing his offer to Mussolini and its rejection. The occasion was a humiliation for Eden which intensified his dislike of Italy. His Parliamentary statement aroused strong opposition at home: Anglo-Italian tension increased and British press comment was vociferous against the Government – mainly because the Zeila offer looked like pandering to a potential aggressor and ignoring the Covenant of the League of Nations.

With the Eden debacle in Rome the British Government were in a quandary. They had little option but to support the League of Nations

---

[d]This report by Sir John Maffey, commissioned on 6 March 1935 following the secret Laval-Mussolini understanding on 7 January, stated: 'No vital British interest is concerned in Ethiopia except the head waters in Lake Tana and the Nile Basin.'

if Mussolini were declared an aggressor by the Council, however essential Italian cooperation was for the Stresa anti-German front. British supporters of the League had held the Peace Ballot in early 1935 when public opinion had been aroused by the Italian threat to Abyssinia. The result was announced by Lord Cecil[e] at the end of June. Ten million people declared they were in favour of economic sanctions and, if necessary, military measures against any nation which attacked another.

In Britain supporters of the League argued with passion and sincerity. The League of Nations Union, headed by Cecil and Professor Gilbert Murray and one million strong, proclaimed the inviolability of the Covenant under which all the member states of the League were committed to take economic sanctions against Italy if she attacked Abyssinia. As a result of the Union's astute organization, every MP's postbag contained many letters from constituents urging sanctions backed by nearly all the Labour and Liberal MPs including Lloyd George, and by the *Daily Herald*, *Manchester Guardian* and the *Daily News*.

The anti-sanctions lobby was predominantly Right-wing. Most of the Conservative MPs were lukewarm about the League. They were backed by Oswald Mosley and General Fuller, the Fascist military historian, though Austen Chamberlain and Winston Churchill were prominent Tory supporters of the League. Mussolini's point of view was emphasized in the monthly *English Review* which carried a regular article by Sir Charles Petrie, and raucously by Lady Houston's *Saturday Review*. The *Daily Mail*, the *Morning Post* and the *Daily Telegraph* were pro-Mussolini.[31]

Stanley Baldwin, who had succeeded MacDonald as Prime Minister, was cautious. Sensitive to public opinion, he had been shocked by the massive pro-League verdict of the Peace Ballot. Hoare and Eden searched for a compromise solution. While during the summer Italian and English diplomats had been trying to resolve the dispute within the framework of the League, the Italians claimed that this would not be difficult provided the Abyssinians knew they would get no help from Britain and France. Vansittart, still pro-Italian and strongly anti-German, had little faith in the League as a peace-keeping force. He was only enthusiastic for sanctions if they could be a dress rehearsal for similar action against Germany in the event of her violating neighbouring frontiers, but he was realistic enough to know

[e]Viscount Cecil of Chelwood was President of the League of Nations Union. He had sat (as Lord Robert Cecil) as an MP 1906–23.

collective resistance by the smaller European states against a militarily strong Nazi Germany was unlikely. He backed every effort to find a compromise solution which would satisfy both Mussolini's ambitions and the dignity of the League. Uppermost in his thoughts was always the danger to Europe from Hitler once the Stresa front was broken.

Laval dominated French foreign policy and was pro-Mussolini. He was an unsatisfactory ally for Britain; almost certainly he received subsidies from the Duce, as did various French national newspapers. He had to tread softly because, as in Britain, a considerable body of French opinion looked on the League of Nations as its best bulwark against German aggression. Laval had been told by Mussolini that he was determined to invade Abyssinia unless his demands for a mandate were met, and Laval was ready to help him in every way. He was in constant close personal touch with the Duce.

In July and August the situation became more and more tense. Italy sent an army of 800,000 to Italian Somaliland and Eritrea on the Abyssinian borders, and the Duce made no secret of his intention to invade. Britain and France were unable to agree on any offer which would satisfy him, and on 22 August Hoare told the Cabinet that there would be a 'wave of public opinion against the Government if we failed to stand by the League and take sanctions against Italy in the event of an invasion'. Reluctantly Baldwin and the Cabinet agreed, with the reservation that 'we must keep in step with the French' and avoid 'trying to force nations to go further than they wished'.[32] Armed with this cautious mandate, Hoare and Eden went to Geneva for the meeting of the League at the beginning of September 1935.

Hoare's much-publicized speech to the Council on that occasion was surprisingly firm and out of keeping with his attitude both before and after. The speech was accompanied by a temporary concentration of the British Fleet at Gibraltar and according to the Vansittart-Hoare correspondence they wanted to 'take every possible precaution to prevent the possibility of a mad dog act giving the Italians any advantage'. Hoare promised that Britain would back the League in 'steady and collective resistance to all acts of unprovoked aggression'. The speech had a dramatic effect on world opinion and was generally interpreted to imply that the British Government had decided to stop Mussolini even if it meant war. The League of Nations lobby in the United Kingdom was delighted, as were the smaller European states. The British Cabinet, however, had neither the intention nor the resolution to carry out such a threat.

Hoare's speech had been drafted by Vansittart. Hoare stated in his memoirs that he had not intended his speech to be such forthright support for League of Nations action. He had also to try to force Laval to choose for or against Italy. Laval was firmly on Mussolini's side; he only gave lip service to the ideals of the League.[33]

On 19 September Laval told Baron Aloisi, the head of the Italian delegation at Geneva, that there was no question of Britain closing the Suez Canal or of taking military sanctions. On 23 September Hoare confirmed this by sending a personal message to Mussolini that there had been 'no discussion of closing the Suez Canal or military sanctions'.[34]

At the League the Committee of Five had been set up to try and work out a compromise solution. It had made slow progress, mainly because the Rumanian Titulescu and the Russian Litvinov opposed any large cession of Abyssinian territory, without which there was no chance of placating Mussolini. Still, by the middle of September its efforts to satisfy Mussolini were near to success. The Committee reported on 18 September and recommended a comprehensive system of League supervision and control of Abyssinian territories. This could well in the event have approximated to an Italian mandate, because privately it was communicated to Mussolini that Italy would have the lion's share of control. Abyssinia was prepared to accept, and the Italian diplomats were conciliatory. There is evidence that Mussolini nearly agreed.

The report included the words: 'The representatives of France . . . and Britain are prepared to recognize a special Italian interest in the economic development of Ethiopia. Consequently these Governments will look with favour on the conclusion of economic agreements between Italy and Ethiopia.' Laval was prepared to go far further, but Titelescu and Litvinov made this impossible.[35]

Aloisi, in despatches on 18 and 19 September, implored his Government to accept the proposals of the Committee of Five. He pointed out that Britain would never agree to any solution which did not provide for the continuation of the Abyssinian empire in name and the great advantage of the present proposals was that they could be revised in five years, when Italy could make another 'leap forward' as the French had done with their Protectorate of Morocco after the Treaty of Algeciras in 1906. Aloisi also cited the advantages of reconciliation with the rest of the League in 'the deplorable circumstances of an Anschluss between Germany and Austria'. He held a meeting of all his delegation and the Italian politicians in Geneva, who unanimously supported his entreaties to Mussolini to agree to the

Committee of Five's solution 'in principle'. Aloisi also pointed out in his despatches that once Italy had accepted in principle, pressure could be put on Britain and the other powers to allow a working Italian majority on the League institutions who would in future administer Abyssinia.

Baron Astuto, a member of the Italian delegation at Geneva, telephoned to the Foreign Office in Rome and spoke to an official who was a dedicated Fascist. He tried to persuade him of the advantages of Italy's accepting the Committee of Five's proposal. The official replied: 'Yes, the frame is excellent, but there is no picture of the man inside' – which meant Mussolini would not get enough personal glamour. To this Astuto responded: 'We are in Geneva to look after the interests of Italy, not to make collections of family pictures.' He was sacked for this remark. Aloisi was also out of favour and in his own words 'driven out of the service' as soon as the Ethiopian problem was not on the agenda at Geneva.[36]

In Rome Mussolini hesitated. Then he ordered Aloisi to refuse to continue negotiations with other countries for an amicable settlement. Probably a powerful factor in making him do so was a premature disclosure in a London newspaper which suggested he would never accept the Committee of Five's proposals. Instead on 3 October he started a war against Abyssinia. Addis Ababa was bombed and 100,000 Italian troops attacked over the frontier from Italian Eritrea and Somaliland.

This was a mad dog act by Mussolini. As Aloisi had told him, he could have secured the essential parts of his colonial ambitions by diplomacy at the League. The whole world was shocked. Since 1918 Europe had been living in the hope that major wars were a thing of the past; civilized nations had outlawed armed conflict for ever by the creation of the League. Mussolini was reviled as a threat to the hard-won peace which followed the 1914–18 fighting. Outside Italy he was looked on as an ogre and from then on there was a feeling that he could never be trusted.

The League of Nations assembled on 5 October, and on 9 October agreed, with Hungary and Austria abstaining (because of their special position *vis-à-vis* Italy), to apply sanctions against Italy. Hitler was delighted. However, it was agreed at Geneva that negotiations with Mussolini should proceed in the hope that an agreed settlement would make sanctions unnecessary.

Mussolini's attack on Abyssinia gives ground for feeling that it might have been impossible ever to satisfy him. But such was the British military weakness that no policy other than luring Mussolini back into the anti-Hitler camp was feasible. Chamberlain in his private minutes often referred to Mussolini as 'the lesser devil' but it was clear after 1 October 1935 that there were two mad dogs in Europe and the outlook for peace was grave only a few months after the Stresa accord had seemed so promising.

Mussolini felt that he must give the Italian people a military triumph in return for their economic sacrifices to pay for rearmament, and he wanted the glory of a successful war to popularize the Fascist regime. He knew that Britain would not risk a war with Italy without firm promises of French support, and Laval had made it plain to the Duce these would not be forthcoming. He knew, too, that the war was popular with the majority of the Italian people on the grounds that Britain and France with valuable African colonies were denying the Italians their same right to an African empire. When the Italian armies took Adowa, they were avenging their humiliating defeat there in 1896. The Italian nation was overjoyed.

Laval met Eden in Paris on 1 October and said he favoured a League mandate given to Italy for all the non-Amharic portions of Abyssinia, and League assistance for Abyssinia proper with Italian participation. Laval wanted this proposal put forward as an Anglo-French proposal. Eden responded that it would be 'scarcely possible' to put this forward as we would be rewarding an aggressor. Laval replied that it went no further than the Committee of Five proposals amended and approved by Britain at Geneva on 16 August. Here the Frenchman was not far wrong, and now the Duce had softened his terms slightly.

During the conversation Eden told Laval he was most disturbed at the hostile attitude of the French press to Britain, and that in Britain there was 'grave anxiety about the French attitude', although it was found hard to believe 'the French would not stand shoulder to shoulder with us'. Laval's reply was that France must not be judged by the press: 'French opinion was much divided.' However, he promised tendentiously to seek to get a mandate for economic sanctions in spite of both a divided Cabinet and a divided French public.

On 24 September Hoare had asked Corbin, the French Ambassador in London, whether Britain could count on military support from France if Italy attacked after sanctions started. Corbin did not deliver the reply until 8 October, and it was that Laval would need 'consultation et accord' before rendering assistance. Vansittart minuted that it was not an honest reply and that Laval wanted 'a loophole for French inaction if we got into trouble'. On 7 October Flandin, the former Prime Minister and a member of Laval's Cabinet, but no friend of Laval, had told Hugh Lloyd Thomas, the British Minister in Paris, that the average Frenchman had no faith in the League and that no French Government would risk war to carry out obligations under the Covenant. Vansittart minuted: 'This is an exceedingly grave statement coming from the late French Prime Minister . . . he is probably speaking the truth.'[37]

Even more grave was a request by Laval to reduce the British concentration of the Fleet in the Mediterranean because Italy could allege it was unjustified: Laval said he reserved his right not to come to the help of Britain if Mussolini attempted a mad dog attack on her, although he would honour his obligation once British forces were normal, thus denying the Duce 'his specious plea that our ships constituted a menace to Italy'.

Hoare reported this to the Cabinet on 16 October, adding that the French Admiralty had refused to discuss cooperation with the British naval attaché in Paris. The Cabinet, apart from Eden, was already lukewarm about sanctions. Now it was clear to them that Britain would have to take the lead over sanctions at Geneva without any proper backing from France, her most powerful ally. Worse still, there was now doubt whether France would come to Britain's aid if she were attacked by Mussolini.[38]

At this Cabinet Hoare and other members claimed that Eden was 'giving the impression' at Geneva that he was making all the proposals for sanctions and the French were constantly wrangling with us. Accordingly the Cabinet authorized Hoare to send a message to Eden in Geneva that the Cabinet were extremely worried by Laval, and 'ask you to go as slow as possible'.[39]

Hoare was also authorized to tell Laval that had Britain felt confident of French naval cooperation and the use of French ports in the event of Italian aggression, she would have sent fewer reinforcements to the Mediterranean. The Cabinet recorded that if Italy attacked Britain in the Mediterranean France might refuse cooperation on the grounds that the British Fleet had been 'provocative'. They decided that until the French situation was cleared up not to apply new sanctions.[f]

Yet this same meeting of the Cabinet approved a General Election to be held on 19 November with dissolution on 19 October. The only honest course for Baldwin would have been to tell the nation that our sanctions policy was subject to French support – just the type of

---

[f]Hoare also reminded the French Prime Minister that he (Laval) had agreed to the British naval reinforcements in the Mediterranean, and said that unless Britain was satisfied with the French attitude there could be no question of withdrawing them. The fact that Laval had originally agreed and then reneged is evidence of how deeply he was in the Duce's pocket.

decision that Baldwin hated making. Instead he launched the Conservative Party into the election on a false prospectus of all-out support for League sanctions. Yet with the disarray of the Opposition and the indications of recent by-election results, he should have had no grounds for fearing an electoral defeat.

At the next Cabinet meeting, on 23 October, Hoare said he had received a very lengthy answer from Laval (heavily leaked to the French press) and that it was 'satisfactory'. Satisfactory or not, the French note required Britain to reduce her forces in the Mediterranean. Perhaps Hoare thought this did not matter because he also told the Cabinet that he had sent an official (Maurice Peterson, Head of the Abyssinian Department) to Paris to help our Ambassador work out a settlement with Laval which would satisfy Mussolini.[40]

On 17 October, a fortnight after the invasion started, Mussolini told the French Ambassador in Rome he would settle if the Committee of Five's plan applied to the old kingdom of Abyssinia, and that for the non-Amharic part (the conquered territories) 'instead of international help, the help would be Italian'. He also stipulated that there must be a reasonable and generous rectification of frontiers in Ogaden and Danakil in Italy's favour. Drummond communicated this news to London and Peterson minuted: 'Signor Mussolini's latest ideas appear to me to be much more encouraging than anything we have before had.' Vansittart added: 'This seems to me a distinct step in advance . . . we should endeavour to give an encouraging tone to our communication.'[41]

Thus even after the war started the British Government in defiance of their election programme, were contemplating a settlement which would reward Italy for her aggression. Mussolini, with good reason, thought he could strike a bargain with Britain on the unwritten understanding that Italy – and particularly Bari Radio[g] ceased to try and interfere with British interests in the Middle East in return for a free hand for Italy in Abyssinia. He tottered for a few weeks on the brink of such an understanding.

In spite of Hoare's Cabinet statement on 23 October, only the previous day he had emphasized to the House of Commons that we would support the League although our involvement would be limited – no military measures, only economic sanctions, and no blocking of the Suez Canal. In the debate Baldwin reiterated the Government's support for the League, although he also argued for rearmament.

[g]Bari Radio continually broadcast vicious propaganda complaining of British activities in Egypt.

Ignoring the fact that Hoare had been authorized to cook up with Laval a deal in favour of Italy at the expense of Abyssinia, Baldwin opened his election campaign with a broadcast setting out the Government's support for collective security through the League of Nations, and pointing out that there were risks if we imposed sanctions. We might be attacked; therefore we must also have limited rearmament. This was the Conservative line throughout the 1935 Election, and Government spokesmen, particularly in reply to questions, stressed their commitment to the League of Nations and their determination not to let Italy reap the rewards of aggression against Abyssinia.

After discussions with Laval and St Quentin, Head of the French African Department, Peterson came up with an agreed draft plan which gave Italy a large zone in Abyssinian territory for exclusive economic development.

Peterson had been instructed to use the Committee of Five's proposals (so nearly accepted by Mussolini on 18 September) as his text, but he went beyond these and produced a draft under which the British and French Government would suggest to Mussolini a settlement on the lines of a special regime for the non-Amharic territories (which were defined as 'depressed by wars, slavery and famine, so that the Central Abyssinian Government had been unable to administer them properly'). This would virtually amount to an Italian mandate, but, as the draft pointed out, it would be difficult to get agreement at Geneva to a mandate. Instead nominally the area would be under League supervision but security would be assured by a Foreign Legion under Italian command. Additionally Italy was to have exclusive economic development in the south, and the conquered territory and sovereignty of all the Danakil and Ogaden country south of the 8th parallel were to be ceded by Abyssinia to Italy. The Abyssinian army was to be disbanded. In return Abyssinia was to be given a port (in British territory), either at Assab or Zeila.[42]

Hoare, in the middle of his election campaign, replied to Laval that he did not want exclusive Italian control but he was ready to agree to concede to the Italians an appropriate share in 'the personnel both of the Central Commission at the capital and of the administration of the provinces', and that he would agree to the proposed boundary changes. He did not want a Foreign Legion but a gendarmerie, and thought Abyssinia would not want a port and corridor enclosed by Italian territory. This meant Zeila in place of Assab. Hoare concluded:

'To sum up, we feel the right and least complicated road to a solution is by a simple exchange of territory, which on this basis clearly entails a large advantage to Italy.'

Peterson left Paris on 27 October. Hoare had told his Ambassador to 'ascertain if Laval will agree to recasting', in which case Peterson would return. In the end the only difference between Laval and Hoare was over 'exclusive control' or 'a major share' of the officials.[43]

Eden and Hoare broke off from the election campaign to go to Geneva, where they met Laval on 1 November. Laval said he was disappointed at the British reply to the Peterson draft, but that he had found out from Mussolini that he was anxious for a settlement. Laval asked for Zeila to be given by Britain to Abyssinia. Hoare replied he would like the Committee of Five's proposals for the central part of Abyssinia (this meant almost Italian control), and to settle the rest by territorial concessions. If Eden disagreed with this reward to Mussolini, this would have been the time for him to protest. He did not.[44]

In his talk with Laval, Hoare said he hoped Italy would, as a gesture, withdraw one division from Libya where Italian troops threatened the British in Egypt. How well the Laval-Mussolini bush telegraph worked is shown by the fact that two days later the Metauro Division began embarking for Naples from Tripoli. Baron Aloisi in Geneva saw Hoare who told him Britain was anxious to continue talks, and the odds looked well on an agreed settlement of the Abyssinian war. The Italian press commented that Laval was being stopped by the British because of electoral reasons.

In the November discussions at Geneva the Canadian delegate, Dr Riddell, for some reason raised the question of oil sanctions. Vansittart minuted: 'These if implemented seriously could have been disastrous for Mussolini.'

Hoare and Eden returned to England on 3 November. The election campaign was going well for the Conservatives, and at a meeting in Hoare's room on 11 November Peterson was told that as soon as the election was over negotiations with Laval would be resumed for a simple exchange of territory and a plan of assistance for Abyssinia with Italian participation – amounting almost to an Italian mandate.[45]

On 14 November the Conservatives under Baldwin were returned again with another steamroller majority. Both Hoare and Eden stayed in the Cabinet in their former roles – Hoare as Foreign Secretary, Eden as Minister for League of Nations Affairs.

Suddenly Mussolini, scared by the threat of oil sanctions, became more belligerent. He threatened to break his alliance with France and leave the League, and hinted that he might bomb the French Riviera. At the same time he moved troops to the French frontier. The Foreign Office became apprehensive that while relatively little separated Britain from agreement with Mussolini, the two countries might drift into war. Drummond's signals from Rome were more and more disquieting.

From Berlin too, on 13 November, Phipps reported that Germany was living in a state of war, and that military expansion would be followed by territorial expansion and we had 'no policy to stop them'. Vansittart told Hoare: 'There is not a week to lose.' Phipps emphasized that Abyssinia 'was not the only pebble on the beach . . . the present Ethiopian imbroglio is mere child's play compared with the (German) problem that will not in the very distant future confront His Majesty's Government.'[46]

Meanwhile the League officials began to plan the oil sanction so dreaded by Mussolini. The Committee of Five responsible was due to meet on 6 December. On 23 November Vansittart told Hoare and Eden that 'we must not have the oil sanction or the Duce will make war on us', and followed it up by saying it would be 'suicidal' to proceed with oil sanctions 'unless we have full and concrete arrangement with [the] French' (for military support).

On 30 October Drummond reported that the Duce had told him that if Italy were faced with 'the choice of being forced to yield or war he would definitely choose war, even if it meant that the whole of Europe went up in a blaze'. Drummond duplicated this message four weeks later, which indicates how seriously the British Ambassador took Mussolini's threat. On 21 November from the British representative to the Vatican came news that Italian bishops and clergy – unchecked by the Pope – were all expressing strong resentment of sanctions.[47] The Italian nation was enthusiastically uniting itself behind Mussolini in favour of the Abyssinian war, and sanctions were regarded as a hostile act inspired by Britain.

The British Cabinet became so alarmed by the threats of an Italian attack in the Mediterranean and by Laval's refusal to come to Britain's aid that on 26 November the War Office, in view of the possibility of an Italian attack on Egypt from Libya, despatched tanks and an infantry brigade, with supporting troops from home reinforcements, to Egypt and authorized the calling up of some volunteers from reserves. Two days later it was reported by the Chiefs of Staff that there were grave shortages of anti-aircraft ammunition and 'no hope whatever that any would become available within a reasonable period of time'.[48]

Baldwin's attitude was what he had repeatedly told Hoare: 'Keep out of war, we are not ready for it.' Baldwin thought

if Mussolini broke out there would be more killed in Valetta in one night than in all the Abyssinian campaign up to date and until we got agreement with the French we would have to go single handed fighting Italy for a month or so. French mobilisation would have led to riots. They are not ready in the air for mobilisation. Malta is the only harbour apart from those of the French where you can take ships with our wounded.[49]

With Baldwin and Vansittart panicky about an Italian attack, Hoare rightly concluded that he must try for peace almost at any cost, and Eden acquiesced. Mussolini was unpredictable; the Italian nation was now anti-British and if fighting started between Britain and Italy the only beneficiary would be Hitler.

On 21 November Hoare and Eden had authorized Peterson to go back to Paris to continue his quest for a compromise peace plan with Laval. With Eden present, Hoare had told Peterson not to engage in tripartite talks with Italian diplomats but to confine himself to the French. Hoare and Eden were agreeable to an 'exchange' of territory, but Peterson was told to be cagey about Italian personnel participating in the League's plan for assistance. If pressed on this point Peterson was to refer home for instructions.

On 25 November Peterson reported from Paris that the minimum terms which Laval expected Mussolini would accept were: (1) Outright cession to Italy of the whole of the Tigre including Makale; (2) Frontier rectification of Ogaden and Danakil which 'would probably not, at least in the case of Ogaden, involve cession *in toto*'; (3) Creation of a very large special zone in southern Abyssinia bounded by the 8th parallel on the north and the 37th meridian on the west. This zone was to remain nominally under the 'Emperor's sovereignty', but 'Italy must be assured of complete control from the point of view of economic development and colonial settlement'. It meant the Emperor giving up an enormous amount of territory, and Peterson stated although in theory it was to be administered by an Italian chartered company, in fact it meant cession to Mussolini.

In return the Emperor was to receive the port of Zeila in British Somaliland. It was to be a 'carve up', with Mussolini receiving what he wanted of the Emperor's territory. Peterson wrote that 'the present suggestion completely eliminated League control while making maintenance of Ethiopian sovereignty no more than a transparent fiction'.

Scrivener,[h] who had recently been at the British Embassy in Addis Ababa, minuted on Peterson's memorandum: 'One wonders whether in the light of Laval's evident intentions to be more Italian than Signor Mussolini, the continuation of these conversations will serve any *really* useful purpose.' And Oliphant[i] commented: 'It has all along been decided that we should try and hold the scales between Rome and Addis Ababa and not expose ourselves to a possible charge of tilting them in favour of Rome.'

Instead Vansittart was enthusiastic. He considered the terms were

the best we can hope for; we should be very happy if the Italians accepted . . . We shall never get the Italians out of Adowa (the S of S. has always been convinced of this too, I think) and we ought not to try . . . I would authorize Mr. Peterson to go ahead at once . . . If we can convince the French I would be prepared to go Rome next . . . we, I think, might use General Garibaldi here.[j]

Eden ignored Scrivener's and Oliphant's reservations, minuting:

I agree with Mr. Peterson's (1) and (2) [cession of Tigre and Manakale plus Ogaden and Danakil to Italy] subject of course to the proviso we have always made and must always maintain that a settlement must be acceptable to the three parties, Italy, Abyssinia and the League. How large the area might be for the Italian chartered company would have to be a matter of bargaining. The Emperor could never agree to one third of his territory, or more, being so dealt with.

Thus Eden raised no substantial objections to the principle of the proposed agreement which was to become the Hoare-Laval Pact. Hoare certainly took it that Eden concurred, minuting: 'I agree. Let us proceed for the present on the lines of the last two minutes [Eden's and Vansittart's].' Accordingly, on 28 November a telegram was sent to Peterson in Paris to negotiate with Laval an agreement on those lines which might satisfy Mussolini.[50]

On the same day General Garibaldi bypassed Grandi, the Italian Ambassador in London, and secured an interview with Vansittart. He told Vansittart that Mussolini wanted a mandate for Italy over all non-Amharic territory (which Peterson was suggesting), and in return

[h]Patrick Stratford Scrivener (b. 1897) was in Addis Ababa December 1933 to April 1935, when he was posted to the Foreign Office in London.

[i]Sir Lancelot Oliphant (b. 1881) was an expert on the Middle East and an Assistant Under-Secretary in 1935.

[j]Grandson of the liberator of Italy. He was in London as Mussolini's secret personal envoy.

Abyssinia should be given the ports of either Zeila or Assab by Britain.
In addition he wanted a League of Nations mandate over Addis Ababa
and the Amharic nucleus around it, with the majority of the League of
Nations officials being Italians. The French Prime Minister and
Peterson had not suggested Italian majority participation in the
League mandate over the Amharic territory, and in the end the
Hoare-Laval Pact excluded this demand.[51] A note of the Vansittart-
Garibaldi conversation was circulated to the whole Cabinet, who
expressed no horror at the idea of an Italian majority on the staff of the
League of Nations administering the mandate over the heartland of
Abyssinia; a fortiori the Hoare-Laval Pact must have been acceptable
to them. From the Garibaldi and Peterson reports it therefore seemed
the dispute was almost solved, because Mussolini wanted little more
than Britain and the French were prepared to concede.

On 30 November Peterson reported from Paris that he and the
French diplomat St Quentin had come to an agreement approved by
Laval which accurately represented Hoare's views. It included cession
of Adowa and Adigrat to Italy, and a very large special economic zone
in the south under Italian control. Peterson signalled two days later
that Laval was sounding out the Duce about the plan.[52]

A Foreign Office report to the Cabinet favoured the Peterson-St
Quentin proposals subject only to the qualification that the Tigre area
should not be firmly ceded to Italy for two or three years and in the
interim should remain indeterminate under a League Commission.
This Commission would have been Italian dominated, but Eden raised
no objection.

Baldwin was in a cleft stick. He had just won the election by
pandering to the country's almost religious devotion to the League and
by giving a false promise to halt Mussolini by sanctions, although he
had known right through the election campaign that Hoare and Eden
were negotiating to offer Mussolini rewards in a compromise peace.

Eden, in any case, had compromised heavily over concessions to
Italy, and on the 29 November had told some of his Cabinet colleagues
that oil sanctions should be postponed until we saw what happened
with the Peterson-Laval negotiations in Paris. The Cabinet decided to
postpone oil sanctions and to continue negotiations with Laval. Hoare
told the House of Commons on 5 December: 'The change of date [of
the meeting to discuss oil sanctions] means no weakening
whatever . . . It does . . . give a further opportunity for an intensive
effort to bring about a peaceful settlement.'

At the 2 December Cabinet the Chiefs of Staff again pinpointed the unpreparedness for war with Italy, and warned if hostilities broke out 'the French might not support us' and Germany would either send her army into the demilitarized Rhineland zone or exploit the situation in Austria or Czechoslovakia. Eden alone argued strongly in favour of oil sanctions against Italy, insisting that only by stopping Mussolini through the Covenant of the League of Nations would we ever be able to stop Hitler. Baldwin was cautious and would not agree to fix a date for oil sanctions to be operative. On that day Vansittart warned: 'We must be sure of our ground, i.e. Italy not making war on us before we embark on oil sanctions . . . suicidal to press on with oil sanctions unless we come to a full and concrete agreement not only with the French, but with the other military powers concerned.' Hoare warned: 'No AA guns available for the defence of Alexandria . . . only thing that could deflect an Italian attack would be to attack Italian bases and North Italy. We should require not only facilities for our own aircraft but active co-operation by the French airforce in attack and defence against counter attack.[53]

The archives reveal that the whole Cabinet, including Eden, on 2 December approved the Peterson proposals[k] and believed it was most likely that Hoare and Laval could make an agreement acceptable to Mussolini under which the League would agree to hand over vast tracts of the Abyssinian empire to Mussolini under the pretext of a Trading Company, and give Italy economic control over nearly all this territory. They all hoped this would end the Abyssinian war and re-establish the Stresa front.

Hoare said that his doctor had told him he must have a holiday in Switzerland. He decided to stop off in Paris en route for Switzerland, taking Vansittart with him, and to try to clinch the deal with Laval. In their autobiographies both Vansittart and Hoare state that Vansittart was on leave in Paris in the first week of December. Actually Vansittart was busy in the Foreign Office at that time, working for a favourable outcome for the Peterson-Laval talks.

Hoare's memory is also at fault when he says in his autobiography that he ought to have called a special Cabinet before he went to Paris. His plan was discussed at length and approved by the Cabinet on 2 December and he was only told to bring the peace plan back to the Cabinet if there were any difficulties. Indeed on 2 December Hoare

[k]As soon as the Foreign Office files were made available in the Public Record Office an Oxford historian, R. A. C. Parker, made an exhaustive examination of them and wrote: 'After the Hoare-Laval plan was condemned and abandoned, other members of the Cabinet began to treat it as a strange and personal aberration of Hoare's. In fact the Cabinet gave him a free hand in advance, and afterwards approved of what he had done.'[54]

wrote to the King asking for permission for himself and Vansittart to be out of the country together and in this letter he stated: 'If, as I hope, M. Laval and I agree upon a basis for a peace negotiation, Vansittart will stop on in Paris for a day or two in order to clinch the details.' On 6 December Vansittart told the French Ambassador in London: 'The problem is to find reasonable and even generous terms to Italy.'[55]

All went well when Hoare and Vansittart arrived in Paris on 7 December. They plunged into discussions with Laval who made it clear that Mussolini knew what was going on and was happy about the suggestions. Hoare agreed to surrender to Mussolini more territory in Tigre and to offer Abyssinia a port either in Asab or Zeila plus the economic monopoly for Italy under League supervision of a large zone in the south and south west. Laval telephoned the proposals to Mussolini who told him they were acceptable. As soon as the agreement was signed Vansittart congratulated Hoare on having stopped the Abyssinian war and re-established not only the Anglo-French front, but also on having brought Mussolini back into the Stresa front.

Hoare (under pressure from Vansittart) and Laval had surprisingly agreed that the terms should be transmitted immediately to Mussolini, but only later to the Emperor. Hoare had also agreed that Abyssinia should not be allowed to build a railway along the corridor carved out of British Somaliland to the port at Zeila. This was to be the subject of hysterical press comment later but was no surprise either to the British Cabinet or to the Emperor.

Hoare signalled on 8 December a full account of the talks with Laval. Vansittart also reported by telephone. Thus the Foreign Office was well briefed on the negotiations. Yet in his memoirs Eden claimed that he was astonished when on the morning of 9 December Peterson brought him a four-page document in French initalled 'SH-PL' giving the details of the agreement. This document remains in the Foreign Office files and was the agreement to be expected in the light of the Cabinet discussion on 2 December.[1]

A special Cabinet was held on 9 December to consider Hoare's proposals. Hoare had gone on from Paris to Switzerland, but he had sent a letter to the Prime Minister strongly recommending the acceptance of the proposals.[56] Eden did not tell his colleagues of any

---

[1] In his memoirs Eden wrote: 'The terms went beyond any which Peterson had earlier been authorised to accept.' In the letter accompanying the document Hoare wrote the proposals came well within the framework discussed at Geneva by the Committee of Five and were on the basis 'we had agreed in London'. Hoare is correct, and Eden wrong according to the archives. This is also Parker's view.

'astonishment'. He only asked for 'two amendments'. One was that the Emperor should be informed of the full text of the proposals at the same time as Mussolini, and the other was a minor one involving the procedure at the League of Nations in Geneva. Eden stated that he expected the question of the oil sanctions would now be postponed, and explained to his colleagues with the help of maps that the whole of the territory which the Emperor was to cede was non-Amharic, and that he was receiving compensation by an outlet to the sea.

Eden confirmed that he supported the Foreign Secretary's proposals although they might prove distasteful to some countries at the League. He added that 'Laval wanted to interpret the proposals as generously as possible for Mussolini' and that there were doubts whether French cooperation over sanctions could be relied on, particularly if Mussolini accepted the proposals but the Emperor of Abyssinia refused. The Cabinet agreed with Eden that the Emperor must be informed of the proposed peace terms at the same time as the Duce, but that the Emperor should be strongly pressed to accept them.

The next day Vansittart from Paris told Eden by telephone that Laval was ready to send the text of the proposals to Haile Selassie on the understanding that if Haile refused there would be no question of oil sanctions. Eden told him that the Cabinet insisted on the terms being sent to Addis Ababa but added: 'It seems very unlikely that oil sanctions would now materialize unless Italy refused the proposals'; but the Cabinet would not pledge themselves to oppose further sanctions in new conditions. According to Vansittart, Laval eventually agreed that evening but with bad grace because the French Premier wanted to tell the Duce oil sanctions were dead if Italy agreed, and the proposals officially went to Rome and Addis Ababa. Mussolini, of course, had known all about them at the weekend from Laval.

Eden, at the Cabinet held on the next day, 10 December, agreed to support the Hoare-Laval Pact at the League of Nations. The Cabinet recorded that they were 'the best terms which could be obtained from Abyssinian point of view from Italy', and if Britain had rejected the terms France would not have gone with sanctions. Eden concurred and signalled to the British Ambassador in Addis Ababa that he should urge Haile to accept, and 'on no account lightly to reject them'.[57]

A red herring now appeared about the French demand that the Abyssinians must not construct a railway from British Zeila or Assab to the interior.

In 1906 the tripartite treaty between Britain, France and Italy committed Britain and Italy not to build a line in competition with the

French line from Djibouti to Addis Ababa. Laval and Peterson considered it reasonable that Abyssinia should join in this guarantee if she acquired a port in British Somaliland. Peterson pointed out on 16 December that 'the world has suffered enough from superfluous railways in the last six years without setting up a duplicate system in East Africa'. He also disclosed that Haile Selassie held a 'substantial shareholding' in the Djibouti line and thus an interest in higher profits. Anyway, Abyssinia was at liberty to construct a line from Zeila, the most probable port, to join the French railway at Djibouti, and the two ports were not far apart. Haile Selassie had bought his shares in the French railway knowing it would have a monopoly, and there is no evidence he objected to this clause.

Advised by Peterson, neither the Cabinet nor Eden thought the prohibition of the railway was of importance, although *The Times* was to produce a leader 'Corridor for Camels' which incensed the pro-League lobby in Britain.[m] It was a brilliant headline but the writer was not briefed about the prohibition in the 1906 Tripartite Agreement, nor about the Emperor's large shareholding in the existing railway. Anyway, Eden authorized further telegrams to Addis Ababa asking the Emperor to accept the terms after the inclusion of the clause about the railway.[58]

According to Sir George Clerk, the British Ambassador in Paris, on 15 December Laval was sure that if the oil embargo were imposed Mussolini would fight. This view was substantiated by what he termed the 'sober and reasoned' reports of Drummond which pointed to some desperate act of war by Italy if the oil embargo came into effect. Hoare was aware that he could not rely on immediate full support from France if Britain was attacked, and the Defence Chiefs had reported an acute shortage of ammunition. Clerk emphasized that public opinion in France was getting more and more opposed to the 'exercise of pressure on Italy', and the French press was becoming poisonously anti-British. France was determined not to go to war with Italy, and for Britain to try and force France to fight against her will would have risked a break with France with disastrous consequences for the League of Nations.

---

[m]The *Times* leader was written by Robin Barrington-Ward, then deputy editor and later editor, according to his biographer Donald McLachlan (*In the Chair, The Times 1927–1948*). 'The leader said: "Emperor to be informed at a covenient moment (probably when he had recovered from the shock of dismemberment) that he was forbidden to build a railway along the corridor." It was apparently to remain no more than a patch of scrub, restricted to the sort of traffic which has entered Ethiopia from the days of King Solomon, a corridor for camels . . .' Barrington-Ward ignored that Zeila was quite unsuitable as a rail head. It only had a jetty where dhows could tie up and ships up to 2,000 tons used to moor two miles out.

Unfortunately the French press obtained full details of the Hoare-Laval plan from a leak in the French Foreign Office and immediately there was a furore in the British national press. This produced a public outcry against the proposals.

From the news leaked in Paris *The Times* wrote on 14 December 1935: 'It is proposed to hand over to Italy effective ownership and control of a good half of Abyssinian territory.' This was more or less true, but a small price to pay for bringing Mussolini back into the anti-Hitler camp. But public opinion would not have it without a resolute and convincing defence of the proposals by Baldwin and the rest of his Cabinet. This they never got. Without a proper lead from the Government it was hailed by a large majority of the British public as an outrage and a complete abandonment of election pledge and support for the League; the Hoare-Laval agreement was dead.[59]

There was a storm of protest from Conservative MPs who were themselves inundated with complaints from indignant constituents declaring that their votes had been obtained under false pretences in the General Election. The pressure from the Conservative backbenchers brought, in the words of Professor Toynbee, 'the Government to their knees' and 'the mastery of the people over the Government was proved by the sensational demonstration of the prevailing public opinion'.

The *Economist* wrote on 14 December:

Conservative members were perplexed, confounded . . . for many of them a few weeks ago won their seats no doubt in all good faith – largely on the strength of assurance to the electors that the Government, if returned, would stand firmly for vindication of the League covenant in accordance with both the spirit and the letter of Sir Samuel Hoare's September speech at Geneva.

Seventy MPs who took the Government Whip put their names to critical motions in the House of Commons. One Junior Minister, Geoffrey Shakespeare, threatened to resign and Harold Macmillan had recalled: 'MPs supporting the Government could not reconcile themselves to so rapid a change so soon after the election with their election speeches still warm on their lips.'[60]

In America responsible newspapers condemned the proposals – in the words of the British Ambassador – 'unanimously, completely and unequivocally'. It was called 'an iniquitous bargain' and 'a plan which must bankrupt the collective system and act as incitation to other ambitious states . . . It is a vindication of the Italian Government's aggression, and represents such terms as might have been exacted after victory'; 'an international disgrace'. It was everywhere in America taken that this was the end of the oil embargo.[61]

Little account was taken by journalists that the Hoare-Laval talks were conditioned throughout by Britain's own naval, military and air weakness and by Laval's support for Mussolini – with his clear intention to refuse both to support Britain's demand for sanctions against Italy and to give military support if Italy attacked Britain.

On the Tuesday morning Samuel Hoare suffered rather more than a mishap. Within minutes of skating on to an ice rink kept empty for him at Zuoz in perfect sunshine he fell down and broke his nose in two places. The doctor told him that he must not travel for fear of infection. Seldom had a Foreign Secretary been so urgently required in London, but Hoare, always worried about his health, stayed in bed in Zuoz while the sympathetic Baldwin told him not to interrupt his holiday. It was a decision both were later to regret.

Parliament was perplexed when it met after the General Election. Baldwin told the House of 'hidden truths' and said it was premature to disclose anything until the matter had been before the League and examined by Italy and Abyssinia. His lips were 'not unsealed' but he could have made a case and 'guaranteed that not a single member would go into the Lobby against us'. Eden said the League of Nations had asked France and Britain to find such a solution. The Opposition spotlighted correctly that the Government had abandoned the policy on which they had been elected.

Afterwards Hoare was sure that Mussolini would have agreed, and that Laval had a definite nod from the Dictator. Drummond saw the Duce on 11 December at 5.30 p.m. and wired back to London in the middle of the night:

Mussolini has not yet made up his mind what to do and feels very keenly his responsibility . . . I still think, although I cannot be certain, of course, that we shall secure his acceptance in principle if the question of oil embargo threat can be overcome. If Committee of 18 [those responsible for oil sanctions] were to adjourn . . . he would, I believe, consider such an arrangement sufficiently satisfactory.

Hoare and Laval were on the brink of ending the Italian-Abyssinian war, in which case Italy would have returned to the Anglo-French camp leaving Hitler isolated, and the risk of the Second World War would have been greatly diminished. Mussolini was on the point of accepting the Hoare-Laval proposals.[62]

Eden went to Geneva where the proposals had a poor reception. The smaller nations felt that if Mussolini was rewarded now the League would have no chance of saving them from Hitler's aggression later. Eden then changed his line and became a violent opponent of the Hoare-Laval plan. He reported on 12 December from Geneva: 'Impression which Paris proposals have made upon public opinion here is even worse than I had anticipated.'

Hoare arrived back in England on 16 December unwell. He landed at Croydon and went home to bed. In his absence Eden had drafted what amounted to the death warrant of the plan. The Cabinet on 17 December, with almost incredible disloyalty to Hoare, authorized Eden to go back to Geneva with a message that the Government were no longer pressing acceptance of the Paris terms.

On 18 December the Cabinet met without Hoare, and decided they could not back France in banning Abyssinia from building a railway down the corridor to their new port.[63] Chamberlain[n] advocated a strong defence of the Hoare-Laval plan arguing, with justification, that it followed the lines of the Committee of Five's proposals. After the Cabinet, Chamberlain saw Hoare in bed and warned him of the Cabinet's doubts about the proposals in face of the public outcry. Hoare stuck to his guns and said he wanted to make a vigorous defence of his plan in the Commons, which he claimed did not depart 'radically from the Peterson agreement which had been reported and approved by the Cabinet and was the alternative to war or the abandonment of oil sanctions'. Chamberlain agreed with him. Then Baldwin and Eden followed to the bedside, now strongly opposed to the plan, and Hoare reluctantly agreed to Eden's draft for Geneva which buried the plan. Hoare accepted the Cabinet had reneged on his plan and he must resign.

Baldwin was in a panic. It looked as if the Government might fall. Elliot, Ormsby-Gore, Stanley and Duff Cooper told Baldwin Hoare should resign, but Chamberlain was furious at this suggestion.

On 18 December, the full Cabinet met in perhaps the most complete disarray of any Cabinet in this century. Eden was not present. The record of the proceedings is preserved but the key points were left blank in the typescript and written in by Hankey, the Secretary to the Cabinet, in his own handwriting. After all the Cabinet had approved both the draft Peterson proposals and the agreed Hoare-Laval text and submitted it to Mussolini, Abyssinia, and the League for acceptance, so their only honest course if they were to repudiate, was resignation. This Baldwin would not do at any price although, as Attlee pointed

[n]He was then Chancellor of the Exchequer and clearly about to succeed Baldwin as Conservative Prime Minister.

out, he had won the election on one policy and immediately carried out another.

To the Cabinet Baldwin stressed his worries over a sudden Italian attack on Britain, and his fears that Laval would not come to our aid. Chamberlain made it clear that Hoare would never change his mind about the correctness of his action in Paris, although he agreed because of public opinion the Government could not adhere to his plan. Chamberlain stated that Hoare had been greatly misled 'by his staff'.

Kingsley Wood (Minister of Health), Oliver Stanley (Education), Jim Thomas (Colonies), and Walter Elliot (Agriculture) were all against Hoare and wanted him to resign and speak from the back benches. Duff Cooper (War) also wanted resignation. Only Lord Zetland (India) backed Hoare in a woolly statement. Lord Percy (Minister without Portfolio) was also against Hoare, and Simon (Home Secretary) said the plan must be repudiated. Halifax and MacDonald thought Hoare should resign. The Prime Minister concluded that he was not 'rattled' although it was a worse situation in the House of Commons than he had ever known. He finished the meeting saying he had not yet made up his mind.[64]

Baldwin soon made up his mind. He sacked Hoare and held his Cabinet together, giving the false impression that Hoare had no mandate to come to the agreement with Laval and that Eden had opposed it all along. Baldwin would have liked Hoare to recant and remain in the Government, but the Foreign Secretary courageously refused. Hoare contended for the rest of his life that nothing else would have satisfied Mussolini and stopped him joining the Hitler front.

Meanwhile Mussolini in Rome was playing for time before accepting or refusing the plan. He arranged a meeting of the Grand Council of the Fascist Party for 18 December, obviously to accept. As soon as Hoare resigned, Mussolini cancelled this meeting because there was no point in accepting if Britain was going to renege, as Eden's attitude in Geneva indicated. Hitler's feelings could only have been of relief: the agreement had been a most unpleasant surprise for him as he knew it would re-create the united Stresa Front against him, now strengthened by the Franco-Soviet pact.[65]

Grandi sent Hoare a letter thanking him for his 'kindness and understanding'. What would have happened if Mussolini had accepted and the British Government stood by Hoare? Public opinion might have ousted the Baldwin Government, but in view of their steamroller majority and the determination of the Conservatives to cling to office, there would not have been a dissolution, only a reshuffle and perhaps a change of leadership. For all the brave talk at Geneva, no other country was prepared to risk war with Italy. The public could have been made to believe by Baldwin that the real danger was Germany, not Italy, and that sanctions apart from oil would never bring Mussolini to his knees, while oil sanctions meant war.

In place of Hoare the anti-Italian Eden became Foreign Secretary. Eden tried to impose oil sanctions but was frustrated by Roosevelt, and by February USA oil exports to Italy were three times the normal flow. Late in February the Cabinet on Eden's insistence agreed to an oil embargo, but because of the French it was never operated.

In January and February 1936 Eden tried for an agreement with Germany and intended giving permission for German troops to reoccupy the Rhineland to be his bargaining counter. However, on 6 March Hitler moved in to the Rhineland in defiance of Versailles, and Abyssinia was no longer the focus of Europe. Mussolini proceeded to obliterate Abyssinia, and from then on was hostile to Britain. It was the worst of both worlds.

2

Uniting the Dictators
1936 – 1938

Sanctions against Italy lingered on for months to poison Anglo-Italian relations. At Geneva the Committee of Eighteen even discussed extending the embargo to oil and at the Committee meeting on 3 March 1936 Eden said the British Government was prepared to accept any decision to which the Committee might come, and was in favour of oil sanctions. Baldwin had backed Eden in the Cabinet on 26 February, and with only Runciman and Eyres Monsell dissenting the Cabinet approved oil sanctions provided other members of the League did the same.

Now the Rhineland became the focus of attention. By the Treaty of Versailles Germany had been forbidden in perpetuity to put troops in the Rhineland or to fortify it, and this had been reaffirmed by the Treaty of Locarno. The French had occupied it in accordance with the Treaty of Versailles until withdrawing their troops in 1933; now it became clear that Hitler was contemplating moving into the demilitarized zone. Flandin, the French Foreign Minister, consulted with Eden in January and February 1936 about the danger of such a move, but Eden refused to give him any assurance that Britain would support the French in military action in the event of such a flagrant breach of Locarno and Versailles. On 4 March in Geneva Flandin told Eden that the imposition of oil sanctions against Italy 'would create a grave situation almost certainly involving the departure of Italy from the League' and an agreement between Hitler and Mussolini that German troops could occupy the demilitarized Rhineland zone.

Flandin was right. Eden, however, was considering allowing the remilitarization of the Rhineland as a bargaining counter in a wider agreement with Hitler. On 17 January he had reported to the Cabinet: 'Hitler's foreign policy may be summed up as the destruction of the peace settlement and re-establishment of Germany as the dominant power in Europe.' At the same time he had circulated Phipps's reports from Berlin. In one of these Phipps had written:

... On every side giant military establishments are springing up ... Enormous aerodromes either finished or under construction march, sometimes for miles, with the main road ... military cars and lorries painted in camouflage colours mix with civilian traffic. In the air the ceaseless hum of aeroplanes bears witness to the expansion of the German air force ... That military expansion will be followed by territorial expansion goes without saying.

The Cabinet's conclusion was that rearmament should be hastened, and an effort made for a *modus vivendi* with Germany.[1]

On 3 February Vansittart wrote a memorandum that Germany's ambitions could only be satisfied by giving her some of Britain's African colonies. Otherwise Britain would have to agree 'to dismember the territory of other European nations, which could not be contemplated'.[2] In Eden's view the cession of colonies was only one of several possible options. He stated in a paper discussed by the Cabinet on 17 February that he wanted consideration of an air pact between Germany and Britain; remilitarization of the Rhineland; and recognition by Britain and France of the special interests of Germany in central and eastern Europe. He gave no details of how he imagined Hitler's ambitions to the east could be catered for without impinging on the sovereignty of Poland or Czechoslovakia. A week later (24 February) he wrote to Phipps: 'It seems to be coming clearer and clearer that before long we shall be making a supreme effort to reach an understanding with Germany.'[3]

Eden had already impressed upon the German Foreign Minister, von Neurath, at a meeting in January, that Britain was anxious for an early agreement to limit air armaments, and had hinted that remilitarization of the Rhineland could be a *quid pro quo* for Germany's agreeing to arms limitation. On 14 February he told the Cabinet that

taking one thing with another, it seems undesirable to adopt an attitude where we would either have to fight for the zone or abandon it in the face of a German reoccupation. It would be preferable for Great Britain and France to enter betimes into negotiations with the German Government for the surrender on conditions of our rights in the zone while such surrender still has got a bargaining value.

This weakness in face of Hitler's belligerency was not challenged by his colleagues.

On 6 March Eden, in defiance of Flandin's clearly defined wishes in their conversation at Geneva two days previously, asked the German Ambassador in London 'if they could start serious discussions' on an air pact 'through the usual channels', and made it obvious that he was

ready to throw in remilitarization of the Rhineland as a make weight.[4]
As a diplomatic ploy this was embarrassingly short-lived: the next day
the Germans dramatically reoccupied the Rhineland, amid enormous
enthusiasm from the population.

Hitler accompanied the invasion by illusory peace offers. He said
Germany was ready to rejoin the League of Nations and he offered
twenty-five-year non-aggression pacts to Belgium, Holland and
France. Naively Eden told the German Ambassador that Germany's
intention to rejoin the League was 'most important'. His position in
Cabinet was that Britain should discourage French military action
against Germany; he was also opposed to sanctions. Phipps in Berlin
was far more positive in denouncing the German breach of faith to the
German Foreign Minister.

Hitler claimed the Franco-Soviet Pact justified remilitarization of
the Rhineland because it was incompatible with Locarno. Eden went
almost half way to agreeing with him, telling the Cabinet that

although I deeply deplore repudiation of a Treaty freely negotiated, yet it is
clear to me that there are certain very important offers contained in the
German communication – notably the non-aggression pact with France and
Italy to be guaranteed by Great Britain and Italy and the offer to return to the
League. I told the French Ambassador and the Belgian Chargé d'Affaires we
should say and do nothing to make the situation more difficult pending the
consultation.[5]

On 7 March 1936 Albert Sarraut, who had replaced Laval as Prime
Minister of France, made a firm speech to his Cabinet which he
intended to be followed by partial mobilization of the French army.
General Gamelin, the French Commander-in-Chief, said it would be
six weeks before he could be ready to send an army adequate to expel
the Germans; this, and Flandin's reminder that Eden on 4 March had
refused to give an assurance of military help, caused Sarraut to find
himself in a Cabinet minority. Hitler's action had violated both
Locarno and Versailles, and if France had mobilized and Hitler had
not immediately withdrawn his troops, under the terms of both
treaties Britain would have been obliged to go to the help of France.
The divided French Cabinet, however, never put Britain's treaty
obligations to the test.

The next day Eden went to Paris to consult with the French and
Belgians. Flandin demanded economic, financial and military sanc-
tions against Germany. Eden refused, although the French and
Belgians argued strongly that Germany must withdraw if the Locarno

powers jointly stood firm.[6] Indeed we now know from the German documents that if the French had invaded the Rhineland the Germans would have withdrawn, although there might well have been fighting. A war in 1936 over the Rhineland might not have led to the fall of the Nazi party, but it must have severely dented Hitler's popularity; and it was this that made it impossible for the moderate German generals to thwart his plans for an all-out war.

With the failure of sanctions against Italy there was little enthusiasm amongst the other members of the League for sanctions against Germany. Poland especially, and the Scandinavian countries, were lukewarm. Only Belgium and France demanded action. France, so hesitant over Italian sanctions, was now militant for sanctions against Germany, while Eden, who had been prepared to risk war by sanctions against Italy, showed none of the same firmness against Germany. The British press, too, seemed unaware of the extent of the threat that Hitler's bad faith represented to the peace of Europe.

The Council of Locarno powers met at St James's Palace on 16 March. Flandin had an interview with Baldwin who categorically informed him he would not involve England in any measures which might lead to war: 'Britain is not in a state to go to war.' At a Cabinet meeting on 12 March Baldwin had said the French should be told military action was inappropriate as being 'out of proportion to what Germany has done'. Eden agreed, and in his report to the Cabinet said the Council of Locarno powers

should give Britain, France and Italy a mandate to negotiate with Germany an air pact, settlement in eastern and central Europe (it won't amount to much) on the basis of unilateral non-aggression pacts offered to Hitler and Germany's unconditional return to the League . . .

The essential thing will be to induce or cajole France to accept the mandate . . . The strength of our position lies in the fact that France is not in the mood for a military adventure.

Flandin had arrived at St James's Palace with high hopes that the British politicians would agree to apply the Treaty of Locarno. When his hopes were dashed and he found that the British Government was determined to repudiate its Locarno obligations, he burst into tears and at one moment during the proceedings threatened to return to Paris.[7]

With France ready to stop Hitler by force, the precious opportunity was let slip by the pusillanimity of Baldwin, his Foreign Secretary and the Cabinet. The British Chiefs of Staff were deeply pessimistic, reporting on 18 March:

POSSIBLE DESPATCH OF AN INTERNATIONAL FORCE TO RHINELAND
It would be purely symbolic; infantry would be peace strength, e.g. no anti-tank guns, armoured cars, tanks which they would need for war . . . 5 Brigades, 20 Battalions could be sent . . . if war broke out we should not with this prior commitment be able to mobilize any troops to refortified France or Belgium on land for a considerable time.

The Chiefs of Staff and the Cabinet ignored the fact that the French army could easily throw the Germans out of the Rhineland and the Germans were too weak to start a war. The twenty battalions Britain could send would have delighted the French Government and completed the discomfiture of Hitler. Neither Baldwin nor Eden, however, saw it that way.

The French made another effort to stiffen Eden on 8 April at a Geneva conference with Flandin and Paul Boncour (Minister of State). Flandin asked Britain to prepare sanctions against Germany for having breached the Treaty of Versailles. Eden refused and asked if France would apply sanctions if Germany fortified the zone. Boncour said they would, and Eden said Ribbentrop had given no promise not to fortify. Flandin did not exclude refortification as part of a general settlement with Hitler, although they would need some 'general security arrangement going beyond the terms of the Covenant'.[8] To this Boncour replied that if the zone was refortified sanctions must be applied, as against Italy. Eden then observed facetiously that Germany had not yet invaded France. Boncour retorted that Germany was doing something much worse than Italy – preparing for the invasion of Europe, and that energetic precautions must be taken. Such a robust French line was not to Eden's liking.

At home there were voices to encourage Downing Street's mood of ineffective restraint. Simon wrote a private letter to the Prime Minister saying: 'Make no statement in the Commons which will give the French encouragement to snap their fingers at the Germans. France will be as selfish and pig headed as France always has been and the prospect of agreement with Germany will grow dimmer and dimmer.' As Baldwin's one-time Foreign Secretary, Simon was still influential with the Prime Minister. He was also writing just what Baldwin wanted to read.

The Colonies backed the Baldwin-Eden appeasement line. Australia said war now would 'find little support', and the Australian Government wanted a formula over the Rhineland 'leading to a general settlement'. South Africa said the Union Government would condemn war and expressed strong disapproval of action by France; it felt 'the world should move away from Versailles'.[9]

At a meeting on 12 March of the Conservative Parliamentary Foreign Affairs Committee (according to the report given to the Cabinet by Lord Dunglass)[a] Lord Winterton[b] and Robert Boothby[c] were hawks. Boothby, who knew a good deal about German internal affairs, said correctly that there was a rupture between Hitler and the Generals. Churchill overstated his hawkish case by declaring that 'all the countries of Europe would hurry to assist France and ourselves against Germany'. Samuel Hoare,[d] Nancy Astor[e] and Colonel Gretton[f] were completely defeatist and both Astor and Gretton said it was 'criminal to embark on war'. Hoare's appeasement speech convinced the majority of MPs present, and Churchill made little impression, Dunglass reported to the Cabinet.[10]

Over foreign affairs Baldwin was still under the influence of Thomas Jones, now retired but at one time Deputy Secretary to the Cabinet. Jones, a member of the Cliveden Set, was pro-German, and the morning after the occupation of the Rhineland he telephoned the Prime Minister from Lord Lothian's home, Blickling, and advised him to welcome Hitler's declaration wholeheartedly, to play down the fact that the entry of German troops was a breach of the Treaty of Versailles, and to accept Hitler's declarations of peace as being made in good faith. Jones's view was that England 'would not dream of going to war because German troops had marched into their own territories', and that Britain had better accept the situation and 'start making a new Locarno with Hitler *vice* Stresemann'.[g]

On 8 April Jones had lunch alone with Ribbentrop and recorded in his diary that he was convinced that Ribbentrop did not want war, and that he and Hitler were in dread of Russia. He told Baldwin that 70% of Tory MPs were anti-French. This was probably correct; about German intentions he could hardly have been more wrong.[11]

Flandin realized sadly that Britain would do nothing about the

[a]Later Earl of Home; as Sir Alec Douglas-Home, Prime Minister 1963–64.

[b]Irish peer, MP for Horsham for forty-five years from 1904. Held Cabinet office 1938–39.

[c]Conservative MP for Aberdeenshire. A former PPS to Churchill, who appointed him to Government office in 1940.

[d]At this time Home Secretary and Lord Privy Seal.

[e]The American-born wife of Viscount Astor. Cliveden, their country house, was celebrated for its political weekend parties.

[f]Lieutenant-Colonel J.C. Gretton was a veteran (since 1895) Conservative backbencher and Chairman of the Bass brewery. Created 1st Lord Gretton in 1944.

[g]Lloyd George had come to an agreement in 1922 with Gustav Stresemann, then Chancellor of the Weimar Republic, which might have led to a revision of the Treaty of Versailles had Stresemann stayed in power.

Rhineland. All that was achieved was five days of staff talks between Britain and France and the despatch of a British questionnaire to Hitler on his foreign policy. The questionnaire was never answered and the staff talks did little more than reveal Britain's abject military weakness, and the ponderousness of the old-fashioned French army. The talks were not resumed until 1939 and the remilitarization of the Rhineland quickly became an irreversible *fait accompli*.

Time was now on Hitler's side. He was rearming quickly, Britain and France desperately slowly. In February 1937 a report from the Ministry of Defence was to show that Germany had 39 divisions ready to take the field against Britain's 2, and 800 long-range bombers against Britain's 48.[12] A much larger proportion of German production – 16.6% against 7% – was devoted to arms and she was a far bigger industrial country. So every month tipped the scales in favour of Hitler. His popularity and the strength of the Nazi party were also increasing steadily. Neither the Foreign Office nor the Cabinet seemed to grasp the implications of this.

Belgium, alarmed by German intentions and the French and British vacillations, withdrew from the French alliance. Given their long frontier with Germany they were understandably apprehensive, but it was a disaster for French defensive plans. The Maginot Line stretched only from Switzerland to Belgium, and now the French had an extended frontier with Belgium which was defenceless if the Germans overran Belgium.

Despite the danger from Germany, Eden refused to try and come to terms with Mussolini and bring him back to the Stresa Front. He tried, in his own words, 'to hold the sanction front together' at a time when Mussolini's support against Hitler was vitally needed by France and Britain. On 6 April Eden told the Cabinet that 'the only effective action at the present stage would be closing the Suez Canal'. He did not press this and the Cabinet rejected the idea, although some Foreign Office officials still felt it might be possible to deprive Italy of victory at the last moment by closing the Canal. Roger Makins[h] on 15 April wrote a minute advocating closure, and Eden commented 'This is stimulating'; but he said nothing about it at the Cabinet on 22 April, when the mood was deeply pessimistic about Abyssinia.

On 29 May Eden conceded in Cabinet: 'that it was not practicable by the maintenance of sanctions to ensure the withdrawal of Italy from Abyssinia'; he would 'circulate a memorandum proposing the end of

[h]Later Ambassador in Washington. Created Lord Sherfield 1964.

sanctions'. On 11 June Chamberlain, without informing Eden, made a speech which obtained great publicity saying the continuance of sanctions was 'the very midsummer of madness'. His statement aroused a storm, and Baldwin ineptly dissociated the Government – a silly move because on 17 June the Cabinet approved 'the immediate raising of sanctions'.[13]

In his diary Chamberlain noted: 'I did it deliberately because I felt that the party and the country needed a lead . . . I did not consult Anthony Eden because he would have been bound to beg me not to say what I proposed.' But to Eden Chamberlain wrote he had been so occupied on the Treasury bench that he 'had not enough time to put his thoughts into a form which he could show me'. The future Prime Minister and his Foreign Secretary were already out of step.[14]

The Labour and Liberal Opposition come out of this period little better than the Government. They called for sanctions against Italy and then voted against rearming. They wanted both the Stresa Front and a League victory over Mussolini through economic sanctions, although once Mussolini had committed his mad dog act of declaring war there was no possibility of saving both.

In the spring of 1936 Ribbentrop had suggested to Jones that Baldwin and Hitler should meet. Jones was enthusiastic and talked to the Prime Minister about it, with the result that Baldwin even agreed to go to Berlin, if accompanied by Eden. The Foreign Secretary was lukewarm. On 18 June, after discussing it with the Prime Minister and Jones at the House of Commons, he rejected the idea. The meeting would have been a disaster because Baldwin relied on Jones and would probably have given Hitler the idea that Britain was no longer interested in Europe.

Although Jones failed with the Prime Minister, he managed to get Lloyd George into Hitler's presence. On 4 September 1936 Lloyd George met the Fuehrer at Berchtesgaden and was well and truly duped – though it should be mentioned that the ex-Prime Minister refused to meet Goebbels and was contemptuous both of alleged German plans to stop profiteering and of Ribbentrop.[15] When they talked Hitler was obsessional about the Bolshevik menace. To his relief Lloyd George did not raise the Jewish problem. After the meeting Jones recorded that Hitler did not seek war with Britain – he desired her friendship: 'If we fail him he will turn to Italy.' Lloyd George wrote in the *Daily Express*: 'The Germans have definitely made their minds up not to quarrel with us again'; and in the *Daily News*: 'Hitler is arming for defence not for attack.'

The British press was sympathetic to Germany after the march into the Rhineland. *The Times* was enthusiastic for Hitler's peace proposals, various Right-wing political magazines such as Lady Houston's *Saturday Review* and the *English Review* carried pro-Nazi articles. Many influential figures in public life were pro-German; Lord Lothian even wrote to Lloyd George on 23 May 1936: 'The only way to peace is justice for Germany.' Within Parliament Thomas Moore[i] formed a pro-German lobby, which included Arnold Wilson, Henry Channon[j] and Nancy Astor. Harold Nicolson, at this time a National MP, wrote to his wife[k] in a letter dated 16 March 1936: 'The people of this country absolutely refuse to have a war. We should be faced by a General Strike if we even suggested such a thing.' Particularly interesting, too, was a letter to *The Times* on 27 March: 'Our Government should rigorously refrain from involving this country in fresh commitments to France, for which there is no popular support.' Its signatories were John Boyd-Carpenter, Anthony Greenwood, P. Heathcoat-Amory, A. J. Irvine and J. C. Smuts.[l]

At the 1936 Berlin Olympics the Anglo-German Fellowship under Lord Mount Temple[m] were entertained by Hitler; Lord Zetland, then Secretary of State for India, was also a guest. Lord Rennell and General Sir Frederick Maurice spoke at the function. Lord Beaverbrook, Lord Rothermere and Lord Monsell (recently retired from the Cabinet) also attended.

The British Government, backed by a considerable section of public opinion, was seeking to appease Germany, and to remove her grievances in the vain hope of peace in Europe and a satisfied Hitler while Germany was still confined to her Treaty of Versailles frontiers. Nothing less than Czechoslovakia, Austria and great chunks of Poland would ever satisfy Hitler. Vansittart realized this, but not Baldwin, Chamberlain or Eden; while Phipps reported from Berlin that Hitler looked on Britain 'as the one country who blocked his territorial

[i] He had been a regular soldier before retiring to enter Parliament in 1925. Subsequently Father of the House; created a baronet 1956.

[j] The American-born socialite 'Chips' Channon, who had married Lord Iveagh's daughter, had become MP for Southend in 1935. He became PPS to R. A. Butler in 1938.

[k] Vita Sackville-West.

[l] The five were friends as undergraduates in the Oxford Union. Patrick Heathcoat-Amory, killed in the war, was uncle of Derick, postwar Conservative Chancellor of the Exchequer. Jan Smuts was son of the South African Field-Marshal. John Boyd-Carpenter became Conservative Minister of Transport. Anthony Greenwood was the son of Arthur Greenwood, the Labour Cabinet Minister, and was himself Secretary of State to the Colonies in the 1964 Wilson Government. Sir A. J. Irvine QC was also a postwar Labour MP.

[m] Ironically Lady Mount Temple was Jewish, a daughter of Sir Ernest Cassel (and mother of Edwina Mountbatten).

ambitions, and that he would eventually take the final gamble of war'.[16] Yet as late as June 1937 an opinion poll showed in answer to the question 'What foreign nation do you like best?' – USA 37%, France 28%, Germany 15% (third). In June 1939 Germany came out at 3%; pro-German feeling in 1937 existed in all walks of life and amongst those of nearly all political opinions except Communists. But after the Anschluss and the brutalities against the Jews it evaporated.[17]

An important diplomatic move was made in February 1937 by Hitler's Economic Minister, Dr Schacht, who in conversation with Sir Frederick Leith-Ross, Chief Economic Adviser to the Government, stressed that Germany needed colonies because of her shortage of raw materials, foodstuffs, fats and oils. Leith-Ross understood perfectly well – as did Schacht, although he would not admit it – that this was in reality a balance of payments problem incapable of political solution by the gift of a colony.

Chamberlain thought that the prestige effect of acquiring a colony would result in future German good behaviour. This naive view was not shared by the Foreign Office – Vansittart called it 'Schacht's little bluff'. This angered Chamberlain, who together with his most influential Cabinet supporters felt that the Foreign Office were missing golden opportunities to satisfy Hitler and preserve the peace of Europe.

Hoare wrote to Chamberlain on 17 March 1937 saying that when Chamberlain was Prime Minister he must not copy

Baldwin's slipshod happy-go-lucky quietism . . . I am convinced that the F.O. is so much biased against Germany and Japan and Italy that unconsciously and almost continuously they are making impossible any sort of reconciliation. I believe that when you are Prime Minister it will be possible greatly to change the European situation.[18]

At a meeting of the Cabinet Committee on Foreign Policy on 18 March 1937 Baldwin was in the chair. He remained silent. Eden proposed that discussions for a 'general settlement' with Germany should be carried out through negotiations with Hitler or von Neurath. What he meant by a 'general settlement' was vague, but he indicated he wanted a new Western Europe treaty to replace Locarno, guarantees to the East Europe powers, a return of Germany to the League of Nations, and international agreement on the limitation of armaments. He said if Germany agreed to most of this, then we would consider returning colonies to her.[19]

Eden ignored a report from Phipps that until the Italian victory in Abyssinia Hitler had wanted an understanding with Britain. Then

British prestige fell so rapidly that he thought an agreement unnecessary; and so decided to push on with the acquisition of Austria and the Sudetenland, and 'the question of the colonies was a sideline'.

On 29 April 1937 Sir Nevile Henderson replaced Phipps, who went as Ambassador to Paris. He interpreted the Cabinet discussions as giving him a brief to reassure Hitler of British sympathy and acquiescence in Germany's territorial ambitions in central Europe. He deluded Chamberlain and Eden into believing that a 'general settlement' would tame Hitler. Henderson, pro-German and anti-Czech and anti-Polish, himself favoured territorial acquisitions by Germany to the east.

When Chamberlain became Prime Minister in place of Baldwin on 28 May 1937 he took the initiative. He had been responsible for a Cabinet memorandum of 2 April on Anglo-German relations:

Herr Hitler's last speech contains certain definite assurances in regard to the peaceful intentions of Germany and Dr Schacht's approaches which have been made with the approval of Herr Hitler cannot be regarded as anything but an invitation to a general discussion.

Chamberlain so loathed the cost of British rearmament which as Chancellor of the Exchequer he had felt would mean ruin for the British economy that he was ready to clutch at straws. He would not accept that the only realistic riposte to Hitler was to put Britain's economy on a war footing and go all out for rearmament. Such a resolute policy would have encouraged the French to do the same, and once Hitler was discomforted there would be a chance of his political downfall and a return to a sane and liberal regime in Germany.

There was no major flare up in Europe in 1937. Chamberlain even wrote to Roosevelt on 26 September: 'At the present moment as far as Europe is concerned I think I may say that it is less menacing than it has appeared for some months past.' It was, however, a year of major international tension with the Spanish Civil War a battlefield between Fascists and Communists, and German rearmament proceeding so fast that the balance of power in Europe was destroyed. Hitler's design to take by force Austria, Czechoslovakia and Poland became more and more evident. At the same time the Cabinet was rashly over-optimistic about Britain's own military strength, believing that in a war with Germany a strong navy and air force would compensate for the lack of troops on the ground.[20]

As the pace of German rearmament quickened Chamberlain became more and more convinced her internal economic situation must become so desperate that Hitler would be forced to do a deal with the West, stop rearming, and generally become docile. The Prime Minister felt that by appeasement Hitler could be persuaded to abandon his arms programme, but for Chamberlain appeasement meant no more than either a colony or fiscal and economic advantages for Germany in east Europe. The term 'general settlement' with Germany was frequently used, but neither the Foreign Office nor the Cabinet would define it. Both 'appeasement' and 'general settlement' became dangerous catch phrases, in continual use in the corridors of power.[n] Vansittart was looked on as an alarmist because he constantly reiterated that only force would stop Hitler.

Was Eden really an anti-appeaser as Foreign Secretary? Although he complained about the slowness of British rearmament he was far from taking the Vansittart line. The Cabinet papers show that he (in Keith Middlemas's words) 'scarcely took part in the Defence debate' which culminated in abandoning plans for a five-division expeditionary force and instead relying on bombers and sea power for a war of defence and siege. This was anathema to the French. Defence costs were actually cut in the 1937 Budget; Eden acquiesced and accepted the delusion of the Chiefs of Staff that by 1939 our rearmament would reach a level of 'comparative safety'.

Meanwhile he remained strongly anti-Italian. Typical was his minute of 5 November 1936:

Does anybody in the Foreign Office really believe that Italy's foreign policy will at any time be other than opportunist? Any agreement with Italy will be kept as long as it suits Italy. Surely nobody now can place any faith in her promises.[21]

Half-jokingly he said to Oliver Harvey[o] on 23 December 1937 that he must prevent his personal prejudice against Mussolini colouring his attitude too much, and he looked on 'Musso' as 'anti-Christ'. Unfortunately Oliver Harvey abetted his chief in this prejudice by saying 'I do too.'[22]

Eden did manage, however, to improve Anglo-Italian relations to the point that in January 1937 the Anglo-Italian 'Gentlemen's Agreement' was signed in Rome. In this both sides recognized the importance of free transit for both countries through the Mediterranean and disclaimed any desire to change in any way the national

[n]Sir Ivo Mallet, then at the German desk, told the author that he and his colleagues constantly pointed out the expression was meaningless, but Eden would never give a definition.
[o]PPS to Eden. Ambassador in Paris 1948–54. Created Lord Harvey of Tasburgh 1954.

sovereignty of territories in the Mediterranean area. Both powers were to cooperate in schemes to limit outside intervention in the Spanish Civil War. Mussolini ignored this last clause.

It was a brief remission. When the British Government invited Haile Selassie to King Edward's Coronation, Mussolini refused to allow Umberto, the King of Italy's heir, to accept, much to the chagrin of the Italian King and Queen. Then press comments on the defeat of the Italian attack on Guadalajara in Spain and a sermon by the Dean of Winchester at a service for the victims of Italian rule in Ethiopia, in which the Dean called Mussolini by inference a madman, worsened relations to the point that the Foreign Office again seriously considered that Italy might go to war with Britain.

It was evident in 1937 that relations between Mussolini and Britain could only be improved by Britain recognizing Italy's conquest of Abyssinia. This Eden categorically refused to do, ignoring the fact that, no matter how unreliable Mussolini might be, France and Britain now desperately needed his support to keep Hitler at bay.

As early as 23 March 1937 Drummond recommended granting Italy *de jure* recognition of her conquest of Abyssinia. Then, Drummond claimed, 'Mussolini would be generous.' Eden said *de jure* recognition must be refused as it was such an important diplomatic bargaining point. Vansittart emphatically disagreed with Eden and wanted *de jure* recognition right away.

On 4 May Drummond pointed out that if Italian sovereignty in Abyssinia still went unrecognized at the League of Nations Council and Assembly at the end of May, the Duce would 'conclude definitely a complete alliance with Germany as her only true friend'. This was the red light; Cranborne (Junior Minister at Foreign Office) and Vansittart endorsed Drummond's view, but Eden again would not have it, minuting: 'Mussolini is a gangster.'

The Ambassador again urged *de jure* recognition of Italy's acquisition of Abyssinia in a despatch dated 5 August 1937: 'The essential condition for any successful negotiations with Italian Government for a general *détente* is recognition on our side of Italian sovereignty over Abyssinia.' Chamberlain agreed, and wrote about this despatch to Vansittart:

We should give *de jure* recognition while it has some marketable value, but we must not offend the French or shock League friends at home. Italians will be quite satisfied if Abyssinia is declared no longer an independent state.

These dictators are men of moods. Catch them in the right mood and they will give you anything you ask for. But if the mood changes they shut up like an oyster. The moral of which is that we must make Musso feel that things are moving all the time.

Chamberlain was right: Mussolini was not only the lesser evil but 'a creature of moods' who by immediate *de jure* recognition might still have been won over to restore the Stresa front and guarantee to try to prevent Austria falling into Hitler's clutches. Eden, however, again rejected *de jure* out of hand, ignoring the view of his Prime Minister. On 11 August he wrote to Halifax from Stanswood, near Southampton:[P]

I am very reluctant to recognize *de jure* conquest. I do not think I could bring myself to any kind of approval of what Italy has done. You will see how strong I am feeling after ten days of sea breezes . . . Come and stay and walk in the pine trees by the sea or play tennis.

Eden and Chamberlain were on a collision course over Mussolini. It was a pity that the break between them did not come at once. Had Eden acquiesced in the Prime Minister's policy or Chamberlain had the guts to sack him in August 1937, Mussolini might not have been finally driven into the arms of Hitler.

It was not to be. In Eden's absence by the sea a long meeting was held in his room at the Foreign Office under Halifax on 10 August. Drummond had come back from Rome and, fortified by his advice, Halifax and the others agreed the status of Abyssinia should be put on the agenda of the next meeting of the League Assembly, and that Britain ought to start talks immediately with Ciano in Rome about *de jure* recognition as part of a general settlement with Italy. In return Italy should be asked to reiterate the Stresa accord to keep Austria safe; to reduce her Libyan garrison; to withdraw volunteers from Spain; to exchange military information; and to stop anti-British propaganda on Bari Radio.

Halifax sent the Office note of the meeting to Eden the next day, writing with it: 'When we talk we shall liquidate the Abyssinian position. We must in some form grasp the Abyssinian nettle.' Eden replied immediately: 'I disagree with the office note. It would be difficult to put all my objections on paper. I will put them to you when we meet . . . we should decline to be rushed into conversations.'

On receiving Eden's reply Halifax wrote to Vansittart: 'This letter disquiets me . . . His attitude is dangerously divergent from the Prime

[P]Halifax, Lord Privy Seal with responsibility for Foreign Affairs, had been left in day-to-day charge of the Foreign Office while Eden had taken a country house for an extended summer holiday.

Minister's . . . onus is on me to say something to Anthony . . . Time is running out.' There is no evidence that Halifax grasped the nettle firmly by telling Chamberlain his only possible solution was to sack Eden.

Halifax went down to Stanswood to stay with Eden, arriving at Southampton in the late afternoon. He was back in the Foreign Office the next day. Although he was himself convinced that Britain could be driving Mussolini into an alliance with Hitler, he made no headway with Eden over *de jure*. He also failed to bring home to Eden the impossible situation which had arisen with the Prime Minister and the Foreign Secretary diametrically opposed on a vital issue. So Eden continued as Foreign Secretary, and recognition of Italy's conquest of Abyssinia was not put on the League's agenda as the Foreign Office meeting had suggested.

Chamberlain wrote to Halifax on 15 August that he agreed with the 'Office' view expressed at the meeting with Drummond on 10 August, but he did not press Eden hard on the urgent need to rebuild Britain's bridges with Mussolini.

On 2 September Eden was back in charge of the Foreign Office, and he circulated a memorandum to the Cabinet stating *de jure* recognition must await a general settlement with Italy. He stressed the Spanish war iniquities of Mussolini and ignored the threat to Austria from Hitler. The Cabinet gave him discretion to choose the moment when he would raise *de jure*. This delay had disastrous effects on Mussolini during the following six months, while the rift between the Prime Minister and Eden deepened.

Eden must have known he was playing with fire. On 2 July Drummond had written:

Is Mussolini working up public opinion for an eventual war with us? I frankly do not know, but if this is his intention he would hardly go about it otherwise than the way he is at present doing. It is unpleasantly reminiscent of the technique used in the early months of 1935 to bring Italian public opinion up to pitch for his Abyssinian adventure . . . Talk about war possibilites was very prevalent in Italian circles 4 or 5 days ago; fathers and mothers were resigned.

Eden immediately wrote to Inskip:[q]

I am sorry this letter was not in my hands for C.I.D. [Committee on Imperial Defence] meeting last week. I was not altogether happy even then at our

[q]Sir Thomas Inskip (later Lord Caldecot) was Minister for co-ordination of Defence and presided at meetings of the Committee on Imperial Defence.

excluding from our hypothesis the possibility of a single handed war with Italy. Had I been in possession of Drummond's letter I would have felt this even more strongly.

At the Imperial Defence meeting on 5 July 1937 Eden had urged that 'Italy should be treated as a potential enemy against whom the C.I.D. should make certain preparations'. At the same meeting the Prime Minister argued Germany was our greatest danger and should have priority in our defence preparations — 'Defence preparations against Italy should be considered of secondary importance.'[23]

In the face of this divergence between Chamberlain and Eden, over whether Mussolini or Hitler was enemy number one, Halifax wrote to Eden on 11 August saying 'time was running out'. The Government had dilly-dallied too long after the Abyssinian conquest was a *fait accompli*, and during the next six months it was to lose any chance of keeping Austria out of the clutches of Hitler. This was exactly Phipps's view just before he left Berlin. 'The only way to keep the balance of power in Europe', he had written, 'was to separate Mussolini from Hitler.'

In the last week of September Hitler and Mussolini met on the Brenner Pass and agreed that Italy would allow Germany a free hand in Austria while Mussolini could do what he liked in the Mediterranean, where Hitler recognized Italian designs on French Tunisia and parts of Egypt. The Stresa Front was shattered.

During the late summer and autumn of 1937 Hitler began to whip up agitation over the Sudetenland. Here many former Prussian subjects had been incorporated in Czechoslovakia by the Treaty of Versailles and the Czechs had not treated this minority well. Eden and Chamberlain took the side of the Sudetenland Germans against the Czech Government.

In November 1937 Halifax went to Germany to see Goering and Hitler. He made the mistake of telling Hitler that there could be

possible alterations in the European order . . . Amongst these questions were Danzig, Austria and Czechoslovakia. England was interested to see that any alterations should come through the course of peaceful evolution and that methods should be avoided which might cause far reaching destruction.

Hitler a fortnight before had told his Foreign Ministry and War Office that subjugating Czechoslovakia and Austria would be his first step towards conquering more territory in the east. Halifax signally failed to warn Hitler that Britain would oppose by force the tearing up of the Treaty of Versailles if Hitler attacked in the east. Thus Hitler took

Halifax's visit as meaning that the British Government were likely to condone his future annexations. The Archives show that both Vansittart and Eden were extremely worried by what Halifax said to Hitler.[24]

Supporters of appeasement in the Government received a fillip when Vansittart was replaced by Alec Cadogan as head of the Foreign Office. Chamberlain thought Vansittart too anti-German; Eden found him bossy. Vansittart refused the Paris Embassy and was 'kicked upstairs' to a new post as Chief Diplomatic Adviser in the New Year of 1938. Here he was kept as much as possible out of the major decisions. On 1 December 1937 Eden told Ribbentrop that Britain would consider the cession of a colony in Germany in return for a disarmament agreement and a 'general settlement'.

This statement by Eden to Ribbentrop followed a visit to London by the new French Prime Minister, Camille Chautemps, and his Foreign Minister, Delbos. In conversations Eden and Chamberlain made it clear that they were lukewarm about resisting Hitler if he tried to annex Austria and Czechoslovakia by force and they agreed with the French that the map of Africa could be redrawn to give Germany back colonies in the interests of the much-desired 'general settlement'. In these conversations with the French Eden showed himself no less appeasement-minded than Chamberlain.

Cadogan advised Eden on 12 January 1938:

If we do not act quickly on this *de jure* recognition we may gradually find ourselves with France, Russia and a few minor satellites the only ones to have withheld recognition. P.M. is extremely anxious for agreement with Duce and attaches great importance to it.

Eden ignored him.

Two days before, on 7 January, the Prime Minister had sent for Cadogan who had warned him 'against opening up with Musso with a personal letter and then leaving the difficulties and possibly the break to Eden'. Cadogan was clearly alarmed by Eden's anti-Mussolini stance.

On 9 January Eden went on holiday to the French Riviera, and on that day he wrote to the Prime Minister: 'I do hope you will never for an instant feel that any interest you take in Foreign Affairs, however close, could ever be resented by me.' Resentment, as it turned out, was something of an understatement.

On 12 January, with Eden away, a secret inquiry arrived from Roosevelt to Chamberlain suggesting calling together the whole diplomatic corps in Washington at the end of the month to try to

improve international relations. Chamberlain did not like this suggestion. Without consulting Eden, he replied that it was not an opportune
moment because we were about to start on talks with Italy and
Germany and this might 'cut across' our efforts for quick results.
Chamberlain added that in the forthcoming talks he would be
prepared to recognize *de jure* the Italian conquest of Abyssinia if Italy
gave evidence of her desire to restore friendly relations, and that before
long we might also begin conversations with Germany.

Eden was recalled from his holiday and was outraged at Chamberlain's reference to granting *de jure* recognition to Italy. The two met at
Chequers and relations were 'strained'. Eden reiterated he 'would not
have *de jure* recognition of the Italian conquest of Abyssinia' and
bluntly reminded the Prime Minister that immediately after signing
the 'Gentlemen's Agreement' Mussolini had sent 4,000 more volunteers to Spain. Conceding *de jure*, Eden stressed, would shock public
opinion in Britain.

Eden proposed that the Government should at once call off the idea
of Italian conversations for fear of offending the United States and
welcome Roosevelt's proposal for a diplomatic conference. The Prime
Minister, very put out, said they must take their dispute to the
Cabinet's Foreign Affairs Committee. The Committee decided they
wanted talks with Mussolini, but compromised with Eden by agreeing
de jure need only be given as a factor in general appeasement.

On 25 January Eden visited Paris and obtained French agreement in
principle to a general agreement with Italy which would include *de
jure* recognition. However, Cadogan recorded in his diary that though
Eden had 'agreed in principle to talks with Musso, he was using every
excuse to run out'.

Ivy Chamberlain, widow of Neville's stepbrother Austen, the
former British Foreign Secretary, was in Rome. She talked to Ciano
and said 'N. C. passionately wants a settlement with Mussolini.' She
reported this to No. 10. Eden, incensed, complained bitterly to
Chamberlain on 8 February. The Prime Minister agreed to ask his
sister-in-law to desist, but added: 'she must not give the impression
that we do not want to have conversations at all.'[25]

Eden wrote to the Prime Minister that Ivy's 'unofficial diplomacy'
placed him in a difficult position:

Mussolini is in an extremely uncomfortable position. He has commitments in
Abyssinia and Spain neither of which is turning out well. He now sees a
Government in Berlin which is comparatively enthusiastic for the Rome-
Berlin axis but which is also apparently determined to pursue a more active

foreign policy in Central Europe with Austria as the first item of intended victims. In such a position we have nothing to gain by showing ourselves too eager [for diplomatic talks with Mussolini].

The Department prepared a memorandum on the probable agenda for talks with Italy. This pointed out that the joint resolution at Stresa about Austria read: 'The three Governments examined afresh the Austrian situation, and recognized the necessity of maintaining the independence of Austria would continue to inspire their common policy.' Against this Eden pencilled, 'Is this a concession at all?'

This pencilled comment, taken in conjunction with his remark to Chamberlain that 'we have nothing to gain by showing ourselves too eager', is evidence that the Foreign Secretary misjudged the menace of a Hitler coup in Austria.[26]

Now a crisis arose over Austria which dwarfed the issue of the Spanish Civil War. On 16 February 1938 Hitler summoned the Austrian Chancellor, von Schuschnigg, to Berlin and ordered him to put the Nazi Dr Seyss-Inquart in charge of the Austrian Ministry of the Interior, including the police. It was clear to Chamberlain that Mussolini had given the green light to Hitler for a German takeover of Austria, and the Prime Minister decided that he must make a last desperate effort to come to terms with Mussolini before Austria fell. He noted in his diary that if Eden would not agree to talks aimed at placating Mussolini urgently, he would part with his Foreign Secretary.

Eden at the time and later in his memoirs emphasized almost exclusively his concern at the bad behaviour of Mussolini in the Spanish Civil War. Nowhere did he indicate that he appreciated the 'threat' to European peace if Hitler took over Austria. Once the German army was in Austria, Czechoslovakian defence plans against Germany would fall to pieces because they were based on defending their well-fortified hilly frontier with Germany, not on fighting a German army along the southern frontier with Austria where the ground would help an attacking army.

Oliver Harvey was at the time Eden's close adviser and confidant. Evidence of Harvey's and Eden's attitude to the Austrian threat comes in Harvey's diary entry on 16 February:

My instinct is not to take Hitler's demands on Schuschnigg too tragically; the prohibition on the Anschluss has been wrong from the start . . . One way or another an Austrian majority has always been in favour of Anschluss, Catholics, Socialists, Nazis, according to the ruling colour in Germany.

Anschluss or at least a satellite Austria is probably inevitable, and to stop it from outside is impossible and indefensible . . . I can't believe the absorption of Austria will strengthen Germany; it should put water in the Nazi wine.[27]

Harvey ignored the surely predictable outrages the Nazis would inflict on the Austrian Jews after an Anschluss and how it would defeat Czech defence plans. The view that Anschluss would be no disaster coloured Eden's thinking throughout his resignation crisis.

Cadogan, too, influenced Eden not to take the threat to Austria as being of major importance, and contradicted Vansittart's more realistic view – which coincided with the Prime Minister's. He wrote in his diary on 16 February:

What is the good of brandishing Austria under Hitler's nose when we can't do *anything* about it? . . . I should not mind if Austria were *gleichgeschaltet* [bust] . . . [On the 17th] We have always known that Germany could swallow Austria. It is no good shouting about it (as Van wants) if we can't stop it, as Van admits we can't.

After the Anschluss was a *fait accompli* Cadogan reaffirmed his outlook: 'Thank goodness Austria's out of the way . . . it was not our business; we had no particular feeling for the Austrians; we only forbade the Anschluss to spite Germany.' Eden was not alone in considering Spain was more important than Austria.[28]

The Foreign Office already had warning that Mussolini was more than ever ill-disposed. On 28 February Drummond wrote that Mussolini would not see Lothian who was anxious to have an interview with him. He had already refused to see Lord Lloyd.[r] Drummond now added that this was because Mussolini believed 'we are still, in our own words, trying to chloroform him and he is determined not to swallow the dope'. It was useless, he added, for anyone to come out to Rome in the hope of seeing the Duce.[29]

Ciano, now Foreign Secretary, was very anti-Hitler and ardently wanted to prevent the Anschluss – which Mussolini had approved in principle at his meeting with Hitler in September. Ciano knew that his father-in-law was not altogether happy with the idea of Hitler's seizure of Austria as it would give the Nazis a predominant position in Europe; but Ciano also knew that only by a sudden change of heart and an immediate generous gesture from Britain could Mussolini be persuaded to take a firm stand against the Anschluss.

[r] A champion of rapid rearmament and an opponent of the Prime Minister's foreign policy.

Accordingly Ciano told Drummond that he had instructed the Italian Ambassador in London to press for an early start of Anglo-Italian conversations 'in view of possible future happenings' – obviously the German takeover of Austria. Then, on 17 February, he gave another strong warning to Ivy Chamberlain after they had lunched together in Rome: she must tell the British Prime Minister that 'time is everything. Today an agreement will be easy, but things are happening in Europe which will make it impossible tomorrow.' Ivy herself added that Ciano was 'completely changed and seemed intensely worried'.

Chamberlain understood from this that Ciano was frightened of a Hitler coup in Austria. A copy of the message was passed to Eden but he did not feel the same urgency about talking to the Duce. He was still opposed to talks which might end in *de jure* recognition of Mussolini's conquest of Abyssinia without big concessions by Mussolini over Spain.[30]

Eden had had a preliminary and inconsequential talk with Ambassador Grandi on 10 February. Meanwhile Chamberlain, unknown to Eden, had been passing messages to Grandi, through Sir Joseph Ball of the Conservative Central Office to the effect that he urgently wanted an agreement with Mussolini and would like talks to start at once.

An appointment was fixed for Eden, Chamberlain and Grandi to meet at 10 Downing Street on 18 February. Eden tried hard to get out of the joint meeting with the Prime Minister, but Chamberlain firmly told him Grandi wanted to come to No. 10. Eden countered with a letter saying he wanted a private talk with Grandi first, when he would ask him about the Spanish withdrawal scheme. Eden also wrote a second letter to the Prime Minister imploring him 'not to commit ourselves' in any way at the meeting with Grandi. This left Chamberlain cold.

When the three met at 10 Downing Street on the morning of 18 February, Chamberlain asked Grandi if all was lost in Austria. Grandi replied that they were only 'at the end of the third act' but from Italy's viewpoint Germany was now at the Brenner and Italy could not be left alone with two great potential enemies, Germany and Britain. When asked what effect the opening of conversations might have on the Italian attitude towards Austria, Grandi replied 'It would give my people more courage.' Eden asked Grandi if Italy would withdraw volunteers from Spain. Grandi said it would be a mistake to hold up Anglo-Italian conversations over Spain.[31]

Grandi left before lunch and Chamberlain told him they would talk again at three. Then in private Chamberlain told Eden that he had decided to tell Grandi that we would open immediate conversations and that Drummond should be asked to come back to London at once to begin preparatory work. Eden emphatically disagreed. Chamberlain said crossly: 'Anthony, you have thrown away chance after chance.' This was the end; Chamberlain wanted another Foreign Secretary. At 2.30 Grandi was told that the Prime Minister was consulting with his colleagues, and he cabled Mussolini that the British Prime Minister and Foreign Secretary were hopelessly divided. The next day, 19 February, a Cabinet was held. Eden argued against talks with Mussolini and in favour of offering a colony to Hitler. Fourteen supported Chamberlain, and four Eden. So Eden resigned, to be replaced by Halifax.[32]

Why did Eden resign? His sticking point was that we must not enter into conversations with Mussolini which might lead to the *de jure* recognition of Italy's conquest of Abyssinia unless Mussolini withdrew his volunteers from Spain. He just did not share Chamberlain's conviction that an urgent agreement with Mussolini was necessary to save Austria from Hitler; he looked on Austria as a cause lost already and of minor importance. He had told Ribbentrop in December 1937 that the Austrian question was of much greater interest to Italy than to England 'whose people recognized that closer connection between Germany and Austria would have to come about sometime'.[33]

A myth has grown up that Eden resigned because Chamberlain would not stand up to the dictators.[s] This is incorrect. Obsessed with Italian involvement in Spain, Eden would not accept Chamberlain's view that it was so much more important to preserve Austria that the Government must try to retrieve the Duce's support. Chamberlain, often wrong about foreign policy, was right about Austria. Eden, for his part, always held that Mussolini was completely unreliable and no real trust could be placed in him. It was a view that history did nothing to contradict.

Malcolm MacDonald,[t] a good friend of Eden and an impartial observer, recorded many years later that Eden came to dinner with him after the Cabinet meeting on 19 February, and said he

could not continue working as a Minister because he did not feel fit to do so; he felt physically unwell and mentally exhausted[u] . . . During our talk I felt

---

[s]It is an entertaining gloss on this view that in January 1938 Eden favoured inviting Goering to London and to watch the Grand National. When the police chief said he could not guarantee Goering's safety in London, Eden wanted him to fly direct to Liverpool. Halifax, who had met Goering quite recently, vetoed Goering's trip out of hand as soon as he became Foreign Secretary.

[t]Son of Ramsay MacDonald, and Secretary of State for the Colonies in 1935 and 1938–40.

[u]Yet Eden was annoyed that Simon and the Cabinet Ministers gossiped that he was mentally and physically ill at this time.

increasingly worried about the state of his mind. His thoughts seemed to be less clear and reasonably coherent than they usually were . . . I decided it would be better if he did resign.

The next morning Malcolm MacDonald went to see the Prime Minister and told him that he thought Eden should resign because 'he was too mentally and physically exhausted to continue working wisely and well in his high office'.[34]

On 20 February Chamberlain announced talks with Italy would begin. He was too late to save Austria. Once the Anschluss was accomplished he wrote to his sister: 'With the Czechoslovakian-Austrian frontier practically open you have only to look at the map to see that nothing France or we could do could possibly save Czechoslovakia being overrun by the Germans if they wanted to do it.'[35]

3
The Fall of Austria
1938

Once Halifax was installed in the Foreign Office, Britain made strenuous efforts to bring Mussolini back to his Stresa stance. Chamberlain and Halifax succeeded in improving relations to the extent that Mussolini stood aside when war with Germany nearly broke out over the Sudetenland six months later.

Anglo-Italian talks took place almost at once but achieved little, although an agreement of sorts was signed in Rome on 16 April. The only thing which could have stopped Hitler annexing Austria was if Britain, France and Italy threatened to interfere with force. In March 1938 Mussolini, because of Eden and Spain, was too far out of step with Britain to contemplate taking a firm stand against Hitler although he did not want the Nazis in Vienna.

The Anglo-Italian agreement of 16 April was only to come into force when the Spanish controversy was settled.[a] Britain insisted on an armistice in Spain followed by substantial withdrawal of Italian volunteeers, but Mussolini rejected this out of hand as he did the other proposed alternatives, so that even by the middle of July Anglo-Italian relations were still bogged down over Spain – now a minor issue compared with the Czech crisis.

Hitler was delighted with Halifax's appointment as Foreign Secretary. From the new Foreign Secretary's recent visit to Germany he knew Halifax was a strong appeaser; indeed Halifax had all but promised him face to face that Britain would not interfere if Hitler pulled off the Anschluss.

After the Brenner Agreement in September 1937 the Austrian Nazis had become more aggressive. Schuschnigg, Dollfuss's successor, found it more and more difficult to govern, and to maintain order he was forced to bring Nazi supporters into his Government. He did, however, make some progress in uniting all non-Nazi Austrians in

[a]This, the Easter Agreement, did not come into force until 20 October – after Munich.

resistance to German demands for a takeover. In order to strengthen his position he planned a popular vote of confidence in Austrian independence from Germany to be held by plebiscite on 13 March 1938. He had consulted with Mussolini, who advised 'extreme caution'.

Hitler knew there would be an overwhelming vote against Nazidom, so on 12 March he ordered German troops across the frontier. Schuschnigg resigned and Hitler declared Austria part of Germany. Immediately the Austrian Nazis began horrible persecutions of the Jews. The outrages were well reported in the *Daily Telegraph*, but Sir Hugh Carleton Greene who was there on behalf of the *Telegraph* told the author that similar copy was sent back to London by the *Times* correspondent but the Editor, Geoffrey Dawson, refused to publish anything derogatory to the Nazis. Chamberlain and Dawson had made an agreement that nothing would appear in *The Times* to anger Hitler.[1]

Most Austrians liked the Germans, their allies in the First World War, although only a minority favoured the Nazis, and German troops were greeted warmly by the majority of the population. Hitler sent Philip of Hesse to see Mussolini in Rome and was immensely relieved when Mussolini raised no objections. The Treaty of Versailles, mangled already by the Anglo-German naval agreement, German conscription, and the reoccupation of the Rhineland, was dead, and the British-Italian entente blocked for so long by Eden was stillborn. Ignominiously, Chamberlain was entertaining Ribbentrop to lunch at 10 Downing Street when the news came of Hitler's ultimatum to Austria.

Grandi later said that Mussolini would have acted 'differently' if it had not been for Eden's intransigence between September 1937 and February 1938.[2] Still, Mussolini would have been in a difficult position. Even if he had moved his troops to the Brenner as in 1934, Hitler was now immeasurably stronger. At the Munich Conference in September 1938 Mussolini told Hitler he would never have dared to use Italian troops inside Austria because of the traditional Austrian hostility to Italy and because of the new strength of the German army.[3] As it was, both Britain and France acquiesced abjectly in Hitler's rape of Austria and never even considered asking Mussolini to prevent it.

On 24 March Chamberlain, apparently unmoved by Hitler's behaviour, told the House of Commons that Britain would only fight in defence of France and Belgium or the British Empire, although possibly 'we might assist a victim of aggression under the Covenant of the League of Nations'. Hitler's aggressive intentions towards the Czech Sudetenland were already unmistakable but Chamberlain stated we would not automatically help Czechoslovakia under the terms of the French-Czech Treaty of 1925. At that stage the Russians were seriously contemplating allying themselves with France and Britain to defend Czechoslovakia, and Chamberlain's Commons speech was ill received in Moscow.

On 18 March the Cabinet Foreign Policy Committee decided they could not have 'recourse to war' against Germany over Czechoslovakia. In the words of Cadogan they felt 'Czechoslovakia was not worth the bones of a single British grenadier'; and Cadogan added, 'they are quite right too.'[4] Oliver Stanley, President of the Board of Trade, told the Committee it was 'impossible to argue that the preservation of Czechoslovakia was a vital interest of Great Britain;· our only obligation to Czechoslovakia was of one League member to another.' Inskip could see no reason why Britain should keep Czechoslovakia in existence because she 'was not permanently tenable and an unstable unit in Central Europe'. Ormsby-Gore[b] felt 'any specific commitment to Czechoslovakia would split public opinion from top to bottom'.

The logical plan to save Europe from the Nazis was a guarantee to Czechoslovakia coupled with an all-out drive for rearmament and an alliance with Russia. Vansittart alone argued for this and, according to Cadogan, damaged his own case by overstatement. This is almost certainly true, taking into account Vansittart's character. He had by now lost most of his influence. Churchill was alarmed and anxious for a hawkish stance but he was powerless.

Czechoslovakia was an artificial twentieth-century state, solely the creation of the Versailles Conference, and carved out of the old Hapsburg Empire. It included in its population Czechs, Poles, Germans, Slovaks, Magyars and Ruthenians. Thus Poland, Germany, Rumania and Hungary all had territorial ambitions there and a vested interest in the collapse of the infant state. The President, Beneš, had promised to treat his minorities on the Swiss Canton system, but had failed to do so; certainly the German minorities in the Sudetenland area had been treated harshly and had legitimate grievances. These Hitler was determined to magnify as an excuse to destroy the Czechoslovakian state and make himself more popular with his own people by annexing territory to the east.

[b]Secretary of State for the Colonies until succeeding his father as 4th Baron Harlech on 8 May 1938.

The British representative in Prague, Basil Newton, reported on 15 March 1938 that 'Czechoslovakia's present political position' was 'not tenable'. This was Chamberlain's view on military grounds regardless of the fact that to allow Germany to take all or part of her was just one more step in the aggrandisement of Hitler.[5]

On 21 March the Cabinet Foreign Policy Committee, met to consider a report from the Chiefs of Staff who had spotlighted the Czech lack of fortifications on the Austrian frontier and the new vulnerability of her munitions centres. They concluded: 'Neither Britain or France could render any assistance to Czechoslovakia and the only direct method of rendering even indirect assistance would be by staging offensive operations against Germany.' They thought it unlikely the French would mount 'an effective attack, and if Germany, Italy and Japan fought a war against us the British Empire would be threatened by an immense aggregate of armed strength, and would be faced with the gravest danger.' Cadogan commented: 'Thank goodness Cabinet firm on doing nothing about Czechoslovakia.'

Stanley told the Committee the effect on France of our attitude over Czechoslovakia would be disastrous, and Halifax said this was also Vansittart's view but 'because France would be shocked was no reason to refrain from a policy of the correctness of which we were fully satisfied'. The French were informed of the British Government's view.[6]

Chamberlain that weekend recorded his gloom in his diary:

The Austrian frontier is practically open; the great Skoda munition works are within easy bombing distance of the German aerodromes; the railways all pass through German territory, Russia is 100 miles away. Therefore we could not help Czechoslovakia – she would simply be a pretext for going to war with Germany. That we could not think of unless we had a reasonable prospect of being able to beat her to her knees in a reasonable time, and of that I see no sign. I have therefore abandoned any idea of giving guarantees to Czechoslovakia or the French in connection with her obligations to that country.[7]

This defeatist attitude dominated all Chamberlain's actions up to and including Munich. The French Government and sporadically Halifax tried to urge him to a firmer line, but without success. Chamberlain felt correctly that the Anschluss was a disaster; now with Austria gone he could think in no other terms than appeasement.

Hitler hoped to annex Czechoslovakia without war. On 28 March he saw Konrad Henlein, the leader of the Sudeten Germans, and told him he was in negotiation with Beneš always to demand more than could be conceded. Beneš relied on France and Britain with Russia in the background. He had the Alliance for Mutual Defence with France of 1925, plus the Alliance with Soviet Russia of 1935 (which did not come into operation unless France acted first), and the Little Entente with Rumania and Yugoslavia. Unfortunately strong elements in Czechoslovakia felt 'Better Hitler than Stalin.'

In spite of thirty-four divisions and powerful fortifications on the German frontier, the Czechs on their Austrian frontier were desperately weak – as Chamberlain and Vansittart had foreseen. There were no fortifications on the vulnerable Austrian side although Beneš frenziedly started to build some. On 15 March the French Committee of National Defence discussed military aid for Czechoslovakia. Gamelin told them the French could 'tie down' some German troops but could not break through the Siegfried Line, they could only attack through Belgium. Still the French Foreign Minister, Paul-Boncour, told Phipps on 24 March: 'A definite warning to Germany [by France and Britain] . . . would be the best means of avoiding war.' Time was 'not on our side' for Germany was 'getting stronger and stronger'. Halifax did not reply, and Boncour left office with Blum on 10 April. The new Premier, Daladier, sacked Boncour because he thought he was too belligerent and took on Bonnet, much more of an appeaser.

On 23 March Halifax told Phipps in Paris:'Our plans, both for offence and defence, are not sufficiently advanced' and he refused the suggestion of the Russians for a conference either in the League of Nations or outside it.[8]

At the end of April 1938 Daladier and Bonnet came to London and urged the British Government to announce it would come to the aid of Czechoslovakia in the event of a German attack. The French already had a clear treaty obligation to defend Czechoslovakia against Hitler, and Daladier said he believed that if the British Government spoke firmly Hitler would climb down.

The British emphasized their commitment under the Guarantee of March 1936 to come to the aid of France, but they could not promise even two divisions for an expeditionary force, and refused naval staff talks for fear of upsetting Italy. Chamberlain said: 'If Germany decides to destroy Czechoslovakia I do not see how this can be prevented.' The French asked if Britain would stand by Czechoslovakia if there was an invasion by Hitler. Chamberlain refused, and said he would urge the Czechs to make concessions to Hitler. All that was decided was that Britain should ask Hitler what he wanted. Two weeks later Henderson told the German Foreign Office that Britain was supporting Germany over Czechoslovakia – only to be rebuked by Halifax who told Henderson that whatever he thought he must not let the impression be created that 'we and others should sit by in all circumstances'.

Henlein came to London on 12 and 13 May on Hitler's orders. His objective in London was to soft soap the British into believing that he was not Hitler's dupe and was genuinely trying for a peaceful solution. Even Vansittart was taken in. He described Henlein as 'far more reasonable and amenable than I had dared to hope' and after his visit recorded: 'If the Germans will desist from blocking tactics, we may really have turned a crucial corner in European history.' Vansittart was soon cured of this illusion.[9]

At this stage Chamberlain sincerely believed that Hitler could be made to accept peaceful solutions, and anyway Germany deserved a good slice of Czechoslovakia. At a party given by Lady Astor on 15 May the Prime Minister told foreign correspondents off the record that Czechoslovakia must give up territory, but that the new adjusted boundaries should be guaranteed by a four-power pact. This was immediately leaked to Canadian and American newspapers, and Hitler felt the British Prime Minister had given him the green light. In his 'four powers' Chamberlain included Italy, not Russia.[10]

After a panic on 20 May that Hitler intended to invade, Czecho-slovakia mobilized 80,000 reserves and moved 400,000 troops to the frontier, and Beneš asked Daladier if he would honour his obligation to Czechoslovakia. Daladier promised to do so and told Britain that he would mobilize at once unless Henderson could prevent Hitler's preparations for war. Whether Hitler intended to attack in May remains a mystery, but Chamberlain was so alarmed that he made up his mind to sacrifice Beneš. A clearly Chamberlain-inspired leader in *The Times* on 3 June declared that the Germans of Czechoslovakia ought to be allowed by plebiscite or otherwise to decide their own future 'even if it means secession to Germany'. This, according to *The Times*, would mean rectification of the injustice of the Treaty of Versailles – which was now Chamberlain's policy. But the Sudeten Germans had not gone there because of the Treaty of Versailles. They went voluntarily from Prussia into the Hapsburg Empire from 1839 onwards to find well-paid work in the coalfields and other industrial development.

On 22 May Halifax, now more courageous than Chamberlain, told Herbert von Dirksen, the new German Ambassador in London,[c] that

---

[c]Ribbentrop had returned to Germany to take up the post of Foreign Minister.

France would attack Germany if Hitler invaded Czechoslovakia even after 'serious acts of provocation by the Czechs'. It would then be 'impossible to see whether Britain would not be drawn into it [a European conflict]'. Dirksen had previously reported to Hitler that the Foreign Office attitude was that Britain would agree to the dismemberment of Czechoslovakia, but that if force was to be used they would definitely go to war alongside France. On 28 May Henderson told Weizsaecker (the permanent head of the German Foreign Office) that Halifax's statement of 22 May which had been given wide publicity in Germany was misunderstood and if the Czechs committed unbearable provocation Britain would not support them but 'leave them to their fate'. Ribbentrop had been so angered by Halifax's statement of 22 May that he had asked Dirksen to get him to deny it. Halifax refused, whereupon Ribbentrop threatened to make it public. Henderson was pursuing Chamberlain's policy in Berlin regardless of the Foreign Office. In any case it was clear from reports from the British Embassy in Prague that Beneš was trying to placate, not irritate, the Germans in the Sudetenland, and Henderson far exceeded his instructions.[11]

Chamberlain was now running far ahead of his Foreign Secretary in his readiness to allow Hitler to absorb parts of the Sudetenland into Germany. Dawson was his mouthpiece and *The Times* published a leader advocating a partition of Czechoslovakia. Halifax for once showed some firmness, and the following letter to Dawson shows how he still hoped the Sudetenland crisis could be solved by agreement between Beneš and Henlein:

Confidential   June 15th, 1938

My dear Geoffrey,
I am rather disturbed by recent references in the "Times" to the desirability of holding a plebiscite in the Sudeten districts of Czechoslovakia. We are, as you know, at present doing our utmost to bring Dr. Beneš and Herr Henlein together on a basis of negotiations for meeting the Sudeten claims within the framework of the existing Czechoslovak state. I think we may claim that, as a result of our pressure, Dr Beneš is now convinced of the necessity of making a really statesmanlike offer to Herr Henlein, who in turn is prepared to give it favourable consideration. Herr Henlein himself is in a difficult position because he is being continually attacked from the rear both by his own extremists and by Berlin on the ground that he is not sufficiently uncompromising in his attitude. Herr Henlein is by nature a moderate, and would, we believe, prefer a satisfactory settlement within the Czechoslovak state to an Anschluss with Germany. In these circumstances, if suggestions of a plebiscite are made in such prominent quarters as the "Times", I am afraid that our efforts to promote a settlement whilst maintaining the existing frontiers of

Czechoslovakia may be seriously compromised. Herr Henlein will be placed in an impossible position if he can be represented as agreeing to terms less favourable than those represented as reasonable by the "Times", whilst Dr. Beneš for his part can hardly be expected to incur the responsibility of offering really far-reaching terms of settlement if they are only to be the stepping-stone to a plebiscite involving the break-up of his state!

I much hope, therefore, that any references to a possible plebiscite may be held back so far as possible for the present! I personally would not altogether exclude the possibility that, if everything else fails, it may be ultimately necessary to fall back on a plebiscite in order to forestall a worse catastrophe, but for the time being I am convinced that the prospects of a reasonable settlement are best served by insistence on the possibility of a solution of the Sudeten question being found on the lines of autonomy within the existing boundaries of the state.

(Signed) HALIFAX

In his reply Dawson was unrepentant so sure was he of Chamberlain's soft line on the Sudetenland.[12]

On 30 May Hitler issued the following directive to his Generals:

WAR ON TWO FRONTS WITH MAIN EFFORT IN SOUTH-EAST

It is my unalterable decision to smash Czechoslovakia by military action in the near future. It is the business of the political leadership to await or bring about the suitable moment from a political and military point of view.

An unavoidable development of events within Czechoslovakia, or other political events in Europe providing a suddenly favourable opportunity which may never recur, may cause me to take early action . . . preparations are to be made immediately . . . it is essential to create a situation within the first two or three days which demonstrates to enemy states which wish to intervene the hopelessness of the Czech military position and also provides an incentive to those states which have territorial claims upon Czechoslovakia to join in immediately against her. (In this case the intervention of Hungary and Poland against Czechoslovakia can be expected, particularly if France . . . fears, or at least hesitates to unleash a European war by intervening against Germany. In all probability attempts by Russia to give Czechoslovakia military support, particularly with her air force, are to be expected.[13]

There is strong evidence that Russia really did intend to fight in defence of Czechoslovakia if the Allies did the same. On 15 March 1938 Litvinov[d] held a press conference for foreign journalists in Moscow and said Russia would intervene in defence of Czecho-slovakia. When asked 'How, without a common frontier?', he replied: 'Means would be found.' When it was suggested that this must involve 'creation of a corridor', he assented, actually repeating the words. In a

[d]Russian Foreign Minister until May 1939.

separate interview with the correspondent of *Le Temps* Litvinov again said 'Means would be found.'[14]

On 10 June Halifax told the German Ambassador in London he was convinced they could get a settlement if they were patient.[15] Henderson in Berlin told Ribbentrop that Britain would stay out of a conflict, and France would do the same, and the British Government was doing everything possible to bring the Prague Government to reason. Hitler therefore believed Britain would stand aside, and on 18 June issued a further directive to his General Staff. While Chamberlain and his Cabinet deluded themselves that Hitler could be stopped by diplomacy and the mythical 'general settlement', the Fuehrer was making firm plans to occupy the Sudetenland by force.

Hitler's directive of 18 June stated that occupation of Czechoslovakia was his immediate aim and from 1 October he would make full use of every favourable political opportunity to realize it. There was no danger of a preventive war by foreign states against Germany, but he would only invade Czechoslovakia if he was sure, as in the case of the Rhineland and Austria, that Britain and France would not intervene. The General Staff were ordered to make full military plans for both Operation Green, invasion of Czechoslovakia, and Operation Red, defence of the west against Britain and France.

Hitler clearly feared Russian intervention, and wrote 'Among the Eastern European powers intervention by Russia is the most likely.' It would probably consist in the beginning of 'mere reinforcement of the Czech Air Force and armaments', but consideration was to be given to Russia starting a naval and air war or even penetration of East Prussia via the Baltic States.[16]

As early as 25 April the German Foreign Office had become aware that the Russians had been talking in Bucharest about Rumania allowing Soviet troops to have rights of transit through Rumania to come to the assistance of Czechoslovakia if Germany attacked. The Germans feared Anglo-French cooperation in these talks. Then a report was sent to Berlin by the German Minister in Rumania that thirty-six Russian bombers were being flown to Czechoslovakia; further confirmation of flights of Russian bombers to Prague over Rumania were received from the same source. Soon after the German Embassy in Warsaw reported that forty Soviet aircraft had been flown by Czech pilots to Prague, and twelve Czech pilots were waiting in Kiev for more aircraft.[17]

How much the British Secret Service knew about Hitler's Directives of 30 May and 10 June is still a matter of speculation, but Cadogan in his diary gives hints of receiving disquieting news during this period. Indisputable evidence, however, soon came from high-up dissident German sources.

Dr Carl Goerdeler, a former Minister and Mayor of Leipzig had been Hitler's original Prince Commissioner, but had turned against the Nazis because of their brutality and warlike intentions. He visited London in early July with the approval of Goering, who wanted a report on the likelihood of a war with Britain, and warned Eden, Halifax and Vansittart that Germany intended to invade Czechoslovakia. He also gave news of the Hossbach Conference held in Berlin on 5 November 1937 when Hitler outlined his plans for military aggression; this became important evidence at the Nuremberg Trials. The Generals Blomberg and Fritsch had criticized this plan and had been replaced by General Brauchitsch who Hitler thought would be more subservient. General Beck, too, the Chief of Staff of the Wehrmacht, was strongly opposed to an aggressive war and remained an implacable opponent of Hitler until he was killed in the 20 July 1944 plot.

The two Directives from Hitler had appalled the more reasonable Generals who knew on military grounds that Germany was not strong enough for a war on two fronts, especially with the Russian threat. They, with Weizsaecker, began to plot the overthrow of Hitler, and started discussions with Goerdeler and other former politicians of the Weimar Republic. This group of generals, politicians and Foreign Office officials sent warnings to Britain, and revealed their plans for a coup. They aroused no response.[18]

On 18 August 1938 Ewald von Kleist came to London on behalf of the opposition. He was a Prussian landowner and the General commanding the Corps at Breslau until 5 February 1938. He saw Vansittart and Churchill, briefed them on Hitler's menacing Directives, and told them that Hitler personally, against the advice of his Generals, had decided to declare war on Czechoslovakia on 28 September. According to Kleist all his friends on the General Staff (except for Jodl, whose views he did not know) were dead against this attack. He warned that the only way to avert war was to threaten Hitler that such an attack would bring the full might of France and Britain against Germany. The opposition felt Germany in 1938 could not fight on both fronts, and the nation's fear of such a catastrophe would enable the Generals to depose Hitler and end the reign of terror. Vansittart accepted Kleist's view and reported to Halifax that the opposition plans unfolded by Kleist were reasonable and corroborated the evidence received by the Foreign Office from 'other sources' (the Secret Service). He was also sure Kleist was correct about the date of attack fixed by Hitler.[19]

Churchill reacted warmly and told Kleist that France and Britain would make concessions to a new German Government over colonies and trade treaties, and did not reject giving Germany the corridor to Danzig, although he feared this might push the Poles into the wrong camp. He gave Kleist a letter to encourage the opposition,[e] and urged Halifax — fruitlessly — to stop Hitler from making war on Czechoslovakia by threatening intervention. In a speech on 27 August he warned that the seizure of Bohemia would produce a second world war.

Churchill himself, who expected a monarchy after the coup,[f] did all he could to bolster the morale of the 1938 anti-Nazi plotters. The recollection of his support at this time must have made his unsympathetic rejection of their overtures all the more disheartening between 1942 and 1944.

Halifax told Chamberlain of Kleist's visit and Vansittart's and Churchill's views. Chamberlain's reaction was dismissive. He wrote on 19 August to Halifax:

Von Kleist is violently anti-Hitler and is extremely anxious to stir up his friends in Germany to make an attempt at its overthrow. He reminds me of the Jacobites at the Court of France in King William's time and I think we must discount a good deal of what he says.

In face of Vansittart's briefing, Chamberlain's flouting of this firm evidence was surely folly.[20]

A discouraged Kleist returned to Germany and reported the British Government's indecision. Generals Beck and Halder, both in top army posts, determined to prevent Hitler's act of madness without British cooperation.[g]

They decided to arrest Hitler at the moment he gave the order to cross the Czech frontier. Brauchitsch would issue a proclamation making himself temporarily the supreme authority in the Reich as Commander-in-Chief, and then an armoured division would be moved to Thuringia in central Germany to prevent the SS troops

[e]This was Kleist's downfall when it fell into the hands of the Gestapo after the Stauffenberg bomb plot in July 1944.

[f]The Kaiser's eldest son, Crown Prince Wilhelm, was prepared to come out into the open.

[g]Halder sent another emissary, Hans Bonn Tottelbach, a businessman with connections in London. He saw Vansittart on 4 September and gave more details of the plot and repeated Kleist's warning — again fruitlessly.

stationed in Munich from travelling to Berlin where the strike against Hitler would take place. General von Witzleben, GOC 23rd Division, would then seize the key government offices and arrest Hitler. The plotters were confident that the bulk of the German public would be so relieved at avoiding another war that there would be enthusiastic support for the coup.

The plotters made detailed plans to deal with Hitler. He was to be arrested and tried by a people's court. Prosecutors had already been briefed; a panel of psychiatrists under Karl Bonhoeffer (father of Dietrich) had made secret inquiries into Hitler's mental state, beginning with his case history when he was in a military hospital. They were confident that he could be certified as insane. This case history of Hitler was kept by the plotters for eventual use, and was discovered by the Gestapo after the failure of the 20 July 1944 bomb plot – with fatal results for some of the leaders of the 1938 plot, who had remained undiscovered for six years.[21]

The plan was feasible and well thought out. The leaders were capable and determined men and – although there is always a risk in any armed *coup d'état* – it was a tragedy it was never attempted. It never occured to Chamberlain or Halifax that the best way to stop the war might be to encourage the anti-Nazis and declare that Britain was in favour of living room for Germany in the east provided she had a democratic Government and ceased to persecute the Jews and minorities.

Hitler had no idea of the existence of the plot. It must have had a reasonable chance of success. Although many young army officers had an almost idolatrous worship for Hitler, the dominant feeling, especially amongst the older generation, would have been to spare Germany from a repetition of the 1914–18 war. Hitler knew his Generals were doubtful of military victory, but he himself was supremely confident that Britain and France would not intervene. The behaviour of Chamberlain, Halifax and Henderson all confirmed him in this belief. Chamberlain's visits to Hitler, the British Government's non-cooperation and its failure to promise automatic hostilities in the event of an invasion of Czechoslovakia combined to destroy the hopes of the conspirators.

In his diary General Jodl wrote:

It is distressing that the Fuehrer has the whole people behind him except the leading army Generals . . . They do not recognize the genius of the Fuehrer in whom some of them still see the corporal of the world war and not the greatest statesman since Bismarck.[22]

Weizsaecker's group of anti-Nazis inside the German Foreign Office included the diplomat brothers Erich and Theodor Kordt. Theodor was in Ribbentrop's private office; Erich was Counsellor at the Embassy in London. Weizsaecker sent a message from the conspirators to Cadogan, and on 6 September 1938 Theo Kordt, called secretly on Sir Horace Wilson[h] and told him of the plot against Hitler. He said that if Britain and France stood firm the conspirators would act on the day Hitler ordered mobilization. The next day Kordt met Halifax, being admitted secretly through the garden door to 10 Downing Street and said Hitler would order mobilization on 16 September with a view to an attack on Czechoslovakia not later than 1 October. Kordt asked Halifax to broadcast to the German nation. Cadogan was present and he noted in his diary: 'That would be fatal' – because he preferred private warnings. Halifax anyway knew that Chamberlain was now dead set on a personal meeting with Hitler. He did not tell Kordt this and took no action on the interview.[23]

Did Halifax refuse to believe that the German High Command were ready to turn on Hitler? The official documents and files are silent. Perhaps some relevant papers are still kept secret or have been destroyed. This double failure to act on either the Kleist or the Kordt disclosures is a severe indictment of Halifax. In 1982 David Astor described it as 'the saddest missed opportunity of the whole hellish experience leading up to World War Two'.[24] On the available evidence it is a reasonable verdict.

Chamberlain conceived two ideas which he felt might solve the Sudetenland problem. The first was to send a mediator to Prague; the second was that he himself should pay a personal visit to Hitler in Germany. Both played into the Fuehrer's hands.

The Prime Minister decided that the former Liberal politician Lord Runciman would be the ideal person to help to produce a settlement in Prague acceptable both to Henlein and his Sudeten Germans and to Beneš.

In July Hitler sent his ADC, Fritz Wiedemann, to London with a personal message to the Prime Minister. This was an assurance that Hitler would not use force if the British Government would put pressure on Beneš to give in to the demands of the Sudeten Germans. Chamberlain gave 'certain assurances' after the conversation to the effect that he was exercising a restraining influence on the Czechs.

[h]Sir John Colville, in *The Fringes of Power*, describes him as 'an *éminence grise* without whose advice the Prime Minister seldom moved' – adding: 'This was not his fault, or indeed his desire.'

Here was appeasement in full swing, and two days later Halifax told Daladier that, without consulting France, Runciman had been sent to Prague on a mission of reconciliation between the Sudeten Germans and Beneš. Faced with a *fait accompli* the French agreed to the Runciman mission, although Daladier had at first objected, saying that such a visit could only encourage Henlein in his demands. Beneš also agreed. Had he not done so, Chamberlain was ready to publish his refusal in the hope it would alienate public sympathy with the Czechs in Britain. The Runciman mission was a nail in the coffin of Czechoslovakia; his presence was evidence Britain was ready to dissolve the State. Runciman went to Prague at the end of July.

In an article in *L'Europe Nouvelle* 'Pertinax' wrote that Runciman was the end of the French Treaty of Alliance with Czechoslovakia, and in the *Nation* the respected British foreign correspondent Robert Dell wrote: 'Hitler has scored again, thanks to his faithful friend Neville Chamberlain. Lord Runciman has been sent to Prague to try to persuade the Czechs to commit national suicide.' These journalists were correct, and Chamberlain was busy implementing his plan to betray Beneš which he had leaked to the journalists at Lady Astor's. In the House of Commons on 26 July Chamberlain declared that Runciman had been sent at the request of Beneš. This was untrue.

On the same day Henderson wrote from Berlin:

The Czechs are a pig-headed race, and Beneš not the least pig-headed among them . . . so long as the Germans trust us and have confidence in the sincerity and impartiality of our effort the battle is not lost . . . we shall have at long last to put our feet down very firmly and say to Beneš 'you must'.

Chamberlain had the Ambassador he wanted.

In Prague Runciman suggested concessions to Henlein by Beneš, to which the Czech leader agreed. Hitler then told Henlein to increase his demands so as to make no agreement possible. In another inspired appeasement leader *The Times* suggested the secession of the Sudetenland without emphasizing that this would deprive Beneš of his fortifications against Germany. The *Daily Mail* and *Daily Express* supported *The Times*, but there were so many protests from the anti-appeasers that Downing Street implausibly denied that the *Times* leader represented the views of the British Government.

Halifax, unlike Chamberlain, suddenly became convinced that no compromise with Hitler was possible over the Sudetenland and that the secret reports received by Cadogan from the plotters were reliable evidence that Hitler was planning invasion. On 8 September he told the Prime Minister he favoured a strong warning to Hitler that infringement of the Czech frontier would mean a European war. Cadogan who was present noted: 'P.M. does not think warning message a good idea. Thinks he should go himself. I agree.' Vansittart was consulted and was strongly against Chamberlain going. Cadogan and Vansittart drafted a warning which, against Chamberlain's wishes, was agreed by the Cabinet on 9 August to the effect that Ribbentrop be told by Henderson that if France became involved in a war against Germany 'Britain could not stand aside'. This was sent to Henderson who was in Nuremberg for the Nazi rally. His response was that such a warning 'would be ill timed and disastrous'. With amazing weakness the Cabinet, strongly influenced by Chamberlain, accepted the Ambassador's advice – with Halifax saying 'It might well have driven Hitler over the edge.'[25]

On the night of 13 September Daladier telephoned Chamberlain and suggested direct meetings with Hitler. Chamberlain leapt at the French suggestion. On 16 September he was at Berchtesgaden in Germany talking to Hitler.[26]

At this time the Poles were anti-Russian and anti-Czech. They were very frightened that once Russian armies appeared on Polish soil they would never evacuate the parts of Poland that had belonged to Czarist Russia. The Foreign Minister was Józef Beck; he had been in a German cavalry regiment in the First World War. He was anti-French and liked the Germans. The Prime Minister, Smigly Ridz, had faith in Beck because he thought he improved relations with Germany. According to the Duff Coopers, who visited Warsaw in 1938, Beck was an alcoholic. An ominous message had come from the British Ambassador (Sir Howard Kennard) in Warsaw on 10 September 1938. He reported that the Poles had little sympathy with the Czechs nor did they feel

the same horror of Nazidom as is felt in democratic countries . . . the one eventuality which might throw Poland into the German camp would be any attempt by the U.S.S.R. to send help to Czechoslovakia across Poland.

What he did not say was how much the Poles hoped Hitler would dismember Czechoslovakia because then they would claim the Teschen – an area of Czechoslovakia previously part of the Hapsburg Empire which was predominantly Polish but had been sacrificed by Poland to Czechoslovakia in 1920 at a moment when Warsaw had nearly fallen to the Red Armies.[27]

Chamberlain and his Cabinet were as anxious as the Poles to

exclude Russia from any part in the Sudetenland dispute and
Chamberlain had maddened the Russians by insisting any treaty must
be through the League. Britain just would not accept Russian aid –
which was the only way of stopping Hitler. Also, by paving the way for
a bloodless triumph for the Fuehrer in the Sudetenland the plans of the
German anti-Nazi conspirators were sabotaged. As long as Hitler did
not have to fight a war on two fronts the German Generals' will to
overthrow him was weakened.

The French Government were now on an anti-Russian and Hitler-
appeasement trail. In Geneva Bonnet told Litvinov that France refused
to take part in staff talks with Russia.[28] Nor had Chamberlain
any intention whatsoever of making an alliance with Russia and he
cold-shouldered the overtures. Some historians contend that Russia
was not genuine, but the evidence to the contrary is overwhelming.

On 12 September, when Chamberlain's visit to Hitler was mooted,
Halifax suggested a four-power conference to solve the Sudeten crisis
to include France, Germany, Britain and Italy – but not Russia.
Vansittart immediately gave this sensible warning:

It would be the thin end of the wedge for driving Russia out of Europe, and
would be completely playing the German game . . . it is Germany, not Russia,
that threatens the physical existence of this country . . . it would surely be
unpardonable folly to assist Germany in driving off the map an associate we
need.[29]

He was right, but Chamberlain and Halifax did not want to hear this,
and Vansittart was ignored. The Government treated all the Russian
overtures so coldly that she became hostile, and within twelve months
Britain was faced by the disaster of the Soviet-German pact which
would not have come about if Russia had been brought into the
Czechoslovakian negotiations in 1938. The Chamberlain Cabinet and
the Tory MPs felt strongly that Russia wanted to stand aloof while
France and Germany bled themselves white in a war. Bonnet, the
French Foreign Secretary, continuously encouraged this view.

On 23 April Stalin sent a message to the Czech Government that
Russia was prepared to defend Czechoslovakia in concert with France.
This appears to have been genuine. On 12 May at Geneva Litvinov
asked the French to get permission for Russian troops to cross Poland
or Rumania.[30]

Litvinov in March had declared unequivocally Russia's intention to
honour her obligation to Czechoslovakia, and he reiterated this at the
League of Nations on 21 September 1938. He told the Assembly of the

League emphatically that Russia intended to fulfil her obligations under the pact with France to assist Czechoslovakia 'by the ways open to us' and asked for immediate consultation between the Great Powers of Europe and other interested states to decide on the terms for a collective démarche. If Litvinov's proposals had been accepted Hitler would certainly not have assaulted Czechoslovakia, but Chamberlain no longer wanted to save her. By ignoring Litvinov the British and French Governments threw away their last chance of thwarting Germany. The British Cabinet was not even allowed to debate the Russian proposal, so anti-Russian were Chamberlain and Halifax.

Chamberlain would not hear of staff talks with Russia because he was already determined to sacrifice the Sudetenland in the hopes of a 'general understanding' with a mollified Hitler, and he dreaded an alliance with Russia in a shooting war which might end with the Soviets in military possession of much of Eastern Europe.

Litvinov's suggestion produced no positive response at Geneva from the British delegates Lord De La Warr, Lord Privy Seal, and Rab Butler (Under-Secretary for Foreign Affairs). They spoke to Litvinov privately at once and he told them that Russia had warned Poland very seriously that she must not attack Czechoslovakia in concert with Germany to recover the Teschen.

Firm evidence that the means referred to by Litvinov in March had been found comes in an important message from De La Warr in Geneva to the Foreign Office dated 15 September 1938:

I saw Foreign Minister of Roumania this afternoon . . . he gave me to understand there was no definite agreement between Russia and Roumania but that, in case of war, supplies would probably pass through Roumania to Czechoslovakia, and he thought there would be no difficulty in such a case in allowing transit especially for aeroplanes. He stressed immense geographical difficulties which stood in the way of easy transit of men and materials across Northern Roumania. There were no convenient railways; a single line railway entailed some 500 miles of devious route to borders of Czechoslovakia . . . Russia's natural line of communication with Czechoslovakia lay through Poland, and if the latter was willing to allow the Russian aid to pass through her territory Roumania could then march and if she did so, so could Yugoslavia.[31]

Halifax told the British delegation to obtain 'precise information' from Litvinov, and on 23 September further evidence of the Russian firm commitment to defend Czechoslovakia came when De La Warr and Butler met Litvinov and Maisky, the Russian Ambassador in London, who had been called to Geneva by Litvinov. They confirmed to the Foreign Office what Litvinov had said in public – that if France honoured her obligation to Czechoslovakia, Russia would fight and come to the aid of the Czechs. In conversation Litvinov had said to the British delegates that he wanted conversations away from Geneva, preferably in Paris, with France, Britain and Rumania and any other small power who could be considered reliable. Litvinov also confirmed that Russia had told Poland that if she attacked the Teschen area the non-aggression pact between Poland and Russia would lapse.[132] Chamberlain at this stage was in Godesberg with Hitler, and he ignored the Russian overtures. Halifax took no steps to initiate Anglo-French-Russian talks about coordinating military plans although these were essential if Czechoslovakia was to be defended.

[i]In his memoirs Butler tried to play down the genuineness of this Russian initiative to intervene against Germany, but the evidence in the British and German archives suggests that Russia was intent on defending Czechoslovakia and would have done so if France went to war.

4
Berchtesgaden, Godesberg and Munich
1938

As Chamberlain left Heston airport for Berchtesgaden on the morning of 15 September 1938, there was a surge of popular support towards him in the newspapers, together with a leap in prices on the Stock Exchange. The German Embassy in London cabled Berlin that they had never witnessed such a sudden change in atmosphere from gloom to elation.

Chamberlain had met the Cabinet the day before and his attitude was that his visit was foremost to secure a 'general settlement' of Anglo-German differences.[1] What exactly he meant by 'general settlement' it is impossible to gather; but he seems to have regarded the Czechoslovakian issue as a minor obstacle in its way. He had no unlimited authority from the Cabinet to negotiate a settlement of the Czechoslovakian dispute; indeed he had promised the Cabinet 'that he would enter into no definite engagement in regard to a plebiscite'.

Not surprisingly the talks between the British Prime Minister and the German Chancellor at Berchtesgaden on 16 September started badly. Chamberlain said there were graver problems than Czechoslovakia to be discussed. Hitler retorted that they must begin with the Sudetenland as the crisis was deepening from hour to hour and there was no point in long diplomatic discussion. The Sudetenland must be solved at once because hundreds of Germans were being killed or injured; if Britain continued to parade her hostile intentions against Germany he would denounce the Anglo-German naval agreement. He went on that he was going to incorporate the Sudetenland into the German Reich and was prepared to risk a general war for a return of the three million Germans in Czechoslovakia. Chamberlain suggested a joint appeal to the two parties in Czechoslovakia. Hitler turned this down out of hand.

The idea of a plebiscite in the German parts of the Sudetenland was never raised. In a firm moment Chamberlain asked why the Fuehrer had let him come if he had already decided to settle the Sudetenland by force, but then dissipated these intimations of resolve by personally agreeing that the Sudetenland should be ceded to Germany. As this far exceeded the mandate Chamberlain had been given by the British Cabinet, he said he would report to his colleagues to see if they agreed with him. In return Hitler promised not to attack during the next few days. As his D Day was fourteen days away, Hitler was conceding nothing. He continued his plans for invasion while Chamberlain went back to London.[2]

At home most people wrongly believed the Prime Minister had prevented Hitler attacking Czechoslovakia. Amid this ill-judged popular enthusiasm Chamberlain allowed himself some elasticity in his assessments of the Fuehrer. To his sister he wrote: 'Here was a man who could be relied upon when he had given his word'; yet he told the Cabinet that Hitler was the 'commonest little dog he had ever seen'.[3]

Chamberlain now decided that he must convince both the Czech and the French Governments that Czechoslovakia should be dismembered. He coined the phrase 'self-determination' for the German majority in the Sudetenland, and claimed this was the only way in which war could be avoided. On 18 September Daladier and Bonnet came from Paris to 10 Downing Street and Chamberlain persuaded them to agree to the 'cession' of the zones of the Sudetenland with a German majority.[4]

The following day Chamberlain artfully told his Cabinet that 'self-determination' and 'cession' were French ideas, not his invention, and they endorsed the plan. A joint Anglo-French message was sent to Beneš calling on him to cede to Germany all Czech territory in which there was a German majority and offering in return to guarantee the rump of the Czech state against a German atttack. Beneš accepted on 21 September. As a result Czechoslovakia was about to lose her fortified frontier against Germany. Chamberlain had carried out Hitler's wishes to the letter.

There was, however, public awareness that Chamberlain was selling out Czechoslovakia to Hitler with nothing in return. At the meeting of the Cabinet on 21 September he was forced to promise that he would break off discussions if Hitler extended his demands for a break up of Czechoslovakia by asking for self-determination for other nationalities within that state.

As soon as Beneš's acceptance was received Chamberlain arranged to meet Hitler again at Godesberg. They met in the Hotel Deesen during the afternoon of 22 September. Chamberlain was confident that now he had met Hitler's demands over the Sudetenland the

German dictator would be more affably disposed towards the permanent 'general settlement' on which Chamberlain's eyes were fixed. He told Hitler that not only could there be a quick solution of the Sudetenland problem, but no plebiscite was necessary because agreement could be reached on what territory was to be ceded to Germany.

Then, to Chamberlain's acute dismay, Hitler made demands in excess of those of Berchtesgaden. He was determined to have the prestige of either a military victory or a triumphant surprise entry. Coldly he told Chamberlain that 'peace could not be firmly established in central Europe' unless the claims of other nationalities in Czechoslovakia were met. This was exactly the British Cabinet's sticking point. Chamberlain said he 'did not wish to dissent' but he was disappointed and puzzled because the Fuehrer was getting exactly what he wanted without any Germans being killed.[5]

Hitler went on with what should have been unacceptable demands. The German army was to replace the Czech army along the fortified frontier, and all Czech troops, police and Czech government institutions were to leave the areas to be ceded at once. Then Hitler would hold a plebiscite and return any areas with Czech majorities because he did not want Czechs in the Reich.

Chamberlain impressed on Hitler that he was having difficulty with public opinion in Britain in meeting even the original demands, and he was 'taking his political life into his hands'. He told Hitler there had been boos at Heston airport the previous day. In fact on 22 September a Mass Observation opinion poll showed only 22% supported Chamberlain and 40% opposed his policy. After a Cabinet discussion the same day, a cable was sent to Chamberlain at Godesberg saying that public opinion was hardening against more concession and it was up to Hitler to make a contribution.

By the end of the day Chamberlain was justifiably depressed and he informed London British objections to Czech mobilization should be withdrawn. He also wrote a letter to Hitler saying he would put the proposal of cession to the Czechs, but he could not agree to the immediate occupation of these areas by German troops because this would be 'an unnecessary display of force'. Hitler replied that because of the 'shameful way' in which Wilson's Fourteen Points in 1918 were disregarded he could only be satisfied by an immediate military occupation.

On the evening of 23 September a second Anglo-German meeting took place. Chamberlain pleaded in vain for some sop to British public opinion. All he could obtain from Hitler was that he would not move before 1 October, which was anyway the earliest date the German armies could be ready to attack. Chamberlain told the Fuehrer that 'a relationship of confidence' between the two had grown up and that he had in mind further and greater problems after the solution of the Czech crisis. Hitler said the Czech problem was his last territorial demand in Europe, and that colonies would not be a matter of mobilization. It speaks distressingly of his gullibility that these statements encouraged Chamberlain.

On his return to London Chamberlain argued for complete capitulation, claiming that Hitler 'would not deliberately deceive a man with whom he had been in negotiation'. He sketched promising prospects for the peace of Europe once there was an Anglo-German understanding.

The inner Cabinet met at 3.30 p.m. on 24 September. They unanimously accepted total surrender. Then Halifax, briefed by Cadogan, stiffened, and at the meeting of the full Cabinet the next day they refused to allow Chamberlain to make any more concessions.[6]

At the Cabinet these notes were exchanged between the Prime Minister and the Foreign Secretary:

Your complete change of view since I saw you last night is a horrible blow to me, but of course you must form your opinions for yourself. It remains however to see what the French say. If they say they will go in, thereby dragging us in, I do not think I could accept responsibility for the decision. But I don't want to anticipate what has not yet arisen.

N.C.

I feel a brute – but I lay awake most of the night, tormenting myself and did not feel I could reach any other conclusion at this moment, on the point of coercing Czechoslovakia.

E.

Night conclusions are seldom taken in the right perspective.

N.C.

Cadogan wrote in his diary: 'I was completely horrified. P.M. was quite calmly for total surrender. Still more horrified to find P.M. has hypnotised Halifax who capitulates totally.' The next morning Halifax said to Cadogan: 'I came to the conclusion you were right, and [this morning] at Cabinet plumped for refusal of Hitler's terms.'[7]

Unfortunately despatches from Phipps in Paris dated 24 and 25 September gave the misleading impression that there was no fight in the French. On 24 September Phipps reported that Flandin had called on him and said all peasant classes were against war, and 'although in case of necessity they would march, their hearts would not be in it. This is confirmed to me by several other sources.'[8] Later the same day Phipps reported his own 'purely personal impression' that

unless German agresssion was so brutal, bloody and prolonged (through gallantry of Czechoslovak resistance) as to infuriate French public opinion to the extent of making it lose its reason, war would now be most unpopular in France. I think therefore H.M.G. should realise extreme danger of even appearing to encourage small but noisy and corrupt, war group here. All that is best in France is against war, *almost* at any price (hence the really deep and pathetic gratitude shown to our Prime Minister). Unless we are sure of considerable initial successes we shall find all that is best in France as well as all that is worst turn against us and accuse us of egging French on to fight what must have seemed from the outset a losing battle.[9]

The next day Phipps wrote that Caillaux, President of the Finance Committee of the Senate, had called on him and assured him that a large majority of French were against war, including a large majority of the Senate, although a small majority of the Chamber might vote for it. Caillaux remarked to him that there might be a different attitude if Hitler 'actually goes to war with the Czechs and pushes into purely Czech territory although even then French public opinion as a whole will be opposed to war'.

These messages from Phipps were out of character. It is strange that he should have taken Caillaux's views so seriously because Caillaux, although a former French Prime Minister, was always pro-German and had gone to prison for being a traitor in the First World War. According to Harvey's diaries, because of these telegrams Phipps was retired earlier than he would have been otherwise.

The disbelieving Cadogan immediately instructed Phipps to obtain the views of Gamelin, Weygand, Pétain, Reynaud and others, and to collect the views of commercial and financial circles respectively from our consuls in France. He added that the Foreign Office did not understand Phipps's reference to

the small but noisy war group here. By war group you surely do not include all those who feel that France must carry out her treaty obligations to Czechoslovakia? If so, what precisely does this group consist of and what does it represent, and what are your reasons for describing it as 'corrupt'?

Harvey commented that the Foreign Office could not credit Phipps's defeatist telegram and insisted that consuls reported direct to London to prevent the Embassy 'doctoring' the messages.[10]

In a way Phipps was right – the French would not fight with great resolution. These messages, however, undoubtedly influenced Halifax towards appeasement at a moment when he was on the brink of insisting that Chamberlain stood up to Hitler.

On the evening of 25 September Jan Masaryk, on behalf of the Czechoslovakian Government, handed Halifax and Chamberlain a memorandum rejecting the Godesberg proposals, which he then denounced at a press conference. *The Times* the next day described the proposals as 'quite incapable of fulfilment,' and printed a letter from Leo Amery decrying them. By now Chamberlain was far more on the appeasement track even than Dawson, and without consulting the Foreign Office asked the German diplomat Kordt to let Hitler know he must not think the Czech rejection was the last word, adding that Downing Street was indignant at Masaryk's arbitrary action. This was one of Chamberlain's most humiliating gestures.[11]

On the morning of 26 September Gamelin told the British Cabinet that the French army would attack from the Maginot Line five days after the war started, and French bombers would attack German industry. He said the French would mobilize five million men and put one hundred divisions into the field. He slightly qualified this, to the unease of the British Chiefs of Staff, by saying that he would, if necessary, retire to the protection of the Maginot Line, 'leaving it to the Germans to break their strength against the permanent fortifications'. This was hardly the *blitzkrieg* required to take the pressure off the Czechs.[12]

Nevertheless, Hitler faltered at Gamelin's statements. He began to reconsider his plans to attack on 1 October, and in the few days between Godesberg and Munich he was nervous and indecisive.

The Dominion Heads of State, meanwhile, were lukewarm, thinking no *casus belli* existed. Chamberlain authorized the mobilization of the Fleet, and air raid precautions went ahead in London. In Berlin, to Hitler's annoyance, a demonstration by three motorized divisions was received without enthusiasm.

On 26 September Hitler spoke at the Sportpalast in Berlin, and announced that after Czechoslovakia he would have no more territorial claims in Europe. Chamberlain took this at its face value and issued a press statement which in effect constituted a promise to Hitler that the Czechs would hand over the Sudetenland.

Secretly, however, Hitler authorized an attack on Czechoslovakia for 1 October and mobilized the five divisions under General Adam facing the Maginot Line. The strain on him was considerable. He knew that if Gamelin attacked in strength the French might occupy large tracts of Germany in the west before he could withdraw his troops from the east. Yet he kept his nerve – with an instinct that France and Britain would not fight, and Chamberlain played into his hands. Extreme firmness by the French and British at this stage would have called Hitler's bluff; nor would he have moved had Russia been likely to intervene.

There was now a divided Cabinet. The Foreign Office was against further appeasement and Halifax authorized a Foreign Office press statement: 'If . . . a German attack is made upon Czechoslovakia the immediate result must be that France will be bound to come to her assistance, and Great Britain and Russia will certainly stand by France.'[a][13]

At the Cabinet meeting of 26 September Chamberlain had accepted that Britain would give a guarantee to France to help her if she went to war with Germany, and in return the Cabinet had authorized him to send his faithful Sir Horace Wilson with a letter to Hitler telling him that the Czechs were likely to reject the Godesberg terms and making 'one last appeal for further negotiations'. If Hitler refused, then Wilson was to tell him 'France would go to war and we would be drawn in'.

Wilson, with Henderson, delivered the message to Hitler on the afternoon of 26 September. The Fuehrer replied that he was determined to smash Czechoslovakia and if the Czechs refused his terms he would attack them. Then there would be war with France and Britain merely because Czechoslovakia refused to accept a memorandum which meant nothing more than the 'fulfilment of pledges already made'. In any event – by negotiation or by force – Sudeten German territory would be under German military occupation on 1 October.

The next morning, 27 September, Wilson told the Fuehrer: 'A catastrophe must be prevented at all costs . . . I will try and make those Czechos sensible.' Hitler said he would welcome that and England could wish for no better friend than him. Wilson gave the impression that Britain would not fight; this was not the majority view of the Cabinet on that day, but of the Prime Minister, who still appeared not to realize what a dangerous opponent he had. The Wilson visit produced no modification of the Godesberg terms; they were worse than the original Berchtesgaden offer.[14]

[a]This was known as the Leeper Statement, being drawn up by Rex Leeper, press officer at the Foreign Office, on Cadogan's initiative without Sir Horace Wilson being involved.

The full Cabinet met at 9.30 p.m. on 27 September after a timid broadcast by the Prime Minister. Wilson, having flown back from Germany, told of his useless encounter with Hitler and expressed the view that if Beneš accepted Hitler's timetable the Fuehrer would cooperate. Duff Cooper said he would rather resign than advise Beneš to accept Hitler's terms, and Halifax, emboldened by Cadogan, refused to agree the new plan. Chamberlain concluded the meeting by saying that 'if that were the general view of his colleagues he was prepared to leave it at that'.[15]

There were now active and visible preparations for war. Duff Cooper had been allowed to mobilize the Fleet; trenches were defiantly dug in Hyde Park. Schoolchildren were being evacuated from big towns and hospitals emptied to deal with the 50,000 air-raid casualties expected in the first few days. In Prague Beneš made ready for war, and France, too, mobilized. Hitler ordered his army to be ready for Operation 'Green' on 30 September.

Late that night a letter came from Hitler to Chamberlain saying that Czechoslovakia must give up her fortified frontier with Germany, and the 'immediate occupation by German contingents demanded by me represents no more than a security measure which is intended to guarantee a quick and smooth achievement of the final settlement'. It contained no concession and emphasized that he would not allow negotiations for the cession of the Sudetenland to be prolonged.

Chamberlain, without consulting his colleagues, decided to ignore their deliberations of a few hours before and wrote to Hitler: 'You can get all essentials without war and without delay.' He offered to come himself to Berlin. He also wrote to Mussolini to ask him to intervene, reiterating that he (Chamberlain) would guarantee that Czech promises would be kept.[16]

The next afternoon, 28 September, the House of Commons met. Chamberlain made a long statement about his futile negotiations, and incorrectly claimed the letter from Hitler received the night before contained 'reassuring statements' – though how this letter could be so construed defeats the imagination. Then a message was brought to him, and he told the House that he, Daladier, Mussolini and Hitler would meet in Munich the next day. Both sides of the House dissolved in wild applause with shouts of 'Thank God for the Prime Minister'. Chamberlain was the hero of the hour as the nation indulged in a short hysterical celebration of relief that the threat of immediate war had been averted.

Chamberlain left Heston airport the next morning, telling

reporters: 'It will be all right this time.' At Munich on the 29th Hitler would certainly have agreed with that prediction – he got everything he wanted. The Munich agreement dismembering Czechoslovakia, giving parts to Poland and Hungary as well as the lion's share to Germany, was signed just after midnight. Hitler's troops were to march in immediately to give him the triumph in the eyes of the German people which he so ardently desired. The rump of Czechoslovakia was a 'sitting duck' for Hitler, and his way into Eastern Europe was open.

The Czech Government was told nothing until the agreement was signed: their fortifications were forfeit and they had no time to remove the mass of their military equipment. Chamberlain never even considered asking the Russians to the conference, and never consulted his colleagues about the likely Russian reaction.

Just before the Munich agreement was signed Russia informed Beneš that she would go to Czechoslovakia's aid single-handed.[17] Beneš stated after the war had started that Litvinov had got the agreement of the Rumanian Government for Russian troops to cross Rumania even if France did not come into the war. This offer, according to Beneš, was refused because he felt the Czech Agrarian Party would not accept Russian aid, fearing their country would become first a battlefield and then a satellite of Russia.

According to the memoirs of Lieutenant-Colonel Peter Paul Donat (one of Hitler's interpreters), Hitler was full of rage against Chamberlain over Munich and said:

Daladier is a lawyer [incorrect] who understands the particulars and consequences. With him one can negotiate clearly and satisfactorily. But this Chamberlain is like a haggling shop-keeper who wrangles over every village and small detail; he is worse than the Czechs themselves. What has he lost in Bohemia? Nothing at all! . . .

[Chamberlain was] an insignificant man whose dearest wish was to go fishing on a weekend. I know no weekends, and I don't fish!

Still, according to the evidence of Schmidt (another Hitler interpreter) at the Nuremberg Trials, when Hitler returned to Berlin he said angrily 'That fellow Chamberlain has spoilt my entry into Prague.'[18]

During the discussions at Munich Chamberlain had been concerned that proper arrangements should be made to safeguard the interests and property of Czechs living in the Sudetenland. His worries were overcome by the promise that an International Commission of British,

French, German and Czech representatives would oversee the takeover. In fact it never operated, nor had Hitler any intention of allowing it to do so.

On the following day Chamberlain, still confirmed in his view that Hitler was someone he could trust, asked for a further interview and talked about Spain, air disarmament, Anglo-German trade, and the whole range of issues concerning Germany and Britain. Hitler showed little interest but agreed to sign the following document:[19]

ANGLO-GERMAN DECLARATION

We, the German Führer and Chancellor and the British Prime Minister, have had a further meeting today and are agreed in recognising that the question of Anglo-German relations is of the first importance for the two countries and for Europe.

We regard the agreement signed last night and the Anglo-German Naval Agreement as symbolic of the desire of our two peoples never to go to war with one another again.

We are resolved that the method of consultation shall be the method adopted to deal with any other questions that may concern our two countries, and we are determined to continue our efforts to remove possible sources of differences and thus to contribute to assuring the peace of Europe.

Signed: ADOLF HITLER

30.9.38   NEVILLE CHAMBERLAIN

It meant nothing to Hitler, but a lot to Chamberlain, who was delighted. All along he had wanted to widen the negotiations away from Czechoslovakia, and he deluded himself that he had established a special relationship with Hitler and laid the foundation of a lasting structure of peace in Europe. He used the unfortunate phrase that at Munich he had secured 'peace in our time'. In reality he had just paved the way for Hitler to seize more of Eastern Europe.

Private letters written by Chamberlain to his sisters and others immediately after Munich give indisputable evidence that he did not believe he had only bought time for British rearmament; he genuinely believed he was ushering in a new era of friendship between Hitler and Britain.

Hitler had been thwarted in his ambitions to see his armoured divisions defeating the armies of Czechoslovakia. However, the German High Command were relieved at having avoided war, and at the Nuremberg Trials General Keitel admitted that they would have had great difficulties in breaking through the fortifications on the Czechoslovakian frontier. The Chief of the Czechoslovakian General

Staff, General Krejci, told the British Air Attaché in Prague on 23 February 1939 that England and France had made a great mistake in not standing up to Germany, and that they had stored up greater trouble for themselves later on. The Germans, he said, were not ready for war in 1938.[20] Certainly the Generals were against it, as was Goering.

According to an authoritative report from the Czech War Office, Germany could not have spared more than seventy-five divisions for the east and their attack on Czechoslovakia and would have had to keep some of these on the Polish frontier.[21] The Czechs had thirty-six divisions. Colonel Petitbon, Gamelin's most trusted staff officer, largely corroborated this by telling the British Military Attaché in Paris on 28 September 1938 that the Czechs had thirty-three to thirty-four well-trained and efficient divisions, and the Germans could not overrun the country quickly without hard fighting. The French War Office said that the morale of the Czech army was high, though on this subject there were conflicting British reports. Mason-Macfarlane[b] told the British Cabinet on 27 September that it was 'not very good. Certainly not if forced to fight alone.' Cadogan commented 'What does he know about it?' This was a reasonable question because Mason-Macfarlane's views had mostly been gathered on one quick trip as courier from Berchtesgaden to Prague.[22]

Soon after the Cabinet adjourned late in the evening of the 27th a message came from Stronge, the British Military Attaché in Prague, that the Czech regulars 'have confidence in their cause, their leadership and their equipment'. Given the support of powerful allies, even if these could not immediately act on their behalf, they would 'render a good account of themselves'. After the war both Stronge and Mason-Macfarlane's deputy, Kenneth Strong, criticized Mason-Macfarlane's hasty judgement which unfortunately influenced the Cabinet towards surrender. As Telford Taylor writes: 'It was seized on with avidity because it was what his listeners wanted to hear.' Chamberlain and Halifax, plus Simon and Inskip, wanted news which would justify capitulation to Hitler.

In addition to a well-equipped army, the Czechs had intensive fortifications along the old German frontier – modelled on the Maginot Line, with heavy concrete fortifications and anti-tank guns. Their Skoda factory was almost the largest armament factory in Europe. Their fortifications on the German frontier were described

---

[b]Military Attaché in Berlin.

and pictured in great detail by the German War Office in 1941: 'Each defended position had independent fortifications in the rear with deep underground entrances and compartments; and there were nine huge fortification complexes.' In a German War Office report dated January 1938, there is a reference to 'the stupendous efforts being made to modernize the army and strengthen the fortifications'.[23] Yet the price of the sell-out was such that, according to Newton, on 1 October guns, ammunition and other war material to the value of 2,000,000 kronen were left behind in the Sudeten zone.[23]

When on 26 September Gamelin saw Chamberlain in London, he told him that the Czech army would give a good account of itself, and even if forced to retire to the east would continue to exist as a fighting force. Later Gamelin told the British Service ministers that the Czech army of thirty-four divisions was a 'good army, good personnel, excellent morale of the people fighting for their lives and an efficient command . . . she could hold out certainly for a few weeks.' According to Stronge, the Czech army was 'probably the best in the smaller states of Europe'. On the same day Daladier told Chamberlain that France was perfectly capable of mobilizing an air force and attacking Germany, and he understood Russia had 5,000 aeroplanes which had done well in the Spanish Civil War; also 200 Russian planes had been flown to Czechoslovakia to be handled by Czech pilots. On 18 September Daladier had told the British Cabinet that in the event of war French squadrons would be sent to Czechoslovakia by air as they could 'menace' Berlin from closer range than Paris. The British Prime Minister made no comment.

The British Military Attaché in Moscow, Colonel Firebrace, reported on 30 May 1938 that his Czech counterpart had told him that the Czechs would resist the German attack on Czechoslovakia with all their strength; that Czech officers were doing attachments with Red Army units, and that Russia had over a hundred divisions. His view was that Czechoslovakia could hold out for three months. The German Military Attaché, who was anti-Hitler, told Firebrace that the Red Army had been good up until 1936, but in the purge 60% of all officers above colonel had gone. He considered Timoshenko and Budjenny the best, but Voroshilov was not a good commander. Under Tuchaevski who was shot in the purge, the Russian army had been a menace to Germany, but not now. According to Firebrace the Russian monthly output of aeroplanes might be as high as 450. The British Committee of Imperial Defence stated Russia could put seventy-five divisions into the field in the west within one month of mobilization, and had 3,500 aircraft, of which not more than 2,000 could be put into operation on the Western Front. Lord Chilston, the British Ambassador in Moscow, was always contemptuous of the Soviets, and wrote that the Red Army was 'incapable of fighting outside Russia.' He was over-pessimistic and knew little about military matters but Chamberlain liked his briefing as it suited his case.[24]

The British Expeditionary Force designed to go to France in case of war amounted to only two regular divisions. They were well equipped by the standards of 1938, and at that date Hitler's army did not have the preponderance of 88mm anti-tank guns, tanks and armoured cars which it had in 1940. Nor was the German infantry in 1938 properly armed with the USA-style Thompson sub-machine guns which were to prove so deadly against the British infantry in May 1940. The Czechoslovakian infantry, however, was well equipped with such automatic weapons – far better than the British or German.

The German Generals were right strategically to tell Hitler that they dare not invade Czechoslovakia if Czechoslovakia was supported by the Allies. If Hitler had done so, after allowing for the divisions he must leave on the Polish frontier and on the Maginot Line, he would have found his best troops bogged down against the Czechoslovak fortifications, and even if the Czechs had to retreat to the east after a few weeks, by then they would have been reinforced by the Russians and Rumanians, so that the Germans would face a long war of attrition. In that case the French, aided by the British, would probably have occupied large tracts of Germany – if Gamelin had mustered up enough courage to attack the Siegfried Line, then incapable of holding back the French army with its huge numerical superiority. The British Chiefs of Staff had estimated on 21 March 1938 that France had fifty-three divisions only after mobilization, but on 26 September Gamelin claimed a hundred.[25]

Chamberlain was always horrified by the prospect of German bombardment of London and other British cities. But the truth was that Hitler in 1938 could not have spared many aircraft to bomb Britain because he would have needed them to support his troops in the east and to defend Germany against Gamelin's attacks in the west. Chamberlain was in despair about the prospect of war, believing that all the improvements in the standard of living achieved during his years as Chancellor of the Exchequer and Minister in charge of Housing would be dissipated. His temperament was such that he was psychologically incapable of examining the military factors realistically because of his terror of a return to the carnage and slaughter of his own generation. Nor did any other member of the Cabinet face the problems realistically, not even the Service ministers. But in the absence of a lead from Chamberlain it was difficult for them, and anyway the French Government was weak and the inscrutable French Commander-in-Chief, Gamelin, on whom so much depended, showed little enthusiasm for his plans to attack the few German divisions in the west, and declined to forecast how far his advance into German territory would proceed.[26]

5
After Munich
1938 – 1939

Between October 1938 and March 1939 opinion polls showed a large majority in favour of Munich, albeit a declining one.[1] Chamberlain received 40,000 letters of support from the public. He asked Dawson to use *The Times* to promote the case for abandoning Czechoslovakia, and the paper published photographs of Nazi soldiers being welcomed by the Sudetenland population. Duff Cooper resigned from the Cabinet; Churchill and Eden protested, but in the Munich debate in the House of Commons only thirty-one Conservative MPs abstained. Chamberlain himself rejected all suggestions of conscription and a Ministry of Supply. He told the Cabinet on 2 October that he felt strongly that because of Munich Britain need not ruin her economy by massive increase in defence spending. Instead he wanted France to extend the Maginot Line to the sea and rejected the Foreign Office calls sponsored by Cadogan for dramatic rearmament.[2]

On 17 October 1938 Halifax told the German Ambassador, Dirksen, that he hoped 'for a further extension of Anglo-German relations'. At the same time he drew attention to press reports of ill-treatment of some Sudeten inhabitants, which drew an uncompromising response from Hitler in a speech two days later at Saarbrucken: 'We cannot tolerate any longer the tutelage of governesses. Inquiries of British politicians concerning the fate of Germans within the frontiers of the Reich or of others belonging to the Reich are out of place.' Although this was intended as a withering snub to Chamberlain, who had set much store by the rights and property of the minorities in the Sudetenland, the Prime Minister still did not question whether or not he had been right at Munich. Sir Charles Petrie, a Right-wing admirer, wrote that in the autumn of 1938 Chamberlain 'entertained a touching belief in Hitler's sincerity'.[3] In mid-October there is perhaps a *frisson* of unease in a letter to his sister: though Munich had 'averted war' he did not believe they were any closer to putting war behind them 'and getting down to the real business of making the world a better place'. He felt the majority of the press was painting Munich in a bad light and frightening people about British unpreparedness.

On 7 November Baron von Rath, Third Secretary at the German Embassy in Paris, was shot by a Polish Jew. Immediately Hitler embarked on a pogrom against the Jews which even Lord London-derry, a leading British Hitler supporter, called 'detestable'. Chamber-lain, with supreme complacency, condoned the pogrom, saying at the Guildhall on 9 November: 'Political conditions in Europe are now settling down to quieter times.' This insensitivity to Nazi anti-Semitism does not in itself imply a conscious attitude towards the Jews, but it was at best unfortunate when taken in conjunction with Chamberlain's rigidity in Cabinet against Jews seeking refuge in Britain from the Nazis. Nevertheless the Prime Minister was beginning to realize that Hitler's attitude was eroding his own electoral popularity, and in private complained that Hitler would not make 'even the smallest sign of goodwill to Britain'. On 14 November the Cabinet Foreign Policy Committee met and were given evidence of Hitler's warlike intentions. They ignored it, and Chamberlain told them: 'We are in no position to frighten Germany.'[4]

Chamberlain's visit to Mussolini in Rome on 10 January 1939 had no concrete results. He had told the Commons on 2 November that he saw it as an important step on the peace path. Now he wrote to his sister that the trip had exceeded his expectations and the possibilities of avoiding another war were greatly enhanced. He was naively pleased at the applause from the Rome crowds.

When the Cabinet met on 17 January the Prime Minister told his colleagues that he was convinced Mussolini and Hitler 'could not be very sympathetic to each other', and he rather doubted if Mussolini knew Hitler's plans. He also said he was favourably impressed with Mussolini's demeanour and attitude, and added that Mussolini had remained absolutely loyal to Hitler in the talks. At the time he had been somewhat disappointed at this attitude, but on reflection he thought it 'reflected credit on Signor Mussolini's character'. Halifax told the Cabinet that he agreed with the Prime Minister that Mussolini's broad instinct was 'for peace'. It proved a somewhat ingenuous judgement. On 4 February Mussolini, in private, outlined his aims to the Grand Council of Fascism. They were to capture for Italy Corsica, Tunisia, Malta, Cyprus, Gibraltar and Suez.

On 25 January Chamberlain told the Cabinet that 'for the moment it would be undesirable that we should enter into a precise and definite obligation to intervene if Holland was attacked by Germany'. The

Cabinet agreed there was 'little scope for acceleration of the Defence programme' – in spite of the evidence given to the Cabinet's Foreign Policy Committee two days before. Then new top secret reports on Germany had been presented by Cadogan, Vansittart, Strang and Jebb.[a] They were highly alarming and even more disquieting than those considered at the previous meeting of the Committee on 23 November, but the Cabinet preferred the soothing syrup from Henderson in Berlin who in his despatches to London claimed Hitler intended 'no more adventures'.[b]

The Committee were told that Hitler was contemplating an 'overwhelming blow at the western powers; it might be an invasion of Holland or a direct air attack on Britain'. Cadogan wrote:

The Germans probably reckon that we should not take up arms in defence of Holland (and this is only too likely to be true), that France and Belgium would not do so . . . once in command of Holland and the Dutch coast Germany would aspire to dictate terms to us.

He wanted immediate talks with the Dutch and for Britain to be ready to

propose some form of arbitration from individuals nominated by say the U.S.A., Swiss, Swedish, Norwegian, Yugoslav and perhaps other Governments. That would doubtless have no effect but if arbitration were rejected or overridden that would give a better *locus standi* for our intervention.

Jebb asserted that

there is incontrovertible evidence that at any rate many of the Führer's entourage are seriously considering the possibility of a direct attack on Great Britain and France during the next few months . . . all our sources are at one in declaring that he (Hitler) is barely sane, consumed by an insensate hatred of this country and capable both of ordering an immediate aerial attack on any European country and of having his command instantly obeyed.[5]

Chamberlain, however, still believed in a diplomatic triumph, and on 25 January no one in his Cabinet insisted on urgent preparations for a European war. On 28 January he made a strongly worded speech in favour of appeasement, and then wrote to his sister that he believed at long last Hitler 'had missed the bus at Munich' and we were in a stronger position than then.

[a] Gladwyn Jebb (created Lord Gladwyn 1960), was at this time Private Secretary to Cadogan.
[b] On what grounds Henderson based his opinions is unclear; at this stage he was a sick man after an operation for a malignant growth on his tongue.

It was wishful thinking. British rearmament was slow except for the development of fighter aircraft and radar. Chamberlain emphasized as late as 21 February 1939 that he was rearming mainly for defence and the biggest effort was to go into air raid precautions and anti-aircraft guns. The War Office argued that the loss of Czechoslovakia left France weaker in relation to Germany and vulnerable, without more ground help, to a German attack through Holland. The Prime Minister ignored the warning and there was no communication between Chamberlain and Daladier over defence. The staff talks with the French, begun before Munich were abandoned.

In October the War Office had prepared a paper for the Cabinet outlining the deficiencies of the field force and the Territorial Army. Hore-Belisha[c] agreed it and sent it to a Cabinet Committee on Defence Preparation and Acceleration set up on 26 October.[6] Ignoring the War Office, Chamberlain told the House of Commons on 1 November: 'We are not contemplating the equipment of an army on a Continental basis.' Hitler was delighted, the French were appalled. No action was taken on the Belisha paper, with Chamberlain telling the Cabinet that Hore-Belisha's scheme 'did not tally with Hitler's next move, which would be eastward, in which case we might not be involved at all'. Not surprisingly some members of the Cabinet were at odds with Chamberlain's opposition to a larger field force.

Thus for six months after Munich the Government, inspired by Chamberlain's optimism, believed that in the event of war with Germany France would defend the land frontier alone. Chamberlain's aim was to harvest the fruits of Munich before the coming General Election, and for him this meant not interfering with either economic recovery or Tory popularity by the higher taxes which would be needed to pay for more rearmament.

Within the Foreign Office Vansittart was muted. Cadogan was defeatist and argued for giving Germany a free hand in the east and containing her only in the west, believing that if Britain built up her air power Germany would not attack France. The Foreign Office and Halifax feared that if Britain committed herself to Russia it would lead to Communism in Germany. Russia knew of the Foreign Office indifference to German expansion in the east, and concluded – with disastrous results – that Britain wanted to set Germany at war with Russia. Hitler himself believed that Britain was 'decadent' and would

[c]Leslie Hore-Belisha had become Secretary of State for War in 1937.

not rearm seriously to check his ambitions. He was quoted, to the Cabinet's dismay, as saying that if Britain did not introduce conscription by the spring of 1939 the Empire would be lost.

The British Government ignored completely the first breaches of faith by Hitler immediately after Munich. On 11 October Vansittart minuted: 'Proceedings of the International Committee have been scandalous. It has simply reproduced Godesberg.' Hitler gave Teschen to Poland without notice and issued ultimata, which Czechoslovakia had to accept, to hand over further areas to Germany, including the historical parts of Taus and seven winter sports resorts. The International Commission, on which Chamberlain had pinned his hopes, literally never functioned. Over the rights and properties of non-Germans in the Sudetenland Hitler behaved as if there had been no Munich accord. He attacked Britain for rearming and told German journalists he no longer placed any value on British friendship. Then, on 2 November, the Vienna Award between Ciano and Ribbentrop carved out an area of South Czechoslovakia and gave it to Hungary without consulting either London or Paris. The Cabinet meeting on 16 November, to consider these developments, postponed any decision and referred the problem to the Foreign Policy Committee, who on 6 December decided to take no action. Chamberlain said in the Commons on 1 November that 'to attack Munich' was to 'foul our own nest'.

The Foreign Office thesis that Germany would attack next in the east was jolted when Beck, the Polish Foreign Minister, went to Berchtesgaden and Ribbentrop to Warsaw to reaffirm the Polish-German agreement of 1934. However, this was just a cover up by Hitler of his plan to dismember Poland – as he admitted later to his Generals when he issued his orders to attack Poland.

Now, with the outlook black, a ray of hope appeared on the horizon. In December 1938 the Foreign Office were informed of a plot to make Goerdeler Chancellor instead of Hitler. Cadogan wrote in his diary: 'If there is anything in it it is the biggest thing in centuries.'

Ashton Gwatkin[d] had kept in touch with Goerdeler who was looked on then by the Foreign Office as the most likely person to overthrow Hitler. Early in December Goerdeler approached Ashton Gwatkin and asked him if he could get an assurance from the British Government that they would not take advantage of any revolution in Germany 'to try and smash Germany', and that the British would

[d]Frank Ashton Gwatkin was Head of Economic Relations at the Foreign Office.

approve the revolutionaries' programme. He added that the new German Government would want to keep Hitler's acquisition of the Sudetenland. The revolution would be spearheaded by the dissident German Generals, but Goerdeler expected he would be Chancellor under the new regime. He asked for the British Government to promise to send a message of support to the revolutionaries as soon as the coup took place.[7]

On 8 December the Kaiser was reported in *The Times* as describing Hitler as

having set up an all-swallowing state disdainful of human dignities and the ancient structures of our race . . . For a few months I was inclined to believe in Nazi Socialism as a necessary fever. But the wisest and most outstanding Germans who were associated with it for a time he has got rid of, or even killed – von Papen, Schleicher, Neurath, even Blomberg. He has nothing left but a bunch of shirted gangsters.

The Kaiser was undoubtedly inspired by Goerdeler and some Generals to make this outburst, and on 10 December Goerdeler's representatives in London called on Ashton Gwatkin at the Foreign Office. They were the German Dr Reinhold Schairer, a well-known educationalist and a close friend of Goerdeler, and A. P. Young, the English Managing Director of British Thompson Houston. Ashton Gwatkin reported:

Dr Schairer attached great importance to the reported interview given by the Kaiser and criticising the Nazis. He saw in this the hand of Dr G.; and regarded it as the first step in the following programme.

As soon as the Generals are ready – and this will depend in the first instance on what G. hears from us with regard to the programme he submitted – arrangements will be made for the Kaiser to go on board a German warship and from there broadcast the nation revoking the abdication of their oath to him (this is very important with ref. to Army loyalties) but referring their loyalty to his grandson Prince Frederick.

The Army would then seize the Broadcast station at Berlin, also the Reichsbank, and declare a Restoration, and the prosecution of the leaders of the Nazi regime. About 2,000 leaders would be arrested at once, and the trials would follow in order to give the utmost publicity to the scandals of the regime. It is therefore, urgent that Dr G. should get a reply, and if possible a favourable reply to his programme by Dec. 18th. A favourable reply from England would be the turning point of his argument with the Generals; and he, Dr S., believes that action would follow almost immediately perhaps between Dec 18th and Dec 31st.

Failing a favourable reply, Dr G. would probably leave Germany, and commence organisation of opposition openly from outside instead of secretly from within.

The leader of the Army people would be von Fritsch, and v. Neurath would be in the plot from the beginning – but not Schacht.

Dr G. himself would probably be Reichskanzler under the new regime.

Cadogan was in two minds in his report to Halifax. He wrote that Goerdeler wanted to show his fellow conspirators that Britain would not take advantage of troubles in Germany 'to try and smash Germany', and 'that any assurance given to Goerdeler would be repeated to the army leaders and thus inevitably get out and unite all Germany behind the Nazis'.

The only message Cadogan thought the Government could send would be that

Our only desire is to live in friendship and peace with a united and peaceable Germany; and we would never attempt to take advantage of any troubles arising in Germany, and we would co-operate and assist any German Government whom we could be assured desired to live at peace with their neighbours . . . If we send a message it should be through Mr. Young who would be ready to go to Germany at any time to meet Mr Go[e]rdeler.

Halifax asked Cadogan to speak to the Prime Minister about it on the next day. After seeing Chamberlain Cadogan minuted:

P.M. would have nothing to do with it. He was very doubtful of Dr. G's scheme; he also took the view that any message to be of any use to Dr. G, and to make the difference between success and failure must expose us to danger from which we might not recover. He definitely said no message should be sent.

Chamberlain's reaction was predictably consistent with his fear of antagonizing Hitler and with his continued ingenuous faith in the Munich promises. In reality nothing he told the German oppposition would have made any difference to Hitler's plans but might have spurred on the Resistance to attempt a coup.

Vansittart saw Schairer and explained that it was not practical politics for an 'authoritative message' to be sent to Goerdeler in these circumstances 'but it must be left to his common sense to know what will be the attitude of HMG to a friendly Government, if it emerges in Germany, and he can himself explain this to his friends.' ·

The approach, which Cadogan took seriously, was kept secret even within the Foreign Office. Sir Ivo Mallet, then private secretary to Lord Halifax, wrote to the author:

Neither while I was in Berlin in 1932–36 nor while I had the German desk at the Foreign Office in 1937–38 did the question of a Hohenzollern restoration crop up. What the German people would have felt if Hitler had been removed by an army *coup* late in 1938 I just do not know. Ashton Gwatkin always thought agreement with the Nazis could be founded on economic concessions such as loans, offers of colonies and other economic concessions. This was totally to misunderstand Hitler and thus I do not attach much weight to his comment. 'A favourable reply from England would be the turning point.'

Chamberlain in December 1938 still clung to his conviction that he could by reaching agreement with Hitler prevent a European war. Ignorant, unwilling to listen, conceited and obstinate he may have been, but at least he was sincere in his endeavours until after 15 March when Hitler's seizure of Prague removed the scales from his eyes. How in those circumstances could Chamberlain have let it be known in Germany that he was in correspondence with, and giving assurances to conspirators who aimed at overthrowing Hitler? It is one thing for an Ambassador abroad to talk to responsible opposition leaders but quite another for a foreign Government to send secret messages of encouragement to a group of underground plotters.[8]

Some might question Mallet's argument that in a one-party tyrannical state it is wrong for a foreign Government to talk to responsible politicians forced to go underground because of the impossibility of offering any visible opposition to official policies. Goerdeler was the nearest approach to a responsible opposition leader. Possibly after the seizure of Prague in March 1939 he might have got a more favourable response from Chamberlain.

On 21 October 1938 Hitler had issued a directive to his Generals to prepare to liquidate the rump of Czechoslovakia while simultaneously defending their western frontier. He sent Ribbentrop to Paris early in December for talks with the French Foreign Minister, Bonnet.[9] According to Ribbentrop, Bonnet told him that Czechoslovakia lay completely within the German sphere of interest.[e] Almost certainly Bonnet gave him a nod that France would not interfere if Prague was occupied by the Germans. The upshot of their talks was an agreement in which Germany abandoned her claims to Alsace-Lorraine.

Thus in the first weeks of 1939 Hitler was set to take the whole of Czechoslovakia and acquire all the Czech army material, which included 1,500 aeroplanes, 450 tanks and the Skoda arms factory, second only in size in Europe to Krupp's.

On 15 March Hitler broke his word given solemnly at Munich and occupied the rump of Czechoslovakia after a stage-managed political revolt in Prague. He claimed he had acted only at the request of Hacha, the Czech President − as with Schuschnigg over the Anschluss. Hacha

---

[e]Significantly, Bonnet later told the British Ambassador in Paris (14 March 1939): 'We nearly went to war last autumn to boost up a state that was not viable.'[10]

ordered there should be no resistance to the German armies, but he did so only because otherwise Hitler had threatened to bomb Prague; indeed Hacha fainted when Hitler threatened him with the destruction of his capital and country by the German troops and air force.

Despite an outcry in the country, Chamberlain told the Commons that Britain had no obligation to defend Czechoslovakia because it was an internal disruption of the state, and that the guarantee related to a 'transitory condition of affairs, and HMG was no longer bound'. He also watered down the draft of the British protest to Germany. Though his Munich policy was in ruins, he still would not admit it; not unnaturally Hitler felt he had the final evidence that Britain would not fight to stop his plans for German aggrandizement.

At last the Prime Minister's weakness all but caused a revolt within the Tory Parliamentary party. According to a letter to his sister, Chamberlain's first reaction to the seizure of all Czechoslovakia was to seek an agreement with Russia, Poland and France so that they would take action if there were renewed German aggression, but Poland refused to have anything to do with Russia.[11]

The anti-Nazis inside Germany were discomforted because the rape of Czechoslovakia made Hitler wildly popular with the German people. He had duped Chamberlain at Munich and succeeded in tearing up the Treaty of Versailles and securing German *lebensraum* to the east. Yet, only the evening before the march to Prague, Hoare – at Chamberlain's suggestion – had made a speech to his Chelsea constituents glorifying 'the golden age of peace and prosperity' that cooperation in Europe would bring because of Chamberlain's triumph at Munich. Cadogan had reported on 11 March on impeccable authority that Hitler was about to take the rest of Czechoslovakia, but Chamberlain must have completely ignored him.[12]

Halifax and the Foreign Office at first agreed that nothing should be done, although Halifax wanted to withdraw Henderson to London for consultation. Chamberlain thought this was 'going too far' but he did agree to postpone a planned trip by Stanley to Berlin. However, within forty-eight hours of Hitler's occupation of Czechoslovakia Chamberlain changed his tune completely. The Rumanian Minister to Britain, Virgil Tilea, panicked the Foreign Office by asserting that within the next few months Hitler would reduce Rumania to vassalage, and had already presented an ultimatum that Germany must have a monopoly of the output of the Ploesti oilfield. The British representative in Rumania, Sir Reginald Hoare, signalled to London that Tilea's story was false and it was denied by the Foreign Ministry in

Bucharest. But Tilea had shocked Chamberlain. In Cabinet the Prime Minister received unanimous endorsement of a change of policy from appeasement to 'joining with friends' in resisting aggression; he saw Poland as the key to the situation. Yet he wrote again to his sister expressing profound mistrust of Russia.

To Chamberlain's annoyance the Russians proposed a conference of Britain, France, Poland, Rumania and themselves to plan 'common action'. This was rejected by Chamberlain and Halifax. Instead, on 20 March Halifax told the Cabinet it was essential to secure the early consent of France, Russia and Poland to a public announcement about stopping German aggression. On 22 March Litvinov told the British Ambassador that Russia would sign such a declaration.[13]

On 21 March there had been a sinister development in Berlin between Ribbentrop and the Polish Ambassador, Lipski, about which the Poles kept Britain in the dark. Ribbentrop told Lipski that the Danzig Corridor dispute must be solved or 'a serious situation would arise'. This was a definite threat that Germany would make war on Poland unless Danzig and the Corridor were handed over.

Two days later Beck suggested to Britain that there should be a secret bilateral security agreement between Britain and Poland. The pact must be confidential and bilateral: open association with Russia might provoke Germany. Beck made no mention to Britain of Ribbentrop's threatening talk with Lipski of 21 March, and hence the British Government at first had no idea it was Poland that was menaced by Hitler, not Rumania.

On 28 March Ian Colvin, the *News Chronicle* German correspondent, flew to London and delivered the bombshell that Hitler intended a *putsch* to take Danzig and the Corridor. Colvin knew all about the Lipski-Ribbentrop talks and the German threat to Poland. He was trusted in Whitehall; he saw Halifax and Cadogan and gave 'hair-raising details of the imminent German thrust against Poland'.[f] Halifax took him to see the Prime Minister.[14]

Colvin explained that the only way to stop Hitler's coup against Poland was to convince him that it was certain that Britain would attack him if it happened, and in that case there would be a good chance of the German Generals, under threat of revolt, persuading him to stay his hand. Colvin added that he was certain that the Generals would have revolted in September if Britain had stood up to Hitler. This, coming on top of Goerdeler's messages in December, was

[f]The German published documents show that Hitler had ordered his military staff to be ready to 'obliterate Poland' by 1 September (Operation White).[15]

convincing evidence of a German opposition ready to act if encouraged by the British. No one in Whitehall, however, paid any attention to Colvin's views about the German opposition.

Almost in a panic the British Government, for fear of a sudden Hitler attack on Poland, gave a unilateral guarantee of military help to Poland if she were attacked by Germany. It was an improvisation finalized in the Foreign Office on 29 March and triggered off by Colvin's arrival in London on 28 March. Chamberlain announced it to the House of Commons on 31 March.

The pledge to Poland abrogated Britain's freedom to negotiate with Hitler the cession of Danzig and the Corridor to Germany; any use of force by Hitler there would be for the Poles a *casus belli* and Britain would have to come to their aid. Chamberlain, in temporary outrage at Hitler breaking his word, had given a blank cheque to the Poles.

He himself never saw it that way; indeed he frequently took personal credit for the pledge to Poland, which – with hindsight – must have been among the more reckless and impractical gestures in our diplomatic history, quite apart from being a denial of everything Chamberlain had done in foreign policy since he came to power. Yet few at home, apart from Lloyd George and Basil Liddell Hart,[g] doubted the wisdom of the Polish move and Churchill, in company with Labour and Liberal leaders, congratulated Chamberlain.

Stalin was horrified by Hitler's invasion of the rump of Czechoslovakia and he and Litvinov were also initially impressed by Chamberlain's guarantee to Poland. Thus Stalin decided to make the offer of a triple defence pact to Britain and France.[16] Russia said she was ready to give military assistance, if the three powers cooperated, to any state in eastern Europe which might be the victim of Hitler's aggression. If this offer had been immediately accepted by Britain there would have been a chance – according to Maisky's view, expressed strongly after the war – of Hitler being overthrown by the German opposition.

Instead Halifax asked Maisky at the preliminary interview whether Russia would give a 'declaration of intent' to resist aggression without either power entering into a definite agreement. This struck the wrong note, and the Russians thought they were being enticed into danger without any guarantee of support from France or Britain if Hitler attacked them. Nor did Halifax's proposal do anything to allay the Russians' long-standing suspicion that Britain wanted Germany and Russia to fight each other.

[g]Doyen of military historians, and unofficial adviser to Hore-Belisha when he was Secretary of State for War.

On 3 May Sir William Seeds[h] saw Litvinov in Moscow and was asked if there was certainty that Britain would declare war on Germany if Rumania was attacked. Seeds hedged. This was a fatal mistake. Stalin thought Britain was stalling and Litvinov, the ardent supporter of an alliance with France and Britain, was sacked from the post of Foreign Affairs and replaced by the less friendly Molotov.[16]

On 8 May Molotov asked Seeds if it was proposed to start immediate military talks with a view to defending Poland and Rumania against Hitler. Once again Seeds procrastinated because he had no clear instructions from his Government. A protracted correspondence between Moscow and London followed. Vansittart's view was that the delay in reaching an understanding would put Stalin into sulks which would be followed by closer Russian relations with Germany, and he wrote to Halifax on 4 May: 'That I regard as absolutely fatal.' He was right. On 27 May Molotov told Seeds he had the impression that Britain and France wanted to continue conversations *ad infinitum* but were not interested in concrete results. Because of Chamberlain's cold response to his offer of a defence pact Stalin felt he must make a deal with Hitler – otherwise he would be left to fight Germany without assistance from the West. The Prime Minister's neglect of the Russian offer of 17 April turned out to be a great mistake. By 16 June Kordt had warned Vansittart that German-Russian negotiations had started, and on 22 May Mussolini and Hitler had signed the Pact of Steel, giving the impression of an Italian pledge of assistance to Germany in event of war although there were secret clauses that Italy would probably not be ready for war until 1942.[17]

Although William Strang was sent to Moscow in June, it was not until 11 August that an Anglo-French mission eventually arrived in Moscow for staff talks with the Russians. The Poles were uncooperative and refused to say whether they would allow Russian armies on their soil in the event of a German attack on Poland or Rumania; with memories of the Bolshevik army advancing to Warsaw nineteen years before, they would not commit themselves to giving permission for a Russian expeditionary force to come to their rescue.

The fatal delay between 17 April and 11 August convinced Stalin that France and Britain wanted him to fight Germany alone. As a *quid pro quo* for a defence pact the Russians wanted to recover as much as possible of former Czarist territory in Poland and the Baltic states.

---

[h]Sir William Seeds was now Ambassador in Moscow. He lasted only a year.

Chamberlain never appreciated this nor how much Russia feared being left alone to fight the Germans. The negotiations dragged on unsuccessfully until on 23 August 1939 Hitler concluded the German-Soviet pact, which amounted to a complete rejection of the West by Stalin and made Hitler's conquest of Poland inevitable.

During this period German conspirators against Hitler were active. Prague had been a shock and they were gravely handicapped by the boost it gave to Hitler's national popularity and to his authority over his Generals, upon whom the anti-Nazis based their hopes of a successful coup. Goerdeler, Schacht and Gisevius went to Ouchy near Geneva to meet an emissary who communicated their plans to the British and French Governments. They made it clear that Hitler was determined to seize the Danzig Corridor by force in the autumn.[18]

The Foreign Office were negative and the Cabinet were not interested. General Beck and General Oster wanted to convey a dire warning to the Foreign Office and contacted Ian Colvin. Colvin met Halifax and Chamberlain on 27 April in the Prime Minister's room at the House of Commons. Colvin said there would very soon be a German attack across the Danzig Corridor seizing Poland's access to the sea, and that the Germans were carrying on an agitation campaign over Polish atrocities against Germans within Poland. Colvin went on at length about the German opposition to Hitler and formed the impression that neither Halifax nor Chamberlain had even been briefed about its existence.[19]

The conspirators were now in great difficulties. They knew an army plot to overthrow Hitler was no longer possible. They recognized sadly that Britain was now so anti-German as a result of the seizure of Prague that she was ready to go to war. They also felt that Britain had given such encouragement to Poland that Poland would now refuse to cede Danzig and the Corridor and would give Hitler more genuine excuses for war by unsympathetic treatment of the German minority in Poland. They were strong nationalists, and not unnaturally refused to promise that a de-Nazified Germany would give up Czechoslovakia or Austria; they could only carry public opinion with them if Britain and France would promise them the territory in the east which Hitler coveted. This was anathema to the Foreign Office.

Two of the younger conspirators were Helmuth von Moltke, grandson of the famous Field-Marshal, and Adam von Trott. Both had strong British connections. Moltke's mother was Scottish, Trott had been an Oxford Rhodes Scholar, a Balliol contemporary of Jo Grimond and David Astor. His large circle of friends included Stafford Cripps[i] and Lord Lothian.

Trott was one of the German Foreign Office plotters inspired by Weizsaecker and Beck who had just sent the German staff officer, Colonel von Schwerin, to London with the message that Hitler would attack Poland later in the summer, and that Hitler believed despite the Polish pact that Britain and France would not fight. Schwerin's job was to make clear to the British that Hitler did not believe Britain was prepared to go to war and that Britain ought to send a battleship to the Baltic to exercise off Danzig, transfer RAF squadrons to France, and replace Henderson with a more militant and less pro-Nazi ambassador. Through Trott, Schwerin met David Astor who introduced him to the Intelligence Department at the War Office.

Whitehall completely ignored Schwerin's message although he talked frankly at a lunch *à quatre* with Admiral Godfrey, Director of Naval Intelligence, General Marshall-Cornwall, high up in the War Office, and James Stuart, a Government Whip representing the Prime Minister. He told them he bore a confidential personal message from Beck that Hitler was bent on annexing Poland in the autumn regardless of the consequences, and the German General Staff were against a war for which they were not ready.[20]

The German Foreign Office plotters now conceived a fantastic scheme. They proposed that Hitler should restore freedom to Czechoslovakia and that in return the Western powers should give him Danzig and the Corridor. They wanted Britain to make this proposal. Then when Hitler was bogged down in this type of negotiation they would attempt to replace him by a coup. Trott was sent to London to sell this idea to the British Government. Thanks to the Astors he had interviews with Chamberlain and Halifax. At the same time Trott told the German Foreign Office that he was going to use his personal connections in London to promote a better understanding of the Fuehrer.

Trott found London tense over the impending war, but he did succeed in convincing the Prime Minister and Foreign Secretary in an interview that there was a German opposition determined to overthrow Hitler. The British Government would not even consider giving the conspirators guarantees that a new democratic Government in Germany would receive favourable treatment from France and Britain

[i]Labour MP. Ambassador to Moscow 1940–42 and later a member of the War Cabinet.

over awards of territory in the east. Neither the Foreign Office nor the Government held any brief for such an agreement although very soon they were ready to give Hitler almost all he wanted.

Although there is evidence that both Chamberlain and Halifax were favourably impressed with the personable Trott, they showed no interest in promising support to an alternative Government in Germany. Neither Chamberlain nor Halifax had lost hope of a deal with Hitler. A speech made by Halifax at Chatham House a few days later may have been due to Trott's talk at Downing Street. In this Halifax said Britain would definitely go to war over Danzig and the Corridor, but would cooperate with a peaceful Hitler over the return of colonies.[21]

David Astor has written that historians have played down the German opposition as not being really worth helping, mainly because of their nationalism and demand for *lebensraum* in the east. But if any Government was to be popular in Germany they had to deliver to the German people freedom from the chains of Versailles, and this meant Polish and Czech territory. Almost no one in London appreciated this crucial point. Most of the 1938 conspirators against Hitler ended up on the gallows after the failure of the 20 July 1944 plot. British and American historians have been unfair in their treatment of their competence and their determination, and above all on their chances of success.

Churchill saw Kleist, von Moltke and Fabian von Schlabrendorff, an anti-Nazi who miraculously survived the July 1944 plot, in the early summer of 1939.[j] Nothing concrete came out of his talks with them except that Churchill became more interested in the existence of a German opposition than did the Government, and of modifying Versailles if there was a liberal democratic peace-loving Government in Germany.[22]

Both the Kordts talked earnestly and confidentially with Vansittart. Again Vansittart was worried by their insistence on *lebensraum* for Germany in the east. When the Kordts warned of the likelihood of a German-Russian deal, Vansittart said 'Keep calm, it is we who will sign an agreement with Russia.'[23] All the German anti-Nazi visitors to London talked about the dangers of the blank cheque which Britain had given to Poland, and this drew reproaches from Vansittart. There

---

[j]Churchill asked Schlabrendorff if he could guarantee a successful action by the plotters. Schlabrendorff said no and wrote after the war that his journey was negative, but in 1949 Churchill told him that his staff had consistently misled him about the strength and size of the anti-Hitler movement during the war.

is no evidence that anyone in high places in London advocated concessions to the German opposition if they could replace Hitler. They were not taken as seriously as Goerdeler had been by Cadogan in the previous December.

Without British encouragement there was little possibility in Germany in the summer of 1939 of resurrecting the conspiracy that had been nipped in the bud by Chamberlain's capitulation at Munich. Witzleben, the key military commander, had been shunted off to Frankfurt from where he could not influence events in Berlin. Halder had blown cold. The German opposition was temporarily a spent force, and without Witzleben at the centre no military coup was possible. Then, at the last moment, on 3 September 1939, General von Hammerstein, a rabid anti-Nazi, was given command of an army on the Rhine. The plotters decided to lure Hitler to Hammerstein's headquarters where they would arrest him. Hitler, who according to the plotters had an uncanny instinct for avoiding danger, suddenly cancelled a proposed visit to Hammerstein's headquarters. There is evidence that history might have been dramatically altered but for that chance alteration in Hitler's engagements.

In a final bid to thwart Hitler, General Georg Thomas,[k] with the help of Goerdeler, Schacht and others, submitted a memorandum to Keitel warning, that if Germany attacked Poland a 'quick war and a quick peace' were an illusion, and that Germany was not equipped for a long drawn out world war. Keitel refused to listen.[24]

At the end of July 1939 Hitler called up his reservists and declared the entire Rhineland and large areas on the Czech, Polish and French frontiers prohibited areas. The British Military Attaché in Berlin sent a serious warning that 'war might' break out. Henderson's reaction was to urge Halifax to force greater concessions out of the Poles.

On 23 May Hitler had told his Generals that war with Poland would entail war with Britain and France. Then, on 22 August, Russia broke off negotiations with France and Britain and signed the Nazi-Soviet Pact of non-aggression. Immediately Hitler told his Generals that Poland would stand alone if Germany attacked her:

Decision to attack Poland was arrived at in spring. Originally there was fear that because of the political constellation we would have to strike at the same time against England, France, Russia and Poland . . . Since the autumn of 1938 and since I have realized that Japan will not go with us unconditionally and that Mussolini is endangered by that nitwit of a King and the treacherous

[k]Head of Military Economic Planning.

scoundrel of a Crown Prince, I decided to go with Stalin. After all there are only three great statesmen in the world, Stalin, I and Mussolini. Mussolini is the weakest, for he has been able to break the power neither of the crown nor of the Church. Stalin and I are the only ones who visualise the future. So in a few weeks hence I shall stretch out my hand to Stalin at the common German-Russian frontier and with him undertake to re-distribute the world.

Our strength lies in our quickness and in our brutality . . . And so for the present only in the East I have put my death-head formations in place with the command relentlessly and without compassion to send into death many women and children of Polish origin and language. Only thus we can gain the living space that we need . . .

Colonel-General von Brauchitsch has promised me to bring the war against Poland to a close within a few weeks. Had he reported to me that he needs two years or even only one year, I should not have given the command to march and should have allied myself temporarily with England instead of Russia for we cannot conduct a long war. To be sure a new situation has arisen. I experienced those poor worms Daladier and Chamberlain in Munich. They will be too cowardly to attack. They won't go beyond a blockade. Against that we have our autarchy and the Russian raw materials.

Poland will be depopulated and settled with Germans. My pact with the Poles was merely conceived of as a gaining of time. As for the rest, gentlemen, the fate of Russia will be exactly the same as I am now going through with in the case of Poland. After Stalin's death – he is a very sick man – we will break the Soviet Union. Then there will begin the dawn of the German rule of the earth . . .

We shall have to take into the bargain the defection of Japan. I gave Japan a full year's time. The Emperor is a counterpart to the last Czar – weak, cowardly, undecided. May he become a victim of the revolution. My going together with Japan was never popular. We shall continue to create disturbances in the Far East and in Arabia. Let us think as 'gentlemen' and let us see in these peoples at best lacquered half maniacs who are anxious to experience the whip.

The opportunity is as favourable as never before. I have but one worry, namely that Chamberlain or some other such pig of a fellow will come at the last moment with proposals or with ratting. He will fly down the stairs, even if I shall personally have to trample on his belly in the eyes of the photographers.

No, it is too late for this. The attack upon and the destruction of Poland begins Saturday [26 August] early. I shall let a few companies in Polish uniform attack in Upper Silesia or in the Protectorate . . . Be hard, be without mercy, act more quickly and brutally than the others. The citizens of Western Europe must tremble with horror. That is the most human way of conducting a war. For it scares the others off.

According to the secret report received a few days later by the Foreign Office: 'The speech was received with enthusiasm. Goering jumped on a table, thanked blood-thirstily and made blood-thirsty promises. He danced like a wild man.'[25]

The full text of the speech was immediately passed by the conspirators to the Foreign Office and was received in London on 25 August. Here was incontrovertible evidence of Hitler's intention and of his brutality towards the Poles. Brauchitsch had refused the entreaties of the conspirators not to obey the orders to attack on the grounds that a declaration of war without the approval of the Reichstag was unconstitutional. The only logical reaction by the British Government was mobilization. Hitler had fixed 26 August for the German army to burst over the Polish Corridor. If Britain was to intervene effectively in the struggle, immediate action was required. None was taken.

By coincidence, and not by intent, the formal Anglo-Polish Alliance was signed on 25 August, but Hitler took it as a deliberate threat of a switch to a stronger policy. Suddenly he realized that his attack on Poland might trigger off a major war; simultaneously Mussolini sent word that in the event of war he would not fight. Hitler faltered. The order to attack was cancelled late on 25 August. The conspirators were jubilant. According to Oster the Fuehrer was 'finished'; Canaris[1] said: 'Peace has been saved for twenty years.' They felt that Hitler would lose prestige and might fall. They were wrong. On 28 August Hitler fixed dawn 1 September as a new zero hour.[26]

Goering made strenuous efforts to stop the war and urged Hitler to make a reasonably generous offer to Poland. At his Nuremberg trial Goering declared that Hitler was abnormal and a complete law unto himself and he, Goering, always had to compete with Himmler and Ribbentrop to have any influence on him. In his evidence Goering indignantly denied that he had danced on the table, but admitted he had led the applause after Hitler's speech. Possibly he showed such pleasure at the announcement of Hitler's warlike intentions on 22 August to improve his standing with the Fuehrer. There is evidence he always had to show 'obsequious humility' to Hitler to get him to listen.[27]

Wohltat, a German industrialist and a friend of Goering, saw R. S. Hudson, Secretary for Overseas Trade, at the German Embassy's request on 20 July 1939. Wohltat told Hudson that economic considerations 'played very little part in the Fuehrer's mind' and that the only person who could get him to see economic arguments was

[1]Anti-Nazi head of the German Secret Service.

Goering. Wohltat said he would report to Goering on his return, and if he could tell Goering that Britain was prepared to see Germany established as a strong economic base, Goering might be able to deflect the Fuehrer from war. However, Hitler felt strongly the only way of continuing indefinitely the advantages of Nazi rule for the German race was by an overwhelmingly powerful army. On 24 July Wohltat met Horace Wilson, who wrote a memorandum for Wohltat on Downing Street paper (obviously with Chamberlain's knowledge) proposing an Anglo-German treaty of non-aggression and non-interference; with a disarmament agreement and trade cooperation, claiming a pact of this kind 'would enable Britain to rid herself of commitments *vis-à-vis* Poland'.[28]

Some accounts of these conversations were leaked to the press and there were rumours of an enormous British loan to Germany to prevent war. Dirksen wrote to Ribbentrop on 18 August that Britain had not pledged herself a hundred percent to support Poland in any conflict, and on 9 August in a memorandum for Hitler had reported that Wilson 'affirmed that the conclusion of an Anglo-German entente would practically render Britain's guarantee policy nugatory . . . and would enable Britain to extricate herself from her predicament in regard to Poland'.[29]

It is clear from the Wilson-Wohltat talks that Chamberlain in July, despite his guarantee to Poland, secretly sought a new understanding with Hitler which would make a defence pact with Russia unnecessary. Thus Hitler had reason to believe that Chamberlain would not be drawn into war over Poland even if the Germans used force. Wilson, according to the Foreign Office archives, did not disclose what he said to anyone except the Prime Minister, and he and Chamberlain bear a dire responsibility for deluding Hitler that we were not 'firm' in our guarantee to Poland. Chamberlain himself did not inform his Cabinet what ideas he was giving to the Germans.

On 25 August Halifax told the Polish Ambassador in London that they must consider a modification of the status of Danzig, subject to international guarantee, and on the same day Makins drew up a memorandum as a basis for starting negotiations on the future of Danzig. Hitler and the British were not far apart.[30]

Goering concluded from the Wilson-Wohltat conversations that Britain was wobbling on her March guarantee to Poland, and he persuaded Hitler to allow Berger Dahlerus to act as an intermediary between Hitler's Chancellery and Downing Street in a last-minute effort to force Poland to cede Danzig and the Corridor without fighting. Curiously Chamberlain and Halifax preferred Dahlerus to Henderson as their intermediary with Hitler.

Sir Frank Roberts,[m] who was then at the German desk at the Foreign Office, told the author he got to know Dahlerus well in 1939; he was introduced originally by British businessmen who had worked with him. He said:

Dahlerus was sincere in trying to avoid war at the eleventh hour. We knew definitely that Goering did not want war. Goering had too many of the good things of life and he wanted to keep his life style, not gamble it all on a war. Dahlerus was a typical Swedish businessman. He had good manners and some charm. I think he was honest, although naive. We thought there was a chance that Goering might have succeeded Hitler, and although he was a devil he was a less warlike devil than Hitler.

Sir Peter Tennant was at the British Legation in Stockholm from 1939 to 1945 and had longer to get to know Dahlerus. His view was not so favourable and he described Dahlerus as 'a professional peace pedlar mainly concerned with enhancing his own self-importance; he was completely unreliable and only out for himself'.[31]

Goering and Dahlerus were on terms of intimate friendship, but Dahlerus proved to be only a fair-weather friend. At the Nuremberg Trial he said that if he had known about Hitler's declaration to his Generals on 22 August that he intended definitely to invade Poland he would not have acted as Goering's intermediary. This is specious. After all Chamberlain and Halifax also knew about Hitler's speech on 22 August and they thought it worth while to continue striving for a peaceful cession of Polish territory.

Dahlerus flew to London on 25 August with a message from Goering which had been approved by Hitler. It confirmed the German Government's desire for an understanding with the British Government, and asserted that Goering would do everything he could to facilitate this. Dahlerus was to say that Chamberlain's speech on 24 August had made a favourable impression on Goering and Hitler. Dahlerus saw Halifax at 6.30 p.m. on 25 August and told him that 'if official negotiations could be brought about they might lead to a peaceful settlement'. Simultaneously Henderson was seeing Hitler.

The next day, 26 August, Dahlerus again saw Halifax, who gave the Swede a personal letter to take urgently to Goering confirming Britain's wish for a peaceful negotiated settlement. Dahlerus flew to Berlin with this and saw Goering. Goering told him to translate the letter into

---

[m]Later Ambassador in Moscow and Bonn. Tennant had taught Scandinavian languages at Cambridge before the war. He was Press Attaché at the Stockholm Legation throughout the war.

German and the pair went to the Chancellery to see Hitler that evening.

Dahlerus was given an interview by the Fuehrer. From his account it is almost certain Hitler was vacillating. Hitler struck Dahlerus as being 'insane', and after fireworks and nonsense from Hitler about U-boat warfare Hitler told Dahlerus to go back to London and say he, Hitler, wanted to bring about an understanding. Dahlerus asked Hitler to give him some idea of his minimum demands for Danzig. Goering opened an atlas, tore out a page and marked in red the Polish areas which must go to Germany. Hitler said Danzig and the Corridor must go to Germany; also Gdynia. Dahlerus told the Foreign Office: 'Mr Hitler himself is not in favour of war but . . . his temper at times is uncontrollable.'

The following morning, 27 August, Dahlerus shuttled back to London by plane. From Croydon he was whisked by Roberts to the Foreign Office and then into Downing Street with Cadogan to see Halifax and Chamberlain.

Henderson also returned to London on 27 August with a report that he had seen Hitler the day before. He had found him calm and ready to tone down his demands on Poland. According to Henderson Britain was to take this 'as an indication that Herr Hitler still desires to avoid war'. This corroborated Dahlerus. On the morning of 27 August the British Prime Minister and Foreign Secretary were hopeful of averting war by negotiating the cession of Danzig and the Corridor to Hitler. They decided to detain Henderson in London while they continued negotiations with Goering through Dahlerus.

The reply sent via Dahlerus was that Britain was willing to negotiate a settlement of Danzig and the Corridor, preferably by direct negotiation between Poland and Germany, and that if other problems were solved and Germany demobilized, Britain would discuss the return of Germany's former colonies. An offer made by Hitler the previous day to Henderson 'to defend the British Empire' was rejected. Dahlerus was told to try and see Hitler and then in Henderson's absence in London to see Ogilvie-Forbes, Minister at the Berlin Embassy.

At 11 p.m. Dahlerus arrived back at Tempelhof aerodrome. Goering decided it would be better if he (Goering) saw Hitler alone. At 1.30 a.m. on 28 August Goering rang Dahlerus to say he had seen Hitler, who welcomed Britain's wish for a peaceful settlement and asked whether Britain wanted a treaty or a pact. He accepted the suggestion that Danzig should be solved by direct negotiation between

Warsaw and Berlin. Goering concluded: 'If Henderson's note corresponds with your report we should reach agreement.'

At 2 a.m. Dahlerus saw Ogilvie-Forbes at the Embassy. Dahlerus briefed him on what had happened, and then breakfasted with Goering. In Goering's private train Dahlerus met General Milch, the air commander, and other military commanders, all now optimistic that war would be averted. Ominously Goering said that Ribbentrop and Hitler still wanted war. At 1.15 a.m. on 29 August Dahlerus was told by Goering's adjutant that Henderson's version had corresponded with Dahlerus's and Hitler had indicated to Goering that the chances of peace were 'good'. The evidence points to Hitler being tempted by the prospect of another diplomatic triumph like Munich, and being held back from war by Goering but pushed into it by Ribbentrop.

Henderson got back to Berlin at 5 on 28 August and saw Hitler at 10.30 with Halifax's communication. Hitler was friendly and calm and told Henderson that he would negotiate direct with Poland provided a plenipotentiary came immediately. Another Munich seemed in sight. Henderson told Halifax this was 'the sole chance of preventing war' and it was 'proof of his [Hitler's] sincerity of his desire for friendship with Great Britain'. Dahlerus told Henderson that if the Poles came to Berlin 'they would be sure of a most friendly reception in view of German desire for better relations with Britain. The Poles must contribute their share to a peaceful settlement.'[32] Henderson sent this message on to Halifax. That evening there was optimism in Whitehall; it seemed as if war had been averted although the price would be cession of Danzig and the Corridor to Germany, with the attendant penalty of an enormous boost to Hitler's popularity.

That day the Poles mobilized – against the advice of the British Ambassador – and this may have been a key factor in pushing Hitler towards war. France advised Beck to go to Berlin immediately; the British Government hoped Poland would enter into immediate negotiations with Hitler, but reiterated they would implement their obligation. Beck refused to go to Berlin.

At 7.15 on the evening of 29 August Hitler and Henderson met again. Henderson, in his autobiography, wrote that he was confident that Hitler was ready to open 'direct negotiations with the Poles'. However, he found Hitler in a very different mood from the night before. Henderson was handed a written document which insisted 'a Polish emissary with full powers' arrived in Berlin the next day, 30

August. Henderson said this was 'an ultimatum' and told Hitler so. This triggered off an outburst from Hitler and gravely disappointed Henderson who had been so agreeably surprised the previous day to find that Hitler had otherwise accepted the British view. It is on the cards that Ribbentrop, who wanted war, had persuaded Hitler to put into his written reply the demand for Polish delegates to arrive the next day. This was the crunch.[33]

Goering sent for Dahlerus and told him he blamed Henderson for infuriating Hitler, and made the point that the German written reply was conciliatory. He also burst out into a diatribe against the Poles and said the German Government were justified in calling for an immediate settlement because of the outrageous behaviour of the Polish Government against the German minority. Later Goering calmed down and told Dahlerus that Hitler was preparing a 'generous offer' to the Poles involving only the return of Danzig and a plebiscite in the Corridor.[n] He drew rough lines on a map to show where the plebiscite should be held – in the areas where there were most Germans. Dahlerus, at Goering's request, immediately flew back to London with this news. He also reported that Goering insisted a plebiscite was a climb down by Hitler.

By 10.30 a.m. on Wednesday 30 August Dahlerus was closeted again with Chamberlain, Halifax, Cadogan and Wilson. At Dahlerus's request, based on Goering's instructions, Halifax cabled Kennard in Warsaw to ask that Germans who caused trouble should not be fired on but arrested; that Germans should be allowed to leave Poland freely; and that inflammatory propaganda should be stopped. Dahlerus stressed that Hitler was at work that day on a 'generous offer' to Poland. The catch, which Chamberlain and Halifax immediately spotlighted, was Hitler's demand that a Polish plenipotentiary should come to Berlin immediately. Did Hitler intend to rupture relations by the demand? We shall never know with certainty. He may have wanted the triumph of announcing to his people that he had gained Danzig and part of the Corridor suddenly and dramatically in a way which showed France and Britain truckled to him, and would go to war only if a Polish plenipotentiary failed to come at once in humility to Berlin.

Dahlerus was asked by the British Prime Minister to go back to Berlin and emphasize to Goering and Hitler, if possible, how anxious the British were for a solution involving the transfer to Germany

[n] To hold a plebiscite instead of claiming the whole Corridor was a climb down by Hitler, but he may only have been trying to make it look as if Poland was uncooperative.

immediately of Danzig and part of the Corridor. Cadogan made Dahlerus telephone Goering from Downing Street and put the suggestion that the Polish-German negotiations should take place not in Berlin, but in neutral territory. Goering said Hitler would not agree and the Poles must, and could easily, send emissaries to Berlin forthwith. This the British accepted.

Dahlerus saw Goering again in Berlin at 1.30 a.m. on 31 August. He assured Goering that London wanted direct Polish-German talks. Beaming all over his face, Goering told Dahlerus that Hitler's note to Poland contained 'most generous terms'; probably Goering himself then genuinely believed that he had averted war. But he warned that with both German and Polish armies mobilized, the risk of a conflagration was still grave.[34]

Meanwhile Henderson and Ribbentrop had met at midnight on 30 August. Ribbentrop was rude and refused to give Henderson the typescript of Hitler's 'generous offer' – merely quoting extracts from it at speed. The British Embassy told Dahlerus of this by telephone while he was with Goering. As soon as Goering heard of it, he said: 'Ribbentrop is sabotaging my efforts to make peace. For God's sake let the British Ambassador have a copy of Hitler's generous terms as soon as possible. The British Government must see it urgently.' This again is evidence that Goering was doing everything in his power to stop the war while Ribbentrop was provoking it. Goering, ostensibly without asking Hitler's permission, gave Dahlerus a copy which Dahlerus presented to Henderson on 31 August at 10 a.m.

Henderson, elated by the prospect of an eleventh-hour agreement, sent Dahlerus round to the Polish Embassy urgently to see Lipski, the Polish Ambassador, with Ogilvie-Forbes. The visit was fruitless. There the Poles were preparing for departure. Lipski said he had no interest in any German proposals because if war was declared the Nazis would be overthrown and 'the Polish Army would probably arrive in Berlin in triumph'.[o] Henderson was appalled.[35]

Dahlerus telephoned London and briefed Wilson on what had occurred, and then went back to Goering who told him the German Foreign Office had intercepted a code telegram from Warsaw to Lipski instructing him in no circumstances to enter into any discussions with the Germans, and that this telegram from Warsaw had triggered Hitler

---

[o]Lipski recorded in his memoirs: 'In order to stop this ghastly business I told him [Dahlerus] I could not understand what the matter was about and asked him to dictate some notes.' Lipski could not understand Dahlerus's role, and could not believe he was the trusted emissary of both the British Government and Goering.

into deciding on war. Goering raved on to Dahlerus about the failings of the Poles. Then, at tea with Henderson, Forbes and Dahlerus, where the atmosphere was cordial, he suggested (with Hitler's permission) that Britain on behalf of the Poles should negotiate with the German Government. Henderson said he would pass on this implausible suggestion. He did not. Goering told Henderson that Lipski was on his way to see Ribbentrop. Henderson pointed out that neither the Poles nor the British Government had seen the terms of the last German offer which he agreed with Goering was 'generous'. Keeping it secret was Ribbentrop's doing. When Lipski saw Ribbentrop he refused to negotiate or say when a plenipotentiary would come. The interview sealed Poland's fate.

Late that evening Ribbentrop sent a statement to Henderson that the direct Polish-German negotiations favoured by the British were impossible owing to the non-arrival of a negotiator. Hitler had been waiting 'two days in vain for the arrival of a Polish negotiator'. This ought to have been the red light for Henderson. Ribbentrop had triumphed with Hitler over Goering; unless Britain and France could frighten Hitler, war was inevitable.

Henderson still would not give up. He cabled Cadogan late on 31 August that the Poles must put themselves in the right by making some sort of gesture or else 'we must all fight'. He added that possibly it would be better to fight. Twenty-four hours before he had signalled: 'I can only urge once more importance of Poland accepting at once proposal for direct negotiations and thereby putting herself right in the eyes of the world.' To this Halifax had replied: 'We cannot advise Polish Government to comply with this procedure which is wholly unreasonable.' At 9.15 a.m. on 31 August Henderson had told the Foreign Office in London: 'I have just been informed on the best possible authority that if nothing happens in next two or three hours i.e. possibly by midday, German Government will declare war in view of Polish general mobilisation and their conviction that Poland prefers to fight rather than negotiate.' His information came from Hassell.[36]

From Rome Ciano telephoned Halifax suggesting Mussolini should ask Hitler to hold his hand; he also told the British Ambassador that war was only a few hours away. Ciano then proposed that Mussolini should call a conference for 5 September to revise the Treaty of Versailles, but the Duce would not agree. The only good news at the Foreign Office on the night of 31 August was that Ciano in Rome told Sir Percy Loraine[P] that Italy would not fight against France and Britain.

[P]Sir Percy Loraine had succeeded Drummond as Ambassador in Rome.

Henderson at midday on 31 August suggested that Halifax should order the Polish Government to insist that Lipski should ask the German Government for the text of Hitler's proposals with a view to sending a plenipotentiary immediately to Berlin. Instead Halifax told Kennard to ask the Poles to approach the German Government through Lipski for an early discussion. At 6.15 p.m. Kennard reported that Beck was only willing to discuss with the German Government the procedure and on what basis negotiations should begin. The Poles were determined to deny Hitler his bloodless triumph.[37]

In contrast to Henderson, Kennard did not like Hitler's 'generous terms' and cabled the Foreign Secretary at 10.25 p.m. that he did not agree the 'terms were reasonable' because *inter alia* the demands were peremptory and humiliating and Poland should not surrender unless discussions took place on a free and equal basis. He added that if Poland's allies accepted these terms as a negotiating basis Poland might resist single-handed.[38]

A despairing Henderson telegraphed to Halifax at 10.45 p.m. on 31 August telling him that the German Government considered their proposals in abeyance if a Polish plenipotentiary did not arrive immediately. He also told Halifax that the German proposals did not 'endanger the independence of Poland', and that he would be 'pessimistic' if Ribbentrop conducted the negotiations, but not if Goering did so. He added that the plebiscite on the Corridor was a climb down from Hitler's original decision to recover the whole of the Corridor. Technically he was correct.

At 12.30 a.m. on 1 September the Foreign Office received from Henderson yet another appeal to recognize Hitler's offer 'was not unreasonable', and the Foreign Office reacted by asking Kennard again to persuade the Poles to accept a document containing the proposals and start discussing the venue and who should take part. So, as the last minutes of peace ticked away in the early hours of 1 September, Henderson was desperately trying to get Hitler's offer accepted, and Halifax was leaning on the Poles to start discussions with a view to handing to Hitler Danzig and the Corridor in a hurry.

Hitler knew all this. If a Polish delegation had come to Berlin it would have been dragooned into accepting Hitler's demands in a humiliating fashion, and Halifax and Chamberlain would have put great pressure on Poland to accept, so that Britain would be relieved of her obligation to fight for Poland. Then Hitler would have stayed his hand. Dahlerus was proving to Hitler how appeasement-minded was the British Government.

Almost certainly the Polish intransigence changed the balance in Hitler's mind and made him decide on war. He was highly nervous at the time. When Henderson had stood up to the Fuehrer at their interview on 29 August it produced something akin to a nervous collapse and his doctor had to be sent for, according to information given at the time to Henderson. Impulsively, on the afternoon of 31 August Hitler made up his mind to stop negotiating and start the war the next morning. Undoubtedly the interception of the telegram from Warsaw to Lipski telling Lipski not to negotiate was a decisive factor.

Strong evidence that Hitler was keeping his options open until the last moment and would not inevitably have invaded Poland comes from General Halder's diary. On the 30 August he recorded that General Brauchitsch's orders were: 'Make all preparations so that attack can begin at 4.30 a.m. on 1 September. Should negotiations in London require postponement, then 2 September. In that case we shall be notified before 3 p.m. tomorrow ... either 1 September or 2 September. All off after 2 September.[39]

Henderson, Halifax and Chamberlain and the Foreign Office wanted Danzig and the Corridor to be returned to Germany immediately, and Henderson put pressure on Halifax to order the Poles to negotiate on this basis. But the Poles never conceded this principle.

Hitler knew that physically Britain could do almost nothing, and he had secret information that the French would not launch a mass attack against the Siegfried Line. But it was Beck, not Hitler, who called the bluff. British appeasement came to an end because Britain had incautiously given a guarantee to Poland and could not wriggle out of it without the Government falling, although the Prime Minister would have been prepared to try.

At 4.30 in the morning of 1 September the German army advanced into Poland and the civilian targets of Cracow and Katowice were bombed. Despite the fighting Henderson thought there was still some possibility of appeasing Hitler, and at 10.50 made the abortive suggestion to the Foreign Office that Smigly Ridz should come to Berlin to act as a plenipotentiary.

Even now Goering hoped to limit hostilities. He and Dahlerus saw Hitler again at around midday but Hitler was, according to Dahlerus, hysterical. Dahlerus telephoned Cadogan who told him the British conditions would be an end to hostilities and withdrawal of German forces to the frontier. Goering temporarily lost interest in peace efforts but the next morning, 2 September, he told Dahlerus that he wanted to inaugurate a new Munich with the aid of Mussolini.

Henderson then sent Dahlerus a note of the Prime Minister's speech in the House of Commons, which Halifax wanted the Swede to show to Goering urgently, because the Foreign Secretary felt it contained the germ of a settlement. Dahlerus told Goering it 'was permeated with a desire to avoid a war', although it declared no negotiations were possible unless Germany withdrew her troops. Goering offered to fly with Dahlerus to London, but this suggestion was not welcome to the Foreign Office unless German troops first withdrew from Poland. According to Dahlerus, Goering had persuaded Hitler to allow the trip as a conciliatory gesture. Goering was finally only silenced by Chamberlain's announcement at 11.00 a.m. on Sunday, 3 September, that Britain was at war.[q][40]

---

[q]Chamberlain said in the Commons on 1 September the delay in declaring war was caused 'by consideration of the Italian Government's proposal', and he, contrary to the views just agreed with his Cabinet colleagues, stressed the possibility of a peaceful settlement.

6

The Phoney War
1939 – 1940

At 7.28 a.m. on 1 September 1939 the Foreign Office learnt that Hitler had invaded Poland at 4.17 a.m. after a trumped up incident in which criminals dressed up in Polish uniforms had been introduced into German frontier posts and barbarously shot dead. Cadogan waited until 9 a.m. before informing the Foreign Secretary, and there was no sense of the urgency which should have resulted from this deliberate attack on an ally. At 11.30, seven hours after Poland had been attacked, the British Cabinet met. The Polish Ambassador, Raczynsky, had seen Halifax at 10.30 and told him it was a clear case of aggression under the Anglo-Polish Treaty of Mutual Assistance. Halifax soothed him, and when the Cabinet met they were more in the mood for overtures to Hitler than for fulfilling their obligations to give immediate military assistance to the Poles. Dahlerus had telephoned the Foreign Office full of Germany's peaceful assertions, and Henderson signalled that Hitler's speech to the Reichstag due that morning might mean a further peace effort.

At this stage the Cabinet would not go beyond a leisurely 'warning' to Hitler via Henderson. Both the British and French Governments were pinning their hopes on another Munich-type intervention by Mussolini, and they totally ignored the reasonable request from Warsaw that the Allies take immediate military action from the air that afternoon to relieve pressure on the Poles. Indeed the Cabinet was not even told about it.

On the morning of 2 September, as Hitler's armies were driving deep into Poland and his air force was bombing Polish towns, Cadogan, on Halifax's instructions, telephoned Bonnet in Paris and said the British Government 'wanted the answer' about what time limit should be given to Hitler; and should there be a Mussolini-organized conference? He also asked whether the retirement of German troops from Polish soil would be a 'prerequisite' of agreement to a conference. The French replied they would deliberate, but the fact that Cadogan was even asking such a question about the retirement of German troops from Polish soil does not say much for Halifax's commitment to his Government's guarantee to Poland.

In London on 2 September Chamberlain was mainly occupied with discussions for the proposed Mussolini conference. This was to revise the Treaty of Versailles and was eagerly applauded by both Bonnet and Halifax. At 6 p.m. Halifax made his last desperate effort at appeasement and rang Ciano to say he would accept a conference but German withdrawal from Poland was 'an essential condition'. Ciano, more realistic, asserted categorically this was unacceptable to the Fuehrer. Yet at 7 p.m. the Prime Minister told the Commons that the Italian proposal was causing delay but that if Hitler would withdraw his forces 'the way would be open' for discussion. His statement was ill received.[1]

For Hitler every hour's delay before France attacked on the Western Front was a bonus, and Ribbentrop made one final effort to keep Britain out of the way through Fritz Hesse, a German journalist in London. He told Hesse to let the British Cabinet know that Hitler would be prepared to move out of Poland provided he received Danzig and the Corridor and Britain acted as mediator in the German-Polish dispute. Hesse saw Horace Wilson at 10 Downing Street during the afternoon of 2 September. Wilson gave him a friendly reception and told him that negotiations could proceed if German troops withdrew from Polish territory. Cadogan minuted: 'These indirect approaches rather reassure me. The Germans must be feeling the draught.' He was wide of the mark. Hitler wanted time to complete his conquest of Poland and the Hesse intervention was only a delaying tactic.[2]

Halifax and Chamberlain were still hoping for a *modus vivendi* with Hitler, but it was too late now for any more appeasement. Angry Tory MPs lobbied other members of the Cabinet, and there was a palace revolt led by Hore-Belisha. At 11 p.m. Chamberlain was given an ultimatum by his Cabinet that he must stop procrastinating and declare war or else he would be defeated in the Commons. Britain had already broken her treaty obligations. Instead of resigning, Chamberlain acquiesced; an ultimatum was sent to Hitler jointly with the French. Chamberlain never considered resignation, judging himself 'indispensable' according to a letter to his sister.

By 11.15 a.m. on 3 September the nation was at war. Chamberlain made a pathetic broadcast. Instead of promising speedy help to the ally on whose behalf Britain was going to war, he spoke of his personal grief. The Poles, however, were delighted and cheered the British diplomats in Warsaw. They had little to cheer about: although they expected immediate help, Britain had no intention of coming to Poland's aid. True, a thirty-man British military mission crossed into Poland from Rumania led by Carton de Wiart[a] and Colin Gubbins,[b] and at midday on 3 September at Lublin they changed into uniform on hearing of the declaration of war. Not until 9 September did a Polish military mission led by General Norwid Neugebauer arrive in London. They found the British CIGS, Ironside, had no plan at all to help Poland. All Ironside could offer was a few thousand old rifles and a few million rounds of ammunition, and he advised them to buy arms from neutral countries such as Spain and Belgium.[3]

The French were equally treacherous to their ally. On 19 May 1939 Gamelin had signed a military agreement with the Polish General Kasprzycki which promised that on the fifteenth day after a German attack on Poland, France would launch an offensive against the Siegfried Line. Gamelin had no intention of doing anything of the sort.

Neither Britain nor France would bomb Germany to help the Poles. Hitler indulged in terror bombing of civilian centres from the beginning of his attack on Poland, but the British Government refused to accept clear evidence of this. Eventually Captain Tommy Davis of the British military mission to Poland returned to London and told the Chief of Air Staff, Newall,[c] that he had actually witnessed the Luftwaffe's indiscriminate bombing. Newall told the Cabinet that in reply the RAF should launch attacks on industrial targets in Germany, but Chamberlain would not have it.[4] Kingsley Wood[d] even told Leo Amery[e] that we must not bomb German 'private property'. Leo Amery's comment was that as Chamberlain so loathed war he was determined 'to wage as little of it as possible'.

Gamelin, too, was against air raids on Germany. He told Ironside and John Slessor[f] that he would 'lean' against the Siegfried Line to 'test its strength'. The failure by the French to honour their pledge to attack Germany on the fifteenth day brought no rebuke from Britain.

General Jodl, in his defence at Nuremberg, stated that 110 French and British divisions 'during our war' against Poland faced twenty-three German divisions and it was only the inactivity of the Allies

[a]Later Lieutenant-General Sir Adrian, he had won the Victoria Cross and been nine times wounded in the First World War.

[b]Major (later Major-General Sir Colin) Gubbins was then a GSO2 at the War Office.

[c]Air Chief Marshal Sir Cyril Newall was Chief of Air Staff 1937–40. Later Governor-General of New Zealand.

[d]Secretary of State for Air.

[e]Secretary of State for the Dominions.

[f]At this time Director of Plans at the Air Ministry. Later Marshal of the Royal Air Force.

which saved Germany from defeat. Keitel, also in evidence, said there were approximately twenty divisions including the reserves in the Rhineland and in the west district behind the lines on the west front in September 1939 as compared with six in 1938. He added: 'A French attack during the Polish campaign would have encountered only a German military screen, not a real defence . . . We soldiers thought the Western powers had no serious intentions because they did not take advantage of the extremely favourable situation.'[5]

By doing nothing, the Allies hamstrung the German Generals who wanted to overthrow Hitler. Worse, the Polish victory obtained at so little cost boosted Hitler's popularity with the German people still further. Hitler, with justification, concluded that Britain's declaration of war was a sham. All that Britain did to help Poland was to send to Constanza, Rumania's main port, fifteen fighter aircraft, seven bombers, 6,000 tons of bombs, 112 Browning machine guns and 2¾ million rounds of ammunition.[6] None reached Poland in time. On 15 September the Chiefs of Staff reported that 'it was futile to despatch war stores to Poland', and the three ships being loaded or in transit were cancelled.

On 17 September, just as the rains had started and the remains of the Polish Army tucked into the Rumanian corner of Poland were able to report some minor military success, the Red Army crossed the frontier and occupied the parts of Poland which had been agreed as theirs in a secret annex to the Ribbentrop-Molotov Pact. The Polish Government, together with the British Ambassador and the British military mission, crossed into Rumania, and Poland ceased to exist. Seeds, on hearing the news, told London: 'I do not see what advantage war with the Soviet Union would be to us although it would please me personally to declare it on Molotov . . . Soviet invasion is not without advantage to us in the long run.'

The Foreign Office immediately pointed out to the Prime Minister that the British treaty with Poland only covered aggression by Germany, and a statement was made in the Commons on 25 August to this effect. Chamberlain was immensely relieved. The Foreign Office also told the War Cabinet that the Russians would occupy the Rumanian border and that Germany would now only be able to attack Rumania via Hungary. A vitriolic leader in *The Times* called the Russian invasion 'a stab in the back'. Chamberlain, at first furious, soon calmed down.[7]

The War Cabinet were divided. Some thought, like Churchill and Hore-Belisha, that Britain must prepare for war with Russia; others agreed with Robert Boothby that without the Russian move German troops would not only be on the Rumanian frontier, but 200 miles further towards Russia. Ambassador Raczynski gave Halifax a note that the Soviet Union had violated the non-aggression pact of 1932, the convention of 1933, and the Protocol of 1934, and that a claim by the Russians that on 17 September the Polish State no longer existed was false. 'All highly relevant, but we do not want to quarrel with the Russians now,' Frank Roberts minuted. That summed up the official view of the Prime Minister and the War Cabinet.

Shortly after Poland had been entirely occupied by the Germans and Russians a barrage of peace proposals reached London. The Cabinet would dearly have loved to start negotiations. Cadogan summarized the Government attitude in a report: 'If Germany will give guarantees to all those countries in Europe who feel damaged by German aggression we are prepared to agree to a conference.' Cadogan also stated significantly: 'We would be unwise to proclaim that we stand for the old boundaries of Poland. Such an attitude would render inevitable a conflict with Russia.' So much for the Government's war aims.

Seeds wrote, and Cadogan agreed, that the part of Poland occupied by the Russians was inhabited by a Russian population while the part occupied by Hitler was entirely non-German. Seeds suggested: 'Would it not be possible to drive a wedge between the two aggressors and perhaps keep this country out of war by suggesting that our war aims are not incompatible with settlement on ethnic and cultural lines?' Ivone Kirkpatrick wrote,[g] and his view was approved by Halifax, that Britain should stick to the Curzon Line (which roughly followed the division of Poland by Russia and Germany) because it would leave 'the predominantly Polish population in the German section' and 'we should stand for an ethnographical and cultural Poland without treading on Russian toes, at all events until the Russians have declared themselves against us.' The advice may have been cynically practical; certainly it had nothing to do with the obligations of alliance.

On 18 November the War Cabinet decided to exclude the Poles from the Supreme War Council, and on 6 December another Foreign Office minute noted: 'We have been very careful to avoid committing ourselves to any guarantee to restore Polish frontiers and to confine ourselves to condemning Russian and German aggression.'[8]

These were the arguments which appealed to Chamberlain, Halifax and the War Cabinet, apart from Churchill and Hore-Belisha. Chamberlain rued his guarantee to Poland which he felt had tied a

---

[g]Now returned to Whitehall, after having been First Secretary at the Embassy in Berlin, where he had not sympathized with the Ambassador's appeasement line.

millstone around his neck. It is abundantly clear from unpublished letters of the Prime Minister that he was now ready to abandon Poland if he could have got out of the war.[9]

Halifax wrote to Lothian: 'Peace feelers come almost every day'; and to Gort: 'A good many peace feelers being put out, all of them tracing to Goering.'[10] Dahlerus was seen at the Foreign Office by Cadogan on 28 and 29 September, having met Hitler and Goering two days before. Cadogan left Dahlerus with the impression that a peace – even with Hitler – could be possible if an independent Polish state were set up. Dahlerus returned to Berlin to communicate this news to Goering and the result was to encourage Hitler to believe the British would never fight. Meanwhile Ribbentrop was letting it be known through the British Embassies in neutral countries that Hitler would agree to an independent Poland and some small autonomous regime in part of Czechoslovakia.[h][11]

On 6 October Hitler delivered what he thought would be a successful peace move. He declared the future of Poland must be settled only by Germany and Russia; he promised to respect the frontiers of Denmark, Belgium and Holland; and he alleged that he had no claims on France and only wanted to bury the hatchet. He asked for a peace conference at which European disarmament, currencies and raw materials could be considered. He gave no hint, however, that he would redress the wrongs done to Poland or stop the persecution of the Jews.

The British Government had to consult the British Dominions and the French before replying to Hitler's offer. Daladier dismissed the overture out of hand, to the consternation of some of his colleagues, but not so the Canadian Prime Minister, Mackenzie King. He had formed a favourable impression of Hitler and the Nazi leaders when he visited Germany in September 1937, and thought Goering had 'an attractive personality'. Mackenzie King believed he had established a personal relationship with Hitler, and as war became imminent in September 1939 had written him a personal letter saying everything could be solved by 'conference and negotiation'. Hitler replied with a friendly letter inviting Mackenzie King to send twelve young students and officers to tour Germany.

On 7 October Mackenzie King suggested to Chamberlain that a committee of neutrals, including the President of the United States, the King of the Belgians and the King of Italy, should be asked to mediate.

---

[h]At that time the German diplomats abroad were on good terms with their British counterparts.

He said that everything must be done to stop the war before the slaughter began.[12] Of the other Dominions, Australia, New Zealand and South Africa, like Daladier, wanted to reject Hitler's peace offer out of hand.

In Britain opinion was divided. The National Peace Council, with Dr Joad, G. D. H. Cole and Sybil Thorndike, wrote a letter to the Prime Minister suggesting a 'truce'. The War Cabinet itself took four meetings to produce a reply to Hitler; and even then it was not fierce enough for Churchill – who produced a much more succinct draft than Chamberlain's actual reply in the House of Commons on 12 October. At least the Prime Minister borrowed one Churchillian flourish: 'Acts not words alone must be forthcoming before we the British peoples and France, our gallant and trusted ally, would be justified in ceasing to wage war to the utmost of our strength.'[13]

Still, Chamberlain's speech was – for him – surprisingly strong. He pointed out that Hitler had vowed repeatedly that his aim was merely to reunite Germans into the Reich, and now he was proposing to govern millions of Czechs and Poles for an indefinite period. He also recalled how Hitler's actions had often been directly contrary to his public statements of policy. He went on:

The repeated disregard of his [Hitler's] word and these sudden reversals of policy bring me to the fundamental difficulty in dealing with the wider proposals in the German Chancellor's speech. The plain truth is that after our past experience it is no longer possible to rely upon the unsupported word of the present German Government . . . Either the German Government must give convincing proof of the sincerity of their desire for peace by definite acts and effective guarantees of their intention to fulfil their undertaking or we must persevere in our duty to the end. It is for Germany to make her choice.

In deference to the timid views of some of his Cabinet, Chamberlain had delivered what he considered to be 'a statement ending on a note of enquiry, rather than on a direct rejection'. Hitler took a very different view of the speech and accused Britain of lies and of being intent 'on the extermination of the German nation'. This, one might have supposed, would have been the end of the peace feelers, but on 14 October Dahlerus bobbed up again, sending to the Foreign Office a letter from Goering dated 10 October saying: 'There can be no conqueror and no conquered and exactly the same problems would have to be considered after the war, with the only difference that there will be millions of dead on both sides, and that it would be sensible to start negotiations now.' The letter was ignored: with the hostile Berlin reaction to Chamberlain's speech Dahlerus's stock at the Foreign Office was temporarily at a low ebb, although soon afterwards he introduced similar proposals that were taken more seriously.[14]

Early in November Queen Wilhelmina of Holland and King Leopold of Belgium made a joint offer to the King of England to mediate. This was well received by a large section of the British public and twenty Labour MPs signed a memorandum asking the Prime Minister to negotiate. One of them, George Lansbury, claimed that 14,000 people wrote to him supporting the Belgian-Dutch offer. However, a row broke out between Chamberlain and Churchill about the reply. The Prime Minister's original draft, Churchill said with reason, amounted to an authorization by the King of England to the other monarchs to open up a channel of negotiations with Hitler. Chamberlain agreed to alter it, but told Churchill that it did not matter what was said since nothing would come of the venture.

Undaunted, Dahlerus continued his efforts. On 20 November, through the British Embassy in Stockholm, he reported that he had had a three-hour conversation in Berlin with Goering, who had proposed a secret meeting on neutral territory between himself and another German representative and two representatives each of the British and French Governments to try and negotiate peace. That this overture was more favourably received at the Foreign Office reflects some Government reassurance at hostilities so far. The war on the Siegfried Line had become a farce with neither side making any effort to fight the other, and the German bomber raids had still not materialized.

Kirkpatrick minuted that Goering,

whose figure, to say the least, is conspicuous, would be unable to attend a meeting unobserved . . . I take it our policy is to spin things out and if the Germans will let us have any proposals which in their opinion could form the basis of negotiations we shall, of course, consider them in consultation with the French.

This was communicated to Dahlerus who promptly relayed it to Goering. It was seen by Hitler as yet another indication that the British did not intend to fight seriously.[15]

Evidently Goering still hoped to end the war by negotiation, while Ribbentrop was prodding Hitler to attack Holland. Although Ribbentrop had told the German Foreign Office that the German Government was no longer interested in Dahlerus sounding out the British, Goering paid no attention;[16] while within the Foreign Office and 10 Downing

Street the Foreign Secretary and the Prime Minister deluded themselves that Goering might replace Hitler and produce a negotiated peace. Of this there was no chance unless Hitler were the victim of a coup or an accident. His popularity with the German nation as a result of the Anschluss and the conquest of Czechoslovakia and now Poland was at a peak, and Goering had always to obey him without argument, or fall.

Sir John Colville was the Prime Minister's Private Secretary at 10 Downing Street and he told the author that the feeling there in the winter and spring of 1939–40 was there would be no real war, with the Germans eventually having to negotiate because the economic blockade would cause them such suffering. Chamberlain made no secret that he was ready to do a deal with anyone in power in Germany except Hitler. Colville felt Chamberlain — largely because of its effects on his own vanity — could not forgive Hitler for breaking his word at Munich, and he believed that the Prime Minister would have tried to make a deal with Goering. But, Colville added, Chamberlain did not have Halifax's confidence in Goering.[17]

Baron Bunde, looked on by the Foreign Office as completely genuine, came to London in December 1939 with peace proposals agreed by Goering. These involved: (1) some form of Polish state; (2) freedom for the Czechs; (3) large loans to the Axis as suggested by the British Board of Trade in spring 1939. Bunde saw Halifax, who told him: 'We have never said we would not make peace with Hitler'; and on the question of loans, 'I know America would help.'[18]

According to Colville, Chamberlain used to say to him: 'We must call a halt before the blood bath starts.' This was also Halifax's line. Typical of the Foreign Secretary's thinking was a letter to Gort on 22 October 1939: 'If Hitler sits back and does nothing, time is running against him on the economic side . . . if things remain stationary until the Spring many of your present anxieties will be diminished.' In November Halifax wrote: 'This pause suits us well enough, both us and the French, for we shall be a good deal stronger in the spring.' This was to ignore the scale of German war production.

In January 1940 the Bishop of Oslo had a long talk with Goering which he reported verbatim to the Foreign Office. Goering told him that 'he would absolutely rather have peace than victory, but he would very much like victory first', and that Germany would never evacuate Poland or Czechoslovakia. The conversation indicated that Goering had now given up hopes of a negotiated peace. This was a disappointment to Halifax who had told Baron Bunde the month before: 'If there is one man who would make peace, I think it would be Goering.'[19]

The only real ray of light was information coming that the German Generals did not want to obey Hitler's orders to attack in the west, but Chamberlain and Halifax refused to believe authoritative reports that Hitler was impatient to start a *blitzkrieg* through the Low Countries and France. The truth is that both the Prime Minister and the Foreign Secretary were quite unsuited to govern in wartime. Their overriding motive was to avoid any repetition of the carnage of 1914–18 and they allowed this to dominate their policy and decisions. They were, unfortunately, for too long all-powerful – very popular with the bulk of their own party, which had a steamroller majority in the House of Commons, while the Labour Party by and large approved the Government's inaction, also believing an economic blockade must bring Germany to her knees. Only Hore-Belisha and Churchill expressed their dissatisfaction, and Churchill's grave concern about the slothful prosecution of the war is documented in his letters to Halifax and others.

Both Chamberlain and Halifax paid a disproportionate attention to the pro-German views of extreme Right-wingers such as Lord Brocket, a pro-Nazi Conservative who had donated large sums to Conservative funds and was a close friend of Chamberlain; the Duke of Buccleuch who had been a popular Tory back bench MP (as Walter Dalkeith); the Marquess of Londonderry who had been Secretary of State for Air in Baldwin's Cabinet; Lord Ponsonby, another former Tory Cabinet member; and the Earl of Darnley. This clique commanded little popular support amongst the electorate although they were influential within the Conservative Party. They bombarded the Prime Minister and the Foreign Secretary with long letters pointing out how badly Germany had been treated by the Treaty of Versailles and asking for peace negotiations on the basis of Hitler retaining the bulk of his conquests. Far from ignoring them, Halifax and Chamberlain consulted each other before replying to their letters. Colville said Buccleuch used to ring up and call at Downing Street although he seldom got through to the Prime Minister. Londonderry was bitter about Chamberlain in letters to Halifax and said he was a 'traitor' because he would not offer Hitler generous peace terms. Typical Londonderry sentiments were: 'Versailles encirclement was a disaster. We should make no secret of the great mistakes made by the Allies during the last twenty years . . . Far better peace terms should be negotiated now than after the chaos and destruction.'[20]

Brocket sent a long hand-written letter to Chamberlain on 27 January 1940. This argued for 'a constructive peace being a duty before the bombing and destruction and fine weather', and complained of 'the appalling taxation which a long war makes necessary'. Brocket also warned that 'a defeated Germany and a dictated peace may mean bolshevism in that country spreading to France and Britain'.

Despite the extreme tone of the letter Chamberlain and Halifax exchanged memoranda about it. In his note to the Prime Minister Halifax betrayed his attitude by writing: 'Can we offer further inducement to the Goering tribe for a reasonable peace? . . . Feelers about reconstructing Poland fit badly with German action in Poland.' Chamberlain's lengthy reply to Brocket, however, finished firmly and sensibly:

Your letter is a plea for peace at any price . . . if we were prepared to pay any price we could get peace for a time. It would, however, be only for a time. I am not prepared to accept terms which would give away just what we are fighting to preserve.

Buccleuch wrote almost weekly and always received considered replies. In a long letter to Chamberlain on 9 February he pointed out, correctly, that we had no military plans for a victory on the Western Front and could only starve Germany out, and that Germany's main objective was not 'Defeat Britain'. This was also the tone of his numerous letters to Halifax, to whom he wrote on 20 February 1940: 'Surely you are greatly in error to have made out that the Poles were almost one hundred per cent in the right and Germany one hundred per cent in the wrong? It should be fifty-fifty.'

Why did Chamberlain and Halifax pay so much attention to these anti-war Tory Right-wingers? They were always careful to give the impression that the anti-war arguments were being closely considered, and that there was not so much difference between the correspondent's point of view and the Government's.[1] Many Tory peers and MPs thought the war was unwinnable and Hitler could still be appeased. The Chamberlain view was that the economic blockade would eventually be successful and then Britain could do a deal with a German Government which did not include Hitler. Lord Bethell considers the Government was frightened of being embarrassed by peace outbursts in the House of Lords. More likely, Chamberlain felt he must keep the Conservative Party together at all costs because if he succeeded in securing a negotiated peace which abandoned much of

---

[1]Such as Chamberlain's letter of 14 November 1939 to Lord Darnley: 'It is always a help to know the views of thoughtful people . . . we are very much on common ground.' He did point out, however, that Britain must have some assurances that Germany would honour any settlement.

Poland and Czechoslovakia he would have considerable difficulty in carrying Parliament with him.

Fortunately for Chamberlain the Labour leaders under Attlee's guidance did everything they could to aid this weak policy; only Lloyd George and the extreme Left ILP opposed it and wanted peace negotiations like the extreme Right. In by-elections the ILP and the Mosley[j] candidates polled only a derisory vote with their anti-war stance. Mosley's telling argument was that the nation had at first been told they were fighting to save Poland. Now it had become a war to destroy Hitlerism, and Britain should not interfere in the internal affairs of another country. Mosley was not interned until May 1940 and he indulged in no treasonable activities.

On the other hand, Maule Ramsay, the Tory MP for Peebles who was the principal organizer of the Right Club, had been engaged in treasonable practices in conjunction with an American, Tyler Kent, employed in the US Embassy. With the consent of the US Ambassador a search had been made of Tyler Kent's room and a large mass of incriminating documents were found, including a sealed packet containing the names and addresses of the members of the Right Club. The Ramsay papers have not been released in the Public Record Office, which makes it impossible to assess how many former appeasers were working for Germany during the Phoney War.[21]

An interesting revelation of Halifax's attitude to German peace feelers can be found in a hitherto unnoticed minute on the Lonsdale Bryans affair in 1940. Bryans, an adventurer, was financed by Lord Brocket to conduct peace talks with any Germans he could find in Switzerland and Rome. He succeeded in making contact with von Hassell, the former German ambassador who was strongly anti-Hitler and prominent in the secret opposition group to the Nazis led by General Beck. Bryans brought back to London a long memorandum on peace terms allowing for expansion of Germany outside her Versailles frontiers, and the stipulation that Britain and France would not attack the Maginot Line during Germany's period of military weakness while a revolution was in progress. He told the Foreign Office that the Nazi party was split and that if Goering became leader instead of Hitler, he and the Generals would be ready for a reasonable peace.

Halifax saw Bryans on 8 January 1940 at the Foreign Office and minuted that he told Bryans:

[j] Sir Oswald Mosley's Fascists represented the extreme Right-wing pro-Nazi element in Britain.

I think Goering is no less of a gangster than Hitler but if Hitler and his entourage Ribbentrop, Himmler, etc. can be got rid of and constitution and liberty were restored to Germany, a new situation would clearly be created in which I personally would be against exploiting the advantage of a revolution by an attack on the Siegfried Line provided the different regime gave us some confidence of honest dealing.

Brocket had implored Halifax to see Bryans, and after the meeting the Treasury put Bryans in funds and gave him a visa so that he could contact Hassell again in Switzerland. His further talks with the German opposition were overtaken by the German invasion of Norway on 9 April.[22]

What is significant about Halifax's minute on the Bryans case is that it confirms that he did not exclude a deal with Goering and, even more important, that he was prepared to negotiate. This was in marked contrast to the Government policy towards German opposition conspirators once Churchill and Eden were in charge of affairs. Had this flexibility of attitude prevailed in the later years of the war when Hitler was obviously losing and the opposition consequently stronger, the war might have ended much sooner.

The Hassell overture was duplicated by Dr Josef Mueller through the Vatican, and Philip Conwell Evans, a British academic with extensive knowledge of Germany, who met Theodor Kordt in Switzerland and was authorized by Chamberlain to confirm that favourable peace terms would be offered to a non-Nazi Germany. These contacts were the last chance of a negotiated peace with the anti-Nazis during the Phoney War.

On 12 January 1940 D'Arcy Osborne[k] wrote that the Pope had had a visit from an unnamed emissary[l] who came on behalf of German Generals wanting to make peace and overthrow Hitler. The terms of peace would include the restoration of Poland and Czechoslovakia but the retention of the Anschluss with Austria. The emissary also stated that 'a great German offensive' had been prepared 'for the middle of February or even earlier'. Osborne told His Holiness the whole thing was 'hopelessly vague'. The official historian says it was not referred to the War Cabinet, but in fact they considered it at their meeting on the 17 January 1940. Their only action was to inform the French Government.

On 7 February the Pope asked Osborne to see him again and told him he had now been approached with a plan to replace Hitler with a 'democratic, conservative and moderate Government decentralized

[k]Envoy to the Holy See 1936–47.
[l]In fact Mueller, a Catholic lawyer. Bavarian Minister of Justice after the war.

and federal'. The Rhineland and Westphalia would remain united to Prussia; Austria would be within the federation, but Poland and non-German Czechoslovakia would be independent. The new Government would try to negotiate peace, and the Pope had been asked whether Britain would accept their plans as a basis for negotiations.

Osborne was instructed to reply that the suggestion of a decentralized and federal Government was of interest and it would be 'useful' if the plotters would develop this 'in concrete terms'. However, the British view was that Austria must decide whether or not she wanted to participate.

Postwar German writers on the Resistance make much of this approach. Professor Ritter suggests that the opposition were 'overconfident' about the army command executing a successful *coup d'état* and that confidence in turn raised expectations in London which then remained unsatisfied and so they were discredited'. However, the British archives show that it was not taken so seriously in Whitehall.[23]

Another revealing record of Chamberlain's attitude to a soft peace during the Phoney War can be found in the record of his talk with the US diplomat and Under Secretary, Sumner Welles. Welles was sent by Roosevelt to Berlin, Paris and London early in 1940 to explore the possibility of a mediated settlement. A conference was held with the Prime Minister, Halifax, the US Ambassador, Joseph Kennedy, and Sumner Welles on 13 March 1940. Welles asked the Prime Minister whether, if satisfactory arrangements could be made for Poland and Czechoslovakia, he would deal with the present German regime. At first Chamberlain said that in his own opinion he could not deal with Hitler, but quickly qualified it by adding that in any case what was quite essential was that 'any settlement should not be such that Hitler could represent it as having been able to get away with it'. Later on in the conversation he contradicted himself: 'If there was complete reversal of Hitler's policy and the freedom of the German people from the Gestapo then we should not be justified in refusing a discussion. But this would be a miracle.' He went on to say: 'We could not be satisfied with any settlement from which it did not clearly emerge that Herr Hitler's policy had been a failure' but there would be no difficulty in giving Germany some sort of preferential economic position in countries adjoining Germany. Halifax's contribution was that Britain would require evidence of German cooperation in Europe whether through the League of Nations or some other organization.[24]

In a letter to his sister Hilda, Chamberlain on 14 March said Welles was the 'best type of American' and he was most flattered when Welles told him that Roosevelt had a deep admiration for him and they 'would understand one another perfectly'.[m] Chamberlain also wrote that the American appreciated that if 'Hitler did not disappear he would have to agree to give up most of what Nazidom stands for'. He thought there was one chance in ten thousand that this might occur, and that the way in which Hitler had talked to Welles 'seems to me significant of a lurking want of confidence at the bottom of his mind'. Chamberlain still had much to learn about the true nature of his opponent.

With Chamberlain in this mood, had Hitler wanted peace in the spring of 1940 he would have found the British cooperative. In spite of his experience over Munich, Chamberlain in August 1939 had been anxious to do a deal with Hitler involving secession of Danzig and the Polish Corridor, and he would have considered favourably terms giving back some independence to a truncated Poland during the first eight months of the war. But now Hitler, intoxicated by his military success in Poland, had no interest in peace; Goering and most of his Generals, including a number who were pro-Nazi, wanted to stop the war but had no power. Before long, with additional military success in Norway and France, any chance of an internal coup against Hitler was to recede still further. Not until the Russian and North African campaigns went sour was there any reasonable prospect that Hitler might be toppled.

Chamberlain's belief that peace could be negotiated with Hitler or his successor as soon as the economic blockade was effective was disastrous for the war effort. There was no sense of urgency, bureaucracy ran riot, and each month Hitler became stronger vis-à-vis the Allies in tanks, aeroplanes and other arms.

In March 1940 Lord Beaverbrook, fully aware of the indecision of the Prime Minister and the Foreign Secretary, suddenly decided to put his weight behind a demand for a negotiated peace with Hitler. Lord Tavistock, President of the British Council for Christian Settlement, had already approached him after the publication of a pamphlet setting out the peace terms which it was alleged (through the German Embassy in Dublin) that the German Government would agree. Beaverbrook had on that occasion replied that he emphatically did not agree. But when Dick Stokes, Labour MP for Ipswich, published a

[m]Chamberlain and Roosevelt never met, although the President sent him a warm invitation to visit America in September 1938 – which the Prime Minister would have liked to accept.

well-argued pamphlet in January 1940 making the case for a negotiated peace, Beaverbrook wrote to say how much he agreed. He promised that if Stokes put such a case at the Labour Party Conference in May the *Express* would be told to report him fully.

According to the Foreign Office archives on 11 March 1940, William Ridsdale[n] minuted Jebb:

I was told today by a reliable journalist that Lord Beaverbrook is intending to promote and finance a campaign in this country for a speedy peace on a compromise basis. With this in view he gave a dinner to three ILP [Independent Labour Party] MPs, McGovern, Jim Maxton and Campbell Stephen and is believed to have discussed with them a campaign throughout the country for which he would provide the money. Beaverbrook is believed to be under the impression that there is a widespread feeling in the country in favour of a negotiated peace provided that there were some change of government in Germany, e.g. Goering coming to the top, and some proposal in regard to Poland and Czechoslovakia which would provide a basis of negotiations.

My informant has the impression that Beaverbrook is acting in conjunction with certain other big money interests.

To this Charles Peake added:[o]

Yes, I have confirmation from a reliable source. Mr. Kingsley Martin, editor of *The New Statesman*, and not apt to be uncharitable to the Left, told me that he is seriously disturbed at the extent to which the left and right wing pacifists are making common cause and according to him making steady progress. He described Mr. McGovern to me as 'dishonest and corrupt'.

Vansittart took it up:

Lord Beaverbrook has been trying this on in France and has caused some sharp and angry protests which have come to me in letters. I have tried to calm these greatly and justifiably disturbed minds by telling them not to attach too much importance to this merchant. But I cannot dismiss it as easily from my own mind. I have, of course, like Mr. Ridsdale and Mr. Peake, reliable confirmation of this. Indeed it is an open secret in advance. Lord Beaverbrook is a buddy of Mr. Kennedy [the United States Ambassador in London] and of most of the 'Money-in-our-time-Brigade' – a detachment of the Fifth Column. If he goes on with this he will do a great deal of damage (1) here (2) in France (3) in the U.S.A. where there is anyhow considerable distrust of us and (4) he will be a great gift to German propaganda. He should therefore be stopped. The Prime Minister and Lord Halifax should send for him together and ask him to drop it, both as a matter of patriotism and

[n]Assistant Press Officer in the Foreign Office.
[o]A Foreign Office adviser to Halifax; later Ambassador to Greece.

commonsense. For the peace he has in mind would only result without fail in our all having our throats cut in a couple of years. I should be glad to know whether this action will be taken.[25]

Halifax did not favour Vansittart's suggestion that he and the Prime Minister should have a heart-to-heart talk with Beaverbrook. He minuted that the best person to talk to Beaverbrook would be Churchill, but there he let the matter drop. Halifax's own views were too close to Beaverbrook's for comfort, and he did not want to be drawn into a controversy with Churchill about a negotiated peace to which he knew Churchill was violently opposed. Churchill, left in ignorance, was to make Beaverbrook Minister of Aircraft Production on 12 May. Had he known of Beaverbrook's flirtation with the ILP and a negotiated peace it is almost impossible that he could have made such an appointment.

In May 1941 a by-election took place in Glasgow. It was contested by the ILP, who were campaigning for peace because Hitler had not yet attacked Russia. McGovern, in a by-election speech, claimed that Beaverbrook had been carrying on his own peace campaign in the spring of 1940 only weeks before he became Minister of Aircraft Production. He said that at a dinner at Stornoway House in 1940 Beaverbrook had told the three ILP MPs that he would support ILP peace candidates in by-elections both financially and by sending special reporters into the constituencies.

In Parliament on 28 June 1941 Churchill defended Beaverbrook, quoting the letter sent by Beaverbrook to Lord Tavistock who had asked for Beaverbrook's help with his own peace proposals in March 1940. Then Beaverbrook had written that he believed in Chamberlain's war policy 'If peace becomes a possibility I feel sure he will do everything in his power to promote it.'

Colville told the author that after Churchill had defended Beaverbrook in the Commons he said: 'Most people will believe Maxton, not Beaverbrook.' Anyway, McGovern was furious. He wrote to Beaverbrook telling him as a man of honour he must admit what happened at the dinner party when 'you made a voluntary offer to give us £500 for every seat we fought'.

Churchill again taxed Beaverbrook, who replied untruthfully that he used to see so many people for dinner each day and talk to so many that he just could not remember what had happened. On this unsatisfactory note the episode ended. It is strange that Churchill remained so loyal to his devious friend.[26]

On 10 May 1940, when it was already clear that the British

campaign in Norway was a disaster, Hitler invaded the Low Countries. Chamberlain resigned and was replaced by Churchill as Prime Minister. It was touch and go whether Halifax got the Premiership instead of Churchill: had he done so, the Government would undoubtedly have made a compromise peace with Hitler – as the proceedings of the War Cabinet provide dramatic evidence.

There was an illuminating report from the American Ambassador, Joseph Kennedy, on 27 May: 'If the Germans made Britain along with France an offer of peace there would be a row in the Cabinet between the 'do or die' group and the 'group that want a settlement'. Although Kennedy considered Churchill and Attlee would stand firm, there were others who thought 'the physical destruction of men and property in England will not be a proper offset to a loss of pride', and that Halifax had told him as early as 16 May that if the French cracked he did not believe that England would fight on alone and that nothing could 'save them from absolute defeat unless the President with some touch of genius and God's blessing can do it'.[27]

Conservative MPs were overwhelmingly in favour of Halifax as Prime Minister, and he was ready to serve. At a meeting in Chamberlain's room at 10 Downing Street on 10 May Chamberlain asked Churchill for his opinion as to whether a peer could be Prime Minister. If Churchill had said 'Yes' Halifax would have been Prime Minister. Instead, Colville told the author, Churchill walked to the window, looked out, and refused to reply.

The Labour Party leaders under Attlee refused to serve under Halifax, and in order to allow a National Government to be formed in this moment of crisis the Tory Ministers, including Halifax, agreed reluctantly that Churchill should become Prime Minister. Even then it was to take all Churchill's resolution to prevent a capitulation to Hitler in the first few weeks of his administration.

Churchill's War Cabinet consisted of five: Halifax continued as Foreign Secretary; Chamberlain was Lord President of the Council, Attlee Lord Privy Seal, and Greenwood Minister Without Portfolio. In addition there were 'regular attenders' including Eden (War Office), Sinclair (Air Ministry – and leader of Liberal Party), and Duff Cooper (Information).

By 25 May France was hopelessly beaten. Weygand's defence line on the Somme had been pierced; there was no hope of a counter-offensive; German tanks were speeding across France and the BEF was retreating towards Dunkirk. At the French War Committee in Paris on 25 May the question of an armistice was mooted at the suggestion of

Weygand. The next day Reynaud, the French Prime Minister, set off for London – not to ask officially for permission from his ally to capitulate, but ostensibly to obtain the support of the British Government 'for concessions to Mussolini in the hope of keeping Italy out of the war' and to explore the possibility of mediation with Hitler by the Italians.

At his first meeting at lunch with Churchill on 26 May Reynaud spoke of the possibility of cessation of hostilities. He got a dusty reply. Churchill said France must stay in the war. Only that morning Churchill had received a depressing preliminary report from the British Chiefs of Staff on the situation which would arise if France dropped out of the war. Churchill did not show this report to his War Cabinet; he feared the effect of it on his appeasement-minded colleagues, Halifax and Chamberlain.

The British Cabinet had already met before Reynaud arrived. Then Churchill had told them he 'doubted whether anything would come of an approach to Italy', but they could consider it after Halifax reported his conversation of the day before with the Italian Ambassador, Bastianini.[28]

On 24 May the War Cabinet had authorized Halifax to say that if Italy remained neutral Britain would take account of reasonable Italian claims at the peace conference, at which Italy would appear 'on an equal footing with the belligerents'. Halifax's talk to Bastianini can only be described as an attempt to bribe Italy to stay out of the war, at the same time importuning Mussolini to persuade Hitler to have a peace conference. Halifax went further than Churchill wanted, telling the Italian Ambassador that 'the Allies would be prepared to consider any proposals which might lead to peace'. Gibraltar, Malta and Suez might be sacrificed to Italy by Britain; Djibouti and Tunis by France. Halifax and the French were ready to internationalize these possessions which, in practice, would mean handing them over to Italy.

On the afternoon of 26 May Halifax saw Reynaud with Churchill and told the French Prime Minister that if Italy would collaborate in a peace which would safeguard the independence of France and Britain the Allies would discuss all the claims of Italy in the Mediterranean – in particular 'the outlets of this sea'. Churchill did not dissent implicitly. On his return to Paris Reynaud reported: 'Halifax agreed, but Churchill took refuge behind the War Cabinet.' So concerned was Churchill on the 26th with the fate of the BEF in France that he was at his most vulnerable point with regard to negotiations with Hitler. As more and more troops returned safely to England, he became more optimistic and opposed to any such move.

Probably the most fateful Cabinet meetings of the century were held in London on 27 and 28 May after Reynaud's departure. Over everything loomed the precarious position of the BEF. On the 27th Cadogan noted: 'I see no hope for more than a tiny fraction of them now that Belgium has capitulated.' This view was widely held in Whitehall.

In Cabinet Halifax's line was that Mussolini was alarmed at Hitler's 'power', and the Government ought to approach him as the French suggested. Chamberlain supported Halifax, who defended himself against attacks by Churchill, saying: 'If we got to the point of discussing a general settlement and found we could obtain terms which did not postulate the destruction of our independence we should be foolish not to accept them.' Churchill was subdued and a telegram was sent to Paris confirming that an approach should be made to Mussolini through the President of the United States.

At a second meeting on 27 May the War Cabinet received the depressing news that Stanley Bruce, the Australian High Commissioner in London, had become defeatist, saying Britain must mobilize Roosevelt and Mussolini before Paris fell. Chamberlain wanted to tell the Dominions 'we should fight on' but with the timorous rider that 'if terms were offered we should consider them on their merits'.

Churchill scoffed at any approach to Mussolini, and said Britain could not get out of her difficulties by concessions to Italy in the Mediterranean and giving back to Germany her colonies; any terms offered by Hitler would prevent Britain continuing with rearmament and the only thing to do was to show Hitler 'he could not conquer this country'. In his view, 'Even if we are beaten we would be no worse than if we abandoned the struggle now.' However, as a concession to Halifax and Chamberlain, he agreed to some approach to Mussolini although he thought talks with Hitler through Mussolini would be futile. Nevertheless Britain must try and help her ally France to keep Italy out of the war.

Halifax now disagreed with Churchill, and declared there were 'profound differences' between him and the Prime Minister. Making an approach to Mussolini bore no resemblance to suing for terms, which the Prime Minister said would lead to disaster. The day before the Prime Minister had been ready to discuss terms 'provided matters vital to our independence were unaffected', and the Prime Minister had agreed 'we should be thankful to get out of our present difficulties even at the cession of territory'. Now the Prime Minister would contemplate 'no course but fighting to the finish'. His own position was that if the country's independence was not at stake he thought it right to accept an offer 'which would save our country from unavoidable disaster'. The Prime Minister infuriated him by telling him that he was talking in 'unreal terms'. Nettled, Halifax retorted 'Suppose the French army collapsed and Hitler made an offer of terms, would the Prime Minister be prepared to discuss Hitler's terms?' Churchill said he would not ask for terms, but if he was told the terms he would be prepared to consider them.

That was the closest Churchill ever got to admitting he was considering capitulation. He was still poles apart from Halifax and Chamberlain, but fortunately for Churchill, Attlee and Greenwood backed him. Halifax was near to resignation, which could have been a political disaster for Churchill in view of Halifax's popularity within the Conservative Party. The Foreign Secretary wrote in his diary: 'Winston talked the most frightful rot, and also Greenwood, and after hearing it all for some time I said exactly what I thought of them, adding that if that was really their view if it came to the point our ways must part.' The discussion was obviously more acrimonious than the official minutes record.

After the second 27 May Cabinet Halifax said to Cadogan: 'I can't work with Winston any longer.' Cadogan replied: 'Don't do anything silly', and urged him before he did anything to 'consult Neville'. This is evidence of how close Halifax came to resignation; yet it must have been a close thing whether his or Churchill's views prevailed. If Halifax had won, the course of European history would have been radically different. Halifax was definitely ready for a peace conference with Hitler.[29]

The next day, 28 May, the War Cabinet met at 4.30 p.m. Chamberlain and Halifax again stated they were in favour of an approach to Hitler through Mussolini with a view to a conference. Halifax said that if Mussolini wanted to play the part of a mediator and could procure terms which would not affect Britain's independence, the Government should consider them – 'We might get better terms before France went out of the war and our aircraft factories were bombed than we might get in three months' time.'

Churchill would have none of this. He replied that Reynaud wanted to get Britain to a conference table with Hitler. If this happened, 'we should find that Hitler's terms infringed our independence and integrity and if we then left the conference table we should find our resolution to fight Hitler would have vanished.'

Chamberlain and the Labour Ministers tended to agree with

Churchill, and Halifax was isolated. The Foreign Secretary again reiterated we should try out the possibilities of mediation 'which the Prime Minister felt was so wrong'. Halifax must again have been close to resignation.

During an interval between 5.15 and 7 p.m., Churchill met in his room in the Commons the other Ministers of Cabinet rank outside the War Cabinet. He said to them: 'I have thought carefully whether I should enter into negotiations with that man. But I am convinced that every man of you would rise up and tear me down from my place if I were for one moment to contemplate parley or surrender.' According to Hugh Dalton, 'there were loud cries of approval and no one expressed even the faintest flicker of dissent'.[30] Fortified by this enthusiastic expression of support Churchill told the War Cabinet that evening he had seen their colleagues and that they had expressed the greatest satisfaction when he had told them there was no chance of giving up the struggle. So Halifax was overruled. The War Cabinet agreed to telegraph Reynaud that this was not 'the right moment to approach the Italian dictator'.

Once it was clear the greater part of the BEF was safe, Churchill would not discuss peace terms. From South Africa General Smuts, too, weighed in with a telegram that 'we must fight alone'. Halifax had argued in vain. There were to be no negotiations with Hitler then or in the future. The Foreign Secretary had shot his bolt in his efforts to end the war on Hitler's and Mussolini's terms.

On 2 June Oliver Harvey noted in his diary that 'Halifax was anxiously exploring possibility of peace proposals à la Lansdowne'; the Prime Minister had 'flatly turned them down'. It was surprising that Churchill made Lloyd George an offer of a place in his War Cabinet on 28 May and again on 19 June: Lloyd George was defeatist and wanted peace negotiations. According to Halifax's diary Churchill intended to get an assurance from Lloyd George that he would never advocate any peace terms which 'would be destructive of our independence'. Another possibility is that Churchill feared that if Hitler triumphed he would be swept from office, and he wanted an orderly transfer of power to those who would try for a negotiated settlement.

For two days the fate of Europe had been in the melting pot as the War Cabinet debated. How close Halifax and Chamberlain were to carrying the day we shall never know. If the BEF had not returned from Dunkirk with far fewer casualties than expected, although without their equipment, the outcome could have been different. The minutes clearly do not tell the full story, but enough can be pieced together to reveal the drama and the divided counsels. Churchill, after he read these Cabinet minutes, ordered that no such full note of the discussions should be taken in future. For the rest of the war the Cabinet minutes reveal no discord.

There was one last flicker from the movement for appeasement and a soft peace with Hitler, which involved Halifax and Rab Butler, then an Under-Secretary. According to the official British historian, differences of opinion 're-emerged three weeks later', and the following is what happened.

Butler was walking through St James's Park on 17 June when he ran into Bjorn Prytz, the much-respected Swedish Minister in London. Butler brought Prytz back to his room in the Foreign Office and had a long confidential chat with him about the likely outcome of the war. Prytz, according to all the British diplomats of that era whom the author has consulted, was completely honest and reliable. He made a broadcast on 7 September 1965 giving the full details of that conversation with Butler. This was reported in the Swedish *Dagens Nyheter* the next day, and in 1984 his dispatch to Stockholm on 17 June 1940 was published for the first time in a Swedish book on foreign policy in the Second World War.[31]

Prytz said that Butler told him 'no opportunity would be neglected for concluding a compromise peace if the chance offered on reasonable conditions'. During the talk Butler was called away to see Halifax, who sent the message to Prytz via Butler that 'commonsense, not bravado, would dictate British Government policy' and that Halifax knew such an attitude would be welcomed by Prytz but he must not interpret it to mean 'peace at any price'. Prytz put in his report from Stockholm that in conversation with MPs it was possible to discern the hope that an opportunity for negotiations with Germany would show itself after the secret session of the Commons on 28 June, and that Halifax could be expected to replace Churchill as Prime Minister. On 17 June Halifax and Butler were still defeatist and many Tory MPs expected Churchill to fall. But as June progressed the Prime Minister was strengthening his hold over Parliament and the nation.

Prytz reported Butler's views to Stockholm in good faith, stating that Britain would only continue the war 'if certain of an ultimate victory'. His report was discussed by the Swedish Foreign Policy Committee which was sworn to secrecy. At that time Sweden was desperately anxious for the war to end as they had been faced with sudden harsh demands from Germany for transit rights for troops and materials through their territory.

The Swedish members of the Foreign Policy Committee immediately leaked the news about Prytz's report, and the Stockholm correspondent of the *News Chronicle* told his paper on 20 June that Butler had said Britain would only continue to fight if certain of victory. Ribbentrop was alerted and asked Marcus Wallenberg to approach Victor Mallet, British Envoy in Stockholm, to find out if the British wanted to negotiate. Mallet reported the leak and the gist of Butler's conversation to London, and was told to tell Wallenberg there was no desire to negotiate.

On 19 June Mallet talked to the Swedish Foreign Minister who asked if Butler's views should be kept secret. Mallet informed London. Butler saw Prytz immediately and told him he had no authority to repeat the conversation of 17 June. Prytz told Butler he thought interested parties in Sweden were trying to cause mischief, and cabled to his Government that his previous report should not be regarded as expressing Halifax's and Butler's views – which were anyway not intended for report to the Swedish Government; but he added the rider that 'pending the result of the secret session the views of H.M.G. had not crystallized'. Butler cabled to Mallet that 'no hint' was intended and Prytz had exaggerated the importance of any 'polite message' conveyed by himself from Lord Halifax to the Swedish Minister on 17 June.

Churchill read the telegrams and was much put out – especially as he had issued a strong directive to all his Ministers that they were at all times to show complete confidence and no signs of defeatism.

He wrote to Halifax on 26 June còmplaining of Butler's 'odd language' and impression of lukewarmness and defeatism:

Private   10, Downing Street,
                                                                    Whitehall
                                                               June 26, 1940

My dear Edward,
    It is quite clear to me from these telegrams and others that Butler held odd language to the Swedish Minister and certainly the Swede derived a strong impression of defeatism. In these circumstances would it not be well for you to find out from Butler actually what he did say. I was strongly pressed in the House of Commons in the Secret Session to give assurances that the present Government and all its Members were resolved to fight on to the death, and I did so, taking personal responsibility for the resolve of all. I saw a silly rumour in a telegram from Belgrade or Bucharest and how promptly you stamped upon it, but any suspicion of lukewarmness in Butler will certainly subject us all to further annoyance of this kind.

                                                               Yours ever,
                                                      WINSTON S. CHURCHILL

Butler must have been close to losing his job in the Government, but he denied giving Prytz any impression of defeatism in a hand-written letter to Halifax on the same day. Clearly he was prevaricating. Here is his not too convincing letter:

Foreign Office,
S.W.1
26.6.'40

Dear S of S,

Thank you for showing me the Prime Minister's letter on the subject of my interview with the Swedish Minister on June 17th.

I feel sure that M. Prytz did not derive any 'impression of defeatism' and I know that he would be glad to give you his own impression of the talk we had if you would care to send for him. Meanwhile his view, and I believe the true view, is included in No. 534 Dipp which I attach and which he and I thought had cleared up the matter.

It has been a source of great distress to the Swedish Minister and myself that this matter should have assumed the wrong significance which it has.

I happened to meet him in the Park and he came into the office for only a few minutes; not being an arranged interview I did not keep a record. You know that I send you records of all my talks and you know that I see most of the Foreign Ministers and transact office business with them. I am prepared for you to ascertain from any of them whether any 'lukewarmness' has been exhibited in my conversation. To suggest enquiring from them may seem odd, but the fact is that our relations are so friendly that this might be the most effective course.

In my public defence of most contentious public policy over the past ten years, and through perpetual heckling I am not aware that I have trembled or been regarded as giving away a single unnecessary point. This instance of my private conversation can only be judged by the Swedish Minister since no one else was present. I do not recognise myself or my conversation in the impressions given.

You may enquire why any conversation with a Foreign Representative took this line at all and why I was reported as saying that 'commonsense and not bravado would dictate our policy'. On meeting me the Swedish Minister has since agreed with me that he opened the conversation by saying that there was more need than ever for successful diplomacy now that Great Britain was left alone to continue the struggle. We ran over the many efforts to improve our position in the international field, and M. Prytz was quite clear that it was in the interest of the neutrals to see an end of the war. I reminded him that if we were to negotiate, we must do so from strength, and that force must be met by force. From this he did not demur and he has since agreed with me that this account of our talk is correct.

It may be that I should have entertained no conversation with M. Prytz on the subject of an ultimate settlement. But I am satisfied that I said nothing definite or specific or that I would wish now to withdraw. I am usually cautious in following the leads of foreign representatives. I can see that in this case I should have been more cautious and I apologise.

I now place myself in your hands. It is essential in the work I do, that there should be absolute confidence between those whom I serve and myself. Had I not been ready to subscribe to the Prime Minister's courageous lead in the House of Commons, I should have felt bound to inform you and to leave the administration.

I feel that I have been placed in a wrong light, but I absolutely understand the Prime Minister's enquiry.

Under the circumstances I await your and the Prime Minister's final opinion after you have read this letter and made any further enquiries.

Yours ever,
R. BUTLER

Halifax wrote to Churchill that they ought to accept Butler's explanation, and Butler's political career was saved.[32] However, it quickly became well known in the Conservative Party that Butler had earned the Prime Minister's grave displeasure by his wish for a negotiated peace. The story was assiduously fanned over the years by Winston's son Randolph, and undoubtedly played its part in preventing Butler from becoming Prime Minister both when Eden resigned in 1956 and when Macmillan resigned in 1963.

7
Mussolini's War
1940 – 1943

Italy declared war on France and Britain in June 1940. It was soon clear she was the weak link in the Axis: an Italian offensive in Greece quickly bogged down in October and November 1940; the RAF ravaged the Italian fleet at Taranto on 11 November; and Marshal Rodolfo Graziani, Commander of the Italian army in North Africa, made no efforts to attack the numerically weaker British army in Egypt. Then with amazing speed General Wavell's British army advanced into Italian Cyrenaica and captured Sidi Barrani, Bardia and Tobruk by 21 January 1941. 90,000 Italians surrendered at Tobruk, and 113,000 at Beda Fomm on 7 February – more than the attacking force.

Reports from Italy told the Foreign Office of sinking morale, powerful anti-Fascist opposition and the desire of the people to get out of the war. Buoyed up by military success early in 1941, the British Government decided on four measures to try to end Italy's part in the war. These were: (1) raising a Free Italian force to fight on the British side (the Garibaldi Legion); (2) establishment of Cyrenaica as a free Italian colony 'to be petted and made prosperous'; (3) bribes to Italian naval officers to induce them to bring their ships to Alexandria and to surrender them; (4) a determined search for an Italian de Gaulle to lead the free anti-Fascist Italians.

All these were embarked on with deadly seriousness. Neither Eden nor Churchill saw fit to refer to them in their autobiographies after the war. This is understandable because they were all abortive and reflect little credit on the acumen of either statesman. It is inexplicable why the official historian of Foreign Policy in the Second World War, Sir Llewellyn Woodward, ignored them. Not only were they important in themselves, but two years later British policy to Italy was completely reversed and this *volte-face*, which was disastrous, is important diplomatic history.

On 22 January 1941 the Southern Department of the Foreign Office issued a confidential memorandum written by William Knight calling attention to the low morale of the Italian POWs, the wish of the Italians in their homeland for a peace, and their hatred of Germany. This was greeted eagerly by Churchill and Eden.

Immediately after the British victory at Beda Fomm Lord Davies, the veteran Tory newspaper magnate, wrote to Churchill and sent him a copy of a letter to Eden advocating the raising of a Free Italian Army to be called the Garibaldi Legion 'to fight against fascism' from Italian prisoners of war in Egypt.[1] Eden liked the idea, and the letter was passed to the Southern Department of the Foreign Office for their comments. Philip Nichols sent the suggestion to the War Office where it was received coldly, but Orme Sargent[a] summed up the views of the Southern Department by minuting that there was much to be said in favour of an effort to organize an anti-Fascist Italian army.

Fortified by the support of his officials, Eden decided to recommend the project to the Prime Minister. After minuting to the Department on 2 February 1941 'P.M. should approve', he sent this memorandum to the Prime Minister on 6 February 1941:

Prime Minister,
Dalton's organisation[b] are with the concurrence of the service departments preparing leaflets to be dropped on Italian Forces if there should be any sign later on that as a result of their dislike of the Germans numbers of the Italian forces are prepared to come over to us.

In the leaflet addressed to *Italian sailors* it is proposed to say:
His Britannic Majesty's Government solemnly pledges itself to give hospitality and protection to you and to your ships in the naval base of Alexandria.

HBMG pledges itself further not to exert the slightest pressure to make you and your ships fight against Germany and Fascist tyranny. Complete freedom of choice will be left to you between taking up the fight against Germany and total abstention from the conflict while putting your ships well out of reach of the rapacious German claws.

The leaflet also states that in both cases Italian sailors (officers, petty officers and men) will receive the same treatment and the same pay as the Royal Navy.

The proposed leaflet to *Italian airmen* urges them to join in the fight for the liberation of Europe from German tyranny and advises them if their machines run the risk of being captured by the Germans to fly them to a British air base.

[a]Under-Secretary at the Foreign Office. Succeeded Sir Alexander Cadogan as Permanent Under-Secretary after the war.
[b]This was SOE (Special Operations Executive), a secret underground organization set up on Churchill's orders on 16 July 1940 to 'sabotage' and 'subvert' the enemy. It was under the Minister of Economic Warfare (then Hugh Dalton). Jebb was the chief executive officer, and the other heads were Sir Frank Nelson, a former Conservative MP, Sir Charles Hambro, the merchant banker, and Colonel Gubbins. There was a constant conflict between SOE and the Ministry of Information, originally SOE was divided into SOE 1 for subversion and SOE 2 for sabotage. SOE 1's title was changed to Political Warfare Executive.

Mussolini greets Hitler at the Brenner Pass

Chamberlain talking to Mussolini at Munich.

Hitler welcoming Chamberlain and Sir Horace Wilson (behind Chamberlain's left shoulder) to Godesberg.

Sir Nevile Henderson and Hitler in Berlin. In between is Hitler's interpreter, Paul Schmidt.

Ribbentrop at a reception in London

Goering

At Munich, left to right: Chamberlain, Daladier, Hitler, Mussolini and Ciano.

EUROPE
1939

Miles

0   50   100   150   200

FINLAND

ESTONIA

LATVIA

LITHUANIA

SSIA

Warsaw

POLAND

many

39

Curzon
Line

To U.S.S.R.
Oct 1939

U.S.S.R.

A

To Hungary
Mar 1939

To Hungary
Nov 1938

RUMANIA

BLACK SEA

Brian MacDermot (left) with Adam von Trott, Pekin 1938

Eden at the time of his resignation in 1938

Carl Goerdeler

General Ludwig Beck

Generals Brauchitsch and Halder

General Keitel

Winston Churchill in 1940

US paratroops of 82nd Airborne Division ready for their drop on Rome airfields, 8 September 1943. The operation was cancelled when they were in the air.

Crown Prince Umberto with an Italian farmer and his wife, September 1943.

Quebec Conference, August 1943. Standing, left to right: Arnold, Portal, Brooke, King, Dill, Marshall, Pound, Leahy. Seated: Mackenzie King, Roosevelt, Churchill.

General Maxwell Taylor with Marshal Badoglio (right) at Brindisi, October 1943.

General Bergonzoli – 'Electric Whiskers'.

Badoglio and Caviglia

Churchill, Roosevelt and Stalin at Yalta. Behind them, left to right: Eden, Stettinius and Molotov.

Eisenhower congratulating Castellano on the signing of the armistice; on the left, Bedell Smith.

Clarita and Adam von Trott

Dietrich Bonhoeffer

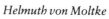

Himmler and Hitler watching troop manoeuvres

Helmuth von Moltke

Sir Frank Roberts

Sir Con O'Neill

Archduke Otto Hapsburg

Sir Geoffrey Harrison

Eva Braun with Hitler

General Hans Oster

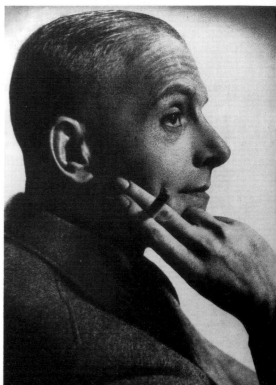

Otto John, one of the few conspirators to escape, with (right) his brother Hans, who was executed.

Major-General Henning von Tresckow

General Erwin von Witzleben

Ulrich von Hassell

Claus von Stauffenberg: taken in 1933

The leaflet further pledges HMG to give Italian airmen who do this the same treatment as that of the R.A.F.

I have no doubt that the line suggested both to the Italian fleet and Italian airmen is the right line. Do you approve? If you do, Dalton's organisation will get ahead with the preparation of the leaflets.

A.E.   6.2.41[2]

On receipt of Eden's message Churchill became enthusiastic and minuted to the Chief of Staffs Committee on 11 February that not only did he agree to raising an anti-Mussolini Italian army in Egypt, but that he wanted to establish Cyrenaica as a free non-Fascist Italian colony to be treated like de Gaulle's colonies, but even better. This treatment of Cyrenaica as a diplomatic bargaining counter recalls, more nearly than anything appropriate to the twentieth century, Prime Minister Addington's bargaining over Malta with Napoleon in the Treaty of Amiens of 1802. Here is the Prime Minister's surprising minute:

Prime Minister's Personal Minute
Serial No. D. 36/1

General Ismay, for C.O.S. Committee
I see no reason why you should not consider raising an anti-Mussolini or Free Italian force in Cyrenaica. Volunteers might be called for from the 100,000 prisoners we have taken. There must be a great many who hate Fascism. We might even rule Cyrenaica under the Free Italian flag and treat it in the same way as de Gaulle's colonies are being treated subject to our military control.[c] Anyhow, I wish Cyrenaica to be petted and made extremely comfortable and prosperous, more money being spent upon them than they are intrinsically worth. Can we not make this place a base for starting a real split in Italy and the source of anti-Mussolini propaganda? We might make it a model of British rule, hold it in trust for the Italian people and have 4,000 or 5,000 Italian troops sworn to the liberation of Italy from the German and Mussolini yoke. This could be run as world propaganda. The matter raises wide political considerations and I am sending a copy of this minute to the Foreign Secretary.

(Intld) W.S.C.   February 11, 1941[3]

Eden did not oppose Churchill's wild project. Lord Gladwyn, then private secretary to Sir Alec Cadogan, told the author: 'In the Foreign Office then we thought it was a good idea and I still think so provided we could have held Cyrenaica.' Eden's acquiescence in 1941 was to be in marked contrast with his rigid refusal two years later to negotiate with anti-Fascists and monarchists who wanted to overthrow Mus-

---

[c]In the unlikely event of Winston Churchill's Cyrenaica proposal coming into effect, Italy would have had a gargantuan Algerian-style situation on her hands after the war.

solini and make peace when Italy had clearly lost her war. In February 1941 he had only recently become Foreign Secretary again, and at first he did not show the same arrogance and contempt for Italy he was later to display.

Electrified by Churchill's minute to the Chiefs of Staff, a Committee chaired by Orme Sargent and composed of representatives from the Foreign Office, Admiralty, War Office, Air Ministry and SOE, met two days later on 13 February at the Foreign Office 'to consider the possibility of a Free Italian movement in Cyrenaica or other Italian colony'. Eden insisted that the Committee should be warned that the Foreign Secretary 'was favourable to the Free Italian Army, but was not so sure that it would be wise to nail the Italian flag to the mast of Cyrenaica, and felt it was a matter which required considerable thought'.[4]

Sir Leonard Woolley, the distinguished archaeologist, was probably the greatest expert on the Arab world in London at that time. He was serving in the War Office and he produced a memorandum for the Committee hotly opposing the scheme. Sargent was at pains to point out that this was only Woolley's personal view.

Memorandum by Major Sir Leonard Woolley, War Office

LIBYA

It is obviously impossible to hand back Cyrenaica to the Italians.
(a) This would stultify in a cynical fashion all our propaganda based on Italian mis-government and oppression in the Colony.
(b) It would lose us all sympathy from Arabs everywhere, who would regard it as a betrayal of the local Arabs.
(c) It would perpetuate the disadvantage from which we have suffered hitherto of having no intermediate air and naval base, other than Malta, between Gibraltar and Egypt.
(d) The loss of Cyrenaica would be not unwelcome to the bulk of Italians, who regard this colony and Abyssinia as disappointing and costly liabilities; it would however be a serious blow to the Fascist leaders whose reputation is involved in the expansion of the Empire.

It is impracticable to establish Cyrenaica as an independent State.
(a) With its mixed population the country could not improvise a government of its own. The only possible head of such a State would be the Grand Senoussi, whose religious prestige could not be translated into political authority without disputes, necessitating external support.

The attachment of Cyrenaica to Egypt would follow historical precedent and would be a logical solution of the problem. It would have many advantages:
(a) It would provide that degree of control which is essential.

(b) It would satisfy the people of Cyrenaica, who would welcome a Moslem government, whatever its shortcomings, and the Grand Senoussi, who has requested Egyptian citizenship.

(c) It would gratify the Egyptians, appealing to the vanity of the King, to the desire for office of the Effendi class, and to the amour propre of the people generally.

(d) It would be generally welcomed by Arabs . . . The Pan-Arabs would see in it a step towards their ideal of union, and would set Great Britain's performance against the doubtful promises of the Axis.

(e) The interests of the native population could be adequately safeguarded. The cession to Egypt would not be absolute but conditional upon Cyrenaica enjoying a degree of cultural autonomy; the authority of the Grand Senoussi under the Crown of Egypt could be assured and defined, and provision made for a percentage of Governmental posts to be held by local inhabitants.

(f) Our own interests would be secured by the condition that we should obtain the lease of one or two air and/or sea bases.

In face of Churchill's enthusiasm for an Italian Cyrenaica and the exciting prospect of whittling Italy out of the war, Woolley's well-argued objections made little headway with the Committee, who endorsed the Prime Minister's initiative. Their findings included: (1) a Free Italian Cyrenaica would make a voluntary surrender of the whole or part of the Italian Fleet easier, and in such an event the families of the sailors might be able to live amongst their countrymen in the Free Italian colony; (2) from the propaganda point of view the existence of a prosperous Free Italian colony would be excellent.

It was also noted, however, that such a decision would be looked upon as betrayal by the Arab population of Cyrenaica who were extremely anti-Italian, and that therefore it might be better to set up the Free Italian colony in Eritrea; also that Cyrenaica could not be self-supporting and had always drawn 'a very large proportion' of its supplies from imports, and the project would be difficult to execute 'in view of the present supply position in the Mediterranean'.[5]

The Financial Department of the War Office took the possibility of a Free Italian Army seriously, and the Permanent Under-Secretary, General Sir Frederick Boschoven, wrote to Strang:

From your experience you will know how large a part questions of pay, allowances and so on, play in the raising of morale of any troops, and I am sure that whoever is responsible will arrange that we on the financial side of the War Office are brought into the picture at an early date.

To this Strang who did not want to get caught up in a discussion of inessential details with a peripheral branch of the War Office, replied:

'All that is proposed at this stage is to consult Wavell on broad question of feasibility.'[6]

The Treasury representative on the Committee commented after the meeting:

It is very difficult to do what the Prime Minister wants. Cyrenaica has always drawn a very large proportion of its supplies from Metropolitan Italy . . . the present supply position will render it very difficult to do what is wished.

Signed: R. A. B. MYNORS

The RAF representative wrote to the Foreign Office after he had read the Committee's conclusions: 'A Free Italian Air Force would be a very dubious asset because there would be no aircraft for them to fly. Eritrea is preferable to Cyrenaica for the project.' The Admiralty wrote that their representative at the meeting thought general feeling was that disadvantages of the proposal outweighed its advantage, and that the published report gave undue prominence to the arguments in favour.

On the Foreign Office file Nichols minuted: 'Grandi might be a go-between between Italy and Britain' – to which Cadogan added: 'and a very slippery one too'. Nichols also noted that the War Office were not too keen on the Free Italian Army idea. Sargent minuted: 'I fear the War Office and General Wavell will think it more trouble than it is worth. This is undoubtedly the case militarily, but from the psychological point of view there would be a great deal to be said for trying to organise such a force.' To this Cadogan added: 'It would certainly only be a psychological force.'[7]

The War Cabinet, in the absence of Eden who had flown to Cairo, approved the report of the Committee, which was printed and circulated to them on 3 March. Accordingly on 7 March the Foreign Office cabled Sir Miles Lampson, the British Ambassador in Cairo:[d]

1. His Majesty's Government have had under consideration the creation of (a) a Free Italian colony in Cyrenaica: this colony to be run under the Free Italian flag and treated, *ceteris paribus*, as are Free French colonies, and (b) the raising of a Free Italian force from among Italian prisoners to be stationed in Cyrenaica.

2. Main advantage of this scheme would be that from point of view of propaganda the existence of a Free Italian colony would enable us to encourage Italians to hope that the future of their country is not necessarily tied up with Germany and Fascism. Secondly it might, if and when the time comes, facilitate the voluntary surrender of whole or part of Italian fleet, since

[d]Later Lord Killearn. He had a great knowledge of Italian affairs.

Italians might find it easier to take their ships to what was still an Italian colony than to an enemy port. Italian fleet might in that case provide an Admiral as leader of the movement. We realise however that largest units of Italian fleet could not be accommodated in Cyrenaican ports.

3. Meanwhile we should be grateful for your views on the following specific points:

(a) Do you consider that a Free Italy movement could be created in Cyrenaica among the existing civil population? (to his Majesty's Ambassador only) Could the large Italian colony in Egypt supply any useful recruits including potential leaders? (to all) No leaders are available in this country.

(b) What are the chances of raising a Free Italian force amongst Italian prisoners of war? What numbers could safely be recruited? Could questioning of Italian prisoners be directed to this end?

(c) What are your views on the above from the purely military/naval/air points of view and from the standpoint of administration, supply and particularly security? In any event His Majesty's Government attach importance to both Italian and Arab population of Cyrenaica being made as comfortable and prosperous as possible under war conditions.

(d) What would be the reactions to these proposals among the Arabs of Cyrenaica, in Egypt, and in the Arab world in the Middle East generally?

4. We shall welcome any further observations you may wish to offer in general. In particular would you see any advantages in setting up a Free Italian movement in Eritrea, rather than Cyrenaica, on the grounds, for instance, that there is no Arab problem in Eritrea, and Italian fleet if it surrendered would be better placed in the Red Sea than in the Mediterranean, and that Eritrea, unlike Cyrenaica, is beyond reach of German bombers?[8]

It was ominous for the success of Churchill's plan that the question of the reaction of the Arabs was raised and that Eritrea was put forward as an alternative to Cyrenaica.

In Cairo the reception was cold. Wavell and his staff held a poor opinion of the value of Italians as a fighting force against the Germans, and a further objection was that if Cyrenaica were to be hailed as an Italian colony it would antagonize not only the Sennussi, who were helping the British militarily there, but the whole of the Arab world. Woolley's views, as expressed to the Foreign Office Committee, roughly represented the thinking in military and government circles in Cairo. Wavell particularly felt that with the menace of a German counter-attack in Cyrenaica the Free Italian Army would be a grave danger. There was also a strong feeling that the frontier of Cyrenaica and Egypt should be rectified in Egypt's favour as a reward for her help against Italy. Eden had arrived in Cairo to consult with Wavell, and he replied to London on 14 March 1941:

I have discussed with Sir M. Lampson, General Wavell and Longmore[e] the question of a Free Italian Colony. Their comments on paragraph (2) of your telegram are as follows:

(a) Existing civil population in Cyrenaica does not afford promising material for a vigorous Free Italy movement. They were chosen as promising Fascist Colonisers and, while they might not offer resistance, their support is improbable and their acquiescence doubtful. Lampson says there is an anti-Fascist movement in Egypt (largely Jews) with about one thousand adherents which is being encouraged as much as possible. But it suffers from a lack of leaders. These could probably only be found amongst Anti-Fascist Italians interned in France if they could be got out. Professor Calosso, who sounds hopeful as propagandist but not as leader, is on his way from Portugal.[f]

(b) Wavell will give his reply as soon as possible on the possibility of raising a Free Italian Force.

(c) Wavell feels strongly that as long as there is a danger of a counter-attack from Tripoli it would be dangerous to experiment with a Free Italian organisation in Cyrenaica.

(d) All were agreed that reactions amongst the Arabs of Cyrenaica, in Egypt, and in the Arab world generally would be unfavourable.

2. For the above reasons, and in particular in the light of Wavell's views, arguments against such an experiment in Cyrenaica seem to be decisive for the time being.

3. We agreed that the arguments in favour of applying the plan to Eritrea are stronger. On the other hand, the effect of an announcement now on the Emperor and patriots in Abyssinia would be bad. It might create a fear that we contemplated some bargain with Italy over Abyssinia and so cool patriotic enthusiasm. While therefore the project for Eritrea will be further considered here, I should be against launching it in East Africa at least until Italian resistance there has collapsed.[9]

Churchill's enthusiasm for a prosperous and petted Free Italian colony in Cyrenaica was stillborn. Nichols minuted:

This is much the kind of answer we expected . . . it looks as if the matter should be put in cold storage until Italian resistance has collapsed in East Africa. It will not be necessary to reconvene a meeting of the Committee to consider this answer.

The Foreign Office accepted that Eritrea was more suitable territory for a Free Italy than Cyrenaica.

[e]Air Chief Marshal Sir Arthur Longmore was AOC-in-C Middle East.

[f]Professor Calosso, when he reached Cairo, ran a daily Allied propaganda newspaper in Italian. On his return to London he broadcast for the BBC in Italian but caused the Foreign Office trouble because he was quarrelsome. He was certainly not a leader.

Now ignoring Churchill's suggestion of an Italian colony in Cyrenaica, the Foreign Office and Wavell in Cairo dragged their feet on the future of Cyrenaica for the rest of 1941. However, the delay was not because of second thoughts about Italy; the argument was whether Egyptians or Sennussi were to rule in Cyrenaica. Eventually, on 8 January 1942, Eden told the House of Commons that the Sennussi help against Britain's enemies had been welcomed and that at the end of the war Sayid Idris and his followers would under no circumstances be placed under Italian rule – thus begging the question of rewarding Egypt with a slice of the former Italian colony.

On 24 March 1941 Wavell signalled to London that the chances of raising a Free Italian force from prisoners of war could not yet be assessed.

Three or four ardent anti-fascists amongst them have expressed the opinion that it might be possible to raise a force of several thousand from them, but this seems optimistic. Such a force, if raised in Egypt, would create serious problems of security, and Eritrea when occupied by us seems the safest place for the formation. The choice of leader is most important.[10]

At that time the British Government expected to find an Italian de Gaulle. The former politicians Sforza, Salvemini and Sturzo were considered amongst the exiles but they were in the United States and preferred to remain there. Also, as the Foreign Office pointed out, they had been out of public sight for seventeen years.

One candidate taken seriously by the British as a possible Italian de Gaulle was the bizarre character General Annibale Bergonzoli, Commander of the Italian 23 Corps, who had been taken prisoner at Tobruk. He had achieved a fleeting renown in the British national press because of his beard, and had become known as 'Electric Whiskers'. He impressed his interrogators temporarily with the strength of his personality and his vivid expression of anti-Fascist sentiments.

In a signal from Cairo dated 24 March 1941, Wavell wrote that Bergonzoli had said: 'Mussolini will not listen to or believe unpleasant truths, and Bergonzoli affirms his dearest ambition is to live so that he can rebel against the rottenness of the present Italian regime.' In a further signal Bergonzoli was reported as saying it would not be difficult to obtain an Italian General de Gaulle, and that military dictatorship – perhaps guided by Marshal Badoglio was the only possible form of revolution in Italy.

Sargent took the comic General Bergonzoli seriously and minuted he should be carefully studied . . . 'if the indications are favourable we might like to try him as leader of the Free Italy Movement.' William Cavendish-Bentinck,[g] Chairman of the Joint Intelligence Committee, wrote to the War Office that if Bergonzoli's credentials were good enough he might be suitable for the post of leader of Free Italy, and he would be preferable to former politicians like Count Sforza, Salvemini and Sturzo who preferred to operate in the safety of the United States. A letter on these lines was sent to the War Office.

The War Office enquiries about Bergonzoli were discouraging. General Davidson, Director of Military Intelligence, replied to Cavendish-Bentinck on 18 April that Major Colwill of the Italian section of the War Office had known Bergonzoli and considered him as rather a mountebank because 'he rushed around paying surprise visits to units and was only rarely in his own office.' 'He rides around on horses, motor cycles and ordinary bicycles paying considerable attention to small details and interfering in the administration of minor units.' Accordingly, Pierson Dixon noted that 'this means we must write off 'Electric Whiskers' as a possible Free Italian leader'. As Wavell suggested no other candidates, the search for an Italian de Gaulle ended.[11]

In April 1941 Rommel launched a successful offensive against Wavell's forces and threatened Egypt. Wavell blew very cold on the idea of a Free Italian Army. In May reports to the Foreign Office showed Italian morale was improving fast because of the Axis success in the Western Desert, despite the surrender of the Duke of Aosta at Addis Ababa. Dixon minuted on 22 May: 'Far from collapsing, Italy is now likely to gain in spirits and lie comfortably back while the Germans do all the work in the Mediterranean.'

SOE, however, would not give up hope. Commander Martelli of their Italian Department continued to argue for a Free Italian Army in spite of firm evidence that the German successes in the desert had made the climate much less favourable. Martelli wrote on 7 June 1941:

No patriotic Italian will risk his life and reprisals against his family only to help Great Britain to win the war. The appeal must be launched in the hopes of Italian independence and her survival as a great power after the war. In other words, without making ourselves ridiculous we cannot ask an Italian POW to join the British Army, but we can ask those who sympathise with us

[g]Later (1977) 9th Duke of Portland.

to enrol in a Free Italian force which fights for the liberation of Italy. In the first case they would be traitors; in the second, patriots.

He also enclosed a memorandum written by Freya Stark and Colonel Thornhill forecasting with absurd optimism that two-thirds of Italian prisoners of war would be anti-Fascist, and that they should be put under sympathetic Maltese guards.

This did not meet with favour in the Foreign Office. A meeting was held on 25 July at the Foreign Office attended by General Brooks,[h] Leeper,[i] Jebb, Sargent, Nichols and Dixon. It was decided, to the annoyance of SOE, to stop all political propaganda amongst Italian prisoners of war in Egypt because of the adverse conditions for successful propaganda there. However, a mission to India was authorized to investigate the possibility of raising a Free Italian Army from prisoners of war there. India, unlike Egypt, was well away from Rommel's advancing Axis forces.[12]

As late as 20 October Eden wrote to Sir Archibald Sinclair, Air Minister, to ask if air passages could be arranged for India for Commander Martelli and Colonel Thornhill and others 'to influence the minds of Italian prisoners of war favourable to the Allies and see if material is available to form the nucleus of a Free Italian Army in India'. Nothing materialized out of India, but this signal is evidence that Eden favoured throughout 1941 a Free Italian Army.

The Duke of Aosta (Amedeo), cousin of the King of Italy, was the Commander of the Italian forces in Ethiopia and he was taken prisoner in May 1941 when Addis Ababa fell to the Allies. Francis Rodd[j] proposed that Britain should try and negotiate with Aosta to bring Italy out of the war. The Foreign Office were in two minds about offering him the throne if he could topple Mussolini, but Eden turned this down out of hand; instead he wanted to negotiate the release of Aosta in return for General O'Connor, an outstanding British General captured in the desert by Rommel – but noted the Government must not let the enemy know how anxious it was to get O'Connor back and should claim other Generals as well, and 'if we got too many Generals back it would be ill received by other ranks of prisoners of war.'[13]

The most influential anti-Fascist conspirators known to the Foreign Office were Marshal Caviglia, Cabruna and Count Comito. Caviglia had enormous prestige because of his part in the Italian victory over

[h]General Dallas Brooks was liaison officer for SOE with the Chiefs of Staff.
[i]Now head of Political Warfare Executive (formerly SOE 1).
[j]Francis Rodd (2nd Lord Rennell 1941) served as Major-General Civil Affairs in Middle East, East Africa and Italy in the Second World War.

Austria in 1918. He was always anti-Fascist and a strong monarchist. Comito was a business magnate with many British friends. Cabruna, who had the Gold Medal, the highest Italian decoration, was a well-known First World War aviator and as a friend of Gabriele d'Annunzio had taken a prominent part in the Fiume effort after 1918.[k] He had held an important position in the Italian police.

Other conspirators' names revealed by the Secret Service to the Foreign Office were the Contessa Nina Colonna and the Marquis Visconti Venosta who, it was revealed at the Verona trials of Mussolini's opponents in January 1944, was a key conspirator in the overthrow of the Duce by the King on 25 July 1943.

In January 1941, after Caviglia had been given a code name by the British Secret Service, he was denounced to the Fascist secret police by a relative, Ines Pescarmona. She was a fanatical Fascist and lived near him at Finale near Savona. She said that Caviglia had discussed with the King how to overthrow Mussolini and win the support of the Army for an anti-Fascist coup. She also said that Caviglia was in continual touch with the British outside Italy, and a plotter against Mussolini.

The Duce did not act on this information, although it reached his desk, because the local police chief at Savona near Caviglia's home generously put in a further statement that Pescarmona should not be believed as she was 'hysterical'. This was incorrect, and her statement of 9 January was accurate. Throughout the war Caviglia was in touch with the British Secret Service. On visits to Rome he had secret talks with King Victor Emmanuel about ending the war by overthrowing Mussolini, and had contacts with many senior naval, air force and army officers who were strongly royalist and anti-Fascist. Either by good luck or because of the sympathies of officials in high places, Caviglia, although suspected of treachery by Mussolini, was never arrested. When he died in March 1945 Mussolini authorized a State funeral.

Pescarmona also declared that a Finale advocate, Renato Wuilermin, shared Caviglia's views and was an accomplice in his treachery to Mussolini, as were the Marshal's nephews. This was also true. Wuilermin and three of Caviglia's nephews were arrested by the Fascist police in December 1942. The previous month Caviglia's house had been searched by the police, but he had hidden any incriminating papers. Simultaneously the German War Office made

---

[k] Fiume was seized illegally in 1919 by a private Italian army led by d'Annunzio, and held until the following year to great popular acclaim.

enquiries about him through Rintelen, their Military Attaché in Rome. Wuilermin was released when Mussolini was deposed in July 1943 and was killed fighting with the partisans near Milan.

Leeper wrote to the Italian Department of the Foreign Office on 24 April 1941 disclosing that the Air Attaché in Berne, Air Commodore 'Freddie' West, VC, had through Secret Service sources discovered the existence of 'a Free Italy Movement inside Italy, of which we have never heard anything before', and that Caviglia had been given the code name X 18 (Comito was X 17 and Cabruna X 19). He added that the 'Free Italy movement' had received 'a temporary setback because of Rommel's successes in Libya'.[14]

West, a flying hero of the First World War, handled the Italian intelligence at the Berne Embassy in his capacity as Air Attaché. Bilingual in Italian, he had previously been at the Rome Embassy and went straight to Berne when Italy declared war on Britain. In an interview with the author he stated that Comito, who was managing director of Snia Viscosa, the textile firm of Milan (owned by Courtauld), was by far his best and most trusted informant. According to West, Comito was violently anti-Fascist and pro-Ally but he was handicapped to a certain extent because his boss, Franco Marinotti, the Chairman, was 'in cahoots' with the Germans, and although he professed anti-Fascist views was not in West's view to be trusted. Comito sent a continuous stream of anti-Fascist emissaries to Berne who informed West of what was happening in Italy. He also used to ring West up to give him news. For example, when the RAF carried out the large-scale air raid on Milan in August 1943 Comito telephoned and said: 'The boxes of oranges have not been broken' – indicating the raid was a failure, which news West transmitted to the Air Ministry.

West never met Caviglia and his information about him came mostly from Comito. Nor did he have much contact with Cabruna, though he knew him as 'a very nice man and a great flier'. The code names were attached in London, and according to West were not of much significance.

The Contessa Colonna spent most of the war at the Palace Hotel in Lausanne, making occasional trips to Rome from where she brought back reliable information. West and his wife saw her constantly and were on very friendly terms with her. She was strongly pro-Ally and anti-Fascist, and a good source of information.

In early 1941, with Italy tottering after the appalling defeat of her forces in the desert, the British Government went on another wild goose chase – to bribe the officers commanding Italian naval ships to surrender to the Allies and come to Alexandria. The crews would be guaranteed the same wages and living conditions as the Royal Navy, and in addition large sums were to be sent to neutral countries for the upkeep of their dependants until the war was over.

No evidence exists to connect Caviglia, Cabruna or Comito with a plot to sell Italian warships, and West said he knew nothing of it. He did, however, have offers in Berne to 'buy' the Italian fleet which were not taken seriously, and even on one occasion an American millionairess offered to buy the French fleet for the British in conjunction with rich friends. This last suggestion was treated as a joke.

The Admiralty learnt through their Naval Attaché in Stockholm, Captain Henry Denham, that there was grave discontent in the Italian Navy. They would prefer to surrender the fleet to the British than let the Germans take it over, provided the officers responsible could have a guarantee that their families would be safe in Portugal or in another place occupied by the Allies. This was reported to Churchill who agreed that if any Italian ships surrendered voluntarily the crews could have the same pay as the Royal Navy.

The Italian fleet episode began with a talk between a Swedish businessman, J. H. Walter, and the Press Officer at the British Legation in Stockholm, Peter Tennant, and Denham on 24 November 1940. Walter had been instrumental in selling four old Italian destroyers to the Swedish Government in 1939, and he had close contacts with the heads of the Italian Navy. The two Britons were sure Walter was in the confidence of dissident senior naval officers in the Italian Admiralty in Rome who were anxious to take Italy out of the war.

He told the British officials of acute discontent amongst the officers of the Italian Navy and so impressed them that they sent the following telegram to the Admiralty on the same day:

Addressed to D.N.I.
MOST IMMEDIATE

(1) Swedish businessman informs us that an Italian who appears to be here on official business and left Rome November 17th has assured him of following:

(a) Germans during past two weeks have been exerting pressure on Italians to give way to *German military occupation of country* and to turn over their fleet to Germans.

(b) With growing anti-war feeling in Italy senior Italian Naval Officers are aware of this possibility of surrender but are unable to resist unless presented with alternative.

(c) The alternative in their minds to surrender fleet to Great Britain and for them and their families to proceed to Portugal or Allies so as to be certain of no reprisals by either Italian Fascists or Germans.

(2) Italian representative returns Italy Wednesday November 27th and it would be possible to contact him before he leaves should you wish to.

(3) Information regarding Swedish informant and if possible identity of Italian representative will be telegraphed as soon as possible.

24.11.40

On 25 November the Admiralty replied to Denham promising every help to the crews of ships who surrendered, and guaranteed the ships safety in ports under British control with no obligation on the crews to fight against the Axis, together with a promise of escorts for any merchant ships with families of the crews on board, hospitality for naval and civilian fugitives, plus the same pay as the Royal Navy for any Italian sailors who wanted to fight on the British side.

The Admiralty had discussed their reply with Halifax, the Foreign Secretary, and the Prime Minister, who was enthusiastic, and minuted he wanted to take a personal interest in it. It had been approved at the meeting of the War Cabinet on 25 November. Pierson Dixon of the Foreign Office noted: 'This seems too good to be true to me.'

Three other conferences took place between Denham, Tennant and Walter at Stockholm on 25 November, 28 November and 6 December, all in Denham's house. Walter confirmed that the Italian businessman referred to in the despatch of 25 November had returned to Rome on 27 November and informed his senior naval contacts that the British Government was ready to negotiate and open up a channel of communication between them and London. He asked for a deposit of £3,125 and promised to return this sum if the enterprise failed. The Stockholm Legation reported this to the Foreign Office, adding that they had heard from other reliable sources of clashes between Fascists and the Civil Service and that influential Italians were anxious to make contact with the British.

The Foreign Office sent the £3,125 to Mallet in Stockholm, and at the same time a MI6 agent was sent to Stockholm to make enquiries about Walter's genuineness. He approved the handing over of the money to Walter, who set out for Rome via Moscow and Riga on 23 January 1942 promising the British in Stockholm that he would contact the Admirals Cavagnari, Riccardi and Parola and other anti-Fascists.

On 6 March Stockholm signalled to London that Walter was back from Rome and that:

1. He states that he has been in touch indirectly with Cavagneri [*sic*] and other prominent anti-Fascist Naval representatives to whom British Admiralty terms for the surrender have now been communicated. Though it is thought in anti-Fascist circles that Cavagneri may at later date join with Triumvirate of Grandi and Badoglio, Cavagneri at present time has suffered much criticism among the younger element of the Navy, for his share of responsibility in Taranto disaster.

2. Riccardi has [?] his Italian intermediary there is now no question of Italians allowing their Admiralty or Fleet to come under German control.

3. There is every desire among the Navy generally as amongst other circles to avoid assisting the Germans. Possibility for surrender to the British though not at present feasible may present itself later when prompted by future events.

4. Channel of communication to Italy will remain open and our intermediary is prepared to go again.

5. Further details of the proposals will be telegraphed shortly.

This was followed two days later on 8 March by:

1. Swedish Intermediary's report still incomplete.

2. My impression from him and through another representative source is that surrender of Naval units is at present impracticable because it is impossible to safeguard the families of personnel. There is also feeling of dishonourable conduct among this section of Naval Officers at leaving the country in the present hour of defeat especially when the country is verging on coming under German control.

3. What anti-Fascists hope is that we would not exploit our victory vindictively when final Italian defeat comes but rather concentrate upon saving Italy from German domination. It seems if this is our intention it might be exploited and made conditional upon Navy conforming to our wishes.

4. Unique opportunity now offered to convey direct message to Higher anti-Fascist representatives. Message must reach me by 1500 Monday 10th.

These messages produced a flurry of activity and consultation between the Prime Minister, Eden and the First Lord of the Admiralty.[1] The next day at 7.40 p.m. the following signal was sent to Mallet in Stockholm from the Foreign Office:

Following message may be given to Swedish intermediary to pass on to his anti-Fascist contacts:

[1]A. V Alexander. He had held the office previously in 1929–31.

We re-affirm our previous offer that we shall gladly receive any units of the Italian Fleet that may come to us, and we will do our best to escort merchant ships with families.

If a real effort is made by the Italian Fleet to avoid falling under German control and evidenced by the sending of important units to British overseas ports, this fact would undoubtedly weigh with us when considering terms of peace with Italy, and we should do our best to save Italy from German domination both before and after the final peace conference.[15]

This promise of softer peace terms was exactly what Walter claimed his Italian contacts needed. On 14 March an even more exciting message came from Stockholm about the Italian fleet. For the first time a price list was produced showing variations from $15,000 for a torpedo boat to $300,000 for a battleship; on top there was to be compensation for families of the officers of surrendered ships so that they could start up in new professions. The signal read:

ITALIAN NAVY

1. During the recent visit to Rome Swedish intermediary has been constantly in touch with Italian representative and a certain officer serving at the Italian Admiralty, said to be representing some 20 senior officers, wishing to wrest the Italian Navy from influence of Fascist and German regimes.

2. British proposals for surrender were considered, but for various reasons it was not deemed feasible to evacuate families of crews of war ships en bloc as was at first thought.

3. Italian intermediary contended that a) families of some prominent officers must be evacuated to certain foreign countries and should receive some grant. b) Officers and crews of surrendered warships would eventually require compensation for their families to start them in new professions later on.

4. Italian representative then proposed the following terms: a) British Admiralty to pay in dollars for ships surrendered.

Battleship.	300,000.
Heavy cruiser.	60,000.
Light cruiser.	50,000.
Destroyer.	50,000.
Submarine.	25,000.
Torpedo boat.	15,000.

b) should it be found more practical to sabotage warships half the amount to be paid for the benefit of active members who carry out the work.

c) the above payments to be made after the war or to any person, persons or body officially approved when proof is furnished that warships have been definitely surrendered or disabled.

d) an immediate deposit of 600,000 dollars to be lodged in United States Bank up to 15% of which to be available now for providing assistance under paragraph 5 a) to evacuated naval families whose names and destination would be communicated.

5. Our considered opinion is that a) basis of payments bears little relation either to potential value of the warships or bonuses to active parties, but it is not possible for us to discuss this.

b) the acceptance of the scheme in principle would enable us to telegraph at once to put it into execution and we consider there is anyhow a chance of its coming off.

c) at the most British Government would only stand to lose the 15% of the deposit, though even this is most unlikely as each case of financial assistance is to be judged on its merits.

d) Swedish intermediary though running considerable risk is prepared once more to attempt another visit to Italy if necessary though he is not blind to his own chances of handsome reward in the event of success, he is the one person we are ever likely to find here with the essential contacts in Italy, real guts, love for this type of adventure.

Note. Contents of Foreign Office telegram of 9 March were handed to independent anti-Fascist now returned to Italy. In undertaking delivery of message he predicted genuine appreciation to be expected at the tone of the message and would do his best to confer in naval quarters.

It is interesting that Mallet should now describe the international go-between Walter as having 'real guts and love of adventure', because in December Mallet had told the Foreign Office Walter was a man 'with the shadiest of reputations. I have made a number of enquiries about him and I have never heard a word in his favour.' After the war Denham and Tennant wrote: 'We judged him to be a courageous adventurer with a genuine commitment to the defeat of the Nazis and with a standard business ethic no worse than that of most of his countrymen.' Of course Walter was in the game for money, and he received 50,000 kronor from the British which was brought to Stockholm by a Royal Marine officer, Colonel Cordeaux, but this was confiscated by the Swedish secret police just as Cordeaux was about to hand it to the Italian intermediary. Walter was sentenced to imprisonment for espionage, but acquitted when Italy changed sides.

Walter had to sue the Swedish Government for his commission on the Italian warships they bought through him before the war, and obtained 300,900 kronor through the courts. Through this sale he made his high up contacts with the Italian Admiralty.

Sargent minuted: 'It is curious that it should have taken the Emissary from the 5 March, when he first reported his return to

Sweden, until the 14th to submit this detailed message. Why the delay, I wonder?' That question can never be answered.

Churchill wanted to accept, and minuted accordingly to the First Lord of the Admiralty, who expressed the view that the chances of success were small, but the necessary payments were so small compared with the importance of the prizes to be gained that the gamble appeared to be worth while.

On 19 March the Foreign Office replied to Mallet in Stockholm: 'While chances of the scheme succeeding appear slight, we accept it in principle. You are authorised to telegraph at once to put it into execution.' On the signal Churchill scrawled:[16]

> Admiralty   )   This all seems fantastic.
> Foreign Office)   w.s.c.   20.3.

Recently published Italian sources indicate that the Italian contact at the Admiralty in Rome may have been Admiral Parola, and that Arturo Riccardi, Chief of the Naval Staff and Under-Secretary for State for the Navy was involved. However, the evidence so far produced is flimsy.

The Italian prospects of victory were immeasurably improved when Rommel opened his desert campaign in April 1941 and drove the British back almost to the Egyptian frontier. On 22 June 1941 Hitler had attacked Russia and at first it looked as if Germany would have an easy victory. Communism was unpopular in Italy and public opinion veered to the view that their best exit from the war would be through an Axis victory, with the vast majority of Italians hoping for a Hitler victory over Stalin. In April Hitler's army brought the disastrous Italian-Greek campaign to a successful conclusion; this brought more optimism in Italy about an Axis victory.

At the same time Mussolini was warned of traitors within his ranks. An anonymous letter was sent to him: 'Duce. You have a traitor in your ranks. Grandi is on the side of the Allies.' Once suspicions were aroused, the Fascist police, helped by the Gestapo, interrogated and imprisoned leading naval and military persons suspected of treachery. The conspirators had temporarily to go to ground. According to Denham's memoirs the Swedish police intercepted one of Mallet's signals to London and told the Germans, who in turn alerted the Italian police.

By July the Italian authorities were reassured and no longer feared a serious plot. On 15 July Mallet cabled to London from Stockholm:

1. Owing to release from prison of certain naval officers our channel of communication has again been restored and should now be maintained. Italian emissary has arrived recently with assurances from certain Italian Naval

officers that, as soon as time is ripe, procedure detailed in my 1811 of March 14th will be put into execution. He return [*sic*] on July 19th with promise that British side of the bargain still holds good.

2. He reports following recent naval developments

  (a) Sudden slackening of German control of navy at the outbreak of the Russian war. This happened at a time when German interference had almost brought Admiral Riccardi to point of resigning.

  (b) Several Italian naval officers have been relieved of their appointments and reprisals taken against them. This is borne out by another reliable source.

3. Details of recent developments are expected next week on the return of another of our Italian contacts.

On 19 July 1941 the Foreign Office cabled back: 'Our side of the bargain still holds.'[17] That was the end of the affair. No more messages came from Stockholm about it, and the Foreign Office files went silent.

With hindsight Denham felt that Walter may have been 'partly bogus' and possibly no intermediary existed to travel from Stockholm to Rome in June 1941. However, he felt sure there was an Italian emissary in Sweden in January 1941 and that the original overture was genuine. The price list for the ships was dictated by Walter from his head and he had no document setting out the schedule. Even at the time this made Denham feel suspicious.

Sir Peter Tennant told the author that he felt throughout the talks Walter was completely genuine. According to Tennant, Mallet made the enquiries in all the wrong places about Walter's character – from Marcus Wallenberg for instance, and other Swedes in Government circles who were trying to do Walter out of his commission on the genuine sale of the Italian destroyers to Sweden.

At the time of writing he agrees there is doubt about the July 1941 suggestion, but he is not convinced that Walter was a fraud. He has been in touch with Swedish police about Walter since the war and he considers any case against him far from proved. Tennant believes the Italian emissary may have been either the conductor Vittorio Gui or the courier from the Italian bank who collected the money for the Italian destroyers sold. Definitely Vittorio Gui saw British Secret Service agents in Stockholm in March 1942 and also in December of that year. He produced much information about internal conditions in Italy and his remarks showed that he was extremely anti-Fascist.

Commander Barrow-Green, RN, then Chief of Naval Intelligence Italy, led a small mission to Italy after the war to enquire into this plot. No documents about this are to be found in the Public Record Office, but on his return Barrow-Green told his friends that although the Italians concerned would not talk, there was some evidence of the existence of a plan to surrender the Italian ships at Alexandria after Wavell's Beda Fomm victory. He is alleged to have said that further inquiries would bring 'libel actions against H.M.G. from Italian families'.[18]

It is not surprising that any Italians identified as being concerned refused to talk, because after the war there was a surge of resentment in Italy at the harsh surrender terms imposed by the Allies and only disclosed in the autumn of 1945, so that many who had been plotting the exit of Italy from the war in the time of Mussolini felt they had been let down. As a result they did not want it known that they had acted as 'traitors' to the Italian war effort. For example, General Castellano who signed the armistice in 1943 on behalf of Badoglio wrote: 'The armistice which the Allies forced us to sign was far from generous, and did not conform to the promises made to us through Allied propaganda which turned out insincere.'

Professor Alberto Santoni has published articles on 'the surrender' in Italian and believes there was a plot. This is queried by other Italian historians. Whatever the truth, there is no doubt that grave discontent existed in the Italian Navy early in 1941; and after Graziani's defeat a surrender of ships may well have been on the cards. Whether such efforts continued after Rommel's victory over Wavell, it is impossible to say. Sir Peter Tennant has cooperated with Santoni in his research for a book on the subject.

Admiral Massimiliano Marandino, Head of the Italian Institute of Naval History, has declared that in his archives there is not a scrap of evidence to support Professor Santoni's claims. He considers it was a plot by the British Secret Service who intended to let documents fall into the hands of the Germans so as to create trouble between Italy and Germany.[m19]

The Foreign Office agreed on 7 April 1941: 'Our propaganda should be that Hitler was going to take over the Italian fleet, and spread such rumours and try and make direct contact with officers of the fleet.' The BBC was told that the Government's strategic objective was 'surrender of Italian fleet and air force, or certain units of it'. The BBC was asked to paint the image of a powerful Free Italian movement outside Italy to make it easier for Italian officers to surrender the fleet without a feeling of treason against Italy.

---

[m]Alberto Santoni, who formerly worked as assistant to Marandino at the Institute, has written to the author that he does not agree with the Admiral.

Professor Franco Bandini has done considerable research both in the British and Italian archives. He writes that he is positive there were contacts between the British Secret Service and the Admirals Domenico Cavagnari (who was sacked by Mussolini on 8 December 1940) and Arturo Riccardi (both former Heads of the Italian Admiralty) and Badoglio and Grandi at the end of 1940 and in early 1941. He is sure that they received 'certain official assurances' from the British Foreign Office about the treatment of the Italian fleet if it surrendered.[20] He believes that in 1940 Riccardi promised Britain, like Admiral Darlan with the French fleet, that the Italian fleet would never fall into German hands. Certainly the evidence that the War Cabinet in December 1940 authorized leaflets to the Italian fleet asking them to surrender adds force to his argument. Bandini believes that the talks petered out because they had begun in a period of Italian gloom after the RAF had sunk many Italian ships in their air raid on Taranto and the Italians looked like being driven out of Cyrenaica. In the spring of 1941, however, prospects were much rosier for the Axis and meanwhile the plot had been discovered by the Fascists so that quite a number of Italian naval officers involved had been arrested. In his view the German attack on Russia on 22 June 1941 finished off any 'surrender' efforts and then 'as if by magic, the luck of the British went into reverse'.

The main historical importance of the British documents from Stockholm, quoted above, is that they are evidence that in 1941 Eden and Churchill were enthusiastic to persuade the Italian fleet to surrender. Yet in 1943, when Italy's plight was far worse, no helping hand at all was extended to dissident Italian army and navy leaders.

Churchill's hopes for a Garibaldi pro-Ally Italian league, a free and prosperous Italian Cyrenaica, and the bribing of Italian naval officers to surrender their ships were linked to a separate peace with Italy. Wavell's victory at Beda Fomm had aroused hopes that Italy might desert Hitler. The Foreign Office kept on receiving reports of lowered Italian morale and the War Office even made plans for a seaborne landing in Sicily (INFLUX) to exploit the disaffection. SOE in Egypt bolstered up these hopes by reporting the anti-Fascist sentiments of the Italian prisoners, but the Italian leaders in exile were weak.

At the beginning of 1941 Churchill was ready to offer Italy the opportunity to become a great power again after the end of the war and to sacrifice the Senussi and antagonize the whole Arab world. However, by the summer of 1941 the Government's strenuous efforts to break down Italian resistance had signally failed. From then on the British Government's attitude was that Italy was just a minor satellite of Hitler's Germany and not an independent power in the world war.

On 25 December 1940 Churchill had broadcast to the Italian nation that Mussolini alone was responsible for the war between two traditionally friendly countries, and invited the people of Italy to overthrow the Duce. At that time and for the next six months any worthwhile overtures of peace from the Italian opposition would have been well received in London. None came.

Eden changed to a hard line with Italy during the summer of 1941. On 18 July the Southern Department submitted a memorandum to Eden which marked the end of any possibility of a soft peace with Italy. It pointed out that although the Italian people were not particularly heartened by the Axis victories in the desert, Greece and Russia, they now looked on the Germans as the probable victors. Italy therefore had no choice but to become a vassal of Germany. The Italian armed forces were against the war and the Fascist regime, but they had been too permeated by Fascists to take any revolutionary action. There was nothing to be hoped for from the King. This memorandum was circulated to the War Cabinet and approved together with a note from Eden on 11 August:

'Apathy and war weariness are the salient characteristics of the prevailing mould in Italy. Chances of knocking Italy out of the war (i.e. separate peace) can now be discounted since the Germans would certainly forestall any such move in Italy by converting the present moral occupation into a physical occupation of the country. But the more depressed and restless the Italians become the less effective is the Italian contribution to the German effort, and the greater the Germans policing responsibilities in Italy become.

The moral of all this is that even though we cannot now hope to knock Italy out, we should not relax efforts to hit metropolitan Italy by air and from the sea whenever opportunity occurs. Each blow against Italy is a blow against Germany.[21]

The Foreign Office papers on which Eden based his War Cabinet memorandum contained a note: 'Italian morale was much less good than might have been expected after the long series of Axis victories.' Eden wrote to Sinclair, Secretary of State for Air, on 6 August 1941: 'I should like to draw your attention to the desirability of hitting Italy whenever possible.' Fortunately for Italy, bombing civilian targets there had a low priority.

In August Cadogan minuted that hopes of a separate peace with Italy were 'moonshine'. Eden agreed, adding: 'We have to win a victory on land in an important theatre before we can catch any of these moonbeams.'[22]

When Roosevelt and Churchill met at Casablanca on 13 January 1943, the tide had turned. The Allies had more than enough troops in Tunisia to defeat the combined German and Italian armies there, and the excess strength was obviously available for an attack on the mainland of Europe within a few months. Not only were the Allies on the path to victory in North Africa, but the Russians had broken through at Stalingrad inflicting undreamt of losses on the Germans.

That week Victor Emmanuel III, King of Italy, decided that Germany was bound to lose the war and that it was his duty to try and make peace with the Allies so as to get the Germans out of Italy. Immediately he became the focal point for intrigues to overthrow Mussolini.

Mussolini, also shaken by the Allies' success in North Africa and the German reverse at Stalingrad, felt either the Axis should make peace with Russia or that Italy should disown Germany and try for a separate peace with the Allies. But Mussolini was still susceptible to Hitler's magnetic powers, and he half believed Hitler's not altogether idle boast that his secret weapons would destroy Britain and force her to sue for an ignominious peace.

Attempts to negotiate with the Allies began from both Fascists and Royalists. The Allies failed to seize these opportunities. Eden was fiercely anti-Italian: Mussolini's behaviour over Abyssinia and his (Eden's) consequent enforced resignation as Foreign Secretary had eaten into his soul. The United States Government was more sympathetic to the Italians, and the important Italian vote was always in Roosevelt's mind. Unfortunately the Italians never realized that a better chance of success lay in Washington than in London. The Royalists had a touching faith in the traditional British friendship for Italy dating back to the Risorgimento. Thus, with the Italian initiatives directed to the British Foreign Office, when the *coup d'état* overthrew Mussolini on 25 July 1943 it was purely an internal Italian affair with no help from the Allies. Prior to July 25 there were five main abortive peace approaches to the British but, only 'unconditional surrender' was offered to Fascists and anti-Fascists alike.

Evidence of Eden's hard line came in November 1942 when Raczynski, the Polish Ambassador in London, saw Sargent at the Foreign Office and told him of an approach from one of Franzoni's[n]

[n]Now Italian Ambassador to Portugal.

subordinates in Lisbon to a Polish diplomat asking whether the British would do anything to make it worthwhile Italy pulling out of the war. 'What were we prepared to offer in return? Could anything be said about Abyssinia?' The Italian contact stated that Franzoni had frequently made approaches to the British Embassy but they had never told him how 'the Allies viewed the situation'.

Cadogan minuted: 'I do not object to the Polish telegram from Lisbon, but I must say whatever is likely to happen in Italy I should not see much utility in following up such feelers.'

Eden's comment laid bare his uncompromising attitude to Italy:

I had much rather kill this stuff and tell the Poles to do the same. We don't propose to make peace with Mussolini and these men are his creatures. The only hope in Italy is a revolution which is just what these men want to avoid. If a whisper of this reached Russian ears results would be very bad, especially with Poles mixed up. Anyway there can be no advantage. I think Poles should be discouraged and we at any rate deprecate the whole affair and refuse to deal with the intermediaries. A.E. 11 Nov. 1942[23]

This was also Eden's stance when a fortnight later Ciano instructed Franzoni to try to open talks with the British Ambassador in Lisbon, Sir Ronald Campbell. The North African landings by the Allies had just taken place and while he was back in Rome earlier in the month, Franzoni asked Ciano, the Italian Foreign Secretary, if he still had hopes of an Axis military victory. Ciano said 'No.' Franzoni then suggested that he should find out the intentions of the British Government in the eventuality of a separate Italian request for peace. Ciano agreed, but he had no plan and not even Mussolini's full agreement. Through a Rumanian intermediary, Jan Pangal, Franzoni sent messages to Campbell in Lisbon. These were relayed to the Foreign Office in London. Eden turned a deaf ear, and on 18 December 1942 wrote to Winant, the United States Ambassador in London, with a copy to Maisky, the Russian Ambassador: '. . . We have decided not to follow up these openings because the Italians in Lisbon are *slaves of the Fascists*, and if we follow up these contacts it will look as if we are not intent on destroying Fascism.'[24]

Here Eden showed a grave ignorance of the stresses within Italy. Franzoni certainly was not a '*Fascist slave*' but an honest patriotic diplomat. The White House took the move much more seriously and replied saying it was a sign of 'important internal Italian political developments'. Eden threw away an opportunity of ending Italian participation in the war during the early phases of the costly North

African campaign. If Ciano's initiative had been seized upon a great number of Allied casualties in North Africa might have been avoided.

In December 1942 the Italian Consul General in Geneva, Luigi Cortese, told his British counterpart that he wanted to open up a channel of communication between London and the new Duke of Aosta,° who was prepared to lead an armed revolt against Mussolini provided: (1) RAF support was forthcoming; (2) an Allied landing in Italy coincided with the revolt to aid in the downfall of Fascism but not to conquer and occupy Italy; (3) the Italian fleet was left intact; (4) the future of the monarchy was guaranteed.

This time Eden agreed the approach was genuine. He informed the United States and Soviet Ambassadors and suggested that Aosta should discuss the plan with the Crown Prince Umberto. Undoubtedly this encouraging message from Eden to Aosta helped to decide Victor Emmanuel to try and overthrow Mussolini and make peace with the Allies. Soon there were to be more Monarchist approaches.

Meanwhile Cordell Hull, the US Foreign Secretary, had officially agreed with Eden that the Ciano-Franzoni Lisbon approach should be snubbed, but the talks with Aosta should be kept going. Hull suggested that the American and British Foreign Offices should define an agreed policy about the acceptability of Italian anti-Fascist personalities. The British ignored this sensible suggestion and the more sympathetic US approach evoked no warmth from Eden. On 14 January 1943 he wrote to Hull that there was no one in Italy who could overthrow Mussolini. The King was a 'docile servant of fascism' and 'only Badoglio at a later date when discontent in the army increased' could do anything. Eden claimed that according to British Intelligence the Fascist party was still united; he told Cordell Hull that the moderate Fascists were 'impotent' and he favoured intensifying the bombing.[25]

In this letter of 14 January to Hull, Eden said it was useless to offer tempting peace terms to the Italian people because the minimum that would attract them would be a guarantee of their pre-war frontiers, and this was not possible because of the claims of Yugoslavia and (surprisingly) Austria. Cordell Hull and the White House disagreed with Eden, but they did nothing to soften the British hard line.

At the Casablanca Conference in January 1943 the 'unconditional surrender' formula was invented. Roosevelt wanted to exclude Italy and so did Churchill. Both men felt, correctly, that the time had come

---

°Amedeo, Duke of Aosta, who had commanded the Italian forces in Abyssinia, died early in 1942. He was succeeded by the Duke of Spoleto (his cousin).

to appeal to the Italian anti-Fascists and that applying unconditional surrender to Italy would defeat their purpose. During the Casablanca Conference, therefore, Churchill sent a signal to the War Cabinet asking for their views on demanding unconditional surrender from Germany and Japan, but not Italy: 'Omission of Italy would encourage break up. FDR likes idea.' In the absence of Churchill, Eden dominated the War Cabinet over foreign affairs and he and Attlee sent back this tough reply: 'Cabinet unanimous that Italy must be threatened with unconditional surrender. Knowledge of rough stuff coming to them should have desired effect on Italian morale.'[26] So unconditional surrender was demanded from Italy until the bitter end with pernicious consequences for the Allies.

SOE in Berne had reported to London on 25 August 1942 that their agent in Lugano, John McCaffery, was in touch with a friend of Badoglio, Dr Rusca (a director of the publishing house of Mondadori in Milan). Rusca had said Badoglio wanted a Free Italian movement to be formed by the British from 'desirable elements' outside Italy. Rusca suggested to McCaffery that General Bergonzoli, still a prisoner of war, should be contacted by a senior Italian officer on behalf of Badoglio. On 15 November McCaffery signalled that Badoglio had told Rusca he would have nothing to do with General Bergonzoli, who was 'a man of straw', but suggested a General Gazzara. Early in January 1943 Rusca travelled from Milan to Lugano and informed McCaffery he had had several conversations with both Badoglio and Caviglia who had made a 'truce' and had jointly chosen General Pesenti to represent them. They asked that Pesenti should be given all facilities for forming a 'Free' Italian Army from prisoners of war and Italian residents abroad. McCaffery sought guidance from London on what line he should take in possible discussions with Pesenti. He was told to talk only on the basis of 'assisting them with their plans' and 'on no account' should he be prepared 'to entertain peace feelers'. On 20 November McCaffery reported that this message had been conveyed to Rusca.

On 1 January 1943 SOE in London told the Foreign Office and the Joint Chiefs of Staff of contacts claiming that Badoglio and Caviglia had a powerful and influential following in Italy and wanted to seize power and set up a military Government on the basis of 'forming an anti-fascist army'. SOE asked for permission to fly Pesenti out from Milan to Cyrenaica to talk to the British Government and start raising an anti-Fascist army from Italian prisoners of war in North Africa. SOE in Berne signalled:

The courier could travel only from Berne to Rome with difficulty, and it is essential an answer is given by 12 January on which date the courier arrives in Berne. Pesenti gives full discretion whether after his flight news should be made public or kept secret.[27]

Pesenti came from a well-known Genoese family and was a talented musician. He was always strongly anti-Fascist and a bitter opponent of the war. He was military commander of Somaliland in 1941 and after General Cunningham's successful attacks in the Jerba sector in February of that year he decided Italy had lost the war in East Africa. He told his commander-in-chief, the Duke of Aosta, that they ought to ask for a separate armistice on the Abyssinian front as all was lost. Aosta was furious and they had a flaming row in which Aosta told Pesenti he ought to be shot for treason. Instead Pesenti was sacked, and he flew safely back to Italy while Aosta became a prisoner of war.

Only a month before the war had started Pesenti had been in South Africa and there is little doubt that he was in contact with the British Secret Service while he was commanding Italian troops in East Africa in 1941. Churchill told the Chiefs of Staff in March 1941: 'We might receive armistice proposals from the cut off Italian garrison in Ethiopia.' This almost certainly was inspired by a message from Pesenti.[28]

Badoglio and Caviglia were now making a concrete offer of collaboration with the Allies. Eden produced a memorandum for the War Cabinet meeting on 18 January 1943, in Churchill's absence at the Casablanca Conference in North Africa.

PROPOSAL RECEIVED FROM CERTAIN ANTI-FASCIST ELEMENTS IN ITALY

Memorandum by the Secretary of State for Foreign Affairs

S.O.E. have for some time been in touch, through an intermediary, with Marshal Badoglio and Marshal Caviglia in Italy.

2. It now appears that Marshal Badoglio is willing at the right moment to take over and establish a military Government. He wishes to send an emissary, General Pesenti, to Cyrenaica to discuss with His Majesty's Government co-ordinated action from outside and inside Italy, aimed at the overthrow of the Fascist régime.

3. Marshal Badoglio is probably the most likely Italian personality to lead a successful anti-Fascist movement and to attract the most sympathy and support inside Italy. Marshal Caviglia, who commanded the Italian army at the battle of Vittorio Veneto, is now about 80 years old, but between them they would probably have a powerful and influential following of anti-Fascist elements in Italy. General Pesenti does not appear to have played any part in

politics which renders his choice for the present purpose suitable. He was General Officer Commanding in Somaliland from 1939 till January 1941 when he was recalled to Italy for a reason unknown.

4. Marshal Badoglio asks for no assurances regarding the future. All that he asks is (1) that General Pesenti should discuss with us co-ordinated action to take place at a given moment; and (2) that General Pesenti should be given facilities for recruiting a force from among the Italians resident abroad and prisoners of war.

5. The disadvantage in agreeing to Marshal Badoglio's suggestion would be that if General Pesenti succeeds in forming a force we shall be committed to supporting him and the two Marshals. This might be embarrassing if subsequently it was felt that some other personality was more likely to succeed in forming an anti-Fascist movement than these two Marshals. We should also run the risk of being saddled with a nondescript force of doubtful military value, which might indulge in unwelcome political activities and try to extort undesirable political concessions from us.

6. The advantages in agreeing to allow General Pesenti to come out of Italy would be (a) we should obtain valuable information about conditions and the situation in Italy and the extent of underground movements; (b) if General Pesenti succeeded in forming an Italian force outside Italy its existence might have considerable effect on discontented elements in Italy; (c) it would be useful to have a force on the lines of the 'Garibaldi' force if and when Allied operations take place in Italy, especially as a man of Marshal Badoglio's standing might be of value to us when the crack in the Fascist régime approaches.

7. I should not, however, be in favour of agreeing in advance to Marshal Badoglio's two points, because I think it would be unwise of us to pledge ourselves before we had been able to form an opinion as to General Pesenti's credentials in the matter of discussing co-ordinated action with him or as to his personal qualifications for rallying Italian prisoners of war and refugees.

8. Provided, however, that it is made clear that we cannot discuss any conditions with Marshal Badoglio's emissary in Switzerland, and that General Pesenti must be prepared to come out unconditionally, I consider that advantage should be taken of the approach which has been made to us and that S.O.E. should proceed with the scheme.

9. If General Pesenti does come out, special arrangements will have to be made as to how and by whom he is to be interviewed, and I would wish to stipulate that at any such interview no offers should be made or undertakings given to him without previous reference to the Foreign Office.

10. If it is decided to respond to the approach, we should no doubt inform the United States and Soviet Governments.[29]

On Eden's advice the Cabinet decided on 18 January 'without further instructions from them no response should be made to Marshal Badoglio and Caviglia'. As Eden had written to Hull on 4

January 1943 that only Badoglio could bring Mussolini down, it is strange that a fortnight later he should have wanted to reject negotiation out of hand.

Military Intelligence and SOE were anxious to make use of the Pesenti channel for information about military movements and internal events in Italy. The War Office put pressure on the Foreign Office to bring Pesenti out. Accordingly Eden sent the following memorandum to Churchill on 17 February. It is reproduced in full because it reveals clearly Eden's hostility to Italy which prevented an early peace with Mussolini's opponents.

P.M./43/26.
MOST SECRET.
PRIME MINISTER.

I propose to bring the matter up in the Cabinet on February 18th, (I must be there the day) and in view of the secrecy of this subject I should be very grateful if it could be discussed by members of the War Cabinet alone. I also propose to raise the following point:

The proposal in my paper to the Cabinet WP (43)27 of January 14th was that Marshal Badoglio's emissary must come out unconditionally, and that it would be made clear that we cannot discuss any conditions with him. There is no question of varying this. But I am quite certain that, if we do get in touch with this emissary (or indeed the emissary of any other serious party in Italy) we shall at once come up against the question, what hope are we prepared to hold out in regard to the future of Italy? Our present line is to make no promise whatsoever, but merely to offer Italians (through our propaganda) the alternatives of sinking or surviving. We do not promise them a suit of clothes or food. We hope that this tough line, supplemented by heavy raids and the threat of invasion, will suffice to frighten the Italians out of the war.

But if we want to go further and get some group in Italy to co-operate with us on that basis, I realise that we shall have to hold out at least some hope in regard to the future of Italy, in order to secure their co-operation. But there is nothing very definite we could promise the Italians. We can give them no comfort about their overseas possessions. We cannot guarantee the territorial restoration of metropolitan Italy, owing to the pledge we have given to the Yugoslavs to espouse their claim to Istria after the war.

The United States Government, however, are clearly anxious that some ray of hope should be held out to the Italians about their future, and I have just received from Hull a formula which I think would meet the case. It is as follows:

We should hold out to the Italian people, without making any specific political or territorial commitments, the hope that Italy, as a nation, will survive after the defeat of the Fascist Government and that neither we nor our Allies have territorial amibitions with respect to such territory as is and always has been essentially Italian.

A second thing we could say to the Italians is that they will enjoy the benefits of the Atlantic Charter, particularly the liberty to determine their own regime and access to the trade and raw materials of the world.

P.W.E. consider that it would help our propaganda to Italy if they were allowed to modify our present tough line to the extent of holding out some hope to the Italians about their future on the lines indicated above. While I consider that in any serious discussions with emissaries from groups inside Italy it would be necessary as a minimum to go as far as this, I am not entirely convinced that it is necessary to take the same line *yet* in our propaganda. Given the Italian character, I fancy we are most likely to achieve our object of getting Italy out of the war by sticking to our present tough line, reinforced by heavy bombing and the threat of invasion. Premature and unrelated promises would be interpreted by the Italians as a sign of weakness and would certainly be exploited to our disadvantage by the Fascist propaganda machine.

I had already informed the United States Government (through Winant) of Marshal Badoglio's approach.[29]

Churchill squiggled on the document: 'A Cabinet before you go. 18.2.43.' It was originally fixed to be taken at the Cabinet meeting on 22 February, but it was postponed because the Prime Minister could not attend. No urgency was given to this glittering opportunity and the Cabinet did not consider it for another twenty-eight days. By then it was too late.

At the meeting of the War Cabinet on 18 March Eden was absent but the Under-Secretary, Richard Law, said the Foreign Secretary was strongly in favour of getting General Pesenti to leave Italy provided he came 'unconditionally'. The general view of the Cabinet was that it would be right to establish contact with Pesenti provided no commitments were entered into without prior authority from Ministers. The Cabinet noted they would be unlikely to get much value from proposed Italian forces to be set up outside Italy, and that dealing with Badoglio who had commanded the Italian forces in Abyssinia 'might have political repercussions'. However, they authorized the Foreign Office to inform SOE they could proceed with their scheme to get Pesenti to Cyrenaica. He never came – although he was expected, according to this letter from Major Roseberry, head of the Italian Section of SOE, to the Foreign Office, dated 7 April:[30]

With reference to the proposal to receive General Pesenti to ascertain with Marshal Badoglio plans to do, we are now advised that our message agreeing to the approach being made has been passed to Badoglio's emissary who has gone to Rome to inform the Marshal.

We are informed that a reply may be expected at the end of this week.[31]

Before he left for Washington, Eden minuted that it would be better not to lay stress on 'Atlantic Charter but confine ourselves to holding out the hope that Italy would survive as a nation after the defeat of the Fascist Government'.

Bianca Ceva, the Italian historian, knew Pesenti well at the time and she has recorded that he was in touch with French anti-Fascists who continually travelled from Switzerland to Milan. According to her Pesenti was not to be flown direct to Cyrenaica, but to Berne and then to London. She confirmed that the aeroplane to fly Pesenti to Switzerland was ready at a Milan military airport for many weeks although petrol was scarce. However, the pilot was eventually arrested and the risk became too great for Pesenti.[32] Certainly he never went to Switzerland in 1943.[P]

With hindsight it is clear that a God-given opportunity to liaise with Badoglio and the anti-Fascist and monarchist forces was thrown away by rejecting the Pesenti offer in January when he could easily have been flown out. With his help plans could have been concerted for an Allied military takeover of Italy as soon as Mussolini was arrested and the Fascist Party overthrown. This could have been unknown to the Germans.

In December 1942 and January 1943 the Italian Army in Tunisia was, according to Field-Marshal Montgomery, Commander of the British Eighth Army in North Africa, fighting harder than ever. Once Italian soldiers heard of a move by Badoglio to raise an anti-Fascist force from prisoners of war their morale would have been seriously damaged and they might well have left the Germans in the lurch. No such consideration appears to have entered Eden's thinking, and his Foreign Office advisers forgot or overlooked the information they had received in 1941 about Caviglia's links with the British Secret Service in Berne.[33]

Badoglio and Caviglia's activities after they heard the War Cabinet had refused to negotiate with them remain a mystery, though undoubtedly they kept in touch with British agents. This was discussed by the Italian diplomatic historian Mario Toscano at a conference on the Resistance in Rome in 1964. Neither he nor the other historians could throw any real light on the matter; nor did Badoglio see fit to enlighten us in his memoirs, and Caviglia died in 1944.

Caviglia and Pesenti stayed in Milan; Badoglio was in Rome. Although both Marshals were bitterly opposed to Mussolini and

[P]According to Ceva, for identification purposes Pesenti was to carry no papers, only a book by Pascal.

Fascism, they hated each other. The quarrel went back to strategy in the First World War during the Battle of Caporetto. Nevertheless they seemed prepared to work together to rescue Italy from her plight.

In the second half of 1942, with the Axis military defeats, Mussolini's hold on the Italian people weakened fast and there was a dramatic revival of clandestine anti-Fascist political activity in Rome. Ivanoe Bonomi, the last Prime Minister of Italy before Mussolini came to power, held frequent meetings with leading politicians of pre-Fascist days, including Orlando and De Gasperi.[q][34]

Bonomi also discussed with Badoglio and Caviglia plans for a *coup d'état* by the King to bring down Mussolini. On 2 June 1943 he presented these plans personally to the King and also talked to Umberto, the Crown Prince, who gave Bonomi more encouragement than his father.

Bonomi wanted the King to arrest Mussolini and dissolve the Fascist party; the King should then take over direct power backed by the Generals and the Army. This was the only practical solution to Italy's predicament because the heads of the armed forces (apart from General Cavallero, Supreme Commander)[r] were loyal to the King, and Cavallero had been sacked by Mussolini in February 1943 as a scapegoat for the military failure in Africa. Bonomi and his associates believed with good reason that the Italian Army could save Italy from the clutches of Hitler.

While the Bonomi group were plotting with the Right-wing Badoglio in Rome for a Royalist coup, another group of former politicians and intellectuals in Milan had formed the Party of Action (Partito d'Azione). The leader was Ugo La Malfa (later Prime Minister). The group was Left-wing and much influenced by Socialists. They considered themselves the heirs of the Giustizia e Liberta Group of opponents of Fascism who had waged vigorous underground warfare ever since Mussolini came to power, in spite of murders and imprisonment by the Fascists. The most famous members had been the Rosselli brothers, assassinated by Mussolini's agents in France in 1938 because their anti-Fascist activities in Paris were becoming a menace to him. They were bitter against the King because of his collaboration with Mussolini in 1922 and his passivity in face of

---

[q]Orlando was Prime Minister during the First World War; De Gasperi was to be the most successful Italian Prime Minister of the post-Second World War period.

[r]Cavallero claimed after the 25th July coup that he had turned anti-Fascist but was arrested by Badoglio. When, after Mussolini's return, the Germans insisted that he should become commander of the Italian Republican Army, he committed suicide. Almost certainly he wanted to throw in his lot with the anti-Fascists.

Mussolini's unconstitutional action in January 1925 and his 1940 declaration of war on Britain and France.

It was impossible to establish any open political organization because the Fascist secret police (Ovra) were too active and the Party of Action was, in fact, not much more than a political discussion club. However, in January 1943 they succeeded in distributing widely a Left-wing anti-Fascist newspaper, *Italia Libera*, which was strongly anti-monarchical and anti-Vatican and critical of former politicians who wanted the King to overthrow Mussolini and return to the rule of the House of Savoy.

From Rome the Bonomi group in reply circulated a rival secret journal, *Ricostruzione*, which appealed to anti-Fascists to unite to overthrow the Fascist tyranny either with or without the help of the monarchy. In it Bonomi emphasized how desperately important it was to save Italy from the 'extreme catastrophe' of a German invasion.[35]

The Party of Action was hopelessly unrealistic. So fanatical was their opposition to the monarchy that they refused any part in a plot by Badoglio for the King to overthrow Mussolini. This they claimed would mean 'the substitution of Fascism by neo-Fascism'. Thus they ignored the fact that a German occupation of Italy following the collapse of Fascism must be inconceivably worse than a Royalist Right wing Government containing ex-Fascists which could be voted out of power as soon as it was possible to hold a general election.

Bonomi had continuous contact with the Party of Action, who afterwards declared their main objective in these talks was to alienate Bonomi from the monarchy and Badoglio, and to weaken any Royalist anti-Fascist movement which carried the inherent risk of 'Fascism without Mussolini'.

In October 1942 La Malfa and his associates suggested to Bonomi that he should go on a British submarine from Lisbon to London where he would proclaim himself the legitimate leader of democratic anti-Fascists. He should ask the Allies to recognize him as the head of a Gaullist-style Italian Government in exile with the help of prominent anti-Fascists living in America, like Sforza and Salvemini[s] who had formed the well-publicized anti-Fascist Mazzini Society and with the philosopher Croce (then in Naples) as President of a Republic. Bonomi, more realistic, refused and continued to plot the downfall of Mussolini with Badoglio through a Royalist coup.[36]

La Malfa has related that in order to put the Allies 'on guard against the efforts of Victor Emmanuel to save the monarchy by establishing an

---

[s]Sforza was a former Foreign Minister who had fled from Mussolini; Salvemini was a prominent Socialist intellectual in exile.

alternative form of moderate Fascism' they prepared a memorandum which was sent to Sforza in America and published in the *New York Times*. This document was Left-wing because of Communist influence within the Party of Action. It included proposals for wide-scale nationalization of industry and made a bad impression on the Allied Governments who wanted nothing to do with a 'Gaullist' Italian Government based on anti-Fascists in exile in America; the Italian experts in the British and American Foreign Office thought them lacking in support in Italy, because they belonged to a past era.[37]

In April 1943 the Party of Action made their first direct contact with the Allies through McCaffery. The emissary was Prince Filippo Caracciolo, the Italian Consul General in Lugano. After the war Caracciolo held office in several Italian Governments and wrote two books of memoirs. He made no mention of his SOE contacts in 1943. The harsh treatment of Italy by the Allies was almost certainly his reason for silence.

Accompanied by his American wife he called on McCaffery in Berne and explained that he was the representative of the Party of Action, and that the foundations of the party had been laid within the Banca Commerciale Italiana by Ugo La Malfa. Caracciolo went on to say that the party consisted of 'Left-wing radicals' who were strongly anti-monarchy and wanted nothing to do with Badoglio or any other military leader.

McCaffery immediately decided the approach was important, and arranged for subsequent meetings to be held in Caracciolo's villa in Lugano; there Caracciolo was joined by La Malfa in further discussions. The two made it clear to McCaffery that the party hated 'not only the King personally but the concept of the monarchy, and they made no distinction between the Royal House and its servant Badoglio'. McCaffery reported this to London and was instructed to tell them that the Allies would aid and abet any efforts to sabotage the German war effort but would give no guarantes of any sort about peace terms for an Italian anti-Fascist Government if Mussolini were overthrown. However, McCaffery was able to facilitate communications between them and the anti-Fascist exiles in America, like Sforza. He pointed out to La Malfa and Caracciolo that the Party of Action did have one aim in common with Badoglio – they both wanted to create a free Italian entity overseas.

Eventually La Malfa and Caracciolo gave a reluctant consent to cooperating with Badoglio in a coup, although they insisted they must retain complete freedom of action concerning him and the monarchy 'when the great evils of Nazism and Fascism' had been overcome. By agreeing to this La Malfa was exceeding the mandate given to him by his colleagues in Milan. This may explain why La Malfa never referred to these negotiations with McCaffery after the war.

At the end of May La Malfa found he was in danger of arrest in Milan and he came to Lugano and lived in a house there belonging to his friend Rino de Nobile, a rich member of the Party of Action who after the war became prominent in Italian politics. Caracciolo was given the code name 'Captain Phillips' and according to a Foreign Office minute in May 1943 'Captain Phillips frequently travelled from Switzerland to Milan and Rome and was in contact with Badoglio'. Eventually La Malfa and Caracciolo agreed to go to London, and Caracciolo bravely took up residence in Geneva where Victor Farrell, a British Secret Service agent, lodged him in his house. McCaffery produced British passports for La Malfa and Caracciolo and arranged for four British companions to travel on the same train through France to Lisbon so that the whole compartment would be full.

At the last moment La Malfa baulked. He found he had only been invited by the War Office, and he feared he might appear to be a British agent, not the representative of a political party. Despite strenuous efforts by McCaffery and by SOE in London, Eden refused a formal Foreign Office invitation to La Malfa, and so an important opportunity for contact with the responsible Italian opposition was thrown away. McCaffery has recorded that once the invasion of Sicily had begun on 10 July 1943 La Malfa would have gone to London 'without conditions' but 'the moment had passed'. One of La Malfa's problems was that while he was reluctantly prepared to cooperate with Badoglio in a Royalist coup d'état many of his political colleagues were strongly opposed to such a move.[38]

Another important Right-wing anti-Fascist, Adriano Olivetti, contacted McCaffery quite independently in June 1943.[t] He told McCaffery that he had discussed with the Princess of Piedmont a plan by which the King and the Crown Prince should abdicate and allow a Regency Council to be set up until the Princess's son came of age. This, according to Olivetti, would appease the critics of the monarchy.

McCaffery reported to London that Olivetti had contacted Caviglia and Badoglio and met the underground political parties both in Rome

[t]Adriano Olivetti was the son of the founder of the famous typewriter company. After the war he started a small intellectual movement aimed at conciliating Christian faith and Socialist ideals – without much success. He was a close friend of many members of the Party of Action and Giustizia e Liberta. He was not a rigid opponent of the monarchy and Badoglio as were the Socialist members of the Party of Action.

and Milan. Convinced that Olivetti's plans were genuine and feasible, McCaffery took Olivetti to see Allen Dulles of OSS in Berne (the US counterpart of SOE) and together they agreed to Olivetti's request that he should be allowed to try and organize negotiations with the Allies through Hugh Montgomery, First Secretary to the British Legation to the Holy See in the Vatican. McCaffery informed Montgomery of this.

McCaffery also made plans to transport Olivetti to London; as a Scotsman he was tickled at Olivetti's 'sportsmanship' in suggesting that a RAF plane should land on Lake Vivarone near his home to collect him. In July, however, Olivetti – who knew that a coup against Mussolini was imminent – unfortunately became 'impatient' and, according to McCaffery, 'jumped the gun' and on two occasions went beyond his brief and had to be 'reprimanded'. Then, without McCaffery's knowledge, Olivetti went to Lisbon for conversations with persons unknown without telling SOE in Switzerland. On his return to Italy he was arrested by Mussolini's secret police, only to be released from prison a few days later when Fascism was overthrown on 25 July.[39]

Air Commodore West told the author that in Berne they were gravely handicapped in their negotiations with Caviglia and Badoglio by the formula of unconditional surrender. They were ordered to tell dissident Italians this was the only basis on which the British Government would treat with them after the Casablanca Conference. West said that in Berne they immediately held a conference with their Italian emissaries to discuss the effect of unconditional surrender. They all felt it was a disaster for their plans to bring Italy out of the war with the help of the anti-Fascists. According to West, McCaffery expressed it best by saying: 'The Italians want a peace but they are a proud nation and will not accept *umiliazione* [humiliation]. I am *cento per cento* [100%] sure that unconditional surrender will wreck our plans.'

It was ludicrous to expect SOE to cause 'disruption' in Germany and Italy if they were not allowed to encourage enemy aliens amongst the anti-Fascists and anti-Nazis by hopes of a satisfactory future for their country after an Allied victory. Yet Eden was adamant that no individual apart from those under his direct control at the Foreign Office should say anything about a possible peace.

This had come to a head in January 1942 when a Foreign Office telegram from Barcelona stated that, according to Secret Service agents five important former Fascists in Italy were ready to organize resistance to Mussolini, as they believed Italy had lost the war. This telegram was passed to Jebb, who was head of SOE. He suggested to the Foreign Office that SOE should send the head of their Italian section to Spain to contact an emissary from these anti-Fascists to see whether these men could be fitted into 'our general scheme for subversion in Italy'. Jebb made it plain in a letter to Cadogan that he did not 'desire to suggest that S.O.E. should conduct negotiations with any really important leader in Italy desirous of concluding a separate peace', but his Minister (Hugh Dalton)

thinks it is the legitimate function of S.O.E. to encourage and organise revolution in enemy occupied countries by every means in their power, and seeing that normally such encouragement can only be provided by means of a system of agents it will, he suggests, normally be within the province of S.O.E. to do the spade work until the point is reached when important decisions have to be taken by the Foreign Office on high questions of policy.

This reasonable suggestion provoked Eden to write almost hysterical minutes:

I do not see why S.O.E. even saw this telegram which is marked *Departmental secret* which means what it says, *confined to the Foreign Office*. If it does not mean this I must find some other method in order that I may be allowed to mind my own business. A.E.

In a minute, Loxley, Private Secretary to Eden, pointed out that Jebb received secret telegrams. Eden had asked why SOE even knew about this matter. Loxley went on: 'He is not allowed to enter them on S.O.E. files save with our permission but if he sees one which he thinks has an S.O.E. interest he gets in touch with me or with the Department and asks that S.O.E. should be officially informed or consulted.' In the margin Eden wrote in red ink: 'Well he should not.' In another minute Eden wrote:

I confess I find this quite intolerable. I am responsible to Parliament for foreign policy and as long as that lasts I am not prepared to share the responsibility with Mr. Jebb or anyone else.

I had naturally imagined the telegrams marked Departmental secret were confined to F.O. They must be in future. Can anyone else see them outside? If so, it must be stopped. Are my personal telegrams to Ambassadors shown to Mr. Jebb too?

This particular issue is nothing to do with subversion in the sense of military intervention. Diplomacy, or the conduct of it, must be exclusively my affair. This is one aspect of it. If I am to ask for a Cabinet decision to avail myself of this constitutional right I am prepared to do so.

His reference to the Cabinet arose because Cadogan had sent the Foreign Secretary this minute:

Sir O. Sargent's reference to 'peace feelers' refers to a recent incident in Sweden when S.O.E. officials received such feelers and passed them on to their superiors in London *without saying anything to the mission.*

That was of course wrong. But so long as S.O.E. are entrusted with 'subversion' one cannot say that they are to know nothing of this. To deprive them of all concern in subversion would, I think, require a Cabinet decision.

But I am very doubtful about allowing S.O.E. to send out the head of their Italian section.   A.C.[40]

The papers show that Cadogan discussed the matter with Eden and calmed him down, and at Eden's direction sent out 'certain instructions' about the distribution of Department secret telegrams, and that no further action was to be taken. This undoubtedly meant that SOE were deprived of information about discontented Italians who might have been extremely helpful both politically and in subversive activities.

In spite of this, a report by the Foreign Office to the War Cabinet dated 24 April 1943 showed that useful information was being sent back to London from SOE contacts in Italy. The report reads:

It is not known what support in the army Badoglio would command, but if he were acting in the King's name it could be considerable. Apart from Badoglio the only name which has been seriously mentioned is that of Marshal Caviglia. He is now a very old man but is said to be very active. We know of no other army leaders who might be expected to lead a revolt.[41]

Striking evidence of the *volte-face* over offers of a soft peace to Italian anti-Fascists came in June 1942. Emilio Lussu was a Left-wing Sardinian anti-Fascist with a considerable following in Italy.[u] After operating in Vichy France, trying to save Italian anti-Fascist exiles who were in danger, he went to Lisbon in June 1941. Here he made detailed plans for a guerrilla uprising in Sardinia which he hoped after initial successes would spread to the Italian mainland; and he visited Malta and Gibraltar to talk to SOE agents. From Lisbon he went to America where he tried to enlist the cooperation of leading anti-Fascist emigrés, including Sforza, Salvemini and Tarchiani, but found them unrealistic. He then went to London in January 1941 where he got in touch with SOE. The Italian section of SOE headed by Major Roseberry took up his plans with enthusiasm, and saw in him an admirable agent to carry out subversion in Sardinia and Italy proper.

[u]Lussu had been the leading Sardinian MP after the First World War and was the nephew of a former Italian Prime Minister. Arrested by Mussolini in 1926, he was detained in the Lipari Islands but made a dramatic escape to freedom in 1932. After the war he was prominent in Italian politics.

However Lussu, who was very much a politician, insisted that if he was to risk his life and go into action on behalf of the Allies in Sardinia he must have reassurances about the proposed treatment of Italy by the Allies after the war. Roseberry took Lussu to Sargent at the Foreign Office in June 1942. They had a long talk and Lussu said he would go into Sardinia immediately to raise a revolt provided he had a guarantee that after the war the Allies would allow Italy to keep all her territory, including her colonies which she possessed in 1922 when Mussolini came to power. Lussu was backed in this demand by Hambro and Sporborg of the SOE, but the Foreign Office gave him short shrift.[v]

On 7 June Sargent minuted that Lussu would only go to Italy if he received a promise about Italy's pre-colonial empire, and that 'we cannot touch the project at all and must tell S.O.E. to adapt their plans accordingly'. Cadogan minuted that he agreed, and Eden: 'There can be no question of such a statement and the project must be firmly ruled out.' This was a far cry from the search for an Italian de Gaulle the year before.[42]

The decision communicated in Eden's letter of 14 January 1943 not even to reply to Badoglio's overture was unfortunate because at Casablanca Roosevelt and Churchill had agreed on Sicily and Italy as the next invasion areas in preference to the Dodecanese, the Balkans or the South of France. The Summit concluded that an Italian invasion would tie up fifteen German divisions as soon as North Africa was liberated; even so, some of the planners were not too happy because Germany would regain most of the rolling stock being used to supply Italy with 12 million tons of coal annually, and the operation would drain the Mediterranean theatre of Allied troops, beside needing 1½ million tons of shipping to maintain the Italian economy.

On 11 February Hull replied to Eden's letter of 14 January saying he thought the House of Savoy might provide an interim Government if Fascism were overthrown and advocating a sympathetic line to Italy to "eliminate" her from the war with bombing confined to military objectives. He pointed out that the British had an unparalleled reputation for discriminate bombing of legitimate targets while the Italians had no illusions about the brutality of the Germans, and wanted phrases used in broadcasts like 'the Allies have no intention of

---

[v]Sir Charles Hambro was head of SOE and Henry Sporborg his second-in-command. By now Lord Selborne had taken over from Dalton as Minister of Economic Warfare. He was not as forceful as his predecessor and although close to Churchill had been out of politics for many years and had never held office higher than Assistant Postmaster-General. Selborne was quite unable to stand up to Eden's reluctance to allow SOE to conduct political negotiations in Italy through their underground contacts with anti-Fascists.

destroying Italy as a nation or depriving her of territories which have always been Italian'. He thought 'threats of destruction as a people and a country, unless and until they request an armistice' should be avoided. These were the assurances that Lussu had sought in vain in 1942. Eden minuted 'a good letter', but as will be seen he soon took a much harsher line, especially over bombing.[43]

In the early spring of 1943 the Royal Family made further soundings both in Lisbon and Geneva. Alessandro Marienni, who was on the staff of the Italian Consul General in Geneva (Cortese) was entrusted with the negotiations. He was a confidant of the Duke of Aosta, had been with him on a mission to Iran in 1938 and had been a witness at his marriage. Marienni was helped in his efforts by Giacomo Cicconardi, an Italian foreign correspondent, later a high EEC official. Cicconardi was friendly with Farrell, and they established a code by which messages could be sent to the Duke of Aosta in Lerici. The Duke made it clear to the British contacts that he was cooperating closely with the Crown Prince Umberto, and that the King would be informed of everything.

At first the British requested that one of the Royal Family should set up a Free non-Fascist Government in Sardinia ready to fight with the Allies against the Germans. This was quite impractical because the Germans had strong forces on the island, and some of the Italian forces there were strongly pro-Fascist. Still, the bait of easier surrender terms was dangled by the British Secret Service, on Foreign Office instructions, provided an anti-Fascist Government was created.

The Italians were informed that the United States Government was leaving the conduct of these negotiations to the British. Marienni told Farrell that the Monarchists were considering the practicability of creating a type of Gaullist regime in Sardinia, but that the Duke of Aosta insisted on knowing what better treatment Italy would receive from the Allies. It was extremely difficult to persuade the High Command to change sides unless they knew that advantages would accrue to their country from doing so. Marienni also asked for details of what help the Allied air forces and fleet would give if an anti-Fascist coup took place in Sardinia.

After the war Marienni stated he could get no satisfaction out of Farrell; whenever he tried to establish detailed plans on behalf of the Duke of Aosta for military action he was met by evasion. His impression was that there was no contact between the British Foreign Office and the Allied High Command, and he found that the British response was continually: 'Do something and then we shall see.' No assurance of any kind was forthcoming to the Duke of Aosta over the treatment which Italy would receive if he succeeded in displacing the Fascist regime and allying with the British and Americans against the Germans. Eventually he decided that the Allies would stick to unconditional surrender whatever the Monarchists succeeded in doing. He and his negotiators resented this Allied intransigence but at least the talks confirmed the King of Italy's resolution that he must attempt a coup against Mussolini even though no alternative to unconditional surrender was offered.

As Aosta's agent plodded on in Geneva, Umberto's wife, Maria José, was active on the same tack in Lisbon. She had a passion for anti-Fascist intrigue and talked with Bonomi and other former Italian democratic politicians. They told her in no uncertain terms that as far as they were concerned monarchy and Fascism were inescapably entwined, although she did her best to disabuse them of this idea. Her father-in-law disapproved of women members of the House of Savoy taking part in politics, but he liked the information she brought him. After the fall of Mussolini the King banished her to a distant part of Piedmont from whence, with her children, she escaped in the nick of time to Switzerland out of the Germans' clutches; thus she took no part in the arrangements which culminated in the September armistice.

Maria José was head of the Italian Red Cross and her talks with wounded soldiers in hospitals had convinced her that Italy was ready to get rid of Mussolini. She first made contact with D'Arcy Osborne, the British Minister in the Vatican, and in the autumn of 1942, before Alamein and Stalingrad, she heard through the Vatican that Sir Samuel Hoare, the former Foreign Secretary and now British Ambassador in Madrid, wanted to tell the Italians that if they withdrew from the Axis Italy would be well treated with economic aid after the war. There is no evidence that this was more than a personal expression of opinion. Maria José immediately told her father-in-law but got a dusty response. Perhaps then, before Alamein, he still hoped the Axis would win.

She next made contact with Salazar, the dictator of Portugal. Through her friendship with the Portuguese Minister at the Vatican, Antonio Pacheco, she was able to send the Italian banker Mattioli to see Salazar, who wanted a Union of Latin States after the war. In June Salazar sent a secret message to the Princess that he was ready to act as intermediary between the Allies and Italy. In fact the Italian War Office had broken her cipher messages sent through Pacheco at the Vatican, but did not tell Mussolini. On 17 July 1943 the Princess sent another emissary, Emo Capodilista, to Salazar, and Salazar told the British

Ambassador of his arrival on 19 July. But it was too late. After the fall of Mussolini six days later, Churchill told the Portuguese dictator that he would have nothing to do with any Italian negotiator unless he was the accredited representative of a new Italian Government. Had Salazar approached the Americans, he might have had better luck; it so happened that he was on better terms with the British Ambassador.[44]

Eden was most displeased when he learnt that the RAF had dropped leaflets on Rome at the beginning of June offering the Italians 'peace with honour'. Cardinal Maglione, Head of State at the Vatican, in D'Arcy Osborne's absence on leave in London sent for his First Secretary, Montgomery, to read out the leaflets to him. How, he asked could Britain reconcile 'peace with honour' with 'unconditional surrender'?

Montgomery was instructed by the Foreign Office he need not try to explain the discrepancy, and Harold Macmillan in Algiers was firmly told to prevent the repetition of this phrase in future leaflets as it was 'not to the liking of Eden or Brendan Bracken, the Minister of Information'. Macmillan was told by Eden: 'I hope you will prevent in future the use of similar phrases which are politically ambiguous and therefore undesirable.'[45]

His Holiness sent for D'Arcy Osborne as soon as he got back from leave and expressed his concern at the difference between 'peace with honour' and 'unconditional surrender'. Eden was unruffled, and when he heard Cardinal Maglione had also asked what the British were doing to safeguard the art treasures of Italy he said Maglione was Italian and the Italians should have thought of this before they declared war.[46]

On 18 July Mussolini suddenly decided to approach the Allies and see what terms he could get if he abandoned Hitler. He sent for Bastianini his Under-Secretary at the Foreign Office, and gave him the go ahead to renew Ciano's 1942 contacts in Lisbon. It was a mad mission. With the invasion of Sicily under way and Allied plans made to follow this up with the invasion of the mainland, how could the Allies do a deal with Mussolini which would stab the anti-Fascists in the back?

Bastianini went to see Cardinal Maglione and asked for a passport for a leading Roman banker, Luigi Fummi, so that he could travel to London via Lisbon. Fummi was told to follow the same contacts as in 1942. He saw Campbell who asked the Foreign Office if he could send him to London, but then came the news of Mussolini's fall on 25 July and his credentials as a negotiator for the Duce were valueless. Eden did not want to know about him.[47]

On 25 July 1943 the King arrested Mussolini and made Badoglio Prime Minister. A plot had been concocted by the Monarchists and anti-Fascists, and Grandi had successfully moved a motion at the meeting of the Grand Council of Fascism the day before critizing Mussolini. This was passed with a substantial majority and gave the King the excuse he needed to depose the Duce, who by now, because of the setbacks in the war, had largely lost his popularity. The Fascist party ceased to exist overnight.

8

Italy after the Armistice
1943–1944

The Allies were taken by surprise by Mussolini's arrest: Eden had relied on reports from D'Arcy Osborne, who was too closely cloistered in the Vatican to be in touch with Italian opinion. On 24 July 1943, the day before Mussolini was arrested, Osborne wrote to the Foreign Office: 'I do not expect any serious or successful movement from any quarter against the Fascist Government . . . typhus and famine are more probable.'

The industrial magnate Alberto Pirelli had in early July gone on a mission to Switzerland with Mussolini's approval to try to explore the possibility of Switzerland being an intermediary in peace moves. On 24 July Eden was sent a report from the Italian Department of the Foreign Office that Pirelli had said in Switzerland: 'The King will replace the Duce within a month.' Eden wrote on it in red ink: 'Italians of Pirelli's type have a lot to learn. A.E.' Yet, even as the Foreign Secretary was writing this note, the Fascist Grand Council was sitting and plotting the Duce's overthrow. Eden had misjudged the strength of the movement against Fascism and upon him lies a heavy responsibility for the failure of the Allies to land in Italy immediately after the 25 July coup, when they could have forestalled a German occupation. When the King set up the Badoglio Government he expected an immediate response through the links already established in Geneva and Lisbon. No messages came from the Allies.[1]

On 25 July Hitler was as much taken by surprise as the British and the Americans. 'Badoglio has taken over – the blackest of our enemies,' he declared, and he was desperately worried that in agreement with Badoglio the British and Americans would suddenly arrive by sea and air in Italy. This the Allies could have done with ease.

At that moment there was only one German division in central Italy, the 3rd Panzer Grenadier; it was incompletely equipped and possessed few tanks. In addition General Student had some elements of a parachute division. Four German divisions were fighting in Sicily and had been severely mauled. There were two armoured divisions in Southern Italy originally designed for Sicily, but because of the transport situation and later because of the likely fall of Sicily they remained in their barracks.[2]

In the House of Commons on 27 July Churchill said:

The only consequence of the Italian Government staying under the German yoke will be that in the next few months Italy will be seared and scarred and blackened from one end to the other . . . we should let the Italians, to use a homely phrase, 'stew in their own juice' for a bit and hot up the fire to the utmost.

This persuaded Hitler that he need not occupy Rome immediately, but German divisions started to move over the Brenner to occupy Italy with 'Viva Duce' written on their helmets. The Germans also issued their own currency, as in occupied countries.

Churchill's speech spotlighted for Badoglio and the King of Italy the difficulties they would have on changing sides. Grandi, who had engineered the overthrow of Mussolini, wanted an immediate switch with the Italians fighting the Germans alongside the Allies; but Badoglio dilly-dallied in the vain hope that Italy might stay neutral for the rest of the war. The realists in his Government knew that Grandi was right but could not persuade Badoglio how urgent it was to come to terms with the Allies. When Grandi was consulted by the King, Badoglio ignored the advice.

The King had toyed with the plan of entrusting the Government to Caviglia instead of Badoglio. Had he done so, Italy would have tried to join the Allies immediately. Caviglia was a stronger and more decisive character and from the start of the war had wanted to change sides.[a] As it was, however, the Allies threw away the prize which was theirs for the asking during the first fourteen of Badoglio's thirty-five days of rule – the secession of the Italy home army, air force and fleet intact, with the minimum interference by the Germans. Instead, both the British and American Governments began a long haggle over the armistice and peace terms. No one in high places, except Macmillan and Eisenhower seemed to realize what a wonderful opportunity was slipping away. The demand for unconditional surrender added to the delays.

As soon as the news of Mussolini's downfall reached the Foreign Office, Jebb wrote a sensible memorandum pointing out that if the Government persisted in unconditional surrender it would find it

[a]Sir William Deakin has produced evidence that the King chose Badoglio instead of Caviglia because Caviglia was a strong Freemason and Victor Emmanuel did not like this; also Badoglio was much younger.

difficult to obtain the 'purely military armistice' that was wanted. He wrote:

It is pretty evident that fascism is being liquidated and that the army plus the House of Savoy is making a desperate effort to put itself in a position in which it can obtain what it considers to be 'reasonable terms of surrender' for Italy. But it is equally plain that neither the King nor the Army would consider 'our own terms reasonable'.[3]

Cadogan commented:

It is an awful prospect if it means that when the Italians ask for an armistice there is to be a telegraphic blitz between the Prime Minister, President and Ike, and Ike's Chiefs of Staff and Combined Chiefs of Staff before we can send an answer.

This, regrettably, is what occurred. Eden's adamant line on unconditional surrender drew the reply from Churchill while in Canada for the Quebec Conference early in August: 'Do not miss the bus, and merely harping on unconditional surrender with no prospect of mercy may well lead to no surrender at all.' To which Eden replied 'I quite understand you wish to sugar the pill for the Badoglio Government . . . I feel that having stated so categorically in public we insist on unconditional surrender we are bound to tell Badoglio's emissary we will require this.'[4]

The Americans, the Prime Minister and the Foreign Secretary went on arguing about the details of the surrender document, but would not alter the term 'unconditional surrender'. As a result Eisenhower was unable in August to concert plans with Badoglio to land Allied troops in Italy before the Germans were in a position to oppose them. Not until 26 August did Washington send Eisenhower the surrender terms which he was authorized to sign with Italy, and then only because of British insistence.[5] Thus the new Italian Government found themselves in a vacuum and had to start from scratch in their efforts to change sides – a difficult enough manoeuvre even without the peril of Hitler's desire for revenge.

On 3 August a diplomat, Alberto Berio, was despatched to Tangier, nominally to become Consul General but really to contact the British Consul, Gascoigne, with a secret message that Italy was in the hands of Germany; Hitler could occupy Rome at any moment and unless the Allies stopped bombing the Badoglio Government would fall. The Allies should land in the Balkans or the South of France to take the pressure off the Italian Government.[6] By 9 August, when Berio made contact with Gascoigne's deputy, Watkinson, Churchill was at sea en route to the Quebec Conference, Roosevelt was on holiday, and Eden in the country. No one could deal with the urgent cables from Tangier.[7]

At the meeting of the War Cabinet in Churchill's absence on 11 August, Eden stated that in addition to Berio's approach, two others had been received: one from Marchese D'Ajeta in Lisbon, and another from Signor Bussetti in Barcelona on behalf of the Italian political parties. He felt that the last two approaches should be ignored, but that Berio's was an official approach from the Badoglio Government. He should be told that the Allies insisted on unconditional surrender as a first step and there could be no consideration of negotiation.

Bussetti claimed he was the accredited representative of the former Italian political parties who had been suppressed for twenty years by the Fascists, but Eden considered they could not 'speak' for the Italian Army who were loyal to Badoglio and the strongest group in the country. Meanwhile Macmillan in Algiers was alarmed that unconditional surrender would frighten off the King and Badoglio and sabotage an agreement for an unopposed landing in Italy. On 29 July he had pointed out to the Prime Minister that to force Italians 'to sign very severe terms would demand a military situation which leaves them no choice. A similar set of more attractive terms should be ready in which your promise of an honourable capitulation was more apparent. This is what Ike wants.' This aroused no spark in Churchill who replied that he did not like Eisenhower's recent broadcasts to the Italian people which 'may defeat their own objective by showing the enemy an over eagerness to treat with him. He should not have promised to restore hundreds of thousands of Italian POWs. His lavish offer did not mention our own POWs.'

Churchill, like Eden, failed to appreciate the urgency on military grounds of patching up an immediate deal with Badoglio at all costs to forestall the German occupation of Italy. Macmillan, Eisenhower and Alexander in Algiers were being driven frantic by the leisurely attitude of the British and American Governments.

On 10 August Macmillan annoyed Eden by sending a long 'Armistice Quiz' to London. It included a section 'What a Commander ought to know' and another 'What a Resident Minister ought to know'. It began:

What is the meaning of unconditional surrender? It clearly cannot mean surrender without conditions because London and Washington have for four months been engaged in writing conditions which have reached 42 clauses and are not finished . . . I think the definition must be that the capitulation is Italian and the honourable part of it is British. In other words there is no conflict between honourable capitulation and unconditional surrender.

He went on that Eisenhower should be allowed to sign a document in an emergency which would take Italy out of the war overnight. Neither Eden nor Churchill would have anything to do with his sensible suggestions, and the Allies remained bogged down haggling over the terms of the armistice.[8]

The nearly desperate Italian Government sent a third mission, this time to Lisbon. It consisted of General Castellano and a Foreign Office official, Montanari, nephew of Badoglio, who spoke perfect English. Castellano, with characteristic Italian casualness, had no proper credentials, only a note to the British Embassy in Madrid from D'Arcy Osborne. However, fortunately for Castellano's credit-worthiness his sleeping car at Nice was accidentally hitched on to the Madrid express instead of the Lisbon train and he arrived in Madrid on 15 August at noon. He knocked on the door of the British Embassy and by presenting D'Arcy Osborne's note saw Hoare. The Ambassador reacted well and sent him on to Campbell at the British Embassy in Lisbon.

On 18 August Castellano amid great secrecy had a conference in Campbell's private flat in Lisbon. Present were the Ambassador, Eisenhower's Chief of Staff, Bedell Smith, his British Head of Intelligence, Brigadier Strong, and the American Ambassador to Portugal, George Kennan.[9] The urgency of coming to terms with the Italians was becoming desperate. Eisenhower had fixed 9 September for the Allied landings at Salerno in Southern Italy, and he was convinced this would not be a success if Italians joined the Germans in opposing it.

At the start Campbell asked Castellano if the Italian Government would sign an armistice with unconditional surrender. Much to the surprise of the Allied representatives Castellano replied that he had no authority to negotiate an armistice. He had only come to discuss what help the Allies could give to Badoglio in turning the Germans out of Italy, and to say that the Italians wished to become allies for this purpose.

At this stage the meeting was chilly, but as Castellano began to give valuable information about German army and air force depositions in Italy, the atmosphere improved. Eventually Castellano was told that the more help the Italians gave to the Allies when they landed in Italy, the softer would be the terms of the armistice. At last Eden was bypassed.

In the early hours of the morning whisky was produced, they all became friendly, and Castellano agreed to go back to Rome to see if his Government would agree to unconditional surrender and help the Allies to land unopposed in Italy. He was due to leave Lisbon on 22 August with a homecoming party of Italian diplomats from Chile, as he said he could not travel separately without alerting the Germans. He was given a special SOE wireless set and cipher and told this could be operated by a British agent, Lieutenant Dick Mallaby, who had been captured a few days before at Como in Northern Italy.

SOE, at the request of McCaffery, had dropped Mallaby, a young wireless operator, into Northern Italy on 14 August to provide a wireless link between the anti-Fascists in Milan and SOE in Berne. (When Badoglio had been offered the use of such a link by SOE agents he had replied complacently that he was already in touch with the Allies.) Mallaby was to be attached nominally to one of the SOE sabotage groups operating in Northern Italy. He was bilingual in Italian and had been briefed on all the SOE contacts with anti-Fascists in Italy.

As the RAF bombers crossed Lake Como on the night of 13/14 August on their way to targets around Milan, Mallaby parachuted down into the lake. He was to proceed to an address in the town of Como. The shores of Lake Como are well populated and the residents used to come out to watch RAF raids on Milan as if they were firework displays. The descending Mallaby was clearly seen in the moonlight and soon, according to the Milan newspaper *Corriere della Sera*, boats including military and police launches formed a circle around him. Mallaby cried out in Italian: 'Are you fishermen?' When they did not reply, he shouted at them angrily. The Italians were amazed that a man in his predicament could afford 'the luxury of being annoyed'.

After a few days' imprisonment Mallaby was brought to Rome from where the SOE wireless set functioned well. He quickly contacted Allied Forces Headquarters in Algiers to provide a perfect secret link between the Badoglio Government and the Allies.

Although it was extremely urgent that Castellano should report back to Rome, he had to wait until the diplomats' ship arrived and only left Lisbon on 25 August. He sent two cables to the War Office in Rome which were not deciphered properly, and merely filed. Meanwhile the Badoglio Government, hearing nothing from Castellano, sent to Lisbon another emissary, General Zanussi, together with General Carton de Wiart, who had been languishing in an Italian prisoner of war camp. Carton de Wiart called on Campbell who told him of Castellano's visit and said that under the circumstances he would not receive Zanussi – about whom the Allies were anyway becoming suspicious. The War Cabinet in London cabled to Eisenhower that he had probably been sent by pro-German Italians to 'find out what Castellano was up to'.

On 27 August, however, Campbell saw Zanussi and told him that the Allied Governments were very worried about their prisoners of war in Italy and that if Badoglio wished to get reasonable terms he must safeguard the Allied prisoners of war and not let them fall into German hands. Zanussi said Hitler would use poison gas on Italy if she changed sides – he had said several times: 'Gas is for use against traitors.' The War Cabinet spent some time discussing poison gas and the prisoners of war without coming to any conclusion.

Zanussi had brought no written credentials of any sort, relying entirely on Carton de Wiart, but the Allied Governments decided to entrust him with the full terms of their long surrender document. These were harsh and humiliating to the Italians.

On 29 August he was flown to Algiers, where Macmillan, visited him and found him 'a very well-covered and talkative middle-aged man who made up for his absence of written credentials by the sincerity with which he entered into all plans for compounding with the Allies as soon as possible'. After the conversation Macmillan removed from him the long terms of surrender because he thought, with good reason, that if they got to Rome they might so shock Badoglio and the King that they would refuse the armistice. On 29 August Castellano, back in Rome, sent a message on Mallaby's wireless set that he would come to Sicily on 31 August.

Macmillan had the right attitude. Within days the American and British armies were to undertake a dangerous amphibious landing at Salerno. If the Italian forces were to resist as well as the Germans it could be a disaster. The only way to stop the Italians fighting was to persuade them to accept an immediate armistice regardless of the long-term consequences.

Macmillan was high in Churchill's favour, but Eden was jealous of him. The reaction of the Foreign Office to the news that the humiliating long terms had been removed from Zanussi was extraordinary. Dixon, who was assiduous in taking the Eden line, minuted on 31 August:

GENERAL ZANUSSI AND TERMS OF SURRENDER FOR ITALY
MR.MACMILLAN'S TELEGRAM NO. 1615

The reasons given in this telegram for the decision not to send the comprehensive terms into Italy by the hand of General Zanussi or his companion are of the flimsiest. It is quite obvious that the headquarters, backed by Mr. Macmillan, are out to conclude the Armistice on the short terms and to sabotage the idea of concluding it on the full terms. This, of course, runs directly counter to everything we have been planning for the last two months, and to the instructions in our telegram No. 1722.

It is now presumably too late to set matters right, but at least we ought to know where we stand, in order to explain to the Russians and others. It is quite incorrect to say, as the Combined Chiefs-of-Staff do in FAN 206, that the Russians have agreed to signature on their behalf of the military terms.[10]

Here Dixon was wrong. The US Embassy in Moscow signalled on 28 August that the Soviet Government agreed the terms and Eisenhower could sign on their behalf. Churchill and Roosevelt jointly signalled to Moscow on 2 September: 'We assume you expect us to sign short terms on your behalf.'

Of course Dixon had no idea the amphibious landing in Italy was scheduled for 9 September, but his attitude was procrastinating and legalistic in face of the desperate need to get the Italians out of the war before the attack on the mainland. In Eden's and Churchill's absence at the Quebec Conference, Dixon drafted a reply which was sent to Macmillan with Attlee's approval. It insisted that Castellano should be asked to sign the long terms as soon as he arrived in Sicily, and that if he had no authority to do so he must be told the Italian Government would be expected to do so as soon as possible; and that although the armistice could come into effect by Castellano signing the short terms it must be made clear to the Badoglio Government that the long terms were an essential part of the armistice.

Nothing could have been more likely to cause the Italians to jib, and Eisenhower and Macmillan sensibly ignored Dixon's instructions. In his report to Churchill Macmillan wrote:

The comprehensive document was wisely kept in reserve since it was felt that its introduction at this stage might only lead to further delays which were not in the military interests of the Allies. Castellano and Montinari were persuaded that they should ask their Government to accept the short terms of the armistice.[11]

The Badoglio Government told Castellano to inform Eisenhower that they would accept the armistice terms provided they were announced after a landing 'in sufficient strength'. Badoglio suggested fifteen Allied divisions; having no idea of logistics, he did not realize that this would take months of preparation, and anyway the Allies did not have so many troops in the Mediterranean theatre.

Castellano flew from the Rome airfield at Centocelle to Termini Imerese in Sicily where Bedell Smith, Strong and Zanussi were waiting for him. Castellano was furious to see Zanussi and asked him 'What are you doing here?' Zanussi said he was anxious about the long armistice and wanted to talk to Castellano about it. Castellano said he already knew everything, which was untrue, and refused to listen. This pleased Eisenhower and Macmillan who were anxious not to let Badoglio know anything about the long armistice because its humiliating terms might wreck the negotiations.

Churchill wanted representatives of the Commonwealth and all the Allied nations to be present at a ceremony for the signing of the armistice. This would have compromised the secrecy of the Salerno landings. Eisenhower cabled the War Cabinet in London: 'Our plans must be kept secret or ruin.' With Macmillan's help unwelcome spectators were kept away – which incensed de Gaulle.

Castellano signed the short surrender on 3 September. He was bluffed by Eisenhower because he had no idea that the Salerno landings would consist of only five divisions. Had the Italians known this they probably would not have signed. Eisenhower admitted afterwards he had been bluffing and was heavily criticized for it by Italians after the war. But at last a lifeline was held out to Italy because Alexander agreed to send an airborne and a seaborne division to Rome to help the Italians keep the Germans out of their capital. He generously agreed that these Allied troops could operate under Italian command, which delighted Castellano and softened his attitude to the armistice. Alexander also promised that 82 US Airborne Division should withdraw from their part in the Salerno operation and instead should land on the Rome airfields.[12]

Castellano explained to the Allied chiefs that although 3rd Panzer Division at Viterbo to the north of Rome and 2nd Para Division to the south were poised for a pincer movement on Rome, the Italians had an armoured corps with three divisions, plus two infantry divisions, between Rome and the Germans. He said that on paper the Italians had superiority but there were shortages of anti-tank guns and annunition. General Ridgway, Commander 82nd Division, said that he would airlift fifty-seven anti-tank guns able to penetrate German Mark IV and Mark VI tanks at up to 500 yards, and a hundred anti-tank guns were promised in the seaborne landings.

Castellano suggested that because of German anti-aircraft guns and the difficulty of making sure that no Italian anti-aircraft battery fired on the American transports, the initial landings should be at Cerveteri and Furbara aerodromes, close to the coast north-west of Rome, where the run in would be over the sea. Ridgway at once prepared an outline plan for these airborne operations, which were christened Giant 2.

82nd Division, after taking part in the invasion of Sicily, had been re-formed at Kairouan, Tunisia, from where some units had already embarked for the amphibious Salerno operation. The whole division was urgently ordered to Licata on the south coast of Sicily on 4 September to be ready for the Rome adventure.

Ridgway and his staff worked all night and on 4 September issued their plan for Giant 2 which was given to Castellano. His ADC flew to Rome with it on 5 September in Castellano's private plane. Castellano thought that the Italian War Office would immediately make a detailed battle plan for their armoured corps outside Rome to occupy and defend the airfields in liaison with the Americans, and that the resulting cooperation in battle between the American and Italian armies must lead to the Allies giving generous peace terms as promised at Cassibile.

General Ambrosio, the Italian CIGS, and his War Office staff sat on the plan. They read it, took no action, and passed it on to Badoglio. Castellano was still unaware of the date of the armistice and hence of D Day for Giant 2, but he would have been appalled had he known that his dedicated efforts to rehabilitate Italy with the Allies were being jettisoned by this inertia in Rome. He expected the War Office to leap into action in the crucial few days before the armistice.

Giant 2 specified that 82nd Division would land on D Day at Cerveteri and Furbara aerodromes and on D Day plus 1 there would be parachute drops and heavy equipment landed at Guidonia, Centocelle and Littoria close to Rome on the east. An American infantry force with plenty of anti-tank guns was hastily assembled at Bizerta in North Africa and loaded on to landing crafts and ships. It sailed on 7 September with sealed orders to land on the mouth of the Tiber at dawn on 9 September.

The armistice was to be announced simultaneously by Badoglio and Eisenhower between 6 and 7 p.m. on 8 September; the first airborne landings were to be a few hours later. Before dawn on 9 September British and American seaborne troops would land at Salerno and soon after the amphibious force would reach the Tiber. The Italian Army was to block all approach roads to the aerodromes and protect the passage up the Tiber of the seaborne force.

Giant 2 provided that at Furbara and Cerveteri aerodromes the Italians were to place horizontal searchlight beams pointing due west and Rome radio stations were to broadcast navigational signals. The perimeters of the airfields were to be outlined with amber lights; runways with white lights. A senior Italian staff officer was to be at each aerodrome with one interpreter for each company. The Italians were to provide 23,000 rations, 355 trucks, 12 ambulances, picks, shovels, barbed wire and 120 field telephones, together with a pool of 500 labourers to dig trenches. The airborne troops would bring rations for two days and petrol for one day and be self-supporting in ammunition and medical supplies. Castellano had already asked for all available supplies of high-octane petrol to be sent to Furbara and Cerveteri.

Ridgway suddenly got cold feet about Giant 2 because he doubted whether the Italians would be able to repulse German attacks. He wanted to send staff officers to Rome to report on the feasibility of the operation. Alexander forbade them to leave before 7 September because of the risk of their being captured by the Germans, which might result in the premature leakage of the place and date of the Allied landings.[13] So it was early on 7 September that General Maxwell Taylor, second-in-command 82 Division, and another staff officer, Colonel Gardiner, left Palermo in a British torpedo boat which took them to the isle of Ustica, forty miles north-west of Sicily. Here they had a rendezvous with an Italian corvette.

There was plenty of food and wine aboard and the weather was good. At 6.30 p.m. they tied up at Gaeta, seventy-five miles south-west of Rome. Pretending to be prisoners of war they allowed themselves to be bustled by guards into a waiting car which took them to a small van with frosted windows on the outskirts of Gaeta. On the drive to Rome they were amazed at the amount of civilian and military road traffic which gave the lie to any stories of petrol shortage. They saw almost no German troops, but on the Appian Way there were ominous neat signs with arrows pointing to German units of Student's 2nd Para Division.

After dark they reached the Palazzo Caprara opposite the Italian War Office and scuttled across the pavement trying to hide their American uniforms inside their greatcoats. A lavish dinner was prepared. This and the luxurious rooms were a welcome surprise to the Americans, who had been accustomed for months to nothing but camp beds and field rations; but to their amazement there were no arrangements for an immediate planning conference. No one in the Italian War Office knew the armistice and the air landings were scheduled for the next day, but even so the lack of urgency in Rome seemed incredible after Castellano's businesslike briefing in Sicily.

Not only had Giant 2 not been properly interpreted into Italian and distributed to the divisional commanders concerned, but General Carboni, commander of the corps around Rome, had held no briefing conferences with his own staff or the commanders of subordinate formations. The truth was that Generals Ambrosio (CIGS), Roatta (Army Chief of Staff), Rossi (Deputy CIGS) and Carboni were all terrified of fighting the Germans. Their one idea was to get the Allies to send as many troops as possible to defend Rome for them.

Taylor at once demanded an interview with Carboni, who panicked when he heard the airborne landing and armistice were within forty-eight hours, and that the main Allied landings were not near Rome, but 140 miles to the south at Salerno. By outright lies he convinced Taylor the air landings would be a disaster. At his court martial Carboni confessed that he had not told the truth because he considered it in the interests of the Italian nation to postpone the armistice so that in five days' time new troop dispositions could ensure the success of the US air landings. This was nonsense.

Carboni lied by saying the airfields were 'virtually' in German hands and that the armoured corps was nearly out of petrol and ammunition. In fact there was plenty of petrol in the main Rome depot at Mezzocammino on the Tiber, and the Rome arsenals were full of shells and small arms ammunition.

Taylor was horrified at what he called Carboni's 'alarming pessimism' and at the Italians' failure to prepare for Giant 2 plan. Ambrosio had gone the day before by train to Turin where he was hiding his family's valuables in case Northern Italy became a battlefield. He refused to fly back to confer with Taylor, so the cowardly Carboni had it all his own way.

Carboni showed Taylor an Italian Air Force memorandum claiming it would take them a week to fix the necessary airport lights to the runways although obviously these could have been improvised in half a day. The War Office, according to Carboni, had reported that there were no surplus army trucks available. In fact plenty of lorries and buses could have been requisitioned in a few hours in Rome to meet the 82nd Division's transport needs. Such apathy among the top military staff was a poor advertisement for twenty years of Fascism.

Taylor said: 'Castellano has so deceived us about the Italian military strength that we are on the brink of disaster. A lot of the top brass at Cassabile thought him a trickster.' Yet Castellano had told the truth. Carboni was the trickster. The Americans were whisked off in Carboni's staff car to Badoglio's villa to try to enlist his support in postponing the armistice.

Having passed both German and Italian road blocks with the uniformed Americans sitting well back in their seats to avoid recognition, they found everyone in pyjamas at Badoglio's villa but out of bed because of the air raids. Carboni left the Americans in the car for a quarter of an hour while he argued with Badoglio, finally convincing him by false information that the armoured corps was incapable of defending the Rome airfields. When Badoglio saw Taylor he repeated Carboni's arguments about a lack of petrol and ammunition and the military situation around Rome. He said he would signal Eisenhower asking for a postponement of the armistice. As the Allied convoys were already at sea making for Salerno this was out of the question, because Italian troops and the navy would then resist the landings.

At 1.20 a.m. on 8 September Taylor and Gardiner got back to Palazzo Caprara and sent a signal to AFHQ[b] over Mallaby's radio set postponing the airborne landing. Atmospherics were so bad that it did not reach AFHQ in Algiers until 8 a.m. General Lemnitzer was then ordered to fly to Licata in Sicily to stop the paratroopers. Because of bad navigation he was almost too late, reaching Licata at 4 p.m. Fifty Dakota aircraft on the tarmac were embarking paratroopers, and sixty-three were already airborne awaiting the code word to fly their troops to Cerveteri and Furbara. The amphibious force was at sea with sealed orders to land either at a beach north of the mouth of the Tiber or halfway between the mouth of the river and Rome.

In Algiers a furious Eisenhower signalled to Badoglio that Italy must announce the armistice that day or take the consequences. Badoglio and the King were undecided but at the last moment complied, and by 7 p.m. on 8 September an announcement of armistice had been broadcast by both sides. Unfortunately Eisenhower had already informed both Roosevelt and Churchill that Badoglio had broken faith, which led to the Allies imposing harsher peace terms on Italy.

Thus at the eleventh hour the daring Rome airborne landing was called off. What would have happened if it had taken place? Three months later Bedell Smith wrote to Castellano:

I have given a great deal of thought to our abortive plan for landing an airborne division near Rome . . . I remain convinced as do the officers of our planning staff that had there been in command of the Italian divisions around Rome an officer of courage, firmness and determination convinced of success, the plan could have been carried out.

This was also the strong view after the war of General Westphal, Chief of Staff to Kesselring.[14]

---

[b] Allied Force Headquarters, was Eisenhower's HQ in Algiers.

Churchill told the House of Commons on 21 September: 'We intended to drop a USA Airborne Division simultaneously with the announcement of the armistice to deal with 3rd Panzer, but as the aerodromes around Rome were occupied this was impossible.' He was wrong. Furbara and Cerveteri were free of Germans on 9 September, and in fact Guidonia was used by the Royal Italian Air Force without German interference until 12 September.

There was certainly a danger that Hitler would have bombed and caused severe damage in Rome, but he was conscious of neutral opinion and the consequent loss of life in Rome would have been less than the civilian losses during the year and a half in which the war raged up the whole length of Italy.

If the Americans had landed from the air, morale would have been high in the Italian Armoured Corps and American-Italian unity cemented. Italian troops would have fought far more enthusiastically to drive the Germans out of their home country than they had in North Africa or Russia. The Allied attitude to the peace terms, too, would have been less harsh if the Italians had made a major contribution in the first days of the Allied landings on the mainland of Europe.

Carboni's armoured corps, now left alone to defend Rome against Kesselring's two divisions, fought so successfully that it is clear they could have held Cerveteri and Furbara aerodromes for the four days which it would have taken 82nd Division to arrive in full strength. During this period German troops could not have reached Guidonia or Littoria aerodromes inland. Once the armoured corps, reinforced by the airborne Americans, had made a ring round Cerveteri and Furbara the nearby beaches would have been ideal for seaborne landings if the seaborne force could have been diverted to the north.

Numerically the Italians were stronger than the Germans. Carboni's corps consisted of four divisions – two armoured, Ariete and Centauro – one motorized infantry, Piave, plus the non-motorized Granatieri. On the evening of the 8th troop trains were bringing the infantry divisions Lupi and Re to the Rome area. In addition the low-quality Piacenza Division was deployed along the Tiber and the Rome-Ostia road towards the coast. Unfortunately it was mixed up hopelessly with Student's ferocious para units. Thinly spread out between Anzio and Fiumcino were two badly manned and poorly equipped coastal divisions. Inside Rome was the Sassari Division lately returned from Croatia but only fit for keeping public order. In total the Italians had about 75,000 soldiers against the Germans' 45,000.

Around Lake Bracciano north of Rome the Ariete Division faced

3rd Panzer. In command was the courageous General Cadorna, an outstanding Italian officer later to win fame with the partisans in Northern Italy. Ariete was the second edition of the armoured division of that name lost in North Africa, and Mussolini had given it the best of the latest Lancia armoured cars and the formidable Italian tanks produced by Fiat in Turin. Cadorna for two years had been head of the mounted cavalry and armour warfare school at Pinerolo, and when the division was re-formed on 1 April 1943 he was able to pick the cream of the officers recently trained at Pinerolo.

Ariete were capable of containing 3rd Panzer because they had their full establishment of 45P tanks with powerful 75mm guns, M13 tanks with 47mm guns, self-propelled 75s on M13 chassis, and plenty of mortars and machine-guns. They also had Lancia 269 armoured cars with 47mm guns, and four divisional workshops to keep all this armour in action. Their 135th Artillery Regiment had 149 field guns, and 235th had new self-propelled 105s – the most modern field gun in the Italian Army, although they arrived only the day before the battle. Ariete's crack Recce Regiment, Montebello, was the flower of Mussolini's remaining army. In fire power Ariete were a match for 3rd Panzer and they not only gave them a bloody nose, but they disengaged and withdrew almost without loss – a difficult manoeuvre during a battle.

In the early hours of 9 September intelligence reports made it clear Kesselring was not withdrawing but instead attacking the Italian troops around Rome. Roatta panicked. He told Badoglio that Rome could not be defended and that the Government must flee. At 5.10 a.m. the King, the Queen, the Crown Prince, Ambrosio and other Ministers fled from Rome towards Pescara on the east coast. Roatta soon followed, but first he saw Carboni and ordered him to send the Ariete Division and the motorized Piave Infantry Division to Tivoli south-east of Rome to cover their flight. These divisions were to be ready to move east for an eventual link up with the British Eighth Army – though in reality Badoglio only wanted them to cover the flight of the Government.[15]

Away from Rome, during the night of 8/9 September the Germans suddenly and brutally attacked the Italian Army all over the peninsula and in the Balkans. Most of the troops, taken by surprise and without orders from above, surrendered although the Navy and Air Force stood firm. By midday on 9 September, apart from the divisions around Rome and in Corsica, Sardinia and the Aegean islands, the Italian Army had virtually ceased to exist. Many Italian soldiers were shot or taken prisoner by the Germans; the majority, however, took the announcement of the armistice as a signal to go home as quickly as possible by train, bicycle or on foot.

When Badoglio decided the King and Government should leave Rome he intended originally to set up the War Office and the Government again at Chieti near the Adriatic port of Pescara. There were almost no German troops on the east coast, and there seemed a good chance of a quick link up with the British Eighth Army which had landed unopposed at Taranto. But when the Italian general staff reached Chieti reports of German attacks on Italian troops were so bad that Badoglio decided to summon the Italian corvette *Bayonette* to Ortogna to evacuate the King and Heads of Government to southern Italy. Here they would be protected by the Allied armies.

Under the terms of the armistice Mussolini was to be handed over to the Allies. He was interned in a ski hotel on the Gran Sasso not far from the royal party's line of escape, with no Germans near him, and he could easily have been collected and evacuated to the south with the King. However, with both Badoglio and the King ignoring this important clause of the armistice, Mussolini was shortly afterwards rescued by Hitler and forced to set up a puppet Government in the north of Italy. This failure of the Badoglio Government to comply with the armistice terms over Mussolini had unfortunate consequences both for the Allies and for the Royalist Government because Mussolini used his popularity and prestige to raise a new Fascist army in the north to aid the Germans. This army fought against both the Allies and the partisans, and produced civil war in Italy with heavy casualties on both sides.

The King would not agree to fly out. He was frightened that wherever he arrived in Southern Italy he might find the aerodrome under German control and that, with Fascists amongst the Italian Air Force pilots, once he was in the air he might be whirled away to the north into the hands of Hitler. The Queen had never flown and was scared of aeroplanes.

Late on 10 September the *Bayonette* with the King and Badoglio aboard docked at Brindisi; there were neither German nor Allied troops there, but Montgomery's Eighth Army was not far away to the south. As soon as the legal Government returned to Italian soil it tried to resume its constitutional role. There was not much it could do because four-fifths of Italy was occupied by the Germans.

On 11 September the Italian chiefs of staff sent out signals from Brindisi to the Italian armed forces everywhere: 'Treat Germans as enemies'. It was too late. It could have been a different story had Badoglio had the courage to act on 8 September, but on that night no orders were sent to the Italian Army commanders and they were quite unprepared for the German attacks on them.

The German High Command in Italy reported to Hitler on 14 September that they had completed their operations against the Italian Army, and claimed with reasonable accuracy that fifty-six divisions had been completely disarmed and twenty-nine partially, with the capture of 700,000 soldiers and an immense amount of war equipment.

In Rome the departure of the Government in the early hours of 9 September left a vacuum. Telephone calls from military headquarters asking whether or not they should fight the Germans were answered by junior staff officers who said 'We cannot help you, there is no one here.' The veteran Caviglia assumed power and on 10 September opened negotiations with the German commander; Rome was declared an open city and an armistice agreed under the terms of which the Italian divisions defending Rome were to be disarmed. General Cadorna handed over to the Germans row upon row of Ariete's modern tanks fresh from the Fiat works and the latest armoured cars from Lancia. If they had been sabotaged the Germans would have taken it as an excuse to shoot Italian soldiers. Now they were to be used against the Allies, whereas they should have been in action defending the Rome aerodromes and beaches for massive American landings.[16]

In Brindisi the King lodged in the historic Castle Svevo; Badoglio and his staff officers went to the best hotel – the International – and with the help of local government officials the Government tried to function in gloomy Admiralty buildings near the waterfront. When on 13 September Allied troops arrived from Taranto, the Italian officers had to evacuate the Hotel International because it was requisitioned for an Allied officers' transit camp. Allied Control Commission officers took up residence and the Badoglio Government found it was subject to the Allies on everything, including details of administration. Rigid Allied censorship of radio and press was introduced and there was an absurd row because a radio announcer referred to Victor Emmanuel as King of Albania and Emperor of Ethiopia.

Macmillan and Robert Murphy, the representatives of the British and American Governments, arrived at Brindisi on 14 September together with the former Governor of Gibraltar, General Noel Mason-Macfarlane, who was Head of the Allied Control Commission. Mason-Macfarlane was anti-Italian and thought Italian forces would be of minimal help to the Allies. He virtually ignored Victor Emmanuel, whom he described as 'ga ga', but Macmillan and Murphy with their greater experience of politics recognized that the King had masterminded the fall of Mussolini and were more sympathetic. Macmillan described him as 'a sad and querulous but probably rather obstinate old man'. He thought Crown Prince Umberto, on the other hand, could play 'a useful role'.

A formal meeting between Eisenhower and Badoglio was arranged for 29 September in Malta. Here Badoglio signed the humiliating long surrender terms – fortunately both for Italy and the Allies kept secret from the press. The King was already being attacked by Fascist sympathizers for accepting dishonourable terms, against which Macmillan and Eisenhower had protested in vain. However, Eisenhower softened the blow for Badoglio by giving him a letter stating the terms would be modified according to the extent of the military cooperation given by the Italians in the war against Hitler. Macmillan was particularly bitter against 'unconditional surrender' in the long armistice and said afterwards how he had 'disliked the procedure in Malta which we were forced to go through'.

Eisenhower pressed Badoglio to declare war on Germany with the argument that the more Italian troops contributed to the war effort the more generous would be the eventual peace terms. Badoglio replied that declaring war was the King's prerogative, and as yet the King was against it, but back in Brindisi he persuaded a reluctant Victor Emmanuel to declare war on Germany on 12 October, and Italy was granted the status of co-belligerent. But as the Foreign Office unhelpfully pointed out she was still technically at war with the Allies. Two days later Alexander agreed that an Italian division could go into the line.

In the Commons awkward questions were put about complicity by Ambrosio and Roatta in Jugoslavian war atrocities. Roatta had indisputably given orders to destroy all houses and villages within half a mile of the oil pipeline from Rumania in September 1942. Both were sacked. Badoglio asked for Field-Marshal Messe, a prisoner of war in Britain, to take Ambrosio's place, and he, General Orlando and General Berardi were released and flown back to Italy to try to put some spirit into a new Royalist army.

Soon a sharp conflict between the Americans and the British arose over the Italian Government. Churchill wanted to retain the monarchy with or without Victor Emmanuel because it was a 'unifying factor'. Roosevelt was determined to oust the King because he considered him unpopular with the Italian voters who were important in the coming Presidential elections.

Victor Emmanuel wanted to bring Grandi into the Government but this was vetoed by the Americans although his initiative had been decisive in bringing down Mussolini. Instead Roosevelt added to the King's problems – and in the event to the Allies – by sending back to Italy the eccentric and controversial Count Sforza. He was the leading anti-Fascist personality in the United States and his views had received great publicity there during the war. Roosevelt thought Sforza's support would be a help to him in the elections. Sforza, aged seventy-one had been Foreign Minister in the Gioliti Government in 1919 and 1920, and Italian Ambassador in London until Mussolini came to power. He had remained a Senator until 1927 but then removed himself from Mussolini's clutches by leaving the country. Since 1940 he had enjoyed a special position in the United States as the spokesman of the Italian opposition to the war.

The Foreign Office objected to Sforza's return because he was anti-Badoglio and hostile to Victor Emmanuel. The Prime Minister yielding to Roosevelt's persuasion overruled them and so en route for Italy Sforza stopped off in London on 11 October and had interviews with both Churchill and Eden. Both were disastrous. Churchill described him as 'a useless ga-ga politician whose hostility to the House of Savoy and whose republicanism arises because he sees himself as representative of the House of Milan,' and as 'a foolish played-out old man incapable of facing, let alone riding, the storm; the old fool wants to be king himself.' The Foreign Office had to explain Sforza was not a claimant to the throne, and the Savoy family had not 'jockeyed' the Sforzas of Milan out of power. In any case the Count did not claim direct descent from the Sforza family who had at one time ruled Milan. As Sforza flew out to Naples to stir up as much trouble as possible, Churchill cabled Macmillan: 'Badoglio is the only solid peg, we must hang on to him'; and he repeated his derisory comments.

In response to repeated requests from Roosevelt, Macmillan and Murphy told the King and Badoglio they must broaden the Italian Government. Badoglio offered to resign, and asked the King to abdicate in favour of either Umberto or his grandson aged six. Victor Emmanuel refused and went to Naples to see what surviving politicians were available there from Italy's democratic days twenty-one years earlier. The philosopher Benedetto Croce was the most influential but he refused to join the Government unless the King abdicated. Without Croce's lead no one would serve. One man refused because of fears of reprisals on his family, who were living in Rome. Sforza contemptuously refused even to see the King.

Nevertheless Victor Emmanuel offered Sforza the post of Prime Minister, which he declined. Sforza was frightened of the rising tide of Communism and believed the monarchy and the Italian constitution could only be saved by the King abdicating in favour of his grandson. He told Macmillan in an interview that the Crown Prince Umberto was 'degenerate, weak and dissipated'. Macmillan took the view that Sforza obviously wanted to be Prime Minister with Badoglio a figurehead as Regent.

Sforza sent via Algiers an impudent, ill-written and badly typed letter in English to Eden proposing himself as Badoglio's successor and suggesting the King should abdicate. Although Roger Makins head of Macmillan's office in Algiers, did not think the letter was worth sending on to the Foreign Secretary, it eventually reached the Prime Minister. He cabled to Sforza: 'I am sorry to see how much trouble you are making. You must not count on any support from me.' Cadogan minuted: 'This slap at old Sforza gives me considerable pleasure.'[17]

Meanwhile the division between Churchill and Roosevelt over the Italian Government became more acute. Macmillan advised the Prime Minister that the King's abdication might have an adverse effect on the morale of the Italian servicemen who were helping the Allies. On 4 November Churchill signalled to Macmillan warning against breaking down Badoglio or the King, and two days later he sent a similar message to Roosevelt, adding: 'Sforza will not make Italians fight.' Eisenhower agreed with Churchill, but Roosevelt was determined to topple Victor Emmanuel. However, the Italian Government's position was strengthened when a message came from the six political parties (including the Socialists and Communists), meeting underground in Rome, that they would support Badoglio as military chief if the Government were broadened and elections held after Rome was occupied. At Victor Emmanuel's request Badoglio agreed to withdraw his resignation. On a minute by Cadogan that the King and Badoglio must continue in Government, Churchill wrote: 'First rate' on 6 November, and cabled Roosevelt that

We ought not to countenance any change in Badoglio and King regime . . . Why weaken British and USA soldiers on march to Rome? . . . VE and Badoglio did deliver the Italian fleet and hold the loyalties of large part of the Italian army. Ike inclines to this view.[18]

On 20 January 1944 the first democratic convention since the coming to power of Fascism was scheduled to take place in Bari. Unfortunately the Foreign Office in London only heard about it through the press; Churchill and Eden were furious. On 24 January the Prime Minister demanded that it should be postponed, Eden did his best to get Macmillan to order it not to take place, but eventually it started on 30 January.

It was opened by Croce. Sforza was hysterical against the Government and the King and made a bad impression on the Allied observers, who reported to the Foreign Office that he was 'a trimmer and egotistical windbag'. The conference asked for the King's abdication, called for an all-party Government and appointed a Giunta of aged politicians as an advisory body. Sforza and Croce refused to be members of the Giunta, claiming their 'steadying influence' would be greater outside.

Eden was not pleased at this effort by the Italians at democratic government. He once again betrayed his dislike of Italy by minuting: 'I foresee much trouble with so-called Italian democrats . . . they will claim to escape from all penalties imposed upon King and Badoglio and there is no reason why they should.' Churchill minuted that it would be a disaster if either Croce or Sforza emerged as Prime Minister and 'we lost Badoglio'.[19]

By now it was clear that the Anzio operation was a failure, and with the Germans holding out at Cassino the liberation of Rome was some time off.[c] Roosevelt grew impatient and without consulting Churchill sent a signal to the US representatives on the Allied Control Commission: 'Liberal forces must set up a new Government without Victor Emmanuel.' Cadogan minuted that this bypassing of London was 'amazing'. However, Churchill was firm that the Italian Government must be left alone and reminded Roosevelt how the agreement with Darlan in Algiers had saved many Allied lives.[d] He argued: 'The Italian Army and Navy are cooperating with us and obeying our orders. If you get in new Liberals they may argue with us. A new regime could be a rod for our backs.'

On 12 February Washington and London agreed on no change, although the Giunta had appealed publicly for dismissal of the King and Badoglio. By now Eisenhower had departed to England to take command of the Second Front forces; Murphy had been recalled to

[c]The Allies had made a powerful landing at Anzio a few miles south of Rome at the end of January 1944. Their march to Rome had been halted by the Germans on a line running through Cassino. At first the Anzio landing was successful and it looked as if Rome must fall. But the German defence was so determined that the Allies could not break out. Rome did not fall until June.

[d]Admiral Darlan, a Vichy supporter, unexpectedly agreed to the unopposed entry of Allied troops into Algiers on 8 November 1942.

Washington for consultation, and Eisenhower's replacement as GOC AFHQ, General Maitland Wilson, wanted Umberto to take over from his father, thinking it would be good for the morale of the Italian forces. On 21 February the War Cabinet decided 'No change'. The Prime Minister scolded Wilson for suggesting Umberto and said: 'Wait until you reach Rome. Do not give in to blackmail from Giunta who have no standing.'

Roosevelt tried again and told Wilson the King must go. Churchill contradicted him and told the President he feared a Gaullist situation might replace a tame and helpful Government. Meanwhile the Russians strengthened the King's hand by offering to exchange Ambassadors. Badoglio immediately accepted, to the irritation of the British and Americans who said he had no right to do so without their approval.

In the first week of April Murphy returned from the United States after three months in Washington. He had strict instructions from the President to get rid of the King. On 8 April Churchill yielded and told Macmillan he agreed the King might abdicate in favour of his son provided Sforza was kept out of the highest office. Accordingly Murphy and Macmillan went to see the King in Brindisi. He pretended not to know why they had come, and refused to abdicate. The next day, after long argument and an emotional scene with tears from Badoglio, the King agreed to abdicate on the day Rome was liberated. Then Umberto would become Lieutenant-General of the Realm and commence his rule – not exactly what Roosevelt wanted, but near enough.

The Allies now began to consider a preliminary peace treaty with the Badoglio Government. Badoglio asked for Allied status and to be allowed to adhere to the Atlantic Charter. Eden minuted: 'Not that one please,' but Sargent made the constructive proposals that the Allied aims in Italy must be: (1) to check Communism; (2) to re-create a friendly Italy; (3) to mobilize Italian war resources.

Prospects for a favourable peace treaty were good until unexpected political events took place when Rome was liberated on 4 June 1944, thirty-six hours before D Day in Normandy. The Allied Commander, General Mark Clark, said there would be grave risk of assassination if the King went to Rome, but surprisingly claimed Umberto would be safe. So when at Ravello near Naples on 5 June Victor Emmanuel asked Mason-Macfarlane for an aeroplane to fly him to Rome, Mason-Macfarlane with scant courtesy refused (Macmillan had told him to fly the King to Algiers if he caused trouble). Then, sadly, the

King signed his decree of abdication in favour of his son. Umberto and Badoglio, without the King, flew to Rome with Mason-Macfarlane.

Then the unpredictable Italian politicians put such spokes in the wheels that an early peace treaty was ruled out. At the Grand Hotel in Rome on 8 June all the leaders of the six democratic parties who had been operating underground in German-occupied Rome (including De Gasperi and Nenni, the Trade Unionist), assembled together with Badoglio's Ministers. After a harangue by Mason-Macfarlane Badoglio formally handed back his mandate to Umberto. Badoglio continued: 'I have been asked by the ruler to stay in office.' He was roughly interrupted and told that the new Government must be led by an anti-Fascist of long standing who should be a new man, Bonomi. Badoglio was dumbfounded. He turned to Togliatti, the Communist leader, who confirmed the Communist party were in complete agreement with the other political parties about this. Recovering his dignity Badoglio said: 'I have given to Italy everything I have, and I hand over willingly to my friend Bonomi.'

Umberto was now installed in the Royal Palace on the Quirinal. On 10 June the new Government was formally presented to him. Bonomi had already had a haggle with Umberto over the words of the new oath of allegiance to the crown – always of importance to the House of Savoy.

Then Mason-Macfarlane, who that morning had already vetoed Sforza as Foreign Secretary and accepted him only as Minister Without Portfolio, inflicted another humiliation on the Italians. He told them the new Government must not function in Rome. It must go back to Salerno.

Churchill was furious at the sacking of Badoglio. General Clark had not allowed the British Ambassador, Sir Noel Charles, to go to Rome and Churchill blamed Charles for accepting the ban and instead allowing Mason-Macfarlane to take charge of operations in Rome and to have 'connived helplessly in Badoglio's dismissal'. The Prime Minister said Italy was a conquered country and had no right to form whatever Government she pleased. He told the President that it was 'disastrous' that Badoglio had been replaced by a group of 'aged and hungry politicians'. He told Stalin: 'We have lost the only competent man with whom we could deal.' This certainly was not the view of the Allies' representatives who had to deal with Badoglio, one of whom had recorded 'He only ticks before lunch.'

The Prime Minister complained to Cadogan that 'this has been bungled by that old woman Mason-Macfarlane', but on 14 June 1944

Roosevelt told Churchill 'The Bonomi Cabinet should be installed without delay.' Compliantly Churchill decided to recognize the Bonomi Government on 17 June and Italy was officially at peace with the Allies under a Government of her own choosing.[20]

Mason-Macfarlane was dismissed by Churchill for his part in the making of the Government on the ostensible grounds of ill health – only to take his revenge by returning to public life twelve months later as Labour MP for Paddington where he unseated Churchill's crony Brendan Bracken by a surprisingly large majority.

9

Unconditional Surrender
1943–1945

On 21 June 1940 Hitler signed an armistice with the defeated French now led by Pétain. The terms were diabolically clever. Hitler persuaded Mussolini to postpone Italian territorial claims on France; only the northern part of France was to be occupied by German troops, and the French could keep their fleet. There were none of the humiliating terms imposed by the Allies on Germany in 1918. Hitler appeared deceptively mild.

The bulk of the French nation accepted the armistice with immense relief and Flandin, Pétain's Foreign Minister, claims there was almost unanimous consent. At the Pétain trial after the war Paul Reynaud, who preferred to resign as Premier rather than surrender, testified that the majority of Frenchmen would have voted for Pétain and the armistice if a referendum had been held.[1]

Churchill was determined to scotch any move for a similar compromise peace with Britain which he knew exerted a powerful attraction for Chamberlain, Halifax, Butler, Lloyd George and a number of MPs. At the secret session of the Commons on 26 June Churchill was strongly pressed by MPs to give assurances in his own words that 'we would fight on until the death'. He gave those assurances, and the country and Parliament rallied to him.

A continuation of the war with Britain was most unwelcome to Hitler. He was worried by the Soviet threat in the east, and especially by the danger to his oil supply if Rumania was in hostile hands. By 1 July he had almost decided on a Russian campaign, and ordered Jodl's staff to prepare a study on operations against Russia. At this stage Hitler found it hard to believe Britain would not negotiate peace terms. An illustration of opinion in Berlin at that period is an entry in the anti-Nazi Weizsaecker's diaries in July 1940: 'Churchill resistance is not logical but psychological. He has gone out on a limb and cannot get back.'[2]

For a short time Hitler contemplated invasion of Britain. On 16 July the Adolf Hitler Directive No. 16 read: 'Since England despite her hopeless military situation shows no sign of willingness to come to terms I have decided to prepare a landing operation. The aim of the operation is to eliminate the English homeland.' First, however, the Luftwaffe had to establish air superiority, and the German navy had to wall off the invasion waters with mines. Both operations failed. Germany lost the air war in the Battle of Britain and the invasion scheduled for August was cancelled.[3]

Not surprisingly approaches for a negotiated peace after the fall of France soon came from official German sources. At the end of June 1940 Attolico, the Italian Ambassador to Berlin, contacted the American Chargé d'Affaires there and suggested that the United States should act as intermediary. Hints on similar lines were put out in other European capitals. Then Lovell, a prominent New York Quaker, sent a message to Lord Lothian, the British Ambassador to the United States, from the German Chargé d'Affaires in Washington that he would communicate German peace terms and that Hitler, although certain England was defeated, did not want to destroy the British Empire. The Germans for propaganda purposes tried to insinuate that Lothian had taken this initiative. Churchill ordered Halifax not to reply to either overture.

On 19 July Hitler in a speech to the Reichstag said the war might continue for a long time, and that Britain should accept defeat and ask for terms. Halifax replied that Britain would not stop fighting until freedom for herself and others had been secured.

In August the King of Sweden sent a telegram to King George VI offering his good offices. Nothing came of it. Indeed it outraged Churchill, because the Swedish Monarch had already shown himself pro-German. In July 1940, through Dr Salazar, Prince Max Hohenlohe and the Finnish Prime Minister, messages arrived that Hitler wanted a working arrangement between Germany and the British Empire. With Hitler's complete military victory on the Continent his terms had hardened. No longer was there any mention of an independent state in Czechoslovakia or Poland.

In September 1940, when Hitler's hopes of invading England had vanished and he had secretly decided to attack Russia, he initiated further peace overtures through Stockholm involving Weissauer, a well-known Berlin lawyer, and Eckberg, the President of the High Court of Sweden. Hitler proposed through Weissauer that 'the political independence of the European countries occupied by Germany would be restored excluding Czechoslovakia'. He said nothing about Italian claims; Mussolini was very much a junior partner.

On 9 September Mallet signalled to London that Weissauer and Eckberg had made it clear Hitler offered to create a world divided into two economic spheres – one Continental, dominated by Germany, the other maritime and colonial dominated by the British Empire and the United States. According to Mallet, if Britain gave no reply it would be taken by Berlin as a definite refusal. Probably as a sop to the Swedes, who were desperately anxious for peace negotiations, Mallet was allowed to send a long message to Eckberg. This stated that the British attitude to German peace offers was still that of Chamberlain's speech in the House of Commons on 12 October 1939, and

our intention to prosecute the war had been strengthened by the many horrible crimes committed by the rulers of Nazi Germany against the smaller states on her border and by the indiscriminate bombing of London. It lay with Germany to make proposals to redress the wrongs inflicted on other nations and to give effective guarantees by deeds and not words that Germany could in a general peace restore freedom to France and the other countries which had been deprived of it.

Weissauer replied that he would take the reply as a temporary refusal but he wanted to 'keep the channel open'. That did not appeal to Churchill and no further message was sent to Weissauer through Eckberg.[4]

From overtures to British diplomats in neutral countries it became clear that Hitler hoped that the Allies would give up fighting and endorse his plan of a so called 'peaceful' German hegemony over Europe which would be agreed by Vichy and the Quislings[a] and the few remaining neutral and independent states in Europe.

The Foreign Office interpreted Hitler's offers as a bid for a short breathing space which would be followed by further German aggression and brutality all over Europe. Accordingly the War Cabinet decided they were not interested in the German 'New Order' or any peace offer from Hitler. Churchill made this crystal clear in a speech at the Mansion House on 10 November 1940.

There were no more important approaches from Hitler during the winter of 1940–41, but on 17 February 1941 a message came from Matsuoka, Japanese Minister of Foreign Affairs, offering to 'act as mediator' not only in Greater East Asia, but 'anywhere the world over'. The Foreign Office saw this as a move to slow up British Far East defence preparations. The Prime Minister replied that 'there could be no question of compromise or parley'.[5]

[a]The pro-German faction in Norway, named after their leader.

Meanwhile anti-Nazis and a section of the German Army in favour of peace continued actively to plot the overthrow of Hitler. Their influence had been greatly diminished by Hitler's success in the Low Countries and France, but as the Army learnt about Hitler's plans to attack Russia, some of the Generals who had previously supported Hitler encouraged the conspirators because they thought a reckless move like the Russian adventure must lead Germany to disaster. They wanted a compromise peace accompanied by the removal of Hitler and the replacement of the Nazis by a moderate democratic Government which would retain part of Hitler's conquests. As a result the Foreign Office denigrated them for wanting a greater Germany, although if Britain had been ready to bribe Hitler with the Sudetenland and parts of Poland it seems illogical to have insisted that a liberal democratic Germany should be confined to the Versailles frontiers, since this would have made it almost impossible for them to obtain popular support.

On 14 April 1941 a lengthy document summarizing all the peace feelers since the start of the war was circulated to the War Cabinet by the Foreign Office:

. . . In nearly all these overtures Goering was alleged to be either the prime mover or at least an interested party. It was he, according to the Swede Dahlerus, who hoped to negotiate an honourable settlement after the fall of Poland and to replace Hitler as the real ruler of Germany once peace was signed . . . The other principal element alleged to be in favour of peace was a section of the German Army. These gentlemen were said to fear the outcome of the pact with the Soviet Union and to favour a peace of compromise accompanied by the removal of Hitler . . . They never suggested, however, any detailed basis for discussion, and they never afforded any evidence of their ability to carry out such terms as might be agreed . . . It seems clear however that their influence was greatly overstated by the emissaries, . . . all the proposals amounted to suggesting that we should purchase peace at the sacrifice of the cause for which we had taken up arms. In fact if the various moves are considered together and not in isolation they appear suspiciously like elements in a grand propaganda design aimed principally at testing the strength of the peace school in England and at sowing the seeds of doubt in our minds and in the minds of the less stalwart neutrals.[6]

With hindsight it is clear that this Foreign Office report was completely wrong about the genuine anti-Nazis, but faced with such an attitude from the Foreign Office anti-Nazi conspirators could hope for little from Britain. Not surprisingly a genuine effort in September 1940 by Wirth, a former German Chancellor, and Gessler, Defence Minister during the Weimar Republic, foundered.[7]

Wirth had fled from Nazi Germany and was living in Switzerland – with the unhelpful reputation of being an alcoholic. On 1 September 1940 he told the British Military Attaché in Berne that the German Army had recognized 'the first serious check in Hitler's succession of victories', and that war between Germany and Russia was inevitable in the spring.

On 5 September Wirth saw a Foreign Office official, Leigh Smith, and told him he was making an approach on behalf of the German General Staff and not for Hitler, and asked if he could be given a visa to go to London. Wirth told him that Gessler's group included Brauchitsch and other members of the old General Staff as opposed to Hitler's new 'private General Staff' of Keitel and Jodl. He confirmed that Gessler's group had had a setback because of Hitler's victories in May 1940. He also rashly said that he thought Germany should retain the Channel ports from Dunkirk to Boulogne for a period of years, and a free hand in the east, 'although he indicated they might be prepared to bargain'. This part of the conversation may have been misconstrued according to German accounts published after the war, but it made an abysmal impression in the Foreign Office.

The Foreign Office ordered their Berne representative not to give Wirth a visa for London, and told him that there was every reason to believe Wirth was being used by Hitler. We now know that Wirth was acting on behalf of the conspirators who eventually exploded the bomb on 20 July 1944, and encouragement of Gessler and Wirth would have been well worth while.[8]

Hitler made no further direct offers of peace such as he had made after his lightning Polish campaign and the collapse of France. Nor did the British Government at first see fit to publish their war aims; they were, after all, fighting for existence. Until there was some real prospect of an Allied victory it would have been ridiculous to lay down the geography of postwar Europe. Churchill told his intimates that he was sure that the United States would enter the war and there should be no discussion of terms until America was a belligerent.

With Hitler's abandonment of the invasion of Britain and the partial failure of his attack on Russia, which began on 22 June 1941, the outlook for the Allies improved sharply. Churchill met Roosevelt in August 1941 in Newfoundland and agreed the Anglo-US aims which became known as the Atlantic Charter. This had eight points and considerable popular appeal. Paticularly attractive were points One to Three which precluded 'aggrandizement' by Britain or the United States, or territorial changes against the wishes of the people, and allowed the right of all nations to choose their own form of government. Article Four was a welcome declaration of intent to remove tariff barriers to trade. Five and Six were pious hopes of a worldwide improvement in living standards. Seven was freedom of the seas, and Eight was general disarmament after the war. The Charter led to the setting up of the United Nations Organization in January 1942, and in 1941 it filled the vacuum over Britain's war aims, encouraging the German resistance to feel that the Allies would treat a new liberal German Government generously if they overthrew the Nazi regime and made peace.

Meanwhile the German opposition, temporarily tamed by Hitler's success in 1940, increased their activities and continued to contact British diplomats in neutral capitals. Churchill insisted, however, against the Foreign Office's advice, that the policy should be 'absolute silence': no reply should be made to any overtures, whether they emanated from 'good Germans' opposed to Nazism or from Hitler himself. This was a serious mistake.

At the end of December 1940 Churchill had been sent by the Foreign Office copies of two telegrams from Berne concerning peace enquiries by a Swede on behalf of Goering. He replied brusquely to Eden:

I presume you are keeping your eye on all this. Your predecessor was entirely misled in December 1939. Our attitude towards all such enquiries should be absolute silence. It may well be that the new offensive will open upon us as an alternative to threats of invasion and poison gas.[9]

The reference to December 1939 is to Halifax having authorized Best, a secret service agent, to meet German representatives at Venlo on the Dutch frontier where Best and his companions were abducted. Eden accepted without demur (and without consulting his staff) the order for 'absolute silence'.

At the instigation of the Foreign Office Eden made a lukewarm request to Churchill for permission to respond to German peace feelers on 10 September 1941. He wrote:

You will remember that our attitude towards all enquiries and suggestions concerning peace feelers is at present absolute silence. In the last two months there has been a recrudescence of such feelers:
(a) In July a message was sent by Herr Goerdeler to S.I.S. agent in Switzerland (former burgomaster of Leipzig) suggesting negotiations in Switzerland. Goerdeler claims to be in touch with a group of German Generals headed by Generals Halder and Blakowitz [sic]. We have had messages from him before and are not disposed to trust him.

(b) In August Berne was authorised to transmit a communication from a Dr. Schultze of Zurich to Archbishop of York. This contained a proposal for peace negotiations made on behalf of an undisclosed group of allegedly moderate and influential Germans based on the elimination of the Nazi regime. I have not passed on this message to the Archbishop.

(c) At the end of August a proposal was received through underground channels at Stockholm for negotiations on behalf of a representative and influential opposition movement in Germany known as the Free Reconstruction Movement. This Movement was said to accept all the eight points of the Atlantic Charter except Point 8 which could be basis for negotiation. It was suggested that negotiations should be opened in Sweden with an emissary of the British Government. The S.I.S. consider this to be a genuine approach.

(d) On 6 September a message was received from Dr. Kurdt Schmidt, former Finance Minister in Germany in the early days of the Nazi regime, through a Swedish industrialist saying that conditions in Germany were serious and that he was authorised by Goering to bring over to Sweden the peace terms which Goering now subscribed and to endeavour to communicate them privately to the British authorities.

These overtures acquire rather more significance from the fact: (1) that we have had indication from secret source that some of the leading Generals are beginning to think that it is time to reinsure. (2) That Goering is very despondent about the situation.

I do not think that we should show any interest in these approaches or authorise any British subject to meet any German emissary. But what would you think of authorising in cases (c) and (d) the acceptance of a neutral intermediary? Such messages occasionally throw interesting light on internal difficulties and tendencies in Germany. This, however, is the furthest that I would go.

The Prime Minister replied categorically:

I am sure we should not depart from our policy of absolute silence. Nothing would be more disturbing to our friends in the United States or more dangerous with our new ally, Russia, than the suggestion that we were entertaining such ideas. I am absolutely opposed to the slightest contact.

On the minute Eden noted:

I do agree and am in fact relieved at your decision. The case in favour was, I thought, worth a mention.   A.E.[10]

Churchill penned on Eden's minute: 'Please keep'. Clearly he wanted to make sure that the Foreign Office did not backpedal on his decision that there should be 'absolute silence', and he bears a heavy responsibility for refusing to encourage the anti-Nazi German patriots who might have been able to bring the war to an end. But Eden was weak in the way he failed to press his Department view in face of the Prime Minister's arbitrary judgement.

Why Eden refused to pass on the message to the Archbishop of York[b] is inexplicable. No conceivable harm to the war effort nor the chance of peace could have resulted. His statement that the Foreign Office were not disposed to trust Goerdeler is also difficult to explain. It was not the view of the Department. After all, Goerdeler had made approaches which Cadogan regarded as genuine in Halifax's day. Eden's suggestion that he should respond to the Goering approach but not to Goerdeler's is strange in view of Cadogan's enthusiasm for Goerdeler in 1938.

Sir Frank Roberts told the author that Vansittart had strong contacts with Goerdeler through neutral embassies and

We in the Department did not like 'absolute silence' in response to peace overtures. We felt it was better to go on talking as it would have given us a lot of information. Eden did not bother much about this. We felt it was better to know what was going on.[11]

'Absolute silence' in response to German peace overtures, whether from the German Government or the anti-Nazis, remained the inflexible rule regardless of glittering opportunities being thrown away. For those German patriots plotting to overthrow Hitler and end the war with a compromise peace, there was worse to come.

At his final press conference at the Casablanca Anglo-American Conference on 24 January 1943, Roosevelt announced

Peace can come only by the total elimination of German and Japanese war power . . . elimination of German, Japanese and Italian war power means unconditional surrender by Germany, Italy and Japan. It does not mean the destruction of the population of Germany, Italy and Japan, but destruction of the philosophies in these countries based on conquest and subjugation of other people.[12]

The impact of the words 'unconditional surrender' was disastrous. Goebbels used his propaganda machine skilfully to convince the German people that it was better to continue the war than suffer the horrible privations which would follow unconditional surrender to the Allies.

Many historians conclude that unconditional surrender was a sudden improvisation by Roosevelt. This is incorrect.[13] Roosevelt had worked out the idea in advance, and as Roberts put it to the author:

[b]William Temple. He became Archbishop of Canterbury in 1942.

I think unconditional surrender was originally entirely a Roosevelt idea originating in the end of the American Civil War which he knew would have romantic associations for Winston. Winston felt he must agree because there were so many other issues on which he and Roosevelt were at variance.

In addition there was a general feeling prevalent then that this time Germany must be completely defeated so there would be no repetition of the 1918 legend that the German disaster came from a stab in the back from German socialists, and that this time we should just substitute anti Nazis. At that time, rightly or wrongly, there was little confidence in either Churchill's or Eden's mind that any conceivable German opposition who might have been attracted by the prospect of terms other than 'unconditional surrender' either would or could deliver the goods.

Last but not least, the slogan was thought likely to appeal to Stalin as proof of our toughness and as removing from his suspicious mind the concept that we might want to do a deal with non communist Germany at his expense, and so tempt him to do his own deal as in 1939 with Hitler.[14]

William Cavendish-Bentinck held a senior position in the Foreign Office in 1943 as Adviser to Director of Plans for War. He told the author:

When news of the unconditional surrender formula came through from Casablanca I told Cadogan 'There are two old men out there who have done this without thinking while they were full up with rough red Moroccan wine.' Later my view was that this formula (unconditional surrender) did make the Germans fight harder; on the other hand unconditional surrender led to the complete break-up of the German officer corps and to their being absolutely discredited.

After the First War the spirit of the army remained in Germany. This would have happened after the Second War had it not been for unconditional surrender. If the spirit of the army had remained we would soon have found the German General Staff coming to terms with the Russians, which would have been worse than the present situation. I was not keen on the German Generals and if there had been a Goerdeler Government after the 20 July bomb plot, the Generals would have held the trump cards.[15]

Although the idea was Roosevelt's, Churchill became keener on it than the American President. He would not tolerate any departure from the principle. Yet he faltered in August 1943. A telegram came from the British Ambassador in Ankara, Sir Hughe Knatchbull-Hugessen, that von Papen[c] had told the Turkish Minister of Foreign Affairs that he expected to be summoned to Berlin to replace Ribbentrop and he was considering the possibilities of an approach to the Allies. Hugessen's telegram continued:

[c]German Ambassador in Turkey.

I told Minister for Foreign Affairs that my information was that, in view of Papen's past record, we were not prepared to listen to advances either through or from him and I went on to speak in the sense of Sir O. Sargent's letter to me of May 7th. I added that moreover our terms were unconditional surrender.

Much to the Department's surprise the Prime Minister suddenly blew cold on 'unconditional surrender' and on reading the file minuted to Eden:

FOREIGN SECRETARY   10 Downing Street,
                                                          Whitehall.

All this is quite true, but it might better have been left unsaid. The displacement of Ribbentrop would be a milestone of importance and would probably lead to further disintegration of the Nazi machine. There is no need for us to discourage this process by continually uttering the slogan 'Unconditional Surrender'. As long as we do not have to commit ourselves to dealing with any particular new figure or new Government our advantage is clear. We certainly do not want, if we can help it, to get them all fused together in a solid desperate block for whom there is no hope. I am sure you will agree with me that a gradual break up in Germany must mean a weakening of their resistance, and consequently the saving of hundreds of thousands of British and American lives.   W.C.   14.8.43.

This minute by Churchill is in dramatic contrast to his insistence on unconditional surrender for the rest of the war. It raised hopes in the Foreign Office that there might be some relaxation of the hard line on 'absolute silence' and peace terms, as the following minutes show:

PEACE APPROACH BY VON PAPEN

Minutes

This raises an important question of principle. Hitherto, the guidance given to our Missions abroad, and more particularly to those in posts where peace feelers are likely, has been to stress unconditional surrender quite bluntly. This has, however, already given rise to difficulties in dealing with Italian peace feelers, e.g. at Lisbon, Madrid and Tangier, and various ingenious formulae have been found which mean unconditional surrender without laying too much stress on the actual words. It would appear from the Prime Minister's directive that similar elasticity should also be adopted in regard to German and other feelers. I submit, therefore, that a circular telegram of guidance in the sense of the Prime Minister's minute should be sent to Lisbon, Madrid, Tangier, Ankara, Berne and Stockholm with an explanation to Washington and Moscow.

F.K. ROBERTS
27 August, 1943

Our representatives will be puzzled by the terms of this circular if it is sent.

Would it not be better to let this matter lie? If we get any genuine approach from Germany we shall know how to deal with it, and there is no risk of any of our representatives not passing it on to us if they get one. If the Germans mean to make an approach they will not be deterred by what H.M. Ambassador at Angora [*sic* — Ankara] said about Papen. (Incidentally, we approved his language – C 9134.)

W. STRANG

13/9[16]

Roberts confirmed to the author that in the Department, in addition to being opposed to 'absolute silence', they were also against unconditional surrender. He said Cadogan was particularly strong about this, and Eden did from time to time represent their point of view to the Prime Minister 'but without any force'. He added: 'In my view we were ham handed over unconditional surrender.'[17]

Any hopes aroused among Foreign Office officials by Churchill's minute of the 14 August were short-lived. Eden took little interest and Churchill soon changed his mind.

The three Allied Foreign Ministers met at the Moscow Conference which started on 19 October 1943. They were Cordell Hull, Eden and Molotov. Unconditional surrender was reaffirmed. Yet at the Teheran Conference on 28 November 1943 Stalin expressed the view that unconditional surrender was bad tactics *vis-à-vis* Germany, and suggested that Germany would be more likely to yield if terms of surrender were worked out and made generally known to the German people. Stalin probably had no intention of sticking to any conditions he announced in advance; he just thought it would weaken the German will to fight. Work was begun on a draft; but nothing materialized.[18]

Strong evidence that unconditional surrender was stiffening German morale soon reached the Foreign Office and War Office. In December 1943 the War Cabinet considered a report from the Intelligence Sub-Committee which concluded:

Formula of unconditional surrender as interpreted by Nazi propaganda in default of any explanation by the United Nations is having a big effect in making the Germans afraid of the consequences of defeat to themselves individually and collectively . . . Germans are afraid unconditional surrender means they can expect no mercy from the United Nations; that Germany to the accompaniment of all sorts of horrors would disappear as a nation; they and their leaders must stand together or else both face disaster; there is ample evidence that the propaganda is having some success, particularly amongst the uneducated masses . . . industrialists, bankers and senior civil servants fear not so much the elimination of the Nazi regime to which they do not feel themselves committed, as that it would lead to the destruction of the entire social and economic structure of Germany.[19]

This report, compiled by German experts from newspapers and other evidence culled in neutral countries, was absolutely correct. The effect of unconditional surrender on anti-Nazis desperately trying to recruit for their conspiracy to overthrow Hitler was disastrous. Allen Dulles (brother of John Foster Dulles), who was the most knowledgeable US diplomat on the Resistance, wrote after the war: 'Goebbels quickly coined the telling phrase "total slavery" and very largely succeeded in making the German people believe that was what unconditional surrender meant.' According to the diary of the anti-Nazi German diplomat Hassell, the conspirators were convinced the unconditional surrender formula 'jeopardized and possibly destroyed six years of work by the anti-Nazi opposition'.[20]

Although Churchill and Eden ignored any evidence that the policy might be flawed, Eisenhower, as soon as he took over command of the forces for the cross-Channel invasion on 1 January 1944, demanded that he should be allowed to present the German forces opposing him with a much more attractive picture of the scenario after surrender. Churchill turned down Eisenhower's suggestion categorically. Yet Sir John Colville told the author that Churchill was never vindictive to the German people when talking of plans for the postwar era. Clearly he concluded that if we set out terms they would be so tough that they would either give more scope to Goebbels's propaganda that the Allies would treat Germany with cruelty or they would be false because Stalin would not abide by them. Then Germany after the war could allege they had been betrayed by false promises as in 1918.[21]

This is Churchill's note circulated to the War Cabinet on 15 January 1944 designed to pre-empt any more controversy:

WAR CABINET

Unconditional Surrender

Note by the Prime Minister

1. The expression 'Unconditional Surrender' was used by the President at Casablanca without previous consultation but I thought it right to endorse what he said, and it may well be that at that period of the war the declaration was appropriate to the circumstances.

2. By 'Unconditional Surrender' I mean that the Germans have thereafter no *rights* to any particular form of treatment. For instance, the Atlantic Charter would not apply to them as *a matter of right*. On the other hand, the victorious nations owe it to themselves to observe the obligations of

humanity and civilisation. The statement by the President in his telegram to me, No. 436 of the 6th January, is a very good popular rendering of this conception. See also my remarks at the Guildhall on the same subject.

3. The question is, whether we should go further at the present time in view of the undoubted truths contained in J.I.C. (43) 527 (W.P.(44) 10). It is perhaps well to look at what is actually going to happen to Germany before deciding whether more precise statements would induce them to surrender.

First, they are to be completely disarmed and deprived of all power to re-arm.

Second, they are to be prohibited from all use of aviation, whether civil or military, and from practising the art of flying.

Third, large numbers of persons alleged to be guilty of atrocities are to be handed over for judgment to the countries where their crimes were committed. Premier Stalin mentioned at Teheran that he would certainly require at least 4 million Germans to work for many years in building up the ruin they had caused in Russia. I have no doubt the Russians will insist upon the handing over to them of vast quantities of German machinery to make up in a generous fashion for what has been destroyed. It may well be that similar claims will be made by others of the victorious Powers. In view of the great severity practised upon immense numbers of French, Italian and Russian prisoners-of-war and internees, such retribution would not appear to be devoid of justice.

Fourth, the British, United States and Russian Governments are I understand agreed that Germany is to be decisively broken up into a number of separate States. East Prussia and Germany east of the River Oder are to be alienated forever and the population shifted. Prussia itself is to be divided and curtailed. The Ruhr and other great centres of coal and steel must be put outside the power of Prussia.

Fifth, the entire core of the German Army comprised in the German Staff must be entirely broken up, and it may well be that the Russians will claim that very large numbers of the General Staff of the German Army shall be either put to death or interned for many years. I have myself wished to publish a list of some 50 to 100 outlaws of first notoriety with a view to dissociating the mass of the people from those who will suffer capital punishment at the hands of the Allies and of avoiding anything in the nature of mass executions. This would tend to reassure the ordinary people. But these proposals were scouted at Teheran as being far too lenient, though I am not sure how far Marshal Stalin was serious in this part of the conversation.

4. Enough at any rate is set down above to show that a frank statement of what is going to happen to Germany would not necessarily have a reassuring effect upon the German people and that they might prefer the vaguer terrors of 'unconditional surrender,' mitigated as they are by such statements as the President has made.

W.S.C.

10, Downing Street, S.W.1.
  15th January, 1944.

ANNEX

President Roosevelt's Statement

I made the following public announcement on the 24th December: 'The United Nations have no intention to enslave the German people. We wish them to have a normal chance to develop in peace, as useful and respectable members of the European family. But we most certainly emphasise the word "respectable", for we intend to rid them once and for all of Nazism and Prussian militarism and the fantastic and disastrous notion that they constitute the "Master Race".'

Attlee disputed the Prime Minister's assertion in Paragraph 4 that Britain, the United States and Russia had agreed Germany should be broken up into a number of separate states, and wrote:

PRIME MINISTER

In your note on 'unconditional surrender' with the conclusion of which I agree, I see that you say that the British, United States and Russian Governments are agreed that Germany is to be decisively broken up into a number of separate states. I do not recall that we have ever taken so definite a decision. For myself, while desiring the decentralization of Germany and the severance of certain areas, I am sceptical as to the efficacy of a partition enforced by the victors.

C. R. ATTLEE
25.1.44.

Whereupon the Prime Minister minuted: 'This certainly was the President's view and that of Mr. Stalin. I did not commit myself beyond isolation on Prussia.'

On 31 January Sargent minuted:

The Prime Minister is wrong in saying the U.K., U.S.A. and Russian Governments agreed Germany is to be decisively broken up into a number of separate states because when Cabinet discussed the question on 5 October 1943 last opinion was divided and no decision was taken. The question of united or divided Germany is becoming urgent.

Cadogan noted on the file: 'This matter requires, if possible, an early decision.'[22]

The three-power Foreign Ministers' Conference in Moscow in October 1943 set up the European Advisory Commission, and the British Cabinet formed the Post-Hostilities Committee. Despite their work nothing was agreed about dismemberment of Germany nor about reparations until the Yalta Conference in March 1945, although as a result of the Quebec Conference in August 1944 zones of occupation were finalized with Russia and the United States.

Eisenhower's SHAEF Headquarters in London were unhappy about Churchill's memorandum of 15 January. Eisenhower's Chief of Staff, Bedell Smith, was particularly concerned and he pressed Eisenhower into forcing Charles Peake, the Foreign Office liaison officer at SHAEF, to take the matter up strongly with the Foreign Office.

On 31 January a meeting was held in Cadogan's room at the Foreign Office to consider the Prime Minister's paper. Cadogan said:

Such a pronouncement would be beneficial. Because of the use made by the Nazis of the repudiation by the Allies of Wilson's 14 points is sufficient warning of the long term dangers involved whatever the short term advantages.

Cadogan wanted to persuade Roosevelt and Stalin to agree a pronouncement and pointed out that all the War Office and Foreign Office committees were in favour of such a step. By this he meant the Joint Intelligence Political Warfare and Joint Policy Staff Committees and their sub-committees. On 27 January Cadogan had minuted that he had always been in favour of such a declaration but

I confess the Prime Minister's paper rather shook me. If we are to be even reasonably frank I rather doubt whether the prospect will be rosy enough for the Germans to think it better to close than go on fighting.

Eden minuted: 'I share Sir A. C.'s doubts.'[23]

Peake emphasized to the Foreign Office on behalf of Eisenhower that it would take months before the Declaration softened up the German Army: he wanted the pronouncement made as soon as there was a break in the west wall of the German fighting forces. He suggested dropping 'unconditional surrender' and substituting 'prompt surrender'.

Bedell Smith was emphatic that the psychological moment would be after the bridgehead was well established, and thought that from all the available evidence it would be impossible in default of such a declaration to exploit 'the crisis which would undoubtedly arise in the German army after a successful landing'.[24]

From December to May 1944 the British Cabinet inconclusively debated unconditional surrender with Whitehall. They produced reams of paper, but no agreement about a declaration to the German people was reached before the invasion in June 1944.

On 8 February Eden gave mild backing to Eisenhower, sending this note to the Prime Minister:

PRIME MINISTER

Your note to the Cabinet on Unconditional Surrender, paragraph 3.

I agree with the Chiefs of Staff that it is neither possible nor desirable for us to abandon the 'Unconditional Surrender' formula at this stage, though I do not think we should overstress it in our propaganda. Though I am conscious of the difficulties which you set out, I think a pronouncement by the three Heads of Government would be helpful, if made at the right psychological moment and provided its terms are not such as to expose us later to a charge of bad faith.

The attached draft seems to me to cover, in their broadest aspect, the points which you advance. It avoids any commitment which might prove embarrassing, and at the same time it might be expected to encourage the Germans to feel that even in defeat there was some hope for their future.

If you agree, I would propose to circulate it to the Cabinet.

A.E.   8th February, 1944

Churchill replied:

FOREIGN SECRETARY

By all means circulate it to the Cabinet. But I do not like it at all. I do not think it will attract the Germans. The time would be better chosen if we had won a few victories against their armies. If we are going to take all this territory away from them and shift 6 or 7 million people out of their homes, and if several millions of them are to go and work in Russia, I doubt very much whether we are in a position to give these assurances, bleak though they be.

W.S.C.   9.2.44.

When Eden wrote that he agreed with the British Chiefs of Staff, he was referring to a report by them on 26 January 1944 which claimed that Nazi propaganda had 'converted the formula of unconditional surrender into one of supporting German will to resist'. Illogically they had continued that would be a 'cardinal mistake to abandon the formula now', and that

from a military point of view it would be better before the cross-channel invasion took place to make a pronouncement by the three heads of Government on the kind of future proposed for the German people which concluded 'we shall ensure there will be no economic collapse of Germany'.

Churchill scrawled against 'economic collapse' – 'How can we do this?' w.s.c.[25]

On 13 March 1944 the War Cabinet duly considered Eden's draft. In the interim, on 22 February, Churchill had made a speech to the House of Commons using some of the terms of Eden's draft declaration and pointing out that unconditional surrender 'does not mean that the German people will be enslaved or destroyed'. This was probably intended for internal consumption and had little effect in Germany according to reports received by the Foreign Office from neutral capitals.

This is Eden's draft declaration; it is doubtful whether it was strong or decisive enough to be construed into an important propaganda weapon for psychological warfare.

DRAFT DECLARATION

We, Winston Churchill, Franklin Roosevelt and Joseph Stalin, on behalf of our respective Governments, hereby solemnly declare:

Germany shall be punished for her aggression. Those responsible for that aggression and for the crimes accompanying it must be handed over for punishment. Justice will govern the actions of the United Nations. There will be no mass reprisals against the people of Germany.

Germany shall be deprived of the fruits of her aggression and will be held responsible for all that she has robbed from the countries occupied by her armies and for the loss and damage which she has caused to the United Nations during the war.

German aggression shall not be renewed. The most complete material guarantees will be exacted from Germany to destroy her power of aggression.

Germany will be purged of the National Socialist party system. Prussian domination and militarism will be extirpated.

The military forces of the United Nations will jointly occupy Germany and German civil administration will be controlled and supervised as may be necessary.

It is in the interests of our own people and of the world

(1) that there shall be established in Germany the rule of law and not of arbitrary violence, and a system of education based on truth, not on perverted history. Only thus will the nations of the world be secured from the rise of a new German tyranny, which would again disturb the peace:

(2) that Germany shall not be a centre of economic collapse and consequent chaos, which might infect the world; and

(3) that, when the German people have been purged and regenerated and have shown themselves capable of becoming law-abiding members of the world community, they shall eventually find their place in the world family of democratic nations and in the world system of security.[26]

When the War Cabinet met on 13 March Churchill was hostile to the Foreign Office suggestion. Eden failed to press it strongly although he spoke about 'the immense propaganda value to which Goebbels was turning the anxiety not only of the German people, but of all enemy or ex-enemy countries in Europe as to the action which would be taken by the victorious Allies'. The decision was recorded 'to re-examine the proposal at a later date'. So unconditional surrender was the order of the day as the invasion loomed nearer and nearer.[27]

In a written memorandum circulated before this War Cabinet meeting Cripps suggested alterations to the draft which in his view would emphasize more strongly the difference between Nazis and the German people. Eden thought little of this and minuted: 'The idea of German as opposed to Nazi guilt is more emphasised in our draft than in Stafford's.' Cripps wanted to include 'no mass reprisals against the German people and we do not desire to see the peoples of Germany engulfed in an economic collapse which would infect the whole of Europe'.

All this was shadow-boxing. The only way to undo the damage being done by Goebbels was to announce that unconditional surrender was abandoned and to state what was proposed for a 'liberated' Germany.

Eisenhower refused to accept the War Cabinet decision, and on 19 April told Peake he would raise the matter strongly with the Prime Minister 'at lunch on Monday'. Eden noted that Eisenhower had not managed to raise it 'while I was there, but I had to leave at 3 p.m.'

Sir Robert Bruce Lockhart, Head of PWE., urged the Foreign Office to press for a new declaration. Harrison, at the German desk of the Foreign Office told him the Prime Minister wanted to leave the whole matter to the Americans 'but was opposed to any statement'.

On 13 April 1944 Eisenhower and Bedell Smith took advantage of the presence of Edward Stettinius in London to return to the attack. Stettinius was an American industrialist whom Roosevelt made an Under-Secretary of State and subsequently Secretary of State in December 1944. The American Generals told Stettinius there was accumulating evidence that unconditional surrender was 'strengthening the morale of the German army and people'. Bedell Smith made it clear that it would be impossible in default of a fresh declaration to exploit the crisis in the German Army which 'will undoubtedly arise immediately after a successful Allied landing'.

In advance of D Day SHAEF wanted a definition of unconditional surrender and a summary of Anglo-American principles upon which military government in Germany would be conducted, and an effort to create a mood in the German General Staff as a result of which 'necessary political steps might be undertaken by a German Badoglio for unconditional surrender'.

Once again Peake was asked to convey these views to the Foreign Office, while Stettinius cabled them to Roosevelt on 13 April. Peake informed the Foreign Office that there was real urgency, as at least a month ought to elapse between the first announcement and the proposed summons by the Allied Supreme Commander calling upon Germany to surrender once the breach in the west wall had been established.[28]

On 15 March Cadogan had sent a draft paper for Churchill to circulate to his colleagues about Bedell Smith's and Eisenhower's insistence on clarifying publicly the term 'unconditional surrender'. Cadogan wanted the Foreign Office to send Eden's draft of 8 February to Washington and Moscow as a basis for discussion. Eden was abroad, so Cadogan had to deal direct with the Prime Minister. Churchill flatly turned it down. He did not like the 'generals shivering before the battle' and wanted it left to the Americans. Here is his reply:

SIR ALEXANDER CADOGAN

1. This matter is on the President. He announced it at Casablanca without any consultation. I backed him up in general terms. Subsequent correspondence with the President has shown him very much disinclined to remodel his statements now. He has given us several examples.

2. I have pointed out to the Cabinet that the actual terms contemplated for Germany are not of a character to reassure them at all, if stated in detail. Both President Roosevelt and Marshal Stalin at Teheran wished to cut Germany into smaller pieces than I had in mind. Stalin spoke of very large mass executions of over 50,000 of the Staffs and military experts. Whether he was joking or not could not be ascertained. The atmosphere was jovial but also grim. He certainly said that he would require 4,000,000 German males to work for an undefinite period to rebuild Russia. We have promised the Poles that they shall have compensation both in East Prussia and, if they like, up to the line of the Oder. There are a lot of other terms implying the German ruin and indefinite prevention of their rising again as an Armed Power.

3. On the other hand, they know that Unconditional Surrender was interpreted in a very favourable manner in the case of the Italians, and we see now what the Roumanians are offered if they will turn their coats, as they have so often done.

4. By all means make a historical summary of events and circulate it to the Cabinet. Personally I am not going to address the President on the subject. For good or ill, the Americans took the lead, and it is for them to make the first move.

5. I may say I think it all wrong for the Generals to start shivering before the battle. This battle has been forced upon us by the Russians and by the United States military authorities. We have gone in wholeheartedly, and I

would not raise a timorous cry before a decision in the field has been taken.

6. The Cabinet should certainly consider the matter but we should wait until Mr. Eden's return. It is primarily a United States affair.

W.S.C.   19.4.44.[29]

Roosevelt countered by proposing that he should make a unilateral declaration to the German people. He cabled his draft to the Prime Minister on 20 May. This contained the words:

Only Germany and Japan stand out against all the rest of humanity . . . the Allies do not seek the total destruction of the German people. They do seek the total destruction of the philosophy of those Germans who have announced that they could subjugate the world.

Whether Roosevelt's statement could have been used by clever and determined Allied propaganda to defeat Goebbels's claims is imponderable. It would have been well worth trying, but it was far from the peace terms envisaged by Eisenhower and Bedell Smith, and not what the American Generals wanted to soften up the German fighting forces. Cadogan minuted: 'The statement itself is not bad and generally on the right lines.' Churchill disagreed. Brendan Bracken, Minister of Information, minuted: 'R's draft was sloppy and silly, and no substitute for tripartite declaration we have proposed.' Eden's comment was 'Better be silent before battle.'[30]

On 24 May, with the invasion of Normandy only a few days off and battle tension mounting, the War Cabinet considered Roosevelt's proposed statement and rejected it. Smuts was present and said:

It ought to be postponed until Germany has been thoroughly beaten on all three fronts. We have said nothing to Germany yet since 'Unconditional Surender' – a declaration which has been very bad propaganda from our point of view. Our next word to Germany should be first class propaganda, a document to which Germany would listen, issued at a time when they would pay most attention. This is an inopportune moment.

Eden said the message should be the basis of conclusion of hostilities and be made by the three leaders, because if Roosevelt made a statement alone the Germans would be in doubt about the views of the Russians and the British.

The Prime Minister said the Government should postpone any action until it sensed victory, and the text of the suggested communication might conceivably be taken as a peace offer which must be agreed by the three Allies. The War Cabinet agreed with the Prime

Minister and concluded that it was far too late as an alternative to get a tripartite statement agreed now with Stalin before D Day.[d][31]

Churchill cabled Roosevelt:

I think myself your message might be taken as a peace feeler. Cabinet showed considerable concern at the tone of friendship shown to the Germans at this moment when the troops are about to engage.

At Teheran my suggestion of dismemberment and isolation of East Prussia was considered far too modest for you and UJ. (*Sic* Uncle Joe, *e.g.* Stalin). How are the Poles to be compensated if they do not get East Prussia and certain territories up to the lines of the Oder in return for the Curzon line which the Russians will certainly demand?

We here earnestly hope you will not make it in its present form and above all at the present time. There was also feeling that a document so grave addressed to the enemy should emanate from the three principal Allies. I may add that nothing of this document would get down to the German pill boxes and front line in time to affect fighting troops.

Roosevelt threw in the sponge and agreed with Churchill, so when the invasion started on 4 June Eisenhower was forbidden to make any announcement about a soft peace and the attractions of surrender to German soldiers.[32] Churchill and Roosevelt were both determined to avoid the ambiguities of Wilson's Fourteen Points which gave Germany a good case for arguing she was deceived in November 1918. Neither Churchill nor Roosevelt nor Eden, once the phrase was coined, attempted a proper analysis of what it meant. Surrender of what? By whose Government or Generals? Did it mean destruction of Germany?

Roosevelt, however, was ready to back Eisenhower against Churchill over a battlefield offer of a soft peace. In his memoirs Churchill explained that his principle reason for opposing and alternative statement on peace terms was that 'a statement of the actual conditions' which public opinion would have insisted on would have been far more repulsive to any German peace movement than the general expression 'unconditional surrender'.

[d]On May 26 Stalin cabled Roosevelt: 'The proposed appeal cannot bring a positive effect . . . Return to question when favourable circumstances arise.'

The Morgenthau Plan

1944

At the September 1944 Quebec Conference Roosevelt and Churchill gave another gratuitous boost to Nazi morale. They played into the hands of Goebbels by announcing that after the war German industry was to be destroyed and the country 'pastoralized'.[a]

In August the Foreign Office had been alerted that Henry Morgenthau, the US Treasury Secretary, wanted very severe treatment of Germany after the war, and was lamenting the tendency of American planners to seek to build up Germany economically and to ignore the President's policy of dismemberment.

On 2 September Halifax cabled to London that Morgenthau was urging that the Allied Military Government must not try to help the postwar German economy and thought a 'severe inflation' with its consequent distress would have 'a salutary effect on the Germans' because Hitler had made them forget the economic consequences of the First World War. According to Halifax, Morgenthau was arguing that another collapse of the mark would make the Germans realize war meant 'economic ruin'. Halifax said all this would inevitably be raised at the Quebec meeting between the two heads of state. The Foreign Office view was that Morgenthau was misguided; 'we' must destroy the Nazi system but always remember a starving and bankrupt Germany would not be 'in our interest'.[1]

On 11 September, while Churchill was en route for Canada, the War Cabinet considered the problem raised by Morgenthau. Eden consulted his colleagues outside the War Cabinet and they were all, except for Bevin, opposed to Morgenthau. Eden accordingly telegraphed Churchill on 14 September giving the Foreign Office view.

Eden's cable came too late. He had given the Ministers up to 1 p.m. on 14 September to send in their comments. By then Churchill had already discussed the Morgenthau Plan and, strongly influenced by

[a]Forty years later more or less the policy of the German Green Party.

Cherwell who accompanied him, had come out in favour. A cable from Churchill crossed with Eden's, and in it Churchill said he and Lord Cherwell favoured the plan put forward by Morgenthau and the President to dismantle the steel industries of the Ruhr and Saar and as a result to pastoralize the character of German life. It meant that Britain could export annually to Germany goods to the value of £3 to £4 billion which would otherwise have been produced by Germany herself.[2]

Churchill commented that he approved of the plan because this would make it impossible for the Germans to rearm, and it would have great beneficial effects on the British economy. He seemed able to do without anyone else's opinion. The same day he and Roosevelt initialled the document which went down to history as the Morgenthau Plan. It was a fatal document, which had far-reaching consequences. It stated that the metallurgical, chemical and electrical industries in the Ruhr and Saar must be closed down and dismantled, and that Germany should be converted into a country 'primarily agricultural and pastoral in its character'.

While Eden was in transit to Quebec Churchill cabled the text to Attlee and the Chancellor of the Exchequer and the next day, 16 September, they sent their warmest congratulations to the Prime Minister without mentioning anything about the desirability or practicability of converting Germany into a primarily agricultural and pastoral country. This was in contradiction of the view they had expressed to Eden.

Eden spent only two days in Quebec. He told Churchill he disapproved of the Morgenthau Plan, but Churchill was unconcerned. Attlee raised the Morgenthau issue at the Armistice and Post War Committee who expressed grave doubts and asked the Economic and Industrial Policy Staff to report. Nothing was heard from them until December. Although they reported unfavourably, Eden made no determined effort then or later to have the Morgenthau Plan rescinded, while Churchill continued to favour it.[3]

Cherwell, who had accompanied Churchill to Quebec, agreed enthusiastically with Morgenthau and was in this instance a malign influence on the Prime Minister. Churchill at that stage of the war had become rather servile to Roosevelt, who was providing a much bigger proportion of the war effort than the United Kingdom, and he admitted afterwards he had been precipitate. It was, however, always for the Prime Minister only a peripheral issue compared with the prosecution of military operations.

In his memoirs Churchill writes that he made a mistake in agreeing to the Morgenthau Plan. In excuse he claims he was 'violently opposed' to the plan at first, but Roosevelt and Morgenthau were so insistent that in the end he agreed. He fails to mention that Cherwell was also insistent, and tendentiously claims that he gave his agreement subject to the consideration of the War Cabinet, and that in the event 'pastoralizing Germany did not survive'.[4] Colville told the author that Churchill realized he had accepted the Plan without considering his colleagues' contrary views, but that did not worry him. Colville suspected that Churchill never gave it serious thought, merely initialling it because he was keen on getting Roosevelt, as a *quid pro quo*, to initial his (Churchill's) plan for a 50/50 division of all atomic products between the United Kingdom and the United States. In fact, after Churchill initialled the plan it was never cancelled; it was even put into effect to a limited extent by the Allied Military Government after hostilities ceased.[5]

There was violent controversy in the American press about Morgenthau and Goebbels exploited the gaffe to the full. On 23 September the *Wall Street Journal* wrote that the Treasury had prepared a plan for Germany to be dismembered and stripped of her industrial might. On 4 October Keynes[b] wrote from Washington that Morgenthau would almost certainly be defeated by vehement opposition from Stimson and Hull. But the resultant controversy only spotlighted it was a Jewish plan.[6]

Halifax's despatch from the Washington Embassy on 25 September 1944 revealed how much publicity the Morgenthau Plan was receiving in the American press:

The attribution of the plan to Mr. Morgenthau loads the scales against it.
(a) He is one of the least popular American officials while Mr. Hull, who has fairly clearly admitted the divergence, is one of the most popular (and thereby dramatised it).
(b) Mr. Morgenthau is not regarded as an expert on foreign affairs, while Mr. Hull is so regarded.
(c) Many Americans are patently anti-semitic and therefore particularly inclined to suspect the objectivity of a Jew on Germany . . .
   [An Associated Press article had stated] 'Morgenthau's thesis is opposed by Hull and violently opposed by Stimson;[c] Hopkins[d] is thought to support him (Morgenthau) and Harry White has drawn up plans; the alleged trend of the

[b]Lord Keynes was acting as a roving financial ambassador in Canada and the United States.
[c]Cordell Hull was Secretary of State; Henry Stimson Secretary of State for War.
[d]Harry Hopkins was Roosevelt's closest adviser.

Treasury argument is that elimination of Ruhr industry will boost that of Britain and so make the Beveridge Plan realisable.'[e7]

Two days later Washington reported that Governor Dewey[f] claimed that the publication of the Morgenthau Plan could prolong the war, and that it had weighty support from the Senate's Kilgore Committee on Cartels and National Security. This, according to Halifax, was the most significant statement yet to appear, and he also commented that although Morgenthau was heavily criticized, there was 'no mistaking the increasing sentiment in favour of the tough treatment which the administration were known to favour'.[8]

Immediately Goebbels's propaganda ministry put out the tale, which was widely believed, that 'Clemenceau had said there were 23 million Germans too many, but that now Morgenthau wanted to exterminate 43 million Germans'. Stokes tabled a parliamentary question about the Morgenthau Plan but got an evasive answer. There was little reaction in Britain.

Soon the Political Warfare files of the Foreign Office were full of reports from neutral countries of the tremendous propaganda value to Goebbels of Morgenthau. The German people, by and large, believed that they were going to be treated brutally and forced into starvation. A further Goebbels embellishment was that anyone trying to leave the country after the war would be shot on the frontier. The routine reports from the Political Warfare Executive on German propaganda can have left the Foreign Office in no doubt about the damage being done by Morgenthau.

On 2 October 1944 the Political Warfare report ran:

Greatest prominence given to Morgenthau alleged proposals for the economic subjugation of Germany. Newspapers report, under many headings Morgenthau surpasses Clemenceau who claimed there were 40 million Germans too many ... Morgenthau was described as the leader of the agitation 'who sings the same tune as the Jews in the Kremlin and demands complete annihilation of the German industry, dismemberment of the country and extermination of half the population' ... Roosevelt was reported to have amplified the plans of his bosom friend the finance Jew Morgenthau and developed a programme of pitiless extermination ... Eisenhower's orders to the allied troops on crossing the German frontier were interpreted as no food for the German population plus compulsory

---

[e]Churchill and a large section of the Conservative party thought the Beveridge Plan would throw too much of a strain on the taxpayer because of the cost of extra social services.

[f]Dewey had been a strong contender for the Republican nomination for President in 1940; he secured it in 1944, only to be defeated by Roosevelt. He won the Governorship of New York in 1942.

registration for deportation . . . as a result Goebbels said every house in Aachen [then being attacked by the Americans] should resemble a fortress.[9]

It is improbable that these reports were made known to Churchill. Certainly he seemed unaware of them.

Unfortunately Morgenthau in Washington irresponsibly made statements which could be construed that Germans leaving would be shot by armed guards; he also gave a long list of categories of officials to be executed. Goebbels spotlighted again and again that the author of the Plan was a Jew, and he was successful in producing a revival of enthusiasm for the Nazi Party, almost unbelievable in the light of their crushing defeat in Normandy and their dismal military prospects. There is incontrovertible evidence that indiscriminate bombing and the policy of unconditional surrender immeasurably stiffened the German people's will to resist and the appalling damage and casualties from British and American bombings were interpreted to the German people by Goebbels as an integral part of the Morgenthau Plan.

In Normandy by September 1944 Hitler's armies had suffered a defeat far more severe than the Kaiser's in 1918. Instead of considering surrender, however, Hitler found extra manpower for new divisions and for the manufacture of arms through an intense combing out of all able-bodied Germans and by an unscrupulous use of slave labour from occupied countries. Even twelve-year-old schoolboys were taken out of school to dig fortifications, and the new battalions contained a chilling ratio of schoolboys. By mid October, when six weeks before defeat had seemed inevitable, Hitler had raised twelve new divisions for the Western Front. They included factory workers, shopkeepers and petty officials. Schoolboys transformed overnight into fighting soldiers had known no Government nor faith other than Nazi; fighting for Hitler had a romantic appeal for them and they resisted like demons. All this had become possible because of the gigantic boost to German fighting morale by the Morgenthau Plan, coupled with the sinister threat to the future of all Germans inherent in unconditional surrender.

Morgenthau knew he had an ally in Cherwell, and in November he sent him a memorandum strongly criticizing drafts of policy towards Germany prepared by the British Armistice and Civil Affairs Committee which had been sent to the European Advisory Commission. These drafts show that the Foreign Office and War Office were poles away from Morgenthau's thinking. Cherwell wrote a memorandum to the Prime Minister suggesting that 'in general we should adopt Morgenthau's views'. Both Eden and Sir James Grigg, the Secretary of State for War, were furious; they regarded it as highly impertinent that Morgenthau should approach the British Prime Minister through Cherwell, and that no advice to Churchill about the treatment of Germany should come direct from the US Treasury. Churchill fuelled their anger by minuting to Eden he found Morgenthau's argument 'very cogent'.[10]

Churchill sent an Eden-Grigg minute with their detailed proposals about a sensible reconstruction of Germany to Cherwell who was most antipathetic to it and told Churchill so. However, Churchill delayed six weeks before replying to Eden. Obviously he was unaware of the harm being done by Goebbels's publicity over Morgenthau. Roosevelt for his part, though dismayed by criticisms of Morgenthau, took no further action on the plan but he equally failed to take any steps to halt the adverse propaganda about it in Germany.

When Churchill replied, he wrote that he had been much struck by the depth of feeling which would be stirred by a policy of 'putting Germany on her feet again' – because of the hatred which Germany had aroused – and

it would be a mistake to try to write out on little bits of paper what the vast emotions of an outraged and quivering world would be either immediately after the struggle is over or when the inevitable cold fit follows the hot . . . there is therefore wisdom in reserving one's decision as long as possible.[11]

From America Keynes wrote on 30 November that Roosevelt had not made up his mind about the Morgenthau Plan, and Law wrote to the same effect on 23 December. Nowhere in the archives is there any real trace of concern by Churchill about the propaganda effects of Morgenthau; nor did the Foreign Office or Eden stress their opposition at all strongly. However, Eden minuted on the Report of EIPS in December on the Morgenthau Plan that although he accepted it, 'we would gain little and have to deal with very serious problems of unemployment in the British zone of occupation'; also that 'we need not take any action over the President's proposal' unless the USA raised the matter again.[12]

A false impression arose in British Civil Service circles that the Morgenthau Plan was dead. A Foreign Office minute on 23 November noted that the plan had been strongly criticized in high quarters in the United States, and a War Office minute of the same date said the Morgenthau Plan was 'probably dead'. It may have been nearly dead from the point of view of British officialdom, but it was far from dead as the trump card of Nazi propaganda.[13]

SHAEF in the autumn of 1944 became more and more alarmed about the high morale of the German fighting forces. Eisenhower returned to the attack over a soft peace and demanded the offer of terms which would induce the Germans to stop fighting. He was dismayed by the fighting qualities of Hitler's new armies, and on 21 November he sent a long telegram to London and Washington stating that German resistance was very tough and that unless the phrase 'Unconditional Surrender' could be modified he saw no end to the war except a long and bitter process of fighting. He went on: 'If unconditional surrender must be adhered to, then everything possible should be done by propaganda and subversive means to soften German morale.' He asked London to go into these matters which 'could not be dealt with by SHAEF'.[14]

This message caused consternation and telegrams flew between Roosevelt and Churchill. Their decision was that it was now too late to go back on unconditional surrender, and that at this stage any alteration would be regarded as a sign of weakness. All that happened in London was that Bruce Lockhart was appointed Chairman of a Committee under the Chiefs of Staff to examine the problem, but it accomplished nothing.

On 25 November the Prime Minister telegraphed to Eisenhower: 'It would be a mistake to show the Germans that we are anxious for them to ease off their desperate opposition.' At least this showed Churchill was aware of the high morale of Hitler's fighters, but it is strange that he should veto any attempt to undermine the Nazi grip on the German people. Roosevelt agreed eventually with the Prime Minister, and SHAEF never got permission for their proposed antidote to Goebbels's morale boosting.

At this stage Churchill, Roosevelt and Eden failed to understand the use the Nazis could make of the link between the Morgenthau Plan and unconditional surrender. Eisenhower's message based on field reports of German morale and the abundant evidence from Political Warfare about German propaganda should have made it crystal clear that in order to help towards an early end to the war, unconditional surrender and the Morgenthau plan must be repudiated. The day after Roosevelt received Eisenhower's *cri de coeur* he cabled Churchill that the Combined Chiefs of Staff in Washington would like a declaration to break down German morale. Winston replied that he had consulted all his Cabinet and we all gravely doubt whether such a declaration should be made, and the Germans are frightened of Russian occupation, not Anglo-U.S.A. Uncle Joe [Stalin] wants two million of Nazi youth for prolonged reparations work, and it is hard to say he is wrong. We could not give any assurances without consulting Uncle Joe. If I were a German soldier I should regard such a statement as a confession of weakness.

Roosevelt disagreed, and wanted to issue a statement including: 'We do not seek to devastate or eliminate the German people . . . we seek the elimination of Nazi control and the return of the German people to the civilization of the rest of the world.'[15] Churchill would not have it. Thus at the end of 1944 nothing was decided about pastoralization or dismemberment of Germany. Goebbels's propaganda continued undiminished and the Allies failed to counter it. Meanwhile the defeated remnants of the German army fought as stoutly as ever against both the Russians and the Anglo-US forces, and Hitler's Ardennes offensive at Christmas 1944 nearly recovered Brussels, Antwerp and most of Belgium.

The Foreign Office became more and more worried at the lack of any firm policy about postwar Germany, not so much because of Goebbels's propaganda but in order to have some agreed policy with which to confront Roosevelt and Stalin at the coming Yalta Conference, due to start on 11 February 1945. Accordingly Eden minuted the Prime Minister on 2 February 1945, immediately before the Yalta Conference:

Urgent to co-ordinate policy of major allied powers on future of Germany. EAC set up in 1943 has agreed terms of surrender protocol of zones of occupation control machinery . . . dismemberment amongst other problems not agreed.[16]

He might have defined pastoralization as one of the problems not agreed, but at this stage of the war Churchill was particularly difficult to approach on unsolved problems.

Churchill's reply to Eden during the Yalta Conference was unhelpful:

P.M. TO FOREIGN SECRETARY
Query? Morale?
1. The only bond of victors is their common hate.
2. To make Britain safe she must become responsible for the safety of a cluster of feeble states.
3. We ought to think of something better than these.

W.S.C.   8.2.45.[17]

Although as far back as February 1944 Churchill had asked for a map showing the proposed zones of occupation, nothing was decided about partition of Germany until the Yalta Conference in February 1945. Thus the British and American Governments were under no binding obligation to Stalin not to discuss postwar German frontiers with the German opposition in 1944. Indeed there was confusion in Whitehall. Halifax signalled the Foreign Office from Washington on 7 September 1944: 'What is our policy on partition of Germany? By partition we mean not lopping off East Prussia and Lorraine, but the hinterland?' The Foreign Office replied: 'Partition of Germany is shortly to be considered by Ministers and we can express no view.'

On 9 February 1945 Attlee cabled the Prime Minister at Yalta following a War Cabinet that the Cabinet had not discussed dismemberment nor what precisely was involved, and said: 'We are most anxious to consider the implication before any binding commitment is entered into.' Churchill replied that at Yalta they had agreed to dismemberment but 'if no practical solution can be arranged we should resume our liberty'.

At this period Cherwell was trying to influence Churchill in favour of the Morgenthau Plan and for the harshest possible treatment of Germany after the war. During the Yalta Conference Cherwell told the Prime Minister Germany's standard of life must be reduced . . . 'Please oppose helping German industry to restart . . . fallacies that destruction of German industry would impoverish Europe and the world. Eden and his officials want to limit German military potential with the least possible dislocation of German industry.' The Morgenthau Plan was not exactly dead when Cherwell was briefing Churchill like this at such a critical juncture.

Cherwell continued:

E and IPS produce briefs for Yalta inter alia to reduce German steel production from 26 to 12 million tons annually, prohibit all exports of machine tools, permanent prohibition of manufacture of civil aircraft and synthetic ammonia and methynol ships and ball bearings for ten years. This is less beneficial to us than Morgenthau Plan.

Cherwell continually stressed to Churchill that curtailment of German industry was preferable to reparations, and particularly he favoured destruction of German industry in the Ruhr.[18]

At Yalta Morgenthau was neither endorsed nor rescinded, but the three Allies decided that Germany should be dismembered with Prussia eliminated, and that enormous sums in reparations would be extorted from Germany. This was kept secret and unconditional surrender plus the Morgenthau Plan was all that the German people knew about during the closing months of the war. As a result, Hitler's armies fought on resolutely to their last gasp, prolonging the war to the last possible moment, believing that after defeat their future would be ghastly.

The Anti-Nazi Conspirators
1938 – 1944

There was no real organized conspiracy against Hitler until 1938 despite the immediate creation by the Nazis, after the Enabling Act of 1933, of a police state in which both political opponents and law-abiding Jews were carted off to concentration camps, many of them to be executed without trial.

During 1938, when Hitler's warlike intentions could no longer be disguised, the Army General Staff made plans to overthrow the Nazis to prevent what they felt sure would be a disastrous war. General Ludwig Beck, Chief of Staff until 1938, was a fervent anti-Nazi, as were other German Generals in high places – General Kurt von Hammerstein, Commander-in-Chief from 1930 to 1934; General Franz Halder, Chief of Staff; Field-Marshal Erwin von Witzleben; General Edward Wagner, Quarter Master General; General Georg Thomas, Head of Military Economic Planning; and General Hans Oster, second-in-command to Admiral Canaris, head of the Abwehr (Intelligence). Canaris himself was strongly opposed to Hitler, as were General Friedrich Olbricht, deputy chief of the replacement army, and General Count Erich von Brockdorff-Ahlefeld, the Potsdam commander. Fabian von Schlabrendorff, a lawyer and high staff officer, together with his friend Major-General Henning von Tresckow made determined efforts to overthrow Hitler from prewar days onwards; and in 1944 Field-Marshal Erwin Rommel and Field-Marshal Guenther-Hans von Kluge joined the plot.

Of these only Halder, Schlabrendorff and Thomas survived the war, and Halder's early oppositon to Hitler had become muted with the military victories. The others were all executed or committed suicide, except for Hammerstein who died of natural causes. Sacked by Hitler in 1941, Halder was put in a concentration camp after 20 July 1944 because of his contacts with Beck and Goerdeler. Another plotter, General Ernst Udet, a First World War air ace, committed suicide in 1941 when his anti-Hitler attitude was discovered by the Gestapo.

Closely associated with this influential list of Generals from 1938 onwards were former well-known German politicians from the days of the Weimar Republic. Their leader from the start until the end was Goerdeler. Johannes Popitz, a former Prussian Finance Minister, and Otto Gessler, a former Defence Minister, were also active.

Other prominent persons amongst the conspirators were Count Friedrich von der Schulenberg, President of Silesia; Albrecht Haushofer, Professor of Geography in the University of Berlin; the diplomat Ulrich von Hassell, son-in-law of Admiral Tirpitz; two socialist leaders, Wilhelm Leuschner and Julius Leber; and numerous former members of the centre party of the Reichstag. In addition there was a distinguished group from business and the professions; including Hans Gisevius, a well-known Berlin lawyer who miraculously survived the war. Another lawyer, Hans von Dohnanyi, who was executed by the Nazis worked in the Canaris organization.

Dr Hjalmar Schacht, President of the Reichsbank, had a limited involvement, although ostensibly he toed the Nazi line, and Franz von Papen, the former Chancellor and wartime Ambassador to Turkey, became a party to the plot in 1943. In 1932 as Chancellor he had tried vainly to hold the balance between the Nazis and the other parties in the Reichstag.

They were a band of well-known and respected Germans, many of whom worked against Hitler from 1938 until the bomb plot of 20 July 1944. Yet during the war the British Foreign Office, Eden and Churchill refused to admit that an organized conspiracy existed, despite much evidence to the contrary through neutral countries and the knowledge of its existence before the war.

From memoirs by the few survivors, the proceedings at the Nuremberg Trials and the German documents on the Nazi trials of the plotters, the whole story can be pieced together. General Erwin Lahousen, a plotter and close collaborator of Canaris, gave valuable testimony at Nuremberg. Important books by survivors Gisevius, Ritter and Schlabrendorff were translated into English but were written before the Foreign Office archives were available. In this chapter the published recollections of the survivors have been reconciled with the British Foreign Office archives.

The Foreign Office during the war, and certain British historians since the war, have tried to blacken the character of those Germans who plotted for so many years, asserting they were all too 'nationalist' because they wanted to retain Hitler's conquests of Austria, Danzig, the Corridor and the Sudetenland. Perhaps their reputations have been besmirched as an excuse for the British failure to give them encouragement.

Taking into account the type of police state they were living in, and the popularity of the Nazis and Hitler after his 1939 and 1940 victories, it is remarkable that the plotters were able to keep the conspiracy alive and even make headway during the war. Because of the Gestapo, they could use neither the telephone nor the post – both were tapped. The Gestapo searched people on buses, trains and trams at random, suspects could expect to be tortured, there were paid informers everywhere. It was impossible to start an anti-Nazi whispering campaign because of the ban on communications of any kind. There was only one reliable way of communicating news to other conspirators. That was the London radio, but BBC help was denied.

Temporarily, after the French armistice in 1940, the plotters were at a low ebb. It was Hitler's decision to attack Russia that converted more supporters to their cause. Among the staff of the Central Army Group (to be used against Russia) there was grave concern at Hitler's order that the Russian campaign must be waged in total disregard of the rules of war.

On 16 June 1941 Beck, Oster, Goerdeler, Popitz and Hassell discussed how they could use the dislike of these orders to convince the German Generals of the need to remove Hitler. The senior commanders Halder and Bock would not cooperate in an anti-Hitler coup, although Bock had refused to pass on the infamous orders. However, Tresckow and Schlabrendorff built up a strong following at Central Army Group and when in 1943 Hitler ordered a further reckless offensive against Moscow they decided to act. By then Kluge had replaced Bock as commander of Central Army Group, and he was open to persuasion.Goerdeler, given false papers by Canaris, even visited Kluge on the Russian front. Kluge toyed with the idea of arresting Hitler if he came to the front and instituting a takeover by the Army.

Hitler came on 13 March 1943. General Tresckow put a time bomb on his plane on the return journey, and Kluge in the east and Olbricht in Berlin were ready to seize power if Hitler was killed. Inexplicably the fuse failed. Tresckow covered his tracks by recovering the bomb.[1]

Meanwhile the conspiracy had been gaining momentum. Church leaders, both Protestant and Catholic, had become more and more anti-Nazi and mobilized their resources for propaganda, risking reprisals. The Nazis did not dare to touch prominent clergymen although they closed down many churches to store furniture from bombed-out houses. The middle class was largely Nazi, as were the working people, but the more intelligent became increasingly disillusioned with the outlook as the Afrika Korps surrendered at Tunis on 7 May 1943.

Two of the younger conspirators, prominent in the anti-Nazi movement even before Hitler appeared certain to lose the war, were Helmuth von Moltke, grandson of the famous Field-Marshal, and Adam von Trott, whose early contacts with the British Government have been recounted in an earlier chapter.

Moltke, a lawyer on the German War Office intelligence staff, got in touch with Beck and Goerdeler in Berlin and at Moltke's country house at Kreisau they assembled a group of Right and Left-wing clerics, scholars, businessmen, economists, trade unionists, diplomats and administrators to discuss the overthrow of Hitler and postwar policy. Trott was an active member of this group. They planned a new liberal and democratic Germany and produced a policy 'think tank' known as the Kreisau Circle.

Up to the time of Hitler's declaration of war on the United States on 8 December 1941, Moltke was in continual touch with the US Embassy in Berlin. His anti-Nazi views were well known to the American diplomats and he was a friend of George Kennan who was serving there.[a] Another close friend of those days was Alexander Kirk, Chargé d' Affaires in Berlin up to December 1941. He was Ambassador in Cairo when Moltke travelled to Istanbul in July 1943 and tried to put peace overtures to the Americans. Moltke hoped that he would be able to fly from Istanbul to Cairo to meet Kirk. His hopes were disappointed.[2]

Canaris had facilitated this first trip to Istanbul in July 1943, ostensibly to try and get the Turks to return German boats which had been interned. Moltke sent a message to Kirk that he was there and wanted to come to Cairo to discuss the possibilities of peace, which would first involve the German opposition aiding the Allies to land on the Continent. Kirk refused to meet him, but in order to keep the channel open asked Moltke to come back in December. Papen, the German Ambassador in Istanbul, talked to Moltke but there was no meeting of minds.[2]

In December 1943 Moltke came back to Turkey and wrote a letter to Kirk suggesting again he should come to Cairo where he would give

---

[a]Later US Ambassador to Russia.

him valuable information. The American Ambassador in Turkey refused to forward the letter to Kirk, although he and his military attaché saw Moltke. Unconditional surrender had become the official Allied policy in January 1943, and because of this Kirk, in spite of his personal friendship for Moltke, was forbidden to talk to him.

Nevertheless Moltke sent Kirk a memorandum claiming that a powerful and extremely influential opposition group would aid military operations by the Allies against the Nazis, and that many in the officers corps of the Wehrmacht and the upper ranks of the Civil Service were ready to act against Hitler. The memorandum stated that if a proper agreement about the future of Germany was signed with this group 'a sufficient number of intact units of the Wehrmacht would fight against the Nazis' and simultaneously an anti-Nazi Government would cooperate with the Allies. The headquarters of this 'democratic counter-Government' would be initially in South Germany or Austria and it would be advisable not to subject this area to indiscriminate bombing. The anti-Nazis were also anxious to prevent a Soviet occupation in the east of Germany. Moltke, in the course of the memorandum, disclosed that Trott was one of the conspirators.

The document eventually reached Roosevelt, who asked Felix Frankfurter to look at it. Frankfurter took the view, as soon as he read Trott's name, that it was a decoy by people who were not sincere. Frankfurter in 1937 had initially liked Trott, but radically changed his opinion after they met in 1940. Probably – quite apart from his Jewish anti-German prejudice – he was influenced to some extent by the Oxford don Maurice Bowra. Frankfurter had spent a year at Oxford in 1938, becoming a close friend of Bowra, and at that time Bowra thought Trott a Nazi. So Moltke's efforts were unrewarded.

Trott, meanwhile, was active in approaching the British Government, but he came up against not only Churchill's edict of absolute silence, but a brick wall of prejudice. The minutes of the Foreign Office German desk show there was no goodwill to the anti-Nazis; doubts, too were cast on Trott's genuineness, despite his being vouched for by Lothian and Cripps. Yet in the Foreign Office files (which are well indexed) there existed indisputable evidence about Trott's consistent strong opposition to the Nazis and the existence of the anti-Nazi plot. This was confirmed by Bishop Bell when he visited Stockholm in 1942.

The first document about Trott on the Foreign Office files was in

August 1938 when Lothian wrote to Halifax recommending him to read Trott's memorandum on the Far East:[b]

It comes from a German Rhodes Scholar who being suffocated in the Third Reich went out to the Far East . . . it develops the thesis that England and Germany working together might bring a fair peace to the Far East and that this co-operation might pave the way to better relations in Europe.

The paper reproduced several pages of comments from the Central Department and was read by Halifax. It was proposed to bring it up with the German Ambassador but because of the crisis over the Sudetenland it was shelved in September 1938. It was incontrovertible written evidence that Trott had the full confidence of both Lothian and Cripps.[3]

Trott first met Cripps in 1934 with a German anti-Nazi, the Socialist Meirendorff. Cripps became a close friend and gave him financial help for his trip in 1937 to the Far East. Lord Lothian was also a friend. They met at Rhodes House, of which Lothian was secretary. It was the Rhodes Trust that gave Trott a grant to go to the Far East.

When Trott returned to Berlin early in 1939 he became a friend of Schacht and General von Falkenhausen whom he had first met in China. Through them he heard of the 1938 plot to remove Hitler, and from then on became an enthusiastic collaborator of the conspirators.

From Berlin Trott came to England in June 1939, and through Halifax's good offices had his interview with Chamberlain at 10 Downing Street. Chamberlain remarked that Trott was 'just the type one would like as mediator because he could see both sides'. Yet all Trott's later wartime overtures foundered because the Foreign Office under Eden viewed him with deep antipathy, mistrusting his true allegiances and suspicious that he was merely after a peace settlement under which Germany would receive more than the Versailles frontiers.

In July 1939 Trott, now in the German Foreign Office, concocted a memorandum for Ribbentrop on his English trip and his interviews with Halifax and Chamberlain. Unfortunately no written records exist of his visit to Downing Street in 1939. The memorandum itself was tendentious and represented Trott as a fervent Nazi. He claimed that he found it most amusing to write it, but his position otherwise as a member of the German Foreign Office would have been untenable.

Late in July 1939 Trott went to visit Falkenhausen, now out of

[b]Brian MacDermot, a British diplomat stationed in Pekin at the time, gave considerable help with this document.

retirement and commanding the Dresden district, accompanied by a Foreign Office friend, von Kessel, assistant to Weizsaecker, the anti-Nazi Permanent Under-Secretary at the German Foreign Office. They suggested to Falkenhausen that he should invite Hitler to inspect the fortifications and then assassinate him.[4] Trott also met the former Socialist MP, Dr Julius Leber, and the Kordt brothers, part of the German Foreign Office group of conspirators who had made overtures in London.

As an official of the Foreign Office Trott was able to travel to Switzerland five times during 1940–42. He contacted an old friend, Dr Visser't Hooft, who was in Geneva as General Secretary of the World Council of Churches, and Elizabeth Wiskemann of the British Legation at Berne. He informed them about the German opposition and their activities and plans.

From Visser't Hooft Trott learned that Bishop Bell of Chichester was making a trip in May 1942 to Stockholm. He arranged for Hans Schoenfeld, a German pastor in the Evangelical Church and Director of the Research Department of the World Council of Churches in Geneva, to go to meet him. He also arranged for Pastor Dietrich Bonhoeffer, another friend of Bell, to go to Stockholm as a courier for the German Foreign Office. Bonhoeffer had known Bell intimately for nine years and was an uncompromising anti-Nazi, a mainspring of the ecclesiastical opposition to Hitler.[5]

Bell went to Stockholm at the request of the British Ministry of Information to renew contacts between British and Swedish churchmen. He had a reputation as a pacifist and had publicly criticized indiscriminate bombing, much to Eden's and Churchill's annoyance. He politely wrote to Eden asking for a quarter of an hour's interview on 8 May when he would be seeing Geoffrey Warner of the Central Department.

Eden was not pleased. He scrawled across the Bishop's letter: 'Dept. This seems a strange choice. I thought he was a pacifist.' Eden's private secretary minuted to him:

S/S. I have spoken to Mr. Makins about the Bishop's Anglo-German activities in the past; but he does not think he would do any harm in Sweden. But the Bishop has now asked to see you tomorrow or on Friday; and this might provide an opportunity for you to speak to him about the line he should take in talking to Swedes, etc.

Eden refused to see Bell, but he allowed him to go. It is clear that Bell was *persona non grata* with Eden from the start.[6]

In Stockholm Schoenfeld informed Bell of the existence of a strong opposition to Hitler which had been developing for some time and had existed before the war. He said that the course of the war had given it a chance which it was waiting to seize. The opposition, according to Schoenfeld, was made up of: (1) members or former members of the state administration; (2) large numbers of former trade unionists who had built up a network of key men in the main industrial parts; (3) high officers in the Army and State police, (4) leaders of the Protestant and Catholic Churches, 'exemplified' by the protests against Nazi tyranny by the protestant Bishop Wurm of Wurttemberg and Bishop von Preysing of Berlin.

This opposition intended to destroy Hitler, Himmler, Goering, Goebbels and the leaders of the Gestapo, SS and SA and in their place establish a Government composed of strong groups of those mentioned above. Their programme, of which Schoenfeld supplied a written memorandum, was principally to include: (1) considerable decentralization of German Government; (2) a free Polish and Czech nation and reparations for damages caused by Germany to other nations; (3) national and social life orientated towards Christianity; (4) repeal of the Nuremberg laws and restoration of property to the Jews.

Schoenfeld was later joined by Bonhoeffer who said the opposition hoped to mobilize the army and the nation against the Nazis. They stressed that they were embarking on a highly dangerous project, and that it was therefore 'extremely important to know the Allies' attitude to a Germany purged of Hitler'.

Bell asked Bonhoeffer to give him the names of the chief conspirators. Bonhoeffer replied that they were Beck, Hammerstein, Goerdeler, Leuschner and Kaiser, the former trade union leaders, and that Beck and Goerdeler were joint leaders, while Schacht, Prince Louis Ferdinand (son of the Kaiser) and leading Protestant and Catholic bishops were involved. He also said that there was an organization representing the opposition in every Ministry and in all the big towns, and mentioned Kluge and Witzleben amongst the Army Generals. Finally Bonhoeffer summed up their discussion by asking Bell to get replies from London to the following well-phrased ánd sensible questions: (1) would the Allied Governments, once the whole Hitler regime had been overthrown, be willing to treat with a *bona fide* German Government for a peace settlement as described above, including the withdrawal of all German forces from occupied countries and reparation for damages, and to say so privately to an authorized representative of the opposition; or, (2) could the Allies make a public pronouncement in clear terms to the same effect?[7]

Bonhoeffer told Bell that Trott would be 'ideal' as an intermediary. Bell discussed all this with Mallet who reported to the Foreign Office that 'this was something more than one of the usual peace feelers'. Bell wanted Dr Ahrenstorm of the World Council of Churches in Geneva or Dr Visser't Hooft to go to Stockholm to help as an intermediary. He left a crude code with Mallet so that he could let the intermediary know if there was any point in getting some of the German resistance to come to Stockholm.[8]

As soon as the Bishop got back to London he saw Geoffrey Warner at the Foreign Office, gave him the gist of the conversation and asked to see the Foreign Secretary. The minutes of the relevant files are revealing. Pat Hancock noted that the Secretary of State might explain to the Bishop the Government's attitude to peace feelers, i.e. 'absolute silence'.

Warner minuted: 'The claims sound very exaggerated.' He commented, correctly, that 'this might chime in with the move from Adam Trott via Visser't Hooft who had come from Geneva to London. It will be interesting to hear what the Bishop has to say.' Strang agreed that Eden should see the Bishop, and Cadogan wrote:

What would be interesting would be to see what any group of this kind can *do*. We are not going to negotiate with any Government in Germany that has not thoroughly purged its soul and we must have some convincing of *that* and we have got to be convinced first. Total defeat and disarmament is probably·the only possible answer.[9]

The Bishop's message fell on stony ground. The Foreign Office already knew from other sources of the existence of the plot but resolutely refused to take it seriously or consider how to encourage the anti-Nazis in their aims to overthrow Hitler. Eden saw the Bishop at the end of June 1942, listened courteously to what he had to say, read Schoenfeld's memorandum, and confirmed that some of the names given by Bonhoeffer were known by the Foreign Office. Because other feelers had reached him from other countries he said he had to be scrupulously careful not to enter into even an appearance of negotiations independently of the Russians and Americans. He wrote to Bell on 17 July that no action could be taken. So these overtures from impeccable sources were greeted with 'absolute silence'.

At the end of May 1942 Visser't Hooft came to England carrying with him a memorandum about the views and aims of the opposition, written at the end of April by Trott in Geneva. It was addressed by Trott to Cripps with copies to Sir Alfred Zimmern[c] and Arnold Toynbee.[d] Cripps showed his copy to Churchill who minuted: 'Most encouraging.'[10]

Toynbee handed his copy to Professor Tom Marshall, Head of the Foreign Office Research Unit on Germany at Balliol College, Oxford. Visser't Hooft told Toynbee that at least one member of the group was an official in the German Ministry of Foreign Affairs, and this official (Trott) had told Visser't Hooft that the group believed 'the only effective way of disposing of the Nazis is to kill them in considerable numbers from Hitler, a long way downwards; he and his friends had twice (the first occasion being in December 1940) been on the point of attempting to carry out these assassinations as the overture to a coup d'état'.[11]

Visser't Hooft assented, when Toynbee asked him whether he believed that 'assassination was really part of the programme of Christians in Germany', as declared to him. The Trott memorandum stated 'We believe in the necessity to reconstitute a free Polish and Czech state within the limits of their geographical frontiers.' This meant that after peace Germany would retain the Sudetenland, Danzig and the Corridor – unlikely to arouse enthusiasm in Whitehall.

The memorandum went on: 'We sincerely hope that our inadequate attempt will be met by frank co-operation in the practical task to face a common future beyond the catastrophe now confronting us all.' Seizure of power in Germany was hindered by the following obstacles:

(a) The dire necessity of national defence against the Soviet Union and against anarchical developments on the eastern front as well as the Balkans.
(b) Existing control of the entire national life by police (Gestapo) and the anticipated difficulties of dealing with Nazi remnants and anarchical outbreaks after the Nazi overthrow.
(c) The complete uncertainty of the British and American attitude towards a change of Government in Germany.
(d) The movements of indiscriminate hatred anticipated in the event of a sudden relaxation of control in the occupied parts of Germany.

The last two problems cannot be overcome without international co-operation even at this stage. For obvious reasons we cannot give details of names, dates and programmes.

Marshall asked Richard Crossman,[e] who had been the philosophy

---

[c]Sir Alfred Zimmern was Professor of International Relations at the University of Oxford and had been prominent in League of Nations affairs.
[d]Arnold Toynbee, Director of the Royal Institute of International Affairs, had been one of the British delegation to the Versailles Conference.
[e]Subsequently a Socialist Cabinet Minister.

tutor at New College when Trott was an undergraduate, for a report on him. Crossman wrote on 27 May 1942:

I knew Adam von Trott throughout his period at Oxford, a difficult period of transition from democratic to Nazi Germany. A tall, extremely handsome young man, he was probably the most successful German Rhodes Scholar in achieving popularity both among dons and undergraduates; incidentally he had a great way with women and was able to discard his worshippers whenever convenient. He always claimed to be Hegelian Socialist which meant, in fact, he had vague socialist ideals but came from too good a family to link them with the working class movement in anything but theory. He took his philosophy very seriously indeed; of the quality of that philosophy one can best judge when one remembers that he did not find the Master of Balliol a confused thinker. Indeed I think that the close friendship of the Master of Balliol is due to the fact that in the realm of philosophy each is as high minded as he is woolly.

Adam always found me slightly too earthy in my outlook on politics and I always found him so Hegelian that almost any action could be given its dialectical justification however slippery it might have been. In brief, I did not trust him very far, and he did not trust me.

In either 1936 or 1937 my wife and I during a tour of Germany stayed at Kassel where Adam was supposed to be training as a lawyer. We saw him every day, mostly in the evenings, in a small bar where he spent his time dicing. He was extremely unhappy and torn in mind, and my feelings were even more strongly confirmed that in any serious political conflict Adam's high minded idealism would somehow twist to avoid the really unpleasant decision to work for a revolution in Germany.

The private paper which Visser't Hooft brought from Adam for the personal perusal of Cripps, Temple and Lindsay, is an almost perfect specimen of Adam's thought, ingenuous in its politics and unaware of its intellectual and political dishonesty. On the other hand it probably very truthfully represents a section of the German diplomatic service, army and church inside Germany whose line of thought is reflected outside by such men as Rauschnig, but there would be very little difference in practice between the actions recommended by each.

I believe therefore that the group Adam represents really does exist and that it is of some importance for our Political Warfare and *it could be misdirected by us in ways useful to HMG* [Author's italics]. Adam von Trott is not fully aware of his ingenuousness in politics, can claim a really extensive knowledge of England, and may therefore be able to persuade harder headed men than himself to share his illusions.

This was an unkind report and it was unfortunate for the conspirators that an influential friend of Trott should write that it was unlikely that he would work for a 'revolution in Germany'. The idea, too, that he could be 'misdirected by us' for propaganda purposes indicated that Crossman, who was then working for the German language broadcasts at the BBC, thought he would have little *gravitas* as an active plotter to overthrow Hitler. The Foreign Office naively accepted Crossman's briefing, ignoring Cripps and Trott's other distinguished friends in England.

Cripps saw Eden and asked what was the Foreign Office attitude towards the memorandum. Geoffrey Harrison minuted on 6 June 1942 that the

main new point is that the alleged anti Hitler group is prepared to assassinate Hitler in a coup d'état . . . we can tell Sir S. Cripps that it very probably represents the views of certain elements in Germany in the civil service, army and church. (I am a little doubtful about Labour circles.) On the other hand we do not think the time has yet come for us to intervene directly to encourage this group and we should see active signs of its existence before we should believe it was of real significance. Visser't Hooft is above suspicion.

A week later Harrison became vicious about the document, commenting that it was dangerous for copies to be circulating in Britain. He did not mean dangerous for Trott and the conspirators, but for Allied morale. He went on:

I think I should draw attention to the fact that it is really very dangerous for documents of the nature of this memorandum to be circulating in this country. There seems no limit to the number of copies which may have been made and it can only be embarrassing if influential people are stimulated in this way to interfere in both our policy and political warfare towards Germany. Moreover, M. Visser't Hooft has moved freely in various circles in this country and he will no doubt in all good faith pass on to his contacts in Switzerland the atmosphere which he found here. I am told that he has in fact been met with a very uncompromising attitude from almost all the people he has seen. One or two, on the other hand, may have been tempted to use him for political warfare purposes. In either case the result is unsatisfactory because undirected. It is therefore for consideration whether, as we cannot expect to control visitors of this kind, we should deny them entry at all in future into this country.

I understand that Sir S. Cripps suggested that Miss Wiskeyman [*sic*] should be told to 'cool off' Adam von Trott on the grounds that he is too valuable. It seems to me regrettable that it should be known that Herr von Trott is in contact at all with Miss Wiskeyman [*sic*] and I am very doubtful about asking her to 'cool him off'. In fact I do not think it is, in our interest to do so since his value to us as a 'martyr' is likely to exceed his value to us in post-war Germany.

G.W. HARRISON
12th June, 1942

Makins commented:

I have held up this paper pending a search for further details of Adam von Trott's visit to this country in July 1939, in the course of which he had two meetings with Lord Halifax. But no record of this can now be discovered.

I agree with Mr. Harrison that there are no doubt a number of people in Germany who would endorse this memorandum, but we have really no evidence that they form an organised group. Moreover, it is quite likely that they are being, or will be, used by other more hard-headed individuals, e.g. in the German General Staff, as cover for peace overtures.

I am quite clear, therefore, that it would be a mistake to give a response to these overtures at the present time, and, further, that the indiscriminate circulation of this memorandum and the casual conversations of M. Visser 't Hooft may be rather misleading to all parties concerned. Fortunately, M. van Kleffens took precisely the right line with M. Visser 't Hooft. (See C 5099/G).

I suggest that Passport Control be asked to inform us in advance about the movements of such birds, in order that we may regulate them as far as possible and arrange for dealing with those who succeed in reaching this country.

R.M. MAKINS
12th June, 1942

Sargent minuted his agreement on the same day.

Makins's comment that he agreed with Harrison there was no evidence that 'the authors of the memorandum formed an organised group' was flying in the face of the evidence given by Bishop Bell after his visit to Stockholm. His reference to van Kleffens arose because he, the Dutch Foreign Minister in exile in London, had written to Eden on 15 May after he had talked to Visser 't Hooft and told him he refused to have anything to do with this group and that they were 'very unrealistic in their outlook'. Eden replied that he 'entirely agreed'.

H. J. Van Rojen recorded after the war that in 1942 he and other Dutch Resistance members met Trott when he came to Holland to establish contact between the German opposition to Hitler and the Dutch Resistance. He was convinced of Trott's genuineness and during the course of several clandestine meetings Trott declared there was what could be described as 'a coalition' of certain Hitler opponents including Catholic and Protestant churchmen, social workers, Army officers and Government officials including secret representatives in different Government departments. Trott offered to try to get Nazi sentences against prominent Dutchmen commuted.

Van Rojen and his friends were much impressed with Trott and remained in touch with him and his friend Moltke until the Germans were arrested. Trott's only request to his Dutch friends was that they should keep the Dutch Government in exile in London informed of their contacts with his group and to state that 'his conspiratorial group was intent upon displacing Hitler'.[12] However, Van Kleffens in London succumbed to the prevailing Foreign Office belief that Trott was not to be trusted, and ignored the first-hand evidence of the Dutch underground.

The attitude of the Foreign Office to Trott was one of undisguised hostility. Professor Marshall alone appreciated what was at stake and minuted:

Religious opposition has been growing in Germany . . . Though the details are unreliable the document provides strong evidence that church circles are prepared to collaborate in some way in the initial revolution . . . These people it is alleged have been actively planning the overthrow of Hitlerism by assassination.

Eden consulted with Cadogan, and wrote back to Cripps rejecting his advice about the importance and authenticity of Trott's approach and ignoring the fact that Cripps knew Trott intimately. He reiterated the views of the Department expressed in the minutes, accepted his subordinate's draft letter without alteration, and clearly did not give this issue the detailed consideration it deserved.

Confidential   Foreign Office, S.W.1
                                                                       18th June, 1942

My dear Stafford,
    You spoke to me a few days ago about a memorandum said to have been written by Freiherr Adam von Trott, which M. Visser't Hooft recently brought over to this country. You asked me what we knew of von Trott and what our attitude was towards M. Visser't Hooft and the document he brought with him.
    As regards Visser't Hooft he is, as you know, both European Secretary of the Y.M.C.A. and also one of the joint Secretaries of the World Council of Churches in Geneva. To the best of our belief he is a man above reproach or suspicion.
    The memorandum is an interesting document, and we believe it is quite likely there are a number of people in Germany who would endorse it. We have, however, no evidence so far that they form an organised group, and there is always the possibility that in due course they may be used by more hard-headed individuals, e.g. as cover for peace overtures. We do not ourselves attach much importance as yet to these people, nor do we propose to respond to any overtures from them. Our view is that until they come out into the open and give some visible sign of their intention to assist in the overthrow of the Nazi regime, they can be of little use to us or to Germany.

Baron von Trott, who was a Rhodes scholar at Oxford in the late nineteen-twenties, is a curious mixture of high-minded idealism and political dishonesty. Here is a short summary of an appreciation by a contemporary of his at Oxford. [Then follows an extract from the Crossman report quoted before.] Adam von Trott in fact is not untypical of a number of young Germans in the German Ministry of Foreign Affairs who, profoundly anti-Nazi in upbringing and outlook, have never quite been able to bring themselves to pay the price of their convictions and *resign* from the service of the Nazi regime. Von Trott has an extensive knowledge of England. He was over here just before the war broke out and met Edward Halifax among others.

Yours ever,
(Sgd.) ANTHONY

Cripps received this letter ill, and acidly wrote back to tell his Cabinet colleague that 'he had made a superficial judgement' – a tart reply between members of the intimate War Cabinet.

Gwydyr House,
Whitehall, S.W.1
June 20, 1942

My dear Anthony,

Thanks for your letter of June 18. I know both these men quite well, and I think probably know von Trott a good deal better than your informant since he has spent long periods staying in our house in the past. It is a complete failure to understand either him or what he stands for that dubs him politically dishonest.

As a matter of fact I spent a long evening with him in July '39 when we were both clear that the war was going to break out before the autumn and discussed at great length his attitude towards the Nazi regime. I have also met a very great many of his friends in different walks of life and he has since the Hitler regime came into power maintained a close contact with the working-class movement very much to his own danger.

He felt strongly that it was his duty as a German, in spite of the imminent personal risks, to go back to Germany and remain there while the war was on although he was bitterly antagonistic to the Nazi regime and has always refused to become a member of the Party.

Any such superficial judgement as that indicated in your letter would lead to a grave misunderstanding as regards the outlook of himself and his friends. It is not a question of his bringing himself to pay the price of his convictions by resigning from the service of the Nazi regime, which would have been a very simple solution, like that of many emigrés. He paid the far higher price in risk in refusing to join the Nazi regime, but going back to Germany to fight for the things which he believed to be right.

I only write you these particulars that you may have a better information as regards his personality.

Yours,
STAFFORD

Eden could not bear criticism of his conduct of foreign affairs. Nettled, he scrawled on Cripps's letter 'Ack. Department to see.' That meant that from the Foreign Office point of view the matter was dead.

How little attention the Foreign Office paid to Cripps's vouching for the honesty and sincerity of Trott in June 1942 is shown by a message to SOE three months later dated 27 September 1942 stating Trott was 'an extraordinary suspicious character', although it gave a much better write up to Moltke. The SOE were then enquiring about members of the German opposition with whom it might be safe for their agents to deal.[13]

After Bishop Bell's visit to Stockholm and Visser't Hooft's trip to London with the Trott memorandum a cursory report was circulated to the War Cabinet:

There is good reason to believe that many of these overtures, perhaps the majority, have been inspired by the German secret service which seems to have made a special study of the strategy and tactics of the peace feelers. The purpose is obvious – to try and sow dissension between the Allies and to slow up the tempo of their war efforts . . .

The paragraph 3 of the memorandum of the 14 April 1941, attention was drawn to the alleged readiness of a section of the German army to purchase a compromise peace at the cost of the elimination of Hitler and his replacement by a more moderate Government. While the 'dissident Generals' have continued to play their part throughout the period under review, notably at the turn of the years 1941/42, pride of place has now been taken by an alleged anti-Hitler group, Christian in outlook, which is said to comprise 'decent elements' from diplomatic, military, industrial, ecclesiastical and trade-union circles.

It has remained the policy of His Majesty's Government to respond to such overtures, from whatever quarter, either with absolute silence, or, in the case of neutral Governments, on the basis of the categoric statements by members of His Majesty's Government that they are not prepared to talk peace until the Nazi regime has been broken. A note of encouragement to dissident elements in Germany was sounded by Mr. Eden in his speech on the 8th May 1942 in Edinburgh, when he said:

'The longer the German people continue to support and to tolerate the regime which is leading them to destruction, the heavier grows their own direct responsibility for the damage they are doing to the world.

'Therefore, if any section of the German people wants to see a return to a German State which is based on respect for law and for the rights of the individual, they must understand that no-one will believe them until they have taken active steps to rid themselves of their present regime.'

Foreign Office, July 1, 1942.[14]

There was no discussion of the memorandum by the War Cabinet nor of an accompanying report which gave brief details of other approaches through diplomats in neutral countries. Yet at that time the Germans occupied 1,000 square miles of Russian territory, Egypt was in danger, and the Americans tied down in the Far East by Japanese successes. Would Russians and Americans not have been seriously tempted to agree to a peace with anti-Nazis on the lines suggested by Trott even if Churchill and Eden rejected the idea out of hand?

In June 1942 Moltke managed to transmit through SOE a letter from Stockholm to his close friend Lionel Curtis,[f] giving evidence of the existence of an active opposition. He wrote:

Can you imagine what is is like to work as a group when you cannot use the telephone; when you are unable to post letters; when you cannot tell the names of your closest friends to your other friends for fear that one of them might be caught and divulge the names under pressure? . . . we are ready to help you to win war and peace.

By the same means he wrote to Michael Balfour, a close friend of his, who was a historian working in the Political Warfare Executive of the Foreign Office. He asked Balfour to come to Stockholm to meet him in September or October. Both Mallet in Stockholm and Balfour's chiefs in PWE were agreeable. Balfour tried to get permission to go. It was turned down by the Prime Minister personally; he confused Helmuth Moltke with his cousin Adolf, then German Ambassador in Madrid, who had been instrumental in passing on peace feelers from the Nazis. Balfour has unimpeachable evidence that it was the Prime Minister himself who refused to allow him to go.[15]

On 14 September 1943 Bishop Bell wrote to Bruce Lockhart, Head of the Political Warfare Executive of the Foreign Office, enclosing Moltke's letter and drawing attention to his request for someone thoroughly trustworthy to be placed in the Legation at Stockholm, outside the Secret Service, to establish contact with the opposition without the danger of betrayal implicit in Secret Service contacts.

Bruce Lockhart did not show the letter to Balfour, whom Moltke had particularly asked for as the contact, although he was working in the section; nor did he show it to the head of the PWE German section. What Curtis did with his copy we do not know. By September 1943 John Wheeler-Bennett who wanted no truck with the German opposition, had become deputy to Bruce Lockhart, and this probably explains the failure of PWE to respond to this communication from an

[f]Lionel Curtis, a former adviser to the Colonial Office, was a leading writer on international affairs.

opposition source known to be above suspicion. The overture from Moltke foundered as had Bishop Bell's, Visser't Hooft's and Trott's.

Moltke also managed to send to Cripps news of the 'White Rose' – a revolutionary movement in Munich University. Two students, Hans and Sophie Scholl, had been sending anti-Nazi leaflets through the post for months and calling on the people to rise up against Hitler. In January 1943 they were arrested by the Gestapo, brutally tortured and executed. The Foreign Office were not interested, but Cripps sent a note about it to Churchill, writing on 29 September 1943: 'It is evidence of internal developments in Germany of which we ought to take account in our political warfare.'

Obviously Cripps hoped Churchill would take it up with Eden so that the Foreign Office might approach the anti-Nazi opposition. Winston's reply was unhelpful. He did not take the hint, and merely minuted non-commitally: 'Most interesting, and I do not wonder that Hitler's gang reacted in a murderous way to it.' That was the end of it as far as the Foreign Office was concerned, but both Balfour and Carleton Greene assured the author that they made full use of the White Rose episode in their propaganda broadcasts to Germany.[16]

In his letter to Curtis Moltke said: 'There are those who supported by Goebbels' propaganda and by British propaganda, say if we lose this war we will be eaten up alive by our enemies, therefore we must stand by Hitler.' Moltke also reported that 250,000 Germans were in concentration camps and that masses of Jews were being killed. This is what he wrote about a liaison officer:

Now how can this be done technically? We would have to have a man in Stockholm who knows Central Europe and who, working under the general guidance of the ambassador would have special functions to keep in touch with the various underground movements in Europe, especially in Germany and would have to deal with them on a basis of political discussion and cooperation. We would supply him with addresses here which would contact him with the oppositions in various countries under Hitler. Preferably it should be a man whom I know or about whom I know something, because time is precious and with a stranger it will take some time to get intimate and real personal contact is required . . . the man must be able in certain circumstances to provide one of us with everything necessary to get to Britain and back in a short time, so that if necessary common plans can be discussed viva voce . . . The name must most certainly never appear in writing anywhere.

As far as I am concerned I would, of course, prefer to have Michael [Balfour] here in Stockholm be it as principal or as an adviser to the principal . . .[17]

To this sensible entreaty the Foreign Office turned a deaf ear.

At the end of June 1942 Trott was back in Geneva to find out from Visser't Hooft the reaction in London to his message to Cripps. Hooft had to tell him that the British Government had spurned his overture and there was no alternative to the complete military defeat of Germany. The only ray of light was that Cripps had stressed in a talk with Hooft that he wanted 'further communications'. This reply was a desperate blow to the conspirators but Trott continued his efforts to interest the Allies in the opposition movement. After the war Visser t'Hooft wrote,'The answer I had to take back to Geneva was that the British Government were not willing to give any encouragement to the German resistance and not even ready to enter into any dialogue. I have never forgotten that summer night in my garden when I was trying to find words to encourage Adam who was near despair.'[18]

In January 1943 Trott made contact with Allen Dulles who had been sent to Berne to head the US Office of Strategic Services (OSS), with the special responsibility of keeping in touch with the anti-Nazis. Trott asked Dulles to tell Washington how disappointed the plotters were at the British refusal to offer any encouragement, and briefed him thoroughly on the plot. He wrote a document for Dulles which pointed out that the rejection by the British Foreign Office of his overtures showed 'prejudice' as a result the conspirators would be tempted to turn to the Russians for help in overthrowing Hitler and obtaining peace terms which would ensure 'preservation of the German nation'. This was duly communicated to Washington who repeated it to London, but it aroused no enthusiasm at a moment when Roosevelt and Churchill were alarmed at the danger of Hitler and Stalin doing another deal.[19]

In June 1943 Trott went to Turkey to meet von Papen in Istanbul. Von Papen was informed of the plot and generally in sympathy, but the meeting accomplished nothing, although they had a frank talk. Trott may well have been too Left-wing for Papen.

In Istanbul Trott met an old friend, Professor Paul Leverkuehn, an anti-Nazi and head of the Abwehr there. Leverkuehn asked him on his return to Berlin to try and get Erich Vermehren transferred from the Berlin office of the Abwehr to Istanbul. Trott, with his usual good nature, agreed. It was to have sinister consequences for the plotters.[20]

Trott's next visit in search of an accommodation with the Allies was to Stockholm on 27 October 1943. There he met two attachés from the British Legation, Roger Hinks and James Knapp-Fisher. Trott's purpose in asking to see them was to enquire whether the British and

American Governments, once a revolution had taken place, would give up the unconditional surrender formula and suspend immediately the bombing of Germany. It is hard to see what the Allies could have lost if they promised to give up the bombing after Hitler was overthrown, but the British representatives had been specifically forbidden to give any such assurances, although they expressed sympathy with Trott and the opposition. The British Envoy in Sweden did not even report to London Trott's direct request for an answer to the question about unconditional surrender; he knew too well from Foreign Office directives that the answer must be an unqualified negative, and probably he thought Knapp-Fisher and Hinks had been definite enough already in stressing there could be no deviation.[20]

Mallet reported to London that Trott had given information that the Communists were well organized in Germany and were the only serious opposition; that Russian defeats were easier to bear than the indiscriminate murder from air raids from the west; and that if at the end of the war the Russians had won all the battles while the British and the Americans had destroyed all the cities, the political consequences would not be favourable to the West.

Trott had not chosen the best arguments; with the British commitment to a bombing offensive such criticism was unwelcome in Downing Street. The internal Foreign Office minute on the Stockholm report on Trott was not passed to Cadogan or Eden.[g] Harrison minuted: 'Note the skill with which he propagates the old Communist bogey and generally mixes up fact and propaganda.' This highlights the anti-Trott prejudice in the German Department; his renewed attempt at communicating with the British Government was a complete failure.[21]

Yet the Foreign Office had considerable evidence about Trott's genuineness on their files. Both Lothian and Cripps had vouched enthusiastically for his *bona fides*, and Wheeler-Bennett had written from Washington on 29 April 1943:[22]

Trott was anti-Nazi but strong German nationalist. My view is he is not a very subtle agent of the enemy as some diplomats think . . . At the Virginia Beach Conference of the Institute of Pacific Relations in November 1940 in private Trott declared himself anti Nazi yet maintaining that Germany must keep what she had taken in Poland.

[g]Mallet's despatch would have been circulated to the Prime Minister and Foreign Secretary, but without any briefing they would have ignored it.

Wheeler-Bennett added that the US Foreign Department thought he was a Nazi agent.

As Wheeler-Bennett had known Trott intimately in England before the war, and had discussed him at great length with Lothian when he was in America in November 1940, he might have been even more forthcoming on his behalf. In March 1940 he had written glowingly to Trott as he prepared to leave the United States for Germany:

Let me wish you the greatest of good fortune in the aim which we have in common. May it be achieved . . . I would like to say how much I admire your courage and determination under very trying circumstances. I hope under similar conditions I could match you but I am pretty sure I could not.[23]

Now, two years later, when Wheeler-Bennett could have influenced the Foreign Office attitude towards the German opposition, the steam seems to have gone out of his admiration. As far as the Foreign Office was concerned the recognition of Trott as a German nationalist was the kiss of death.

Wheeler-Bennett, who returned to London from Washington in 1943, was a close friend and confidant of Eden. Typical of his attitude was a paper by him sent on by the Washington Embassy to the Foreign Office in 1943 on 'other Germans'. In it he wrote:

At the conclusion of the war we are not going to be liked by any Germans, 'good' or 'bad'. Any friendly feelings will be unnatural and therefore suspect . . . we should not place ourselves in the position of bargaining with any Germans good or bad . . . this is inherent in the principle of unconditional surrender.

He was commenting on two recently published books on Germany after Hitler by anti-Nazis in the United States.[h] He added there was a rallying point there amongst German emigres who wanted a soft peace. He had talked with Brettauer and Rauschning who argued that unconditional surrender had made a coup in Germany impossible and that Germany must go Communist without a soft peace, and he pointed out that Rauschning wanted to keep Austria and East Prussia as part of Germany after the war.

Professor Marshall rumbled Wheeler-Bennett and commented on the Foreign Office file:

This vitriolic little paper is hardly worthy of its distinguished author. He is shooting at the wrong target. The real point is not whether the German

[h]Rauschning had been a Nazi chief in Danzig but had turned anti-Hitler and emigrated. Brettauer was a wealthy Jew who had escaped from Germany with his fortune in early days of Nazidom, and his large house on the Pacific coast was a meeting place for anti-Nazi émigrés.

emigreés are sincere idealists or scheming nationalists, but whether the German people now in Germany can be converted by kindness (or whether a large proportion of them do not need conversion), as some of the emigrés appear to believe. Mr. Wheeler-Bennett is grossly unfair to the authors of *The Next Germany*. The passage he quotes, if read in its context, is obviously not a plea for an expansion of German frontiers, but a cautious appeal to Germans not to object too strongly to the curtailment of German territory. The authors (I know three of the four quite well) are not nationalists, still less pan-Germans. They are internationally minded socialists. Their weakness is that nationalism enters so little into their thinking that they forget the strength of the feeling that Germany must suffer as a guilty nation. Mr. Wheeler-Bennett seems to think that they reveal the underlying principles of German thought. The difficulty is that they do not. If they did, there would be no German problem.[24]

Trott went to Geneva from 18 to 20 December 1943. Here he met Robert Elliot of the Student Christian Movement who reported to the Foreign Office in London that Trott had declared 'an army coup would produce a new provisional Government which would stop all anti-Jewish discrimination, but would not surrender all German-held territory in Czechoslovakia and Poland'.[25] Predictably, the reference to Germany's retaining parts of pre-war Poland and Czechoslovakia made the Foreign Office officials, if possible, even less sympathetic to Trott, but to Elliot he emphasized that the Allies must not confine a new German Government to the Versailles frontiers, and 'that Germany must have a dominant position in West Europe'.

On the file the Department minuted that they knew Halder was part of Trott's group (this was incorrect) and that Halder's and Weizsaecker's designs coincided with Hitler's and Ribbentrop's so that 'open and clandestine trends of peace proposals have temporarily merged'. The Foreign Office could not have been further from the truth.[26]

Trott also contacted Dulles but the information he sent merely confirmed much of what Dulles had already learnt about the conspiracy from Goerdeler and Gisevius. Dulles sent another accurate picture of the plot to Washington, which aroused no response — although it was fruitlessly sent on to London.[27]

During the early part of 1944 further evidence began to accumulate that something really serious was afoot from the German Resistance. In mid January Lord Selborne, Minister of Economic Warfare, received what he described as 'urgent information' through Switzerland that the German general staff intended to assassinate Hitler, accept unconditional surrender and evacuate Holland. This came from Dr Gerbrandy, the Dutch Prime Minister, and the envoy had been an unnamed German staff colonel. Selborne told Churchill, but Eden would have nothing to do with it and wrote to the Dutch Prime Minister on 28 January 1944: 'Such moves always came from the German secret service and as such were ignored.' Churchill received a copy of Eden's minute and concurred. With hindsight we know it was genuine advance information of the highest importance.[28]

On 9 January Campbell wrote from Lisbon to Roberts:

You may remember Arany, the Hungarian face-massage man who hands Berta bits of paper containing scraps of information let drop by his German clients. Most of his stuff, which I pass to Gledhill, has the appearance of being what the Germans are putting out, although recently he produced what looked like being the correct figures of the casualties suffered by the principal bombed German towns.

The other day I saw him in response to a message which he said he could divulge to me alone. This was what he told me.

He had remained in touch with his one-time Professor (medical) in Germany who had just sent him a message (by the mouth of some German who had come here) to say that a group in Germany composed in part of professors, in part of army officers, was ready to encompass the fall or death of Hitler in order to bring about an earlier cessation of hostilities, and perhaps less harsh terms, provided the principal conspirators were guaranteed asylum in some other country whose nationality they must be allowed to acquire (to avoid the stigma of being Germans) and that they were ensured a livelihood in their country of adoption.

Roberts noted it was 'the usual soft peace move' and told Campbell to ignore the information.[29]

Mallet from Stockholm sent news in the same week of a plan by German ecclesiastics for a new constitution following the overthrow of Hitler. This time Roberts noted: 'The Churches will be the only respectable institution left in the immediate post war state of Germany. It would presumably make difficulties with the Russians.' No action was taken, and no effort made to relate this news to the information brought in 1942 by Bishop Bell about the German Churches.[30]

In April Knatchbull-Hugessen wrote from Ankara that his Belgian counterpart had news of a move by the German military to make peace and they wanted to know what the peace terms were, and that he had told the Soviet Ambassador in Ankara of this. Roberts minuted that Huggeson had handled the matter 'ineptly' because it was for the Foreign Office to decide what should be passed on to the Soviets, and the feeler was 'of no value'.[31]

Everything foundered on the mistrust of Trott by Roberts, Harrison, Harvey and Kirkpatrick. Brian MacDermot told the author that he would have vouched for Trott's truthfulness but he would not have believed that he was anything more than a talker and would have been sceptical about his being an efficient activist. Gordon Etherington-Smith, another member of the Foreign Office, said he had known Trott well in Berlin during the few months before the war started and would have guaranteed his honesty. Yet he had no firm evidence that he was anti-Nazi. But then Trott had to be careful. During his trip to England in 1939 as a member of the German Foreign Office, he had to simulate the pose of being an ardent Nazi except with his closest friends, as otherwise information might have been leaked to the Gestapo and he would have been trapped. The stance deceived Bowra, who wrote in his autobiography: 'I decided that von Trott was playing a double game. My rejection of him remains one of my bitterest regrets.'[32]

Sir Con O'Neill, another diplomat, had also been a contemporary of Trott at Balliol. When they met in 1939 Trott did not dare to tell him of his anti-Nazi work and O'Neill was deceived into thinking he was pro-Nazi because he was in the German Foreign Office. O'Neill himself had resigned from the British Foreign Office at the end of 1938 when he was Third Secretary in Berlin. It was a gesture against appeasement and because he could not bear to work under Henderson, who was prepared to give in completely to Hitler. He was succeeded by Etherington-Smith. This is O'Neill's Foreign Office minute in 1944:

I too knew Adam von Trott pretty well, both in Oxford 12 years ago and in Berlin in 1938 after his return from China. On the whole I endorse the opinion expressed about him in this file. With others, I certainly distrusted him; not least when I came across him during his 'mission' to London a few weeks before war began, in the course of this as is recorded elsewhere among these papers, he met Mr. Chamberlain and Lord Halifax.

I also knew well (not through von Trott) the other man whose name has often been coupled with von Trott's in various reports and who is also discussed in Mr. Wheeler-Bennett's paper – Helmut von Moltke. To him, in my opinion, Mr. Wheeler-Bennett does a good deal less than justice. I thought him von Trott's superior in all respects, of a greater intelligence and integrity, and of far greater discretion. He was in fact a man of very strong character and personality; of equally imposing physique (he was about 6 feet 3 in height). He was not such an indiscriminate Anglophile as Trott, though he knew England pretty well and was called to the Bar here in 1939. But he was a much more profound anti Nazi; and I feel fairly confident in saying of him, what could be said of few Germans, that he must have found the events of

June 1940 as depressing as all Englishmen did. He was also a profound anti-militarist – even more surprising in the head (as he was) of the most famous of all Prussian militarist families. This, I daresay, was a result of a strong puritan and ascetic strain in his character, which may have come from his English (or rather South African) mother. Growing up after the last war, he had of course escaped military service. He practised law in Berlin, and also managed his own large farm in Silesia.

Some question arises in Mr. Wheeler-Bennett's paper as to whether these two men knew each other before the war. They certainly did; I have seen them together. But at that time (1938 and 1939) I think von Moltke distrusted von Trott as much as I did.[33]

When the author showed this minute to O'Neill in 1984 he said he had often thought about it and regretted it. His revised opinion was that Trott was a hero, but that Trott's attitude in 1939 (when he was covering his tracks) was such that O'Neill felt he had made a justifiable mistake. O'Neill could not recall where he got the idea that Moltke mistrusted Trott, and in this he appears to have been completely wrong. Both Christabel Bielenberg[i] and Trott's widow have confirmed to the author that Trott and Moltke trusted each other completely.

O'Neill said that he was working on German reconstruction from 1943 onwards in the next room to Roberts and Harrison, but they never consulted him or showed him the papers about the plot. When the author showed him the documents reproduced in this chapter he said if he had seen them with his recent knowledge of Germany he would have been sure that something really serious was brewing.

David Astor, Trott's oldest close English friend, told the author that he felt strongly that in view of the importance of the information coming from Trott, the Foreign Office should have instituted a type of police operation to establish whether or not he was genuine. He wrote to the author:

If military intelligence or the police took as little trouble to check on their impressions of a suspected person as the Foreign Office took in checking their suspicions of Adam, it would have caused a scandal. Their suspicions were largely concerning his one or two visits to London in 1939. At that time he was in constant touch with Stafford Cripps and myself, and intermittent touch with Wilfred Israel.[j] None of us was ever asked by anyone for our information on what he was talking about and what we thought he was

---

[i] A niece of Lord Northcliffe, she was married to a German lawyer who was closely involved with the resistance movement. She recounted her experiences in *The Past Is Myself*.
[j] A Fellow of All Souls.

doing. Yet all three of us were reasonably honest people who could have given them better information than they had got themselves.

MacDermot's comment was that people like himself and his Foreign Office colleagues were completely unsuited to make the proper inquiries or the judgments as to whether Trott was genuine or not, and he endorsed Astor's view.

Hugh Carleton Greene, before he was expelled by Hitler as *Daily Telegraph* correspondent in 1939, had known Trott well in Berlin. He told the author:

Trott was amazingly indiscreet in conversation – so much so that I began to suspect (wrongly I know) that he was an agent provocateur luring people on to expose their anti-Nazis views. There was justification for the Foreign Office view that he might not be reliable despite his impeccable credentials from Cripps and Lothian, etc. You must remember people do change their views very surprisingly.[34]

Christopher Sykes, in his biography of Trott published in 1969, wrote that the Foreign Office had a dossier on Trott but that it was 'in the main a mass of prejudiced comment and mistaken conclusions, some of it of the most ridiculous kind'. This was speculation by Sykes because the official archives were closed and no one then thought they would be opened until after the year 2000. Now the Foreign Office papers confirm that Sykes's guess in 1969 was entirely accurate.

In August 1942 the Beck, Goerdeler, Trott, Moltke circle had been seriously endangered by the discovery by the Gestapo of a Communist plot inside the Air Ministry. It was known as the Red Chapel and had a loose connection with the Beck-Goerdeler group. Goering, responsible for the Air Ministry, was furious; there were nearly 1,000 executions and a witch hunt was started to find other anti-Nazi groups. The Kreisau group was endangered, as were Beck, Goerdeler and Trott – but Canaris was able to keep the Gestapo at bay temporarily.

Many arrests of Trott's friends were made when the Kreisau Circle was penetrated at a tea party in Berlin in August 1943 given by Frau Solf. She was the fervently anti-Nazi widow of an ambassador. A Gestapo agent came posing as an anti-Nazi and soon collected incriminating evidence against the other guests. As a result, Frau Solf, von Moltke, Fraulein von Thadden, headmistress of a famous girls' school, and Otto Kleip, a former German Consul in New York, were arrested in January 1944, plus two ex-diplomats, Kunzer and

Bernstorff[k] − a deadly blow to the Resistance. All the guests at the tea party were executed, except the Solfs who miraculously escaped.[35]

Trott himself was now in great danger because he had been instrumental in getting a visa for a former Rhodes Scholar nominee, Erich Vermehren (another plotter), to go to Istanbul. Vermehren had been close to Kleip and after the arrests a telegram was sent in March to Istanbul at the instigation of the Gestapo, ordering him to return immediately to Berlin. Instead he and his wife defected to the British. Two other Abwehr agents simultaneously defected to Cairo from Turkey. Just as worrying for Trott were injudicious BBC programmes which had referred to 'a Rhodes Scholar with peace proposals' during his last visit to Stockholm.

When Roger Hinks[l] sent a message from Stockholm that they would like a further talk with Trott, he decided to gamble with death and go. The British Foreign Office, however, only wanted the interview as a means of getting information about internal conditions in Germany and had no intention of starting the negotiations with the German opposition which Trott so ardently desired. Yet this hope had been the only reason for his dangerous journey to Stockholm.

Ewan Butler, a Secret Service agent, has recorded that at the Legation they all heard of Trott's arrival and asked permission from their superiors in London to meet him. Denham, the Naval Attaché, wrote in his memoirs to the same effect.[36] This was sternly refused on the grounds that the policy was 'unconditional surrender' and any contact with anti-Nazis who wanted to get rid of Hitler was forbidden. Butler's postwar comment was: 'The Allies missed a great opportunity.' Tennant, who was press officer at the British Legation in Stockholm throughout the war, told the author that in his view the Foreign Office was 'caddish' in its behaviour to Trott and Goerdeler.

Trott in Stockholm in mid-March 1944 had two long talks with a Frau Almstrom in her flat. She was a safe pro-British Swede. These talks were held at the request of the British Legation who also asked Frau Almstrom to produce a memorandum on Trott's views. This memorandum on the Trott conversations in Stockholm was forwarded to London by Mallet. The main points were:

American bombing in daylight of industrial targets was understood by the German people to be a 'necessity', but the British bombing by night with the object of total obliteration of German cities did the British cause great harm;

---

[k]Gordon Etherington-Smith who knew Bernstorff well in Berlin in 1939 said he was notoriously indiscreet. Con O'Neill said the same.

[l]The art historian, then attached as Second Secretary to the British Legation in Stockholm.

the average German was saying 'the British are as bad as the Nazis; there is as little to be hoped from the English as from the Russians'. He added that bombing strengthened Hitler's cause because all relief for the bombed out was in the hands of the party who appeared as 'civilised people performing acts of charity'. He feared the German people would turn to Russia.

He argued the allied terms for an armistice should be dinned into the ears of the German people day and night over the radio so that Goebbels would not be able to keep them from the German people.'

If a trustworthy member of an Allied Government would let them know what the peace terms were he would disclose the names of the Generals willing to attempt a coup to dethrone Hitler, and it was of vital importance that these terms, even if it reduced Germany to a smaller state than the Versailles frontiers, should not make the German people feel themselves reduced to 'helots'. He recognised the necessity of a total occupation of the country and urged that it should be a joint Anglo-Russian-American occupation. [The Russian advances had considerably reduced Trott's territorial ambitions since his talk in December in Geneva with Elliot.]

He claimed that if the Generals knew the terms they would, if necessary, make the second front a walk over for the Allies and that he had spoken to the Generals about 'this very thing'.

The opposition was well organised but as it had no support from outside it had to keep low. Trott could get permission to come at any time to Stockholm as a contact between the opposition and the allies because he was being treated by a Stockholm doctor for a liver complaint.

He said the military must be used at any rate in the early stages if the whole of Europe was not to fall into a state of chaos from which it might never recover as they were the only opposition with sufficient strength to bring about a successful coup. He did not favour the complete liquidation of the military tradition in Germany as this would lead to deep resentment and a possible rebirth in a far worse form of the military tradition which anyway it is impossible to obliterate.[37]

Finally Trott gave details of life in bombed out Berlin; he said he, as a high official, was allowed the luxury of travelling to work in his own car, but clerks and typists had great travel problems and frequently arrived two hours late. Somehow traffic functioned and still brought the considerably reduced population of Berlin to its offices each day. Berlin was extremely dreary and very empty.

The Foreign Office gave no consideration to the possibility of negotiating through Trott with the opposition in an effort to end the war before D Day. Nothing was said about it to Eisenhower's staff but this time the importance of the Stockholm information from Trott was realized. His reliability, however, was again questioned by Harrison, and the main interest in it was whether or not unconditional surrender was the best tactic.

The minutes reaffirm the Foreign Office attitude to the German opposition:

Although v. Trott, if it is him, seems to be a very good mouthpiece of a certain well known type of German propaganda this report makes interesting reading throughout. He appeals to our humanitarian feelings, points to the dangers of Bolshevism and insists that it would be to our disadvantage to destroy the military tradition in Germany. But his plea for a clear statement of our peace terms is interesting in connection with the recently discussed pros and cons of a Declaration to the German People which was finally turned down by the War Cabinet.

REAY   1/4

This is the sort of stuff we have come to expect from this source.

D. ALLEN   1/4

This is worth reading – provided it is remembered that the source is tainted. I am not impressed with the story of why he is allowed to go so often to Sweden. I still have an open mind as to whether he is a conscious or unconscious agent of the German Secret Service. But his line of talk is certainly dangerous to us.

G.W. HARRISON   1/4

It does not seem to have cut much ice with the Swedish listener. Personally I think there is much truth as well as propaganda in his Para 4 in particular to support recent departmental recommendations that what would strike us as a very negative declaration might nevertheless have a great effect in Germany.

F. ROBERTS   2/4

The marked passages are worth a glance.

O. HARVEY   4/4

We tried one hand at a declaration to the German people but it has been, so far as I remember, at least shelved. I confess I still rather hanker after it. But the timing, as well as the phrasing, is important, and I don't know whether it would come best before the opening of forthcoming operations, or after they have scored an initial success.

A[LEC] C[ADOGAN]   April 4, 1944

This can certainly be examined afresh.

A[NTHONY] E[DEN]   April 6[38]

With great perseverance and courage Trott almost immediately went to Geneva. Here he met Elizabeth Wiskemann who recorded that 'he was a broken man, so worried by the Communists'. Trott contacted Dulles who had recently talked with Goerdeler in Geneva. Dulles signalled to Washington the gist of these talks. In a signal on 16 May Dulles said he was 'convinced of the sincerity of the emissaries', and asked what was the Allied policy towards the Resistance movement and what offers of help could they give. In their preliminary note to the British Ambassador the State Department unfortunately omitted that Dulles was 'convinced' of the emissaries' sincerity, and said Dulles had been told firmly that the US policy was not to entertain such overtures. Here is the note transmitted from the British Embassy in Washington to the Foreign Office on 24 May 1944:

An approach has been made by two emissaries of a German group proposing an attempt to overthrow the Nazi regime. These emissaries claim to represent a group including Leuschner, Socialist Leader and former Minister of Interior in Hesse; Oster, a General formerly the right hand man of Canaris, arrested in 1943 by the Gestapo kept under surveillance after his release and recently discharged from official functions by Keitel; Gordeler, former Mayor of Leipzig, and General Beck. Other German Generals mentioned subsequently as members of this opposition group include Halder, Zeitzler, Heusinger (Chief of Operations for Zeitzler), Olbrecht (Chief of the German Army administration), Falkenhausen and Rundstedt. With respect to Zeitzler it was reported that he had been won over by Heusinger and Olbrecht on the reasoning that he should co-operate in any plan to bring about an orderly liqudation of the Eastern front in order to escape the blame for a military disaster there which he greatly fears.

The emissaries approached an American representative in Switzerland and expressed in the name of the group their willingness and preparation to attempt to oust Hitler and the Nazis. The claim was made that the group would exercise sufficient influence with the German Army to cause certain Generals commanding in the west to cease resistance to Allied landings once the Nazis had been ousted. The condition on which the group expressed willingness to act was that they could deal directly with the United Kingdom and the United States alone after overthrowing the Nazi regime. As a precedent for excluding the Soviet they cited the recent example of Finland who they claim had dealt solely with Moscow.

Cadogan, on behalf of the Department, replied on 8 June: 'Please thank State Department for this information and say: "We fully agree with them in regarding this approach with profound suspicion".'

Harrison had minuted: 'This looks very bogus.' Roberts minuted: 'Very bogus and old friends.' Loxley added fatuously: 'Uncle Tom Cobley and all.'[m] The names of Goerdeler, Leuschner, Oster and Beck should have alerted these officials that something extremely important was brewing, but this last overture from Berne came up against a brick wall of suspicion.[39]

[m]Loxley was then private secretary to Cadogan. He was killed in an air crash on the way to the Yalta Conference. Harrison was originally scheduled to travel on the same plane but at the last moment was switched to an earlier flight as his matters at Yalta were being taken first.

In May Gisevius in Switzerland had told Dulles on behalf of the conspirators that they wanted to surrender to the West only and proposed that the anti-Nazi Generals should let American and British troops occupy Germany while the Russians were held on the Eastern Front. Their proposals included landing three airborne Allied divisions in the Berlin area where local German commanders would cooperate, together with large scale landings near Hamburg and on the French coast; simultaneously anti-Nazi troops would isolate Hitler and the top Nazis on Ober Salzberg. This information was not passed on to London, but such wild and unrealistic plans would have had a stony reception.[40]

In June Dulles received a confidential message through Gisevius giving advance news of the plan to murder Hitler. On 12 July he told Washington: 'Dramatic events may be impending.' He continued on 18 July that it confirmed his previous report about the plot's organization and that they could overthrow Hitler and set up a respectable Government. He said the group wanted to prevent as much as possible of Germany falling into Russian hands, and would call for an ordered retreat from the west and the transfer of the best divisions to the east. His news was immediately communicated by the US Government to the British and the Soviet Embassies, again without result.

On 26 June Trott was back in Stockholm with more news about the plans for the Allies. The US Minister in Stockholm, Herschel Johnson, reported to Washington that Trott ('a reliable person') had given information that the Russians had sent in by parachute a Communist committee, but this had no contact with Trott's resistance group composed of bourgeoise, especially Catholics and former Social Democrats, plus a few ex-Communists and officers, which was now making its own plans for a coup against the Nazis. He added that Trott warned the Allies would find a revolutionary situation in Germany.[41]

Trott also said that the Communist group of resisters had been penetrated by the Gestapo, so his group would not meet them. Leber conferred with them and was immediately arrested – a deadly blow to the Resistance.

Trott had made his June visit to Stockholm because a message had been passed to him in Berlin through Frau Amstrom that the British Legation would like to talk to him. Trott thought that finally the British Government had decided to negotiate with the Resistance. This was far from the case: the British Embassy did not regard Trott as, in their own words, 'a *bona fide* political contact, but merely a source of information about internal German conditions which could be exploited'.

Instead of allowing a diplomat to talk to Trott, a British Secret Service agent, David MacEwan, interviewed Trott at Alstrom's flat alone on 21 June. MacEwan had been one of the MI6 agents at the Berlin Embassy when the war started in 1939 and was an expert on Germany. He was the son of Air Vice-Marshal MacEwan and a friend of the Right-wing tennis star, Gottfried von Cramm, who had in the spring of 1944 visited Stockholm as the King's guest and tennis partner.

The British had cynically asked Trott to come to Stockholm in June 1944 at great risk to his life when all they wanted from him was information about conditions inside Germany which could have been obtained from any traveller from Germany; the British Legation had no intention even of evaluating the possibility of the German Resistance being able to bring the war to an early conclusion. The last English person Trott spoke to before his arrest and execution was MacEwan who knew and cared nothing about the German opposition.

Trott gave MacEwan a memorandum for the British Government. It reveals a resignation to the non-cooperation of the British and the pernicious effects of 'unconditional surrender'. Trott wrote that because of the unconditional surrender formula he could not take the risk of naming the leaders of the opposition, but said they were ready to act and remove the Nazi Government. He must have been unaware that in May Goerdeler had disclosed names to Dulles.

He pointed out that the abandonment of the Atlantic Charter in relation to Germany was being interpreted by many interested in overthrowing Hitler as meaning that Germany would have to exchange 'one lawless tyranny for another', and to their mind it would entail

slicing up of national territory at the instigation of uncontrolled passions in the neighbouring countries violated by Hitler, and arbitrary slave traffic in German workers and soldiers, and denial of the right to mete out justice to Nazi criminals . . . some assurance regarding territorial integrity, some understanding about orderly military demobilisation by the German command in co-operation with Allied control commissions and about the punishment of Nazi criminals by German courts would remove the worst obstacles now barring confidence and contact between this opposition group and the western allies.

He explained that 'to gain effective control of Germany' they would have to rely on senior Generals and the uncorrupted section of the police in the larger cities and certain militant groups of Social Democrats, Reichsbanner and Trade Union movements. His most telling point was that by accepting unconditional surrender now they would be unable later on to counteract the mass slogan of 'having stabbed in the back our fighting forces – a slogan which is bound to recur even more violently and immediately than it did after 1918'.

He confirmed that plans for a coup were at an advanced stage and that a group of political leaders widely representative had been formed to work in close contact with the Generals who were collaborating in the plot, and that some of the political leaders were known in England and had been carrying on contacts in neutral countries. He finished with a plea for the despatch of reliable agents to Stockholm.

Trott left Stockholm in no doubt from his contacts with the United States and British officials that the Allies would insist on unconditional surrender even if the conspirators overthrew the Nazis. That was the end of his journeys in search of an accommodation with the Allies.

When the news of Trott's trial and execution reached the British Legation in Stockholm a terse memorandum stated that 'contact with him had been dropped' in June because he was not prepared to furnish information for 'intelligence purposes' and his sole interest was to establish contact with the Allied powers 'with a view to securing some measures of assurance on the subject of Germany's future'. The Legation note stated that it was known he had seen Willi Brandt, John Scott, the American journalist, and Mr and Mrs Myrdal, Swedish economists who had returned from the United States and were very pro-Ally.

While in Stockholm Trott had two long talks with Willi Brandt – after the war leader of the German Socialist Party. He convinced Brandt that the conspirators would overthrow Hitler, and Trott asked Brandt if he would put himself at the disposal of the new Government. Brandt agreed, and told Trott that accepting 'unconditional surrender' was not too high a price to pay for stopping the war and thus saving hundreds of thousands of human lives. Brandt promised to contact 'several personages in the western camp' to see if they would help the conspirators. Undoubtedly Brandt spoke to members of the British Legation in Stockholm and passed on Trott's messages. Trott had intended to speak to Mrs Kollontay, the Soviet Ambassador in Stockholm, but discovered just in time that the Gestapo had infiltrated the Russian Embassy.[42]

The Foreign Office file on Trott's June 1944 visit to Stockholm is closed until the year 2000 because of MacEwan being a Secret Service agent. However, the Foreign Office has been good enough to let the author know that the London reaction to Trott's memorandum was 'that there should be no further contact' and that a major consideration influencing thinking on this matter was the need to avoid any action which could have jeopardized the unity of the Alliance with Russia.[43]

From this one can guess the type of minutes written on the file and Cadogan's and Eden's dismissal of this gallant final approach. Trott's memorandum coupled with Dulles's May signal from Berne gave a complete and accurate description of the plot and confirmed both the wide basis of the conspiracy, and all the Foreign Office had learnt from Bishop Bell and Visser't Hooft in 1942. It should have been immediately considered by the War Cabinet, but the Foreign Office sat on it.

In June 1944 a meeting of 'interested departments' was held in the Foreign Office 'to discuss whether we could gain any immediate advantage by contacting dissident groups in Germany, or German commanders in the field'. Surprisingly the discussion took place without reference to the danger of such overtures to Anglo-Soviet relations.

The questions discussed were:

(1) Are the stories which reach us of 'dissident' groups in Germany genuine or inspired by the German Secret Service.
(2) If such groups exist is there any organisation or coordination amongst them?
(3) Would it be possible by establishing contact with any group or individual to assist military operations in Western Europe?

The questions were well framed. With hindsight we now know that the answer to all three should have been an unqualified 'Yes', with an urgent call for action to enlist these German patriots in an effort to bring the war to an early end.

Harrison wrote the report which he said represented the generally agreed view of the meeting:

In the early days of the war the majority of overtures were alleged to originate with dissident elements in the German Army which claimed to be anxious to purchase a compromise peace at the cost of the elimination of Hitler and his replacement by a more moderate Government. [These are the Generals frequently referred to by Cadogan in his diary for the early years of the war.]

Pride of place has now been taken by an alleged anti Hitler group, Christian in outlook, which is said to comprise dissident elements from diplomatic, military, industrial, ecclesiastical and trades union circles.

Both the above groups are alleged to desire to come to terms with the West 'to preserve Germany from Bolshevism'. There are also reports of elements both in the army and in the party who look to a settlement with the East.

This was a fair description of the overtures, but Harrison went on to demolish the thesis that an organized opposition existed. The report of 8 June 1944 could not have been more wrong:

The balance of evidence suggests that no organised oppositional group exists in Germany. Furthermore even if one or two small groups do exist, it seems clear that, in the absence of widespread popular support, of which there is not the faintest sign, they would be powerless to render us any service at the present stage. The indications are that these individuals are in fact less concerned with active steps in eliminating the Nazis than in stepping into the Nazis' shoes, when the Nazis have been eliminated. It seems clear therefore that the only direction in which to look for effective action is the German Army . . .

It is highly improbable that anything we can say would interest General von Rundstedt in the slightest degree, until it had become obvious to him that our military operations had succeeded and that we were firmly established in France. By that time our own interest in anything that General von Rundstedt could do would have diminished proportionately. Furthermore, even at that state General von Rundstedt might well not be interested in any bait less tempting than (1) modification (or anyhow amplification) of the terms 'unconditional surrender' and (2) an undertaking to help to 'preserve Germany from Bolshevism'. Such a price would clearly be totally impossible for us to contemplate.

The only possible conclusion seems to be that, quite apart from considerations of high policy, there is no initiative we can take vis-à-vis 'dissident' German groups or individuals, military or civilian, which holds out the smallest prospect of affording practical assistance to our present military operations in the West . . .[44]

Harrison subsequently wrote in a letter to the author:

It seems to me to read rather well 40 years on! I cannot remember the precise context leading to its composition. But in retrospect it seems to me quite natural that an alert young secretary should think it desirable to examine, at the time of D Day, whether there was any political initiative we could take to disrupt life behind the German lines. (1st paragraph of conclusion.) If there were, it would have had to be considered against the long-standing high policy decisions regarding contact with dissident German groups (i.e. unconditional surrender and the Soviet angle). Since it was held that there was nothing to be gained by contact with 'dissidents', military of civilian, any review of high policy did not arise. So far as I recall, there was certainly no feeling that there was accumulating evidence of a conspiracy (as you suggest). The idea is, in fact, dismissed in the memo.

I cannot myself see that consideration, at this particular juncture of events, whether we could use the 'dissidents' to help our military effort was in any way inconsistent with our previous attitude. My minute of 8 June 1944 seems to me to say it all.[45]

Submitting the report to Eden, Roberts minuted: 'The answer was probably a foregone conclusion; but it may none the less be useful to have examined the possibility.'

Harvey wrote: 'I agree with the conclusions. I have little doubt that the Generals will put out the first peace feelers but they will be anti-Russian, and that we may have difficulties with the United States over them.'

Cadogan minuted on 11 June, as Montgomery's invasion of Normandy teetered in the balance:

A very useful paper. As Mr. Harrison says, the upshot was a foregone conclusion. If there is anything in this 'dissidence' which at present I doubt, its sole object is to preserve Europe from Bolshevism, i.e. to help Germany against Russia, which is unthinkable.

Eden merely initialled the file ten days later. It is strange that the Foreign Secretary should have shown no interest in a subject which might have involved an earlier end to the war and the saving of countless lives.

Harrison's conclusions were seriously invalidated by the evidence of Vermehren who had defected in March and had been flown back to England via Algiers. He had been vouched for to the German Department by Dr C. K. Allen, Warden of Rhodes House, who said he had always been anti-Nazi and had been admitted as a Rhodes Scholar to take up residence at Oxford in October 1939. His tale should have been treated with deadly seriousness. It was not. Kirkpatrick wrote to Harvey from the Political Intelligence Department enclosing a note of what Vermehren had said to him, commenting: 'You will not be surprised to see that I do not think there is any money in this German opposition.'

Vermehren had left Germany too early to be aware of the imminence of the bomb plot, but he confirmed what was being learnt from Stockholm and Berne. As Kirkpatrick considered Vermehren 'completely truthful' it is difficult to explain why the Department ignored his evidence. Here is Kirkpatrick's rendering:

Top Secret

THE OPPOSITION ORGANISATION

Virtually all the information which V. possesses comes from Trott, now employed in the Far Eastern Section of the Auswärtiges Amt. Trott is engaged on propaganda work which gives him the opportunity of moving around.

Associated with Trott and an active member is Freiherr Marschall v. Bieberstein, head of the Personnel Department of the Auswärtiges Amt. He is married to a Catholic. There are many other members in the Ausw. Amt whom V. could not name. He does not know either of the brothers Kordt (likely members); nor does he know anything of senior men such as Bülow Schwante. He thought Bernstorff was in touch, but was so carefully watched that he could only be an occasional informant.

Army generals named by Trott as in touch with the movement are Falkenhausen, Blaskowitz, Geyr, Rundstedt and Oster, who is deputy to Canaris. Oster is active; V. thought Canaris was disaffected too, but he could not be positive on this point.

In Catholic circles he mentioned Abs, the banker. The Catholic clergy are in sympathy, but are too carefully watched to be active. The most active are probably the Bishops of Berlin and Fulda.

The S.S. opposition is ultra left wing and is not in touch with or trusted by V's friends.

THE AIMS OF THE ORGANISATION

The opposition want to work their passage home. They plan to get into touch with us, help to accelerate Hitler's demise so that they can claim for Germany proportionately mild treatment. They want the Western Allies, particularly England, to protect Germany from the worst Russian excesses. In particular the whole German nation fear forced labour in Russia. They would not mind forced labour for members of the N.S.D.A.P., but they are afraid of indiscriminate press gangs.

Failing an opportunity of working a passage, the opposition would like to attenuate Germany's fate by taking charge when the collapse comes. A suitable figure would be the Markgraf of Saxony, the eldest surviving son of the late king.

In the face of 'an unjust peace' we could look for the hostility of these people. They would be 'reasonable'. They realised that Germany would have to pay the price of defeat, even the loss of territory. But they would not stand for an oppressive peace of revenge.

THE TERROR

People here do not understand the efficiency and ruthlessness of the Gestapo terror. Even if the Gestapo have been hampered by bombing or dilution, they make up for it by the increasing savagery of the penalties. In the towns listening to the B.B.C. is too dangerous to be worth while. V. agreed that the terror must to some extent cramp the opposition, though it did not deter them from communicating with one another.

V'S RECOMMENDATION

V. urged that we should forthwith get into touch with the opposition. When asked with whom precisely we should communicate – the generals or whom, he replied *not* the generals. He could only suggest Trott.

MY IMPRESSION OF THE CONVERSATION

I consider V. completely truthful. In the course of two hours talk I was unable to detect an untruth or prevarication. I know most of the people he mentioned and his account of them is correct. On matters or on personalities outside the sphere his knowledge he at once admitted ignorance.

But if we accept his information, it seems to me correct the opposition is unlikely to be able to do anything to shorten the war. They are not powerful enough, the terror is too efficient and moreover they would not act unless we gave them assurances which would gravely embarrass us later. At the worst to give them a glimpse into our minds might drive them into the Nazi camp!

I.K.   6.7.44[46]

Kirkpatrick gave a wrong impression. It was a pity he did not have a full transcript made so that the Department could have judged it on its merits. He failed to disclose that he had also interviewed Vermehren's wife.

Vermehren commented to the author when he showed him the memorandum:

I am puzzled by Kirkpatrick's wholly negative assessment of the opposition's ability 'to shorten the war' although it is a both 'adequate and accurate statement' of what my wife and I told him. Kirkpatrick must have been a whole-hearted supporter of the Morgenthau Plan or some other similar project for Germany's eternal humiliation, dismemberment and 'castration' with his remark 'at the worst to give them a glimpse into our minds might drive them into the Nazi camp' (i.e. plans for post war treatment of the German nation.)

The whole thrust of our presentation had been to obtain precisely these assurances which Kirkpatrick says 'would gravely embarrass us later'. It is possible Kirkpatrick, after speaking to us, had become convinced that the opposition once spurred to action by the required minimum 'assurances from the Allies' were quite capable of overthrowing Hitler and asking for peace on 'honourable terms'. Since this did not fit in with Kirkpatrick's personal ideas about the treatment to be meted out to a vanquished Germany he was at pains to minimise the importance of the opposition and its chances 'to do anything to shorten the war' otherwise the Foreign Office might seriously consider revising its attitude and entering into genuine negotiations.[46]

Vermehren was not close to the core of the conspiracy. He knew in general what was going on, but had no specific role; after the war he learnt his name had been pencilled in as a possible candidate for an under-secretaryship in the new Government of Goerdeler-Beck; he was in the Abwehr and posted to Istanbul to help Leverkuehn with Secret Service intelligence. His wife was to follow him but her parents

in Bremen fell under suspicion of the Gestapo because they had
duplicated a copy of the Pope's encyclical. They were arrested, and
Erich's wife was refused a passport to follow her husband. He enlisted
the help of Trott and a passport was produced. However, at the
Turkish frontier she was sent back by the Gestapo to Sofia. Here she
sought help from a conspirator at the German Embassy and flew on to
Istanbul on the official German courier weekly flight.

Vermehren told the author he knew Trott very well and frequently
saw him in Berlin. Trott had enthusiastically sponsored him for his
Rhodes Scholarship at Oxford and had wanted him to go to Balliol.
Frau Vermehren was a second cousin of Papen who asked them to stay
for a fortnight at the German Embassy when they arrived. In Istanbul
the Vermehrens decided to defect and contacted the British Secret
Service who arranged to send them to Cairo secretly.

At first the Gestapo thought the Vermehrens had been kidnapped by
the British, but they bribed a Turkish official who blew the gaff. Then
the Gestapo put out the false story that Vermehren had absconded
with £70,000 of Abwehr money. To clear his name, according to
Vermehren, he gave the full story of his defection to an American
journalist in Cairo. The British, for propaganda purposes, used it for a
broadcast to the German people from Algiers. Vermehren admitted he
told the journalist about there being plenty of 'good Germans' in
important Government positions, and this was repeated in the
broadcast which was not made by Vermehren but by another German
pretending to be him. His family knew it was not his voice when they
heard it.

Once in London, Vermehren told the Foreign Office it would be
against his conscience to do anything to help the Allies directly to win
the war. However the Secret Service official who arranged their escape
from Istanbul told the author he insisted that Vermehren brought him
copies of four days of signals from the Abwehr in Istanbul, and as a
result he found the Germans were using mostly double agents known
to the British. This official added that if Vermehren had refused to do
this he would not have organized his escape, as he required some *quid
pro quo*.

Clarita Trott and the Bielenbergs were bitter about the Vermehrens.
They both wrote to the author emphasizing that after Trott had risked
his life to get Frau Vermehren a visa to go to Istanbul they should have
kept absolutely quiet after they had defected and under no circumstances talked to any journalists. They recall that the broadcast was
definitely in his and his wife's name and stated that his conscience

would not allow him and his wife to stay on in Germany, and also mentioned there were many others like himself in 'high places' who felt the same as he did. As a result Trott had to submit to several tough Gestapo interrogations, and for Vermehren's family it meant concentration camps thereafter until the end of the war.

When Vermehren tried to see Peter Bielenberg after the war, Bielenberg refused to meet him. Christabel Bielenberg wrote to the author that the British at that time used this sort of material most carelessly and mentioned names in their broadcasts which endangered a number of people in the opposition.[47]

After D Day British propaganda beamed at the German population and their fighting forces was hostile to the German Resistance. The Political Warfare Executive of the Foreign Office were given a strong transmitter in Sussex to broadcast to the German Army from D Day onwards. This was called Radio Calais or Soldatensender Calais. In addition a daily newspaper was dropped by the RAF and USAAF and also fired behind the German lines by artillery. This was *Nachrichten für die Truppen*, edited by Sefton Delmer.

Because of the lack of imagination and foresight of Eden and Brendan Bracken (Minister of Information), the contents were, if anything, calculated to stiffen rather than weaken German resistance. Wheeler-Bennett had the ear of Eden and Bracken, and his insistent advice was there were no 'good Germans' and the resistance to Hitler was to be despised. His attitude was accepted by the Foreign Office, Eden and Bracken, and incorporated in the Directives issued to the Psychological Warfare Executive.

Wheeler-Bennett's memorandum of 6 July to the Foreign Office began with the words: 'This paper is written on the assumption that it is the aim of the United Nations that German militarism shall be finally destroyed by methods which render it impossible again to be said that the German army has not been defeated in the field.'

He forecast that there might be a split between the Army and the Nazis when the High Command had to inform the Fuehrer that the war was lost and that the armies in the field could no longer maintain 'any but a rear action'.

At this point the Nazi leaders, realising they have nothing to lose, may wish to order a national suicide and continue the battle into Germany. They may be prepared to scorch the earth not only of the now occupied territories, but of the Reich itself, bringing down all in one gigantic blaze of immolation.

Wheeler-Bennett considered that the High Command of the

German Army would be against 'such a proposal' because their intention was 'to live to fight another day, and thus it must assure its record for the future generations of Germans whom it may wish to train for service, hence its whole inclination will be to prevent the horror of actual invasion being visited upon the German Reich'.

He went on that the task of PWE would be to promote discord without 'encouraging the Army in the belief that having accomplished the overthrow of Hitler they can anticipate any mitigation of the terms of unconditional surrender'.

The memorandum contains one revealing and most disturbing paragraph:

What must be avoided at all costs is that at the close of hostilities the Allies should find themselves obligated or committed to any German Army leaders in any way or that the Allied determination to destroy the military tradition of Germany is in any way impaired.

Wheeler-Bennett's priority was not the humanitarian aim of ending the slaughter as soon as possible with the help of German anti-Nazis, but to continue the war to the bitter end so as to make sure of destroying the spirit of German militarism. The Foreign Office agreed with his views and PWE was instructed to conform to them. Harrison minuted on 11 July (after criticizing Hugh Carleton Greene for emphasizing the split between the 'old school' Generals and the 'Nazified' ones, in a broadcast on 9 July):

I am doubtful if the 'Generals' are any longer in a position to overthrow the Nazi regime . . . If they do, I am very much less afraid of army 'committments or obligations' incurred on our behalf by PWE than of very strong pressure from various quarters – American, Russian, and even British – to parley with the German High Command with a view (a) to finishing the war as quickly as possible, and (b) to prevent chaos breaking loose in Germany.

Roberts minuted that 'we should agree' with Wheeler-Bennett. Harvey also minuted his agreement eight days before the Stauffenberg bomb was to explode.[47]

Harrison sums up the 1944 Whitehall attitude by deprecating 'pressure from those who wanted to finish the war as quickly as possible by parleying with the Germans', and his minute and Wheeler-Bennett's memorandum give an accurate picture of the attitude of the War Cabinet and Whitehall. For them, finishing the war had lower priority than crushing Germany.

On 6 July 1944 Attlee made a speech in the Commons which at last encouraged the resisters, appealing to them to show by active steps they were trying to get rid of the present regime – otherwise no one would believe in their genuineness. This contradicted Churchill's previous statement to the House on 24 May when he reiterated 'unconditional surrender' and said anything different would give the Germans grounds to protest later as they did after Wilson's sixteen points. Attlee's intervention was inspired by Cripps, who alone in the Cabinet was aware of the opposition's potential.

The conspirators, who had been depressed by the negative attitude of the Allies to Trott on his two visits to Stockholm and the lack of any reply from Dulles, were cheered by Attlee's speech. Any faltering by the plotters ended early in July when Rommel and Kluge, in command of the Western Front against Eisenhower, dramatically joined the plot and promised to surrender in the west once Hitler was overthrown.

Claus von Stauffenberg, who had great courage and intelligence, was now the leading activist in Berlin. He was an aristocrat and because of Hitler's obstinacy in face of the military disasters in North Africa had become his deadly enemy. On 1 June 1944 he became Chief of Staff at the General Army Office in Berlin and went to Hitler's headquarters for conferences. He decided that as he was the only member of the inner circle with access to Hitler, he would take it upon himself to kill him. With the help of General Stieff, head of the Organization branch in the Army High Command, he prepared time bombs from British material.

A final conspirators' meeting was held in Berlin on 16 July with Stauffenberg, Berk, Goerdeler, Witzleben and Trott present. Otto John, legal adviser to Lufthansa, had made a last despairing trip to Madrid to try and gain Allied cooperation for the coup. He saw the US Military Attaché, who promised to pass any message on to Eisenhower but warned John that hostilities could not be ended except by unconditional surrender to all the Allies. At the final conference the plotters accepted this definite warning there would be no terms from the Allies. Trott, now optimistic again, and cheered by Attlee's Commons statement and the adherence of Rommel and Kluge, argued that the enemy would treat a complete change of regime as the necessary pre-condition for a different diplomatic attitude.

After Hitler's overthrow Trott was to be part of the delegation to the West, while Schulenberg as a former Ambassador in Moscow would go to the East. At this fateful 16 July meeting the conspirators agreed to a proposal from Stauffenberg to place one or two of his and Stieff's time bombs in Hitler's conference room the next time he went there, and then to proclaim a revolutionary Government.

John told the author that during the final hours before 20 July Stauffenberg was impatient with Goerdeler's and Trott's efforts to communicate with the Allies through British and American diplomats in neutral countries, and had no use for their political memoranda which had been sent to the Allies. Stauffenberg did not want any politician or diplomat to intervene between him and Eisenhower. As a result Stauffenberg was not depressed by the negative results from Goerdeler's negotiations in Berne and Trott's in Stockholm. John told the author:

I was to be his personal go-between with Eisenhower. Stauffenberg wanted soldier to soldier talks with Eisenhower after he had seized power.

I approached the USA Embassy in Madrid and got a personal authoritative promise that any message Stauffenberg wanted to send to Eisenhower after the plot had been successful would immediately be placed on Eisenhower's desk; but the British Embassy in Madrid had told me categorically in January 1944 that they were forbidden to continue contacts with me on behalf of the German Resistance.

On 13 July I heard through the British Embassy in Madrid that the British would not make any effort to get to Berlin before the Russians. This came from Kim Philby. I flew back to Berlin on 19 July and saw Trott but did not see Stauffenberg until the 20th in the War Office after the bomb had failed to kill Hitler.

A few days before 20 July machinery was set in motion immediately to warn all the activists of an early *coup d'état*, and messages were sent to Dulles in Berne informing Washington of its imminence. At this stage Trott and Stauffenberg were close. They met frequently and after 20 July Trott was incriminated because Stauffenberg's chauffeur revealed how often his superior had visited Trott. But there is evidence that Stauffenberg was at cross-purposes with Goerdeler on some aspects of the conspiracy.

In despatches from Berne dated 13 and 15 July, Dulles urged Washington to make a statement similar to Attlee's as his informants had told him the assassination attempt was imminent and that a shadow Government had been formed with a list of respected and well-known names, some of which he reported. Goerdeler also communicated with the banker brothers Marcus and Jacob Wallenberg in Stockholm, asking them to use their contacts to tell the British Government that the coup had been prepared for immediate execution. According to Tennant, who was in a good position to judge, the Wallenbergs had no link with London. Goerdeler thought falsely they had direct contact with Churchill at all times. Perhaps Marcus, who was untrustworthy, deceived Goerdeler.[48]

On 18 July, in a Supply Committee debate in the House of Commons, the rights and wrongs of unconditional surrender and the terrifying consequences of the Teheran Conference on the German people were unexpectedly raised, together with the Goebbels propaganda about it. Eden decided to make an off-the-cuff reply and complained petulantly that he could not give a 're-definition of unconditional surrender' when he had only a few minutes' warning.

He read out to the House part of the Prime Minister's uncompromising statement of 22 February 1944 and ignored Attlee's more generous statement of 6 July. He emphasized that the Government were not going to allow themselves to be put into a similar position *vis-à-vis* Germany as they had been because of Wilson's points at the end of the First World War; and he claimed, with no evidence to support him, that the Government's propaganda to Germany 'has not been unsuccessful'. This is evidence Eden had not read the recent authoritative reports coming to the Foreign Office from the British Legation in Stockholm and via Washington from Dulles in Berne about the strength of the conspiracy and the imminence of a coup. Nor could he have studied the Vermehren interrogation, because nothing could have been more likely to cool off the plotters than this 18 July speech. However, complete reports of the debate via Stockholm and Berne may not have reached Berlin before 20 July. As it was, with the plotters prepared to explode their bomb and seize power, complete silence and unconditional surrender were the order of the day in both London and Washington.

12

The Road to Surrender
1944 – 1945

By the end of June 1944 the Allies were building up supplies and troops at such a rate in Normandy that to any intelligent German General the defeat of the Wehrmacht there could only be a question of time. Thanks to the high morale of most of the German infantry formations and the superiority of their tanks, guns and mortars, Montgomery was prevented from breaking out into the good tank country south of Caen, but the Germans did not have enough armoured formations to hold both the British in the east and the Americans in the west.

Von Rundstedt was Commander-in-Chief in the west, and he and Rommel, Commander of Army Group German Armies in Normandy, pointed out to Hitler at a conference on 29 June at Rastenburg that the Normandy situation was hopeless.[1] Hitler sent away both Field Marshals in a rage, declining even to ask them to stay to dinner, and told them they must hold the front. The next day the frustrated Rundstedt, when asked by Keitel on the telephone 'What shall we do?', replied 'Make peace, you fool.' This was repeated to Hitler who immediately sacked Rundstedt and appointed Kluge in his place. Kluge, an anti-Nazi, had been in touch with the conspirators since 1938, but he was vacillating and indecisive.

After touring the fronts with Rommel, Kluge agreed that German prospects in Normandy were hopeless and that they must convince the Fuehrer of this or put a stop to the fighting on their own.

The plotters had decided that, as soon as Hitler was killed, one of their most influential members, General Karl Stuelpnagel, Military Commander of Paris, should seize Paris in the name of the new Government and arrest all the Gestapo leaders. Probably not more than twenty officers in Stuelpnagel's headquarters were active in the plot, but there were many other sympathizers and the officers of the Wehrmacht were at daggers drawn with the Gestapo, SS and SD in Paris. Two senior staff officers at Rommel's headquarters, Eberhard Finckh and Hans Speidel, were in the plot. Tentatively they discussed the situation with Rommel and found him 'open to persuasion'. Accordingly Colonel Caesar von Hofacker, a cousin of Stauffenberg and Stuelpnagel's aide in Paris, and an active conspirator, went with Stuelpnagel to visit Rommel at his headquarters at La Roche Guyon on 9 July. They talked for several hours and pretended they had been reminiscing about their younger days together in the Army. In reality they were enrolling Rommel in the plot. Rommel was shown the impressive list of prospective Ministers who would make up the Beck-Goerdeler Government; this included well-known former members of the SPD and Centre parties and the Christian Trade Unions.[a] Rommel told Hofacker that the military situation was hopeless and that he was ready to ask Montgomery for an armistice on the day the coup took place. Rommel himself was against the assassination of Hitler; he wanted him arrested and tried.

Finally Rommel agreed that he would be either interim Chief of State or Commander of Chief of the Army temporarily after the *coup d'état*. Rommel and Stuelpnagel gave detailed instructions to Walter Bargatzky, a lawyer on Stuelpnagel's staff in Paris, to draft a surrender document which Rommel could send to Montgomery. According to Bargatzky, Rommel had become so enthusiastic about ending the fighting that there was no holding him back. Bargatzky drafted a document on the lines Rommel suggested; it consisted of a simple request to Montgomery for 'initial secrecy' and 'honourable treatment' of the German troops after the surrender. Bargatzky recommended that the document be taken through the lines by a medical officer.

Bargatzky was also entrusted with drawing up charges against the leaders of the Gestapo, SS and SD in Paris, so that some of them could be executed summarily on Rommel's signature. The charges were to be deportation of French Jews and others to extermination camps, burning synagogues, robbing anti-German French of their property and mass murders in retaliation against French resisters.

After the leaders had been executed there was to be a show trial of the subordinates and Bargatzky had begun work on the necessary evidence and supporting legal documents. The show trial was to take place in the large Casino room in the Hotel Majestic, and the immediate execution of the leaders on Mont Valerien. After the first executions a press and radio announcement was to be made above the signatures of Rommel and Stuelpnagel: 'In the course of the restoration of the German constitution the following were shot dead today.'

---

[a]All but three died after 20 July.

After the war Bargatzky became head of the German Red Cross. In 1984 he told the author that his draft surrender document had been approved by Hofacker on behalf of Stuelpnagel but as everything had to be done in strict secrecy he never learnt whether Kluge and Rommel had agreed the wording. Likewise his charges and proposed press announcements of the executions were approved by Stuelpnagel, but Rommel preferred a full trial before any executions took place.[2]

The day after Stuelpnagel's visit to Rommel, Montgomery's British Second Army began Offensive 'Epsom' against the Germans around Caen. It was partially held, but casualties on both sides were heavy. For Rommel it was the final proof that he did not have the resources to hold both the Americans and the British. On 15 July he wrote a three-page memorandum for Hitler reporting that the situation in Normandy was 'approaching a crisis'; he was short of reinforcements – only 6,000 against 97,000 casualties and 17 new tanks to replace 225. He said his new divisions were untrained and that the Allies had overwhelming superiority in numbers and materials, as well as complete command of the sky.

Our troops are fighting heroically but the unequal contest is drawing to an end . . . the Allies will succeed within fourteen days to three weeks in breaking our thin front and will push far into the interior of France; the consequences will be immeasurable . . . I must beg you to draw the political conclusions without delay. It is my duty to state this clearly.[3]

Rommel's attitude was that he was giving Hitler his last chance to make peace with the Allies, and if this report was ignored he himself would end the fighting in the west. Rommel showed Kluge the letter. There is no doubt that Kluge was a full consenting partner to the Rommel-Stuelpnagel surrender plan. He endorsed the letter to Hitler, writing: 'Unfortunately the Field Marshal is right.' For some unknown reason, however, he did not forward the letter to Hitler for several days.

Rommel had already opened a radio link with the Americans. As a result of negotiations over this line, on 2 July eight German nurses from Cherbourg had been passed through the lines at Sept Vents during a truce lasting from 3.10 p.m. until 7.00 p.m. On 9 July, two German nurses and seven female secretaries were handed over, and German envoys were fed at the American forward headquarters. Severely wounded Americans were returned.[b] On 16 and 17 July

[b]In a written answer to a Parliamentary question on 18 July the Secretary of State for War, Sir James Grigg, confirmed that nine German nurses captured in Cherbourg were returned to the German lines. The German signals are in the archives at Stanford University, California.

Rommel toured his fronts telling selected commanders of his démarche to Hitler and warning them of the likelihood of an armistice.

On 17 July Rommel told Stuelpnagel again that he was ready to act 'openly and unconditionally' as soon as Hitler was liquidated, whether Kluge went along with him or not. Then, as he was motoring home, his car was attacked by British Spitfires. The driver was killed and the speeding car overturned into a ditch; Rommel was thrown out and fractured his skull. The hospital verdict was that he would live but would be out of action for several months.

The conspirators' hopes in the west now rested on the spineless Kluge, who took over direct command of Rommel's group of armies. According to Bargatzky, on 19 July Kluge came to Paris and held a conference at the Hotel Majestic with Speidel and Stuelpnagel. Kluge was informed the assassination was planned for the next day and he agreed to honour Rommel's commitments.

Stauffenberg made his assassination attempt on 20 July at the Fuehrer's weekly war conference at Rastenburg. He flew from Berlin with his adjutant, carrying the time bomb in his briefcase. He set the fuse, put the briefcase under the table, and left. As he was hurrying to the airport he heard the explosion. Hitler was only slightly wounded.

In Berlin the conspirators waited anxiously for Stauffenberg's return. At 3.30 p.m. he reached the War Office in the Bendlerstrasse where he was met by Beck and other staff officers in the plot. They immediately sent out orders drafted in advance for the Army to occupy the Government quarter in Berlin. They also planned to arrest Goebbels and make a broadcast from the radio station as soon as it and Goebbels's Ministry were occupied. Unfortunately the troops were commanded by a Major Remer (a well-known neo-Nazi after the war), who was dedicated to Hitler. When Remer's troops occupied the Propaganda Ministry near the War Office, Goebbels persuaded him to speak to Hitler on the telephone to prove to him that Hitler was alive. Once Remer had heard Hitler's voice he refused to obey the orders from the plotters in the War Office, and the coup in Berlin was finished. The plan to blow up all the telephone exchanges at the Fuehrer's headquarters miscarried and Keitel countermanded all orders sent by Stauffenberg from the War Office. Witzleben, who had come to Berlin to take control, went home saying 'You have bungled the business.' Beck and Stauffenberg were immediately shot on the orders of General Fromm (who himself had been involved in discussions about the plot). Beck, as a General, was invited to take his own life, but mismanaged it.

In Paris Stuelpnagel and his co-plotters had received a telephone message from Stauffenberg at 3.30 p.m. that the coup was 'on' and Hitler was dead. Then they heard on the radio that Hitler was alive. Finally at 6.30 p.m. Stauffenberg telephoned to Stuelpnagel and said briefly: 'All is lost'.

Stuelpnagel decided that as a last resort he would try to operate a coup against Hitler from the west. As planned, he ordered the arrest of the leading Gestapo, SS and SD in Paris. Over 1,000 were arrested by the Army, disarmed and put in prison without violence. With Hofacker, Stuelpnagel set off for the hour's drive to Kluge's head-quarters in a desperate effort to persuade him to come out against Hitler and surrender the Western Front.

Kluge, knowing the attempt would be made on 20 July, had deliberately stayed away from his headquarters until 6.00 p.m. He found one message on his desk that Hitler was dead, together with a later radio report that he was alive. When he telephoned Keitel at Rastenburg and found Hitler was alive, his nerve failed. He told Stuelpnagel that he had only consented to cooperate once Hitler was dead, and this crucial condition had not been fulfilled. He threatened Hofacker and Stuelpnagel with arrest; his Chief of Staff, General Hans Speidel, up to his neck in the plot, was appalled. They had dinner together in icy silence, then Stuelpnagel renewed the argument, refusing to release the Gestapo and SS personnel under arrest in Paris.[4]

Stuelpnagel and Hofacker got back to the Majestic Hotel in Paris at midnight. There they found Hitler's Ambassador to France, Abetz, waiting for them. Bargatzky and others of Stuelpnagel's associates in the Hotel Majestic suggested they should summarily execute the leading Gestapo members – and then make public Kluge's promise to join the coup. By this blackmail they hoped to force him to come out on the side of the plotters. Stuelpnagel refused, and reluctantly released the prisoners; the coup in Paris was over. After midnight the plotters and the Gestapo chiefs drank wine together in the Majestic in uneasy conviviality. Stuelpnagel said the arrests were solely due to an order received from the War Office in Berlin. But the cat was out of the bag.[5]

The next day Stuelpnagel was summoned back to Berlin. He knew what this meant; en route he tried to shoot himself and failed. He, with almost all the ringleaders, including Trott, Moltke, Leber, Witzleben and Goerdeler, were executed by Hitler with appalling barbarity after the mockery of a trial in front of Freisler in the people's court. Schlabrendorff, John, Gisevius, Schacht, together with Bargatzky and a few others, escaped to tell the story after the war.

John, because of his position as legal adviser to Lufthansa, was able to fly to Madrid on 23 July. There the Gestapo tried to kidnap him, but the British brought him to London where he helped the Allied war effort. He told the author that he spent all day on the 22nd in his neighbour's garden watching his front door to see if the Gestapo came to arrest him. He added that he saw Trott on the 22nd and begged him to fly to Madrid the next day. Trott refused because he was still optimistic that the Gestapo might not discover his involvement, and also because he feared reprisals would be taken against his family. According to John these would have been no worse if he had fled. John said that Adam had a valid pass from the Gestapo which would have enabled him to travel on the same Lufthansa plane to safety on 23 July.

The British and Americans were taken completely by surprise at the attempted coup, in spite of the numerous warnings coming from Stockholm and Switzerland from reliable sources. According to their diaries, the CIGS, General Sir Alan Brooke, was flabbergasted, as was Cadogan. On 21 July the Prime Minister was at Montgomery's headquarters in Normandy. According to Brigadier Sir Edgar Williams, who was present, Churchill was completely non-plussed when Montgomery gave him the news of the attempted revolution in Germany. Churchill asked Montgomery and Williams to go through his despatch boxes and as they scrabbled through the papers they found Ultra signals and Intelligence reports all muddled up. From these Williams saw that Witzleben was involved; he had already been told by a high up Nazi deserter that Witzleben was the likely leader of the coup against Hitler. Williams told the author:

I suddenly realised that Winston had come from London with all this stuff in his despatch box unread and that he was 'naked' in face of the possible sudden end of the war. I was amazed that he could have been as unbriefed about what was going on in Germany as he was on 21 July.[6]

Was a battlefield surrender possible? In October 1918 the last Austrian Emperor, Karl, had surrendered to the Italian Army on the Isonzo front by sending forward at first light from the Austrian trenches a captain with two private soldiers and a white flag bearing his message of surrender. The fighting was over by midday. It could have been repeated.

Eisenhower was empowered by Roosevelt and Churchill to accept a surrender and to leave the German Army free. Originally the Russians had wanted all members of German armed forces to be designated prisoners of war if there was a surrender. The Americans held that the Commander-in-Chief must be free to decide which of the German forces would be designated prisoners of war. They were supported by Churchill and after much haggling the Russians gave way.[7]

Thus Eisenhower and Montgomery, without consulting the Russians, could have agreed that Kluge should leave all his guns and heavy equipment in Normandy and withdraw his men into Germany.

Rommel had intended to offer Montgomery (Eisenhower was still at Portsmouth) an immediate armistice and, while the Beck-Goerdeler Government negotiated a peace settlement with the three Allies, the evacuation of all occupied territories in the west and the withdrawal of all German forces behind the Siegfried Line.

Kluge must have thought on the same lines or he and Rommel would have quarrelled. Indeed one of Kluge's staff officers, General Blumentritt, gave evidence that when Kluge heard the false news of Hitler's death he said: 'If the Fuehrer is dead we ought to get in touch with the people on the other side at once.'[8] If Kluge had made an armistice offer it is inconceivable that the Allies would have refused to stop the bloodshed. A ferocious tank battle was raging south of Caen (Goodwood) and the outcome was uncertain; the only certainly was very heavy casualties on both sides.

Churchill and Roosevelt were always fearful that their alliance with Stalin might fall apart, and that Hitler would make peace with Russia behind their backs. If Kluge had surrendered on the Western Front, Britain and America would have been in an overwhelming position of strength *vis-à-vis* Stalin who was still struggling against the powerful German armies in the east. Overnight the danger of a Hitler-Stalin agreement would have disappeared.

The Foreign Office, the Prime Minister's and Foreign Secretary's reaction to the attempted coup was strange. For them there were no 'good' Germans, and it was almost a matter of congratulation that the coup failed. They expressed no regret that they had not assisted the would-be assassins of Hitler to bring the war to an abrupt conclusion – although Churchill, though not Eden, made amends after the war.

Wheeler-Bennett dominated thinking on Germany from his post as Deputy Head of Political Warfare being close to Eden and with access to Churchill. He continually belittled the plotters, as did the German desk in the Foreign Office. Here is the astonishing memorandum of 25 July from Wheeler-Bennett which was sent to Eden and Churchill:

1. Within the narrow limits of our accurate information it is possible to make a certain appreciation of the position resulting from the recent events in Germany, and to deduce certain future developments from it.

2. It may now be said with some definiteness that we are better off with

things as they are today than if the plot of July 20th had succeeded and Hitler had been assassinated. In this event the 'Old Army' Generals would have taken over and, as may be deduced from the recent statement from the Vatican as to the Pope's readiness to mediate, would have put into operation through Baron von Weizsäcker a peace move, already prepared, in which Germany would admit herself defeated and would sue for terms other than those of Unconditional Surrender.

3. By the failure of the plot we have been spared the embarrassments, both at home and in the United States, which might have resulted from such a move and, moreover, the present purge is presumably removing from the scene numerous individuals which might have caused us difficulty, not only had the plot succeeded, but also after the defeat of a Nazi Germany.

4. If it is true that a number of the more distinguished generals, together with such civilians as Schacht, Neurath and Schulenberg, have been eliminated, the Gestapo and the S.S. have done us an appreciable service in removing a selection of those who would undoubtedly have posed as 'good' Germans after the war, while preparing for a third World War. It is to our advantage therefore that the purge should continue, since the killing of Germans by Germans will save us from future embarrassments of many kinds.

For Wheeler-Bennett it was apparently better for the war to continue than for Germany to be spared the humiliation of 'unconditional surrender'. His phrase that it was 'to our advantage if the purge continued' is indefensible besides being inhumane; to suggest Schacht, Neurath and Schulenberg would prepare Germany for a third world war is a wild distortion of the truth. Unhappily, his words 'killing of Germans by Germans' had a strong emotional appeal to Churchill and were used by him in the House of Commons to complete the discomfiture of the plotters.

In the Foreign Office Wheeler-Bennett's memorandum was at first approved by Roberts who, forty-two years later, told the author that he still 'did not entirely disagreee, but would not have put it like that'. His original minute was: 'It all seems sensible and calls for no special comment.' However, a week later he was shaken by a persuasive minute from Marshall:

I am not happy about the opening paragraphs [of Wheeler-Bennett's paper]. They seem to be based on the assumption that the Allies cannot be trusted to pursue a firm and consistent policy towards Germany and that they might succumb to the temptation to accept an offer from a non-Nazi German Government to conclude a negotiated peace. But the failure of the plot has by no means eliminated the possibility of such an offer being made and we ought to be clear what our attitude will be if it is. In my view any new German Government which offered a negotiated peace would, if we rejected the offer, be very soon driven to unconditional surrender, since the internal revolution would weaken Germany's power of resistance. I think this would have happened if the plot had succeeded – or else the new Government would have been displaced by one which would have surrendered. I do not agree that the failure of the plot is to our advantage, especially if it is going to lead, among other things, to the murder of prisoners of war.

If all internal attempts to overthrow Hitler fail, we shall have no German Government with which to deal when the end comes. There will be a state of anarchy in Germany. Consequently it may well be argued that any revolution is to our advantage, provided we do not allow it to weaken our purpose.[9]

On reading Marshall's minute Roberts changed his mind and wrote: 'I agree with Mr. Marshall.'

Harvey wrote in his diary on 30 July:

I am convinced that it was to our interest that this coup has failed. If Hitler had died, we would have had a surge to make peace with the Generals – the rot must proceed further yet. Our enemies are both the Nazis and the Generals. We should make peace with neither.

Obviously he had read Wheeler-Bennett's paper and accepted his argument.

Con O'Neill, when the author showed him Wheeler-Bennett's memorandum in 1984, was visibly shocked; then he saw his initials on the file and recalled that although he had been horrified on reading it forty years before, he had decided to make no protest because of his peripheral position. (He was then only concerned with planning postwar Germany.)

On the night of 20 July Carleton Greene, head of BBC German language broadcasts, was summoned to Bush House to write a news report to be broadcast to the German people, and to the rest of Europe, about the attempt on Hitler's life. On this important occasion, when there was really something to say to the Germans (and they were sensitive to the broadcasts), he was given no briefing at all, much to his satisfaction, from Kirkpatrick or Bruce Lockhart – in authority over him at the Political Warfare Executive. Thinking, quite rightly as it turned out, that some of the Army conspirators might be holding out at various points in Germany and occupied Europe, he began his story with the words: 'Civil war has broken out in Germany'. A few hours later he heard what he had put out was not to the liking of the Foreign Office, who wanted the BBC to take their much more hostile attitude to the conspirators.[c]

[c]When Greene reached Paris early in August 1944 on behalf of the German service of the BBC, he met a very charming French countess who had been Hofacker's mistress. She told him that Rommel had been in the 20 July plot, but swore him to secrecy while Rommel was alive. As soon as the Germans broadcast that Rommel was dead Greene made sure the BBC made it clear to the German people that Rommel had been ready to betray the Fuehrer.[10]

On 21 July PWE issued their directive about propaganda to the German people on what they termed 'the Revolt of the Generals'. It followed Wheeler-Bennett's memorandum of early July, emphasizing that there was no Allied support for 'good Germans' nor any possibility of a negotiated peace, thus cold-shouldering any German Generals who might be thinking in terms of an armistice in the west. Paragraph 3 was sensible: 'Present the revolt as a practical demonstration by the Generals of their conviction that the war is lost, and that Hitler and the party leaders are recklessly prolonging it to save their own skins.' However, paragraph 6 is evidence that the Government was prepared to prolong the war until the German armies were completely defeated in the field:

Do not express or imply Allied support for, or commendation of the dissidents as 'good Germans' or suggest any possibility of a negotiated peace, or indeed any deviation from the Prime Minister's last statement. Our line is still 'unconditional surrender' from competent representatives of Germany and the Wehrmacht. The only question for the German people is whether it comes sooner or later.

The evidence held by the Foreign Office of the wide basis of the conspiracy and the support of many former politicians, civil servants, churchmen and lawyers was ignored. It was actually misleading for the Foreign Office to allow PWE to call it 'the Revolt of the Generals'. Yet Bracken even told Delmer that he was sure the bomb plot was an invention by Hitler. Eden laid down that not only was 'the idea of a propaganda stunt' to be avoided but that rumours of civil war were not to be accepted as valid until further evidence came to hand. The PWE conclusion was that there was 'no political opposition in Germany at present capable of supporting, let alone initiating a revolution'. The Russians, on the other hand, called on the Wehrmacht and the German civilian population to support a revolt[10].

Wheeler-Bennett discussed the bomb plot with Eden before the debate which took place in the Commons on 2 August. Eden also wrote a minute about it to the Prime Minister which is in the Eden papers at the Public Record Office, but closed by the Lord Chancellor for another thirty years. The War Cabinet decided to ignore Cripps and take a line in the Commons completely hostile to the conspirators, and to reject any possibility of a soft peace for a new revolutionary German Government. It is clear from reading Churchill's words that he accepted Wheeler-Bennett's briefing.

Churchill in a long speech made only a short reference to the attempted revolution: 'The highest personalities in the German Reich are murdering one another, or trying to, while the avenging armies of the Allies close upon the doomed and ever-narrowing circle of their power.' He was followed by Greenwood, no longer in the War Cabinet but very influential. He brutally destroyed the aspirations of those opposed to Hitler inside Germany by saying:

Let us never forget that it was largely the military caste that put Hitler where he is today . . . It would be a fatal mistake if . . . we were to present any better terms to the militarists of Germany than we have done to the discredited Nazis. I think the House is more or less agreed about that, and when my Friend says 'No parley' I agree with that. I can conceive no different treatment being meted out to Germany, whether the terms are delivered to the Nazi Party of Hitler or the German military leaders. That I think is important.

Only Richard Stokes and George Strauss dissented from the Government line.[d] Strauss said that

now we knew there is a strong element in the German army which thinks that continuance of the war is foolish and suicidal, we should change our whole policy. How can one expect a movement of that sort to be widespread and broad-based if the Germans have nothing to go on except the repeated cry of 'unconditional surrender' and statements daily by Dr Goebbels over the wireless telling the people that if German is conquered we are going to cut Germany up and do awful things to its men and women?

Stokes intervened to add: 'By the Prime Minister too.'

Strauss was heavily barracked when he went on to say that Goebbels's propaganda claimed that after the Allies victory nine million German people of Upper Silesia, East Prussia and the Sudetenland would be transported. He finished by saying that the Allies should immediately declare their terms 'and help the next crack in Germany to develop into a fissure that will rend the army and nation in twain'. He wrote to the author that he was proud he had made the speech, but the mood of the House was they would not countenance a separate peace with the German opposition.[11]

Stokes argued for a revocation of the Teheran Conference decisions and a return to the Atlantic Charter, with a declaration that it was sincerely meant that the German people should have the kind of Government they wanted after the war. He forecast that the German people would give in 'if they were told . . . not only that they are not

[d]Stokes was appointed Minister of Works after the war (1951). Strauss was Minister of Aircraft Production in the Churchill Government 1942–43; Minister of Supply 1947–51.

going to be shot, but that they have something to hope for.' Like Strauss, Stokes was jeered by both Labour and Conservative MPs.

Eden's speech is further evidence that he ignored or disbelieved the constant stream of information coming into the Foreign Office about the proposed Goerdeler-Beck anti-Nazi pro-peace Government. He said that Germany could not be allowed to choose her own Government after the war and went on:

I cannot conceive that the Nazi-trained German mentality of war which is now unhappily deep in the minds of Germans is going willingly to accept a peace which does not allow a future Nazi domination of Europe. That is a fundamental problem which we must face up to.

These words, ill phrased as they are, reveal Eden's attitude to a soft peace with the anti-Nazis if they seized power. Unlike Churchill, Eden in his postwar memoirs did not discuss the attempts at negotiations by the opposition in Germany, nor unconditional surrender, and it is difficult to avoid the conclusion that he dismissed the German opposition with contempt, believing, like Wheeler-Bennett, that there were no good Germans in 1944; just as for him there were no good Italians in 1943.

As wartime Prime Minister Churchill showed no sympathy to the Resistance. All the same, he paid a generous tribute in 1946 to the sacrifices of the German patriots who went to their death after the failure of the bomb plot:

In German there lived an opposition which was weakened by their losses and an enervating international policy, but which belongs to the noblest and greatest that the political history of any nation has ever produced. These men fought without help from within or from abroad – driven forward only by the restlessness of their conscience. As long as they lived they were invisible and unrecognisable to us, because they had to camouflage themselves. But their death made the resistance visible.[12]

When Schlabrendorff went back to see Churchill in 1949, also at Chartwell, Churchill told him that during the war he had been misled 'by his assistants about the considerable strength and size of the anti-Hitler resistance'.[13]

Eden and his Foreign Office advisors' view about the need to crush Germany was not shared by all in high places in Whitehall. Brooke, the CIGS, was in favour of a strong postwar Germany. If his views could have been put to the conspirators they would have had no difficulty in enrolling enough German Generals in the plot to make sure that Hitler was overthrown and the war ended in the summer of 1944. Here is an extract from Brooke's diary six days after the bomb plot:

Back to War Office to have an hour with Secretary of State [for War – Grigg], discussing post-war policy in Europe. Should Germany be dismembered or gradually converted to an ally to meet the Russian threat of twenty years hence? I suggested the latter and feel certain that we must from now onwards regard Germany in a very different light. Germany is no longer the dominating power in Europe – Russia is. Unfortunately Russia is not entirely European. She has, however, vast resources and cannot fail to become the main threat in fifteen years from now. Therefore, foster Germany, gradually build her up and bring her into a Federation of Western Europe. Unfortunately this must all be done under the cloak of a holy alliance between England, Russia and America. Not an easy policy, and one requiring a super Foreign Secretary.[14]

Even at that time the Chiefs of Staff were considering plans for Germany's help in counterbalancing the Russian military strength in the postwar period. Brooke's reference to the need for a 'super Foreign Secretary' suggests that he had misgivings about Eden's views on the future of Germany.

Grave misjudgements within Whitehall surely occurred. The author asked Roberts, for instance, why, in spite of the fact that Lothian, Cripps and other well-known people had vouched for Trott's sincerity, the minutes show that the German desk at the Foreign Office did not trust him and thought right up to 20 July 1944 he might be a Nazi agent. Roberts replied that the way in which Trott was able to travel around to neutral countries made them suspicious and 'we thought the Gestapo was much more efficient than it was, and no genuine plotter could have had this freedom of movement. We were wrong about the Gestapo.'[15]

The author asked Harrison if, with hindsight, he regretted some of his wartime views. He stuck to his guns:

I always looked on unconditional surrender as an unmitigated disaster, especially from the point of view of Political Warfare, and with hindsight I would have been more compassionate to poor Adam Trott, but we felt that if we in London were told of their plans the Gestapo must know all about them too.

All these German peace feelers were of no interest to us at all because, apart from anything else, we had no faith they could deliver the goods; we thought they were so impractical they could be of no help to the war effort. Our instructions in the Foreign Office were 'no parley' and 'unconditional surrender', so we were just not interested.

I knew Bishop Bell well and saw him frequently. My country house in Sussex was in his diocese. I liked him. He had charm and charisma, but was terribly naive and understood nothing about Germany.[e] He was a red rag to a bull to Eden, and we did not take him seriously.

20 July was a Generals' plot because it was Stauffenberg who tried to kill Hitler. Until after the war we had no idea the conspiracy was so wide-based and included so many politicians. I looked on the emissaries sending messages about peace from neutral countries as agents for the German General Staff, and believed even Keitel and Jodl might jettison Hitler and turn round and try to make peace with us.

At the time of the debate in the Commons on 2 August 1944, the nation was strongly pro-Russian. Neither the House nor the country would have stood for a peace with Germany which did not include Russia. We had all been taught to look forward to a postwar world in which Russia was friendly to the West, and everything was geared to a tripartite peace. Having encouraged the British people to love the Russians you could not throw them overboard, and the War Cabinet felt the country would not be with them in a negotiated peace with a German opposition.

The then more senior Duke of Portland told the author:

Even if Rommel had offered to surrender in July 1944 I am not sure the war would have come to an end suddenly because Roosevelt and Churchill would have insisted on simultaneous surrender to the Russians, and Rommel would not have agreed.

It was worth a lot to break the spirit of the German army; after all, the casualties in the last months of the war were nothing like those my generation suffered in the First World War. Remember too, we might have pushed Hitler into the arms of Russia, and Roosevelt and Churchill were terrified of double-crossing by Stalin.

I was at the British Embassy in Warsaw in 1920 when the Poles took over the Polish Corridor from Germany. The Germans then acquiesced but they told me they would be fighting again one day and it reminded them of Napoleon's temporary rearrangement after Austerlitz, and that 'the spirit of the army' remained in Germany. We killed this in 1945.

The Morgenthau Plan was nonsense. We all knew it would never be implemented but it was not worthwhile having a squabble with the Americans about it. I believe the Germans went on fighting just as much because of fear of the Russians as of Morgenthau. Still we failed to realize the strength of Goebbels's propaganda. At that stage of the war it was not easy to handle the Americans.[16]

After 20 July the ranks of the plotters in Berlin and Paris were shattered by wholesale arrests and executions. Mussolini, through his

---

[e]Hugh Carleton Greene, who was married by Bishop Bell, confirmed that the Bishop gave the impression of great naivety − 'a sort of holy fool who was difficult to take seriously'.

Ambassador to Berlin, Anfuso, intervened with Hitler at Frau Hassell's request to try to save the life of Hassell, with whom he had been friendly in Rome. Hitler refused out of hand. No more overtures came from the German Resistance as the leaders were rounded up and more and more names were extracted under torture from those already arrested. However, Weizsaecker and Kessel had escaped, and now safely installed inside the Vatican with Rome occupied by the Allies, offered to act as intermediaries with Rundstedt.[17] Kluge knew that his number was up because with the Gestapo methods of interrogation under torture he would be bound to be betrayed by the arrested plotters. On the last day of August 1944 the Allied armies, as Rommel had predicted, burst through the thin ring of the German defences in Normandy and swept south. Brittany and Paris were at their mercy. Kluge knew the German armies in Normandy were lost, but Hitler insisted on a counter-offensive at Mortain which produced serious losses to Kluge's remaining Panzer divisions.

There is evidence that despite the failure of the plot and the refusal of the Allies to offer any concessions to an anti-Nazi Government, Kluge then made efforts to surrender. If an olive branch had been held out to him by the Allies, his resolve might have been strengthened and other German Generals might have spurred him on to put an end to the useless continuation of the war.

On 15 August, when his troops were *in extremis*, Kluge disappeared and was out of contact with his staff all day. Hitler said it was the worst day of his life when he heard Kluge could not be contacted. At Hitler's headquarters they monitored an Allied radio signal asking where Kluge was. Kluge's radio truck was silent after 9.30 a.m., and Hitler believed he was negotiating the surrender of the Western Front. After the war Blumentritt confirmed under interrogation that Keitel had told him of the intercepted Allied signal and General Guderian, according to General Milch's diary, said: 'Kluge tried in France to contact the enemy.'

Kluge's son-in-law, Dr Udo Esch, a German army doctor who later gave Kluge cyanide with which to commit suicide, told his Allied interrogators on 27 July 1945 that Kluge had discussed with him the possibility of surrendering the entire Western Front and said 'he went to the front lines but was unable to get in touch with the Allied commanders'.

From the American side there is evidence from Lieutenant-Colonel George Pfann, secretary of General Patton's Third Army, who stated that Patton vanished from his headquarters for an entire day in mid-

August, and when he returned said he had tried to make contact with a German emissary who had not turned up at the appointed place.[18]

Brigadier Williams told the author he could recall the day when Kluge was reported missing, and although he had had no 'share' in peace feelers he warned his 'master', Montgomery, that they might get something from Kluge at any moment, and that he must 'watch his step' if any German Generals came over to their lines. Montgomery, according to Williams, got 'silly' and over-excited with captured German Generals, finding it fascinating to talk to them as they could tell him so much about their troops. In North Africa, when General von Thoma had been captured, Montgomery invited him to dinner; for this he had been criticized in the Commons and Williams said they did not want 'any of that business again'. According to Williams, the information probably came from intercepted German signals through Ultra, and he could not remember hearing anything from the Americans about it.[19]

At 7.30 p.m. on 15 August Kluge was still missing, but late that night he reappeared and said his radio link van had been damaged by enemy aircraft so he had sent on a staff officer alone to the planned rendezvous with other German Generals. Hitler immediately sacked Kluge, ordering him to remain away from the front line until his successor, Field-Marshal Model, arrived. Hitler wanted to make sure there were no more efforts to contact the Allies, and Model was a dedicated Hitler supporter. On his way back to Germany, on 19 August, Kluge committed suicide. His final letter to Hitler contained the words: '. . . My Fuehrer, make up your mind to end the war. The German people have borne such untold suffering that it is time to put an end to this frightfulness.'[20]

As the Allied armies surged across France and liberated Belgium to reach the German and Dutch frontiers in early September, Hitler was able to rally Germany to his cause because the alternatives seemed so appalling. The Teheran Conference was made out by Goebbels as meaning that Germany would be robbed of her eastern provinces and half of her territory with deportations of several million people.

Goebbels's propaganda through the summer of 1944 was that the Allies intended to 'exterminate us root and branch as a nation'. As a result of the Morgenthau Plan German national newspapers warned that their enemies wanted 'to exterminate 30 or 40 million people'. The publicity given to the Morgenthau Plan and the insistence on unconditional surrender, coupled with indiscriminate bombing, produced a revival of enthusiasm for the Nazi party almost unbelievable in the light of the military collapse in France. Under Albert Speer and Karl Saur, arms production soared and a new peak was reached as late as August 1944. The hard line taken in the 2 August Commons debate helped Hitler to resist to the end.

The diaries of Cadogan and Brooke, who were the closest advisers to Churchill and Eden during the war, suggest that neither the Prime Minister nor the Foreign Secretary had time in 1944 to sit back and take proper appraisal of the plot to overthrow Hitler and end the war, in spite of the evidence accumulating in London and Washington.

Eden had been delighted when Churchill asked him to become Leader of the House in November 1942, as he felt this gave him wider authority and experience outside the Foreign Office. However, from then on he was unable to give enough attention to foreign affairs, and Cadogan in his diary describes how difficult it was to work with him.

[6 October 1944] Complete confusion. He can't go on doubling these parts. F.O. can't work like this and he agrees . . . [16 December 1944] A arrived 2.55. Saw him for 5 minutes. What a way to do business. A got back to F.O. at 6.55 to catch 7.18 train to Binderton. I had a word with him while he was flapping about the room collecting hat and coat . . . [8 January 1945] A arrives at 12.30: summons a meeting on Greece 12.45. *What* a way of doing business. This is all one sees of him. He strides about the room gabbling, and I at least can't hear what he says.

Harvey, a close friend and admirer of Eden, noted in his diary that Eden suffered from 'lamentable escapism'. He and Cadogan give a clear picture of an overwrought Foreign Secretary who by coupling the post with that of Leader of the House gave himself too little time for considered decisions.

Both Eden and Churchill were under severe strain in the spring of 1944 when the decisions were made not to issue a declaration to the Germans before D Day and to ignore the growing evidence of an imminent coup by the anti-Nazis. Brooke recorded in March 1944 of Churchill: 'He is losing ground rapidly. He seems quite incapable of concentrating for a few minutes on end.' On 19 April Cadogan recorded:

PM, I fear, is breaking down. He rambles without a pause, and we really got nowhere by 7.40. N. Chamberlain would have settled it in 6 minutes . . . he wasted about 150 man-hours . . . I really am fussed about the PM. He is *not* the man he was 12 months ago, and I really don't know if he can carry on.[21]

Although Churchill took a hard line against the forces trying to overthrow Hitler in Germany, he was more sympathetic towards the

Archduke Otto Hapsburg who suggested using his supporters and friends to organize revolutions in Austria and Hungary.

Otto was the son of the last Austrian Emperor, Karl, and the heir to the throne of the two monarchies Austria and Hungary. When Hitler's armies overran France, with his mother, the Empress Zita, he fled to Lisbon and then to Quebec. He organized Right-wing exiled Austrians into an anti-Nazi group favouring the end of the Anschluss and the restoration of the Hapsburg monarchy in Hungary and Austria. Similar groups of exiles were formed in London and Lisbon under his brothers.

The Archduke had submitted to the American State Department a number of papers discussing Soviet plans for a Communist Austria and his own plans both to organize an anti-Nazi revolt there, and to overthrow the Horthy Government in Hungary and replace it with a pro-Allied Government. These were brought to Churchill's attention when he reached Quebec for the Heads of State Conference in September 1943. The ideas interested Churchill and he saw Otto in Quebec on 31 August 1943.

Churchill said that he personally approved of Otto's views on the future structure of Central Europe, but he was hampered by 'those in his Cabinet who were prepared to make a surrender to Russia'. In return Otto told Churchill that in Hungary at a given signal from the Allies the Nazi sympathizers in the Government and among the deputies would be arrested, and the Regent would resign. Parliament would then declare an end to the war against Britain and America, and Hungary would assume strict neutrality, not allowing German troops trains to pass through her territory, nor allow her airfields to be at the disposal of the enemy. The Germans would oppose this move with armed forces and the Hungarian troops would resist; thus Hungary would pass to the side of the Allies.

Otto emphasized that it would all be done quite constitutionally. He confirmed this to Churchill by letter, writing on 2 September: 'The Hungarian Government is no longer willing to fight with Germany. Horthy is ready to step down. I have contacts with the highest officials.' He continued that the Austrians had contacts with him in Lisbon and there was 'a revolutionary underground there ready to aid the Allies as soon as they approach the Austrian border'. He also raised the question of the return to Austria of the south Tyrol, ceded to Italy at Versailles. With the Italian armistice imminent, he must have been sure of Churchill's goodwill to suggest such a step.

Amazingly, in view of the Government's refusal to embark on negotiations with the proposed Beck-Goerdeler Government in Germany, Churchill was enthusiastic to cooperate with Otto, although he must have known Hapsburg internal support in Austria and Hungary was flimsy and that any such move would antagonize Stalin. His actions therefore with regard to Otto indicate that he intrinsically had little fear of Stalin making a separate peace with Hitler, and that his refusal to acknowledge the existence of the Beck-Goerdeler opposition must have been due to ignorance rather than fear of upsetting the Russians.

Otto told the Prime Minister that potential Austrian revolutionaries would send a courier to Lisbon immediately to talk to him about their plan, and he wanted to send his brother Archduke Charles Louis there from America to meet them. The British Foreign Office, however, would not give Charles Louis a visa to travel on to Britain, and the Portugese insisted on this British visa before they would allow him to come to Lisbon. Cadogan opposed the visa for Charles Louis on the grounds that the agreed Foreign Office view was that it was a mistake to associate the Hapsburgs with the liberation of Europe. Churchill, who felt Otto could help the war effort, was displeased; he did not always care for Cadogan and, when cross, sometimes described him as 'a frozen codfish'.[22] On 7 September he sent the following message to Eden from Quebec:

2. I think it is a small thing to grant the visa. It commits us to nothing. No-one can tell how Central Europe will turn. It would be silly for us to try to force any kind of a king or emperor on them. It would in my opinion be equally unwise, and also inappropriate in a monarchical state like ours, for us to go out of our way to knock any chances of this kind on the head.

3. One of the greatest mistakes made after the last war was the destruction by ignorant hands of the Austro-Hungarian Empire. Considering the ruin into which they have been plunged it may well be that those disillusioned peoples may see a way out of their troubles through some symbolic chief. Pray think this over on large lines. Do not discuss it with our colleagues, for I have no doubt you could easily beat everything on the head. Please try to have a little confidence in my insight into Europe gathered over so many years.

4. Wilson and Lloyd George thought they were ensuring peace as well as gratifying their raw prejudices in driving out monarchy. However if the Wittelsbachs had been substituted in Germany for the Hohenzollerns there would have been no Hitler and no war. Be kind to me in this small matter and let the poor devil have his visa.

Against Churchill's phrase 'Please try to have a little confidence in my insight into Europe' Eden wrote: 'He might have a little in mine.'

W. D. Allen[f] minuted about Churchill's telegram 'It would be a mistake to facilitate these legitimist contacts at present . . . for the Allies to be suspected of encouraging Hapsburg designs would do us more harm than good.' Harrison minuted: 'Support for the Hapsburgs in Austria and Hungary is inconsiderable. In the succession stakes and Russia the Hapsburg name stinks.' Roberts's view was: 'Our other contacts in Hungary and Austria are likely to be much more useful'; while Strang wrote: 'The Ruritanian brothers take themselves too seriously.' Nevertheless the Foreign Office did not feel it worth while opposing the Prime Minister's wishes although they, through the Secret Service and SOE, had contacts with Hungarian and Austrian dissidents of different political affiliations.

Eden replied:

There is a risk that this may complicate our Hungarian negotiations and have other minor unwelcome repercussions, even though Hapsburgs have little enough support in Austria and Hungary. But if you want to help the young man to the extent of giving him this visa, I see no great harm. We can presumably reply to questions that we saw no reason why the brothers should not meet.
2. It is for the Home Secretary to authorise the issue of the visa, but I can take the responsibility of recommending it to him.[23]

Thus Otto's brother got his visa and – against Eden's and Cadogan's wishes – was free to do what he could to further the Hapsburg cause in Austria and Hungary. Otto himself said in a letter to the author that Churchill really 'enjoyed' overruling the Foreign Office over the visa.[24]

Otto talked to Wheeler-Bennett in New York, and on 1 October 1943 Wheeler-Bennett reported to the Foreign Office that Otto was more violently anti-Russian than ever, and had said

the English were blind to the Bolshevik danger as they had been to the Nazi menace. Stalin, he declared, wished to dominate all Europe and most of Asia, and it was not impossible that he would succeed in doing so with the help of Germany whose people and army he was assiduously wooing. It appeared that only Mr. Churchill saw the danger just as he had also foreseen the falseness of Hitler's promises . . . As a parting shot Otto observed that the Polish Prime Minister, Milholajczyk, was such a crook that even Dr. Benes would have to look out for him.

Repeating this was unlikely to endear the Foreign Office to Otto.[25]

[f]Ambassador to Turkey 1963–67.

Nothing transpired from the Churchill-Hapsburg talks because of the opposition of Cadogan and Eden. At the second Quebec conference the next year, Churchill gave Otto lunch on 17 September 1944. In his letter thanking the British Prime Minister for the lunch Otto wrote: 'Any uprising in Austria would be suicidal; all our manhood is scattered in every corner of Europe, but I am ready to take part in one.' He said he was ready to do anything to bring about unconditional surrender in Hungary and Austria, and suggested Cardinal Seredi as head of the Hungarian Government instead of Horthy, who was hated by the Russians. He offered to go to the Swiss border to meet Hungarian delegates; he would call on Horthy and his Government to negotiate surrender, and asked for arms and ammunition for his people. Seredi was pro-Hapsburg. Otto explained to the author why he thought Seredi, who was head of the Church, would replace Horthy as head of the Government:

Seredi's claim to play a key role towards the end of the war is because under the Hungarian constitution the Primate has an important constitutional function. He would have been the logical head of either a transitional Government or he would have been head of state automatically in a period in which Hungary was without a formal Government.[26]

The news of the lunch was leaked to the press, and Cadogan wrote to the Prime Minister on 28 October, in Eden's absence:

I am satisfied the Archduke's interference can only do harm. The support he enjoys in Austria and Hungary is far too small to counterbalance the certain disadvantages we should incur in Soviet Russia, Czechoslovakia and Yugoslavia, not to mention public reactions in this country were we to attempt to make use of him [to promote an uprising in Austria]. I hope that the Americans will act with discretion.

Nothing came of Churchill's second meeting with Otto and the Prime Minister reluctantly accepted the Foreign Office advice. But how keen Churchill was on using monarchist sympathizers in Austria and Hungary to break the Nazi rule can be seen from a minute by him to the Foreign Office dated 8 April 1945. Otto had written to Churchill on 1 March seeking support for monarchist sympathizers in Austria who were organizing uprisings as the Germans retreated. Eden, the Foreign Office and the War Office wanted nothing to do with it. This brought a sharp retort from Churchill:

This war would never have come if under American and modernising pressure we had not driven the Hapsburgs out of Austria and Hungary, and the Hohenzollerns out of Germany. By making these vacuums we gave the opening for the Hitlerite monster to crawl out of its sewer on to its vacant throne. No doubt these views are very unfashionable. If there is no possibility of helping Otto and his brothers I do not see why we should invite them to disclose their secrets.

Eden replied on 13 April:

There is of course much force in what you say about the consequences of the over-hasty dissolution of the Hapsburg Empire at the end of the last war. But for us to attempt now to put back the clock by embarking on substantial military assistance to the Hapsburgs would in my view be both impracticable and dangerous, especially in present circumstances.

2. In addition to the points made in General Ismay's minute of the 7th April, there is a further reason why it would, I think, be unwise to give encouragement to the Hapsburgs. At a time when we are particularly anxious that the Russians should take no action in Austria likely to prejudice the situation before the full Allied machinery is set up there, we must be particularly careful to avoid doing anything likely to arouse Russian suspicions.

3. In the circumstances I can see no alternative to closing the correspondence with the Archduke. That being so, I quite agree that we should not send any further communication asking for particulars of his organisation.

4. If you approve, I will myself send a letter to Duff Cooper[g] explaining why we do not feel able to accede to the Archduke's request, and asking for a suitable message to be conveyed to him.

Churchill admitted defeat on receipt of this letter. He knew his colleagues in the War Cabinet would not want to antagonize the Russians and that they would back Eden against him. He minuted to his private secretaries Colville and Millard: 'No action', and that ended his efforts to make the Hapsburgs part of the postwar European settlement. The correspondence with Otto ceased, as Eden wished.

No copy of Otto's letter to Churchill of 1 March 1945 asking for aid to the monarchist uprising in Austria exists in the archives, and Otto informed the author that for security reasons he kept no copies of any letters he wrote from Paris in 1945. However, he told the author that immediately after the fall of France he was able to make contacts with the monarchist opposition in Austria, and this was due especially to help from General de Gaulle, 'who was vitally interested in the independence of Austria'. Otto stated that he had kept in close touch with the French Resistance and the Gaullist movement during the war years, and once de Gaulle was in control of the French 'machinery of

---

[g]Duff Cooper was Ambassador in Paris where Otto now was; the French Government were helping Otto in his clandestine contacts with pro-monarchy plotters inside Austria.

state' he received considerable help from him. As a result he was able to establish contacts with his sympathizers in resistance movements inside Austria, and was able to 'send in certain persons and bring out others'. The French radio sent coded messages on his behalf, and 'this was particularly important in the liberation phase of Voralberg and Tyrol'.

Otto stressed in a letter to the author that Churchill was his one link and support with the British Government during the war:

Eden was continually hostile to the point where he showed it publicly. It was quite striking when I met Eden in the presence of Churchill how different he was as long as the Prime Minister was present, and how unbearable he became as soon as the Prime Minister had gone. The minutes you are publishing in your book confirm my personal impression at that time.[h26]

Colville assured the author that Churchill was deadly serious in his support of Otto,[i] and in a letter wrote:

I can certainly solve the riddle why Churchill was prepared to negotiate with the Hapsburgs and not with the German plotters. He did not believe that the latter had any powerful support in Germany, but at a time when dividing Germany was still Allied policy Chrurchill thought that a Danubian-state containing Austria, Hungary, Bavaria and perhaps Würtemburg and Baden might be created under the Hapsburgs. He always felt that one of the causes of World War Two was the vacuum left in the Danube valley by the dissolution of the Austro -Hungarian Empire.

On 27 July 1944 Bishop Bell wrote to Eden suggesting there should be a liaison link with the German Resistance in Stockholm, and that Johansson of Sigtuna would be the most suitable. The Bishop thought the Church leaders in Germany would want to communicate with Britain now, and that there was a connection between the 20 July plot and the move towards a revolt 'which I learned in such a confidential way two years ago'. Harvey minuted, and Cadogan agreed: 'We should certainly discourage this; the German Protestant Church is not to be trusted'; and Eden scrawled in red ink across the top of the letter: 'I see no reason to encourage this turbulent priest. Perhaps you will advise me how to reply.'[27] Bishop Bell was told his suggestion did not find favour with the Foreign Office.

---

[h]Sir John Colville records in his diary that in April 1945 Churchill instructed him to see that his views on the Hapsburgs 'were given a wide distribution inside the Foreign Office' which he accused of 'Republicanism'.

[i]Churchill did not refer to Otto in his postwar memoirs. However, shortly after the war was over, when he learnt the Allies were considering capturing or detaining Otto in Brussels, he sent a strong telegram to the British Ambassador vetoing it.

A similar effort, by the Archbishop of Canterbury, was also dismissed. The Archbishop wrote on 15 September asking for facilities for Visser't Hooft, still General Secretary of the World Council of Churches, to come to London for consultations. He added that the Prime Minister of the Netherlands Government in exile in London had also asked for him.

Harrison's response survives in a minute:

M. Visser 't Hooft is European Secretary of the Y.M.C.A. and also General Secretary of the World Council of Churches in Geneva. In character he is by all accounts above suspicion or reproach. None the less the fact remains that he is known in the past to have been in touch with German oppositional groups, in particular the civilian side of the opposition which has probably been eliminated as a result of the purge following the attempted coup of July 20th. When he came to this country in 1942, he brought with him a memorandum from a group of Germans which included Adam von Trott, liquidated a week or so ago.

I have an uneasy feeling that if we allowed M. Visser 't Hooft to come to this country he will get into touch with circles here who are disposed towards a soft peace for Germany. He may supply information not only to the Archbishop of Canterbury but also perhaps to men like the Bishop of Chichester, which it may be inconvenient for them to have, e.g. stories of continued oppositional movements in Germany, especially in Church circles. I should hope therefore that it may be possible to find administrative or technical difficulties which would prevent M. Visser 't Hooft coming to this country until Germany has collapsed.[28]

Roberts added: 'I agree,' and Harvey added his initials to show that he concurred in this outrageous minute. What harm it could do to the war effort if Visser't Hooft talked to Bishop Bell – or even to Strauss or Stokes, the anti-unconditional surrender MPs – defeats the imagination. The Eden line over no 'soft peace' was slavishly followed by the Foreign Office. The Archbishop was firmly told in a letter from Harvey that the visit could not be arranged. When the author asked Harrison why he had minuted that it would be 'inconvenient' for Bishop Bell to be told of continued opposition, he replied:

I would write exactly the same minute today. We did not want to rock the boat by encouraging those who wanted a soft peace. It would have been bad for morale. We wanted to crush the Germans so there could be no recurrence of the events of the '30s. After all, our war casualties were not so great from that time onwards.

The author sent copies of the Foreign Office minutes and the Archbishop's letter to Dr Visser't Hooft, who replied:

I must call 'hypocrisy' that sentence that accuses me of bringing material to England, and especially to the Archbishop of Canterbury, that would be 'inconvenient' for them to know. It is really quite wonderful, that in a war fought ostensibly for freedom over and against a dictator's control of the state, I was to be kept out of Britain because I might tell the truth to the head of the Anglican Church.

Surprisingly, in the autumn of 1944 peace overtures came from Himmler. He was head of the SS and the police in Germany and controlled the Gestapo and the SD. By 1943 he was the Crown Prince who would succeed Hitler, because Goering with the failure of the Luftwaffe was a declining force. Yet as early as 1942 Himmler toyed with the idea that he might overthrow Hitler, become leader of Germany, and make peace with the Allies. In May 1942 and again in January 1943 he tried to open negotiations with the British in Madrid, and the British Ambassador, Sir Samuel Hoare, reported that Prince Max Hohenlohe had said he and Himmler were hostile to Hitler and wanted to make peace. This got a chilly reception in the Foreign Office. In January 1943 Allen minuted: 'If there is anything in this story that Hohenlohe is backed by Himmler, it is an added reason for nothing to do with him.' Harrison's comment was:

Himmler is probably the most hated man in Europe and has no popular backing in Germany. I simply cannot see him either as a rival to Hitler or as trying to negotiate peace with us. Himmler has agents of his own abroad who report direct to him, and Hohenlohe may in fact be his agent in Spain. But as Mr. Allen says, this is simply an added reason for steering clear of him.[29]

Himmler, a stupid man, had no idea how loathed he was outside Germany. Langbehn, one of the leading conspirators, was a friend of Himmler, mainly because their children went to the same school. Since May 1943 he had been negotiating through General Wolff, Himmler's Chief of Staff, about the possibility of a coup in which Himmler would replace Hitler. On 26 August, Langbehn and Popitz, another influential conspirator and former Minister, had an interview with Himmler himself.

Langbehn was a dedicated anti-Nazi, honest and genuine. He lived next door in Berlin to Christabel Bielenberg who told the author he was a man of the highest moral standing and had no intention of allowing Himmler to take control of Germany. He was only seeking authorization from Himmler to go to Switzerland in order to make contact with the Allies on behalf of the plotters; he would have abandoned Himmler if anything had materialized.[30]

Himmler gave Langbehn the necessary authority to travel to Switzerland to meet Dulles, believing he was going to sound out the Allies about a possible change of regime and the substitution of Hitler by Himmler. In reality Langbehn wanted to substitute Hitler with a Beck-Goerdeler Government and to ditch Himmler. Beck and Goerdeler wanted nothing to do with Himmler but did not object to anything which might create confusion in the Nazi ranks.

Langbehn duly contacted Dulles in Berne, but unfortunately Dulles's signal to Washington that 'Himmler's lawyer confirms the hopelessness of Germany's military and political situation and has arrived to put out peace feelers' was intercepted and reported to Hitler. Langbehn was immediately put into restrictive custody on his return to Germany, but Himmler managed to convince the Fuehrer of his own loyalty. Hitler had no idea of what Dulles called 'his flirtation with treason'.

On Hitler's orders Gestapo secret agents made persistent enquiries from the United States Legation in Berne 'to provoke an expression of opinion about Langbehn'. Dulles informed Washington that Langbehn was a private legal agent of Himmler and that the Nazis had discovered he had made clandestine contacts with American officials; his detention in Moabit prison was therefore ordered by the Gestapo. (According to Christabel Bielenberg, he was at first able to do business and receive visitors there.) Dulles added that Langbehn was said to have double-crossed Himmler. Obviously the Gestapo and SS were in dispute over him and he was thought by Hitler's personal entourage to be disloyal.[31]

The information was passed on to the British Embassy in Washington, who reported to the Foreign Office in London 'The message rings no bell with us, but may be of interest at your end.' Here was an important clue to a split between Himmler and Hitler.[32]

During the autumn of 1944 Himmler sent emissaries to Dulles in Berne, suggesting that the Germans should cease fighting in the west and join forces with the Allies in a common front against the Russians.[j] Dulles reported these to Washington but they came to nothing. Using the same channels, two SS Generals, Wolff[k] and Dollman, suggested in February to Dulles that Kesselring would be willing to surrender the Italian Front to put an end to the fighting, regardless

---

[j] This was exactly the same message as that brought by Hess in May 1941, except that Hess alleged that the message came from Hitler.

[k] It was Wolff who managed to stop Italian Jews being exterminated and prevented the scorched earth policy in Italy ordered by Hitler.

of Hitler. These genuine proposals were taken seriously by the Allies. Unfortunately Kesselring, who was in favour of peace, was removed by Hitler to command the Southern Group of Armies in Germany and was replaced by General Vietinghof who would not consider surrender without Hitler's permission.

Himmler persevered. According to Brandenburg, who was Goerdeler's gaoler in the autumn of 1944, he suggested to Goerdeler in prison that Goerdeler should get in touch with Wallenberg in Stockholm and the Zionist leader Weizmann to put peace proposals from Himmler to Churchill, and bring the war 'to a swift and tolerable conclusion'. Goerdeler agreed to act, but said a pre-condition must be that he was set free and allowed to go to Stockholm. This Himmler would not do, but he kept both Popitz and Goerdeler (as well as Langbehn) alive until Hitler's personal staff became suspicious that he was negotiating a takeover and peace through them. Then Hitler gave a direct order for their execution on 2 February 1945.

Concurrently with his overtures to Goerdeler, Himmler enlisted the services of the ubiquitous Dahlerus. Dahlerus visited the British Legation in Stockholm in December 1944 and claimed that Himmler was now the virtual dictator of Germany because Hitler, as a result of his injuries from the 20 July bomb, was incapable of concentrating for more than ten minutes. According to Dahlerus, Himmler had gained the support of 'all the leading military who were non-Nazi by promising to abolish all the Nazi plans and ideals'.

Mallet's despatch to London of 15 December 1944 read:

Himmler hoped to produce a German fighting force of five million men. With these he was confident that he could hold the Russian front, and he hoped to hold the Western Front long enough to cause enough losses of British and American troops to persuade the Western powers to agree to a more reasonable settlement with Germany.

An indication of Himmler's new policy was that during the last four weeks the wives and families of all those who took part in the attempt on Hitler's life, including the family of Stauffenberg himself, had been released and pensioned. It was not generally known that the clean up which followed July 20th also included the arrest and shooting of all those Germans who were attempting to reach a settlement with Russia. Himmler was a great opponent of Russia and was determined to exterminate all those with a contrary view on this question.

Dahlerus then said that he was turning over in his mind the idea of visiting Germany, where he thought he could arrange, possibly through his friends Stegmann and Kloth, to be received by Himmler, and he would take this opportunity to try to find out whether Himmler seriously thought there was any use in continuing the struggle and if not what steps he proposed to take with a view to sueing for peace. Before deciding, however, whether to go to Germany, Dahlerus asked for an assurance that if he reported the result of his visit to us the British Foreign Office would believe what he said. He added that he knew that he had been in our black books and that there had been a move to black list him and he thought that as a result of this the Foreign Office might not believe a word he said; if this were the case there would be no point whatever in his carrying out his plan.[1]

Counsellor then said that he thought it was only fair to make it clear before Dahlerus decided to go to Berlin that whatever proposal Himmler might make there was no chance whatever of His Majesty's Government agreeing to negotiate with him in any circumstances whatever, and that therefore any interest which His Majesty's Government might have in the result of Dahlerus's initiative would be purely of an intelligence nature. Dahlerus said that while he fully appreciated this he thought it possible that Himmler might agree to retire altogether with the whole of the rest of the Nazi gang and leave it to other elements to sue for peace.

Churchill rightly gave this Himmler-Dahlerus approach short shrift and treated it with the contempt it deserved. He minuted Eden with a peremptory instruction to have nothing to do with it.

FOREIGN SECRETARY

Is it not very dangerous indeed for us to get mixed up with people going to and fro from Germany? At any time you may find a garbled version of the story conveyed to the Russians or the Americans. I am seriously alarmed about this telegram, particularly the part marked 'A'. I am sure the Cabinet should be informed before there is the slightest entanglement of this kind. I consider that we should keep ourselves clear of the whole of this business, but if you like it can be brought up at Cabinet this evening.

On 22 October 1944 Cadogan had minuted:

I am horrified of telling Americans we have been trying to muzzle him [Dahlerus]. That will create a much worse impression than any distortion by enemy propaganda; we must not give the Americans any grounds for thinking there was something fishy about our relations with him in 1939.

Roberts replied that there was

nothing in our dealings with Dahlerus of which we need to be ashamed ... but it is embarrassing that he was strongly anti-Polish. His account would support German propaganda that origin of war was Polish intransigence, not German aggression. Should we put his companies on the black list?

[1]In spite of the trust placed in Dahlerus during the frantic days of last-minute appeasement in 1939, his companies had been placed on the Allies' black list of Swedish companies with whom they would not trade. In January 1945 they were taken off it as a reward for Dahlerus's involvement in 1939.

Roberts was quite right that Dahlerus was 'anti-Polish', but what about Chamberlain, Halifax, Cadogan and Henderson during their 1939 dealings with Dahlerus? All four were 'anti-Polish' as well. Cadogan was justified in being concerned lest the Americans should think British relations wiith Dahlerus in 1939 were 'fishy'. Britain used him as a go-between for a sell out of Poland to Hitler, and it would have come off but for 'Polish intransigence'. In 1944 Cadogan was ashamed of the incident and wanted 'to muzzle' Dahlerus because it was a complete clandestine breach of Britain's solemn treaty obligation to the Poles.

On 23 December Eden cabled to Mallet:

I regret that any conversation was held with Dahlerus with reference to his journey to Germany. It is to be expected that the German military counter attack in the West[m] will be accompanied by a deliberate attempt to sow suspicion and dissension amongst the Allies with the object of bringing about a compromise peace with one or the other . . . I must ask you therefore to ensure that in future no member of your staff enters into any discussion of this nature with Dahlerus or with anyone else. In order to make certain that no misunderstanding can arise . . . I am informing the United States and Soviet Governments of this incident. We must expect that a number of peace feelers may be launched and the utmost vigilance is necessary to ensure that no encouragement is given to any.[33]

When Castellano came to Lisbon in August 1943 he was given a wireless set so that he could communicate with Eisenhower's headquarters and negotiate a surrender. Cadogan noted in his diary three days after the bomb plot that he had authorized a wireless set to General Reinhart, the German Commander in Holland, but 'I do not expect anything will come of it.'[34] A radio link was also made available to Wolff in 1945 when he was trying to negotiate the surrender of the Italian Front. However, no wireless set or any means of communication were ever given to Trott or Goerdeler's emissaries. Without any contact with the Allied Governments the German opposition never knew if they formed a Government whether they would get such terms of peace from the Allies as would enable them to survive and get German public opinion to support them.

The following letter which Ludwig Hammerstein, son of General Hammerstein, wrote to the author illustrates the attitude of the anti-Hitler Generals who had the power to topple him.

---

[m]Rundstedt had launched a counter-attack in ʰe Ardennes just before Christmas which threatened to cross the Meuse and retake Brussels and Antwerp.

I discussed the action they planned against Hitler with my father, who died on the 24th April 1943, in March 1943. My father considered action against Hitler to be right in principle, but feared a new 'stab-in-the-back legend' as after the First World War, since neither the troops nor the mass of the German population had correctly recognized Hitler's criminal character and the hopeless military situation. He also warned against underestimating the difficulties of acting against Hitler, which many people were inclined to do. On no account should we act carelessly. A failure would immediately lead to the elimination of all opponents of the Nazis and thus make further action impossible.[35]

Recently the younger generation of German historians have tended to dismiss the Resistance as 'Nationalist and Conservative'. This is incorrect. The plotters were anti-Communist and anti-Nazi and covered a wide spectrum of political opinion, including Socialists and Trade Unionists; in addition they were strongly opposed to anti-Semitism. The Gestapo had discovered complete lists of Trade Unionist and Communist activists, with the result that very few were at liberty and cooperation with them was impractical. The remnants of the Italian political parties wanted no dealings with the Generals in their resistance to Mussolini; the German plotters were more realistic and realized no coup could succeed without the support of the German Army. At first, certainly, the German plotters hoped for some revision of the Versailles frontiers; every German between the two wars wanted this, and until the German frontiers were crossed by Russian and Allied troops it would have been almost indispensable for popular support for a new anti-Nazi Government.[36]

German postwar sources give incontrovertible evidence of the strength and determination of the German conspirators. The British Government was gravely mistaken in not differentiating between 'good' and 'bad' Germans, and thus refusing the conspirators the help they needed to gather more sensible Germans to their cause. German patriots were putting their lives at risk every time they contacted the Allies in neutral countries, but when they did so no helping hand was extended. As it was, the Beck, Goerdeler, Trott, and Stauffenberg conspirators nearly ended the war with their attempted coup on 20 July 1944; if the Allies had helped them they would almost certainly have gathered enough recruits to be successful. The archives show the British Government's behaviour towards them was unjustified; the official line that it was better to continue the fighting than to allow the German opposition to negotiate peace before a complete military defeat is surely indefensible. The pressing need was to stop the bloodshed as soon as possible.

In fairness it must be said that any deal with German anti-Hitler plotters ran the risk of angering Stalin, and might have destroyed the Alliance, but the inescapable fact is that if in the summer of 1944 Rommel or Kluge had surrendered in the west, Britain and America were no longer dependent on Stalin's goodwill.

Wheeler-Bennett's part in the affair is particularly regrettable. He convinced Churchill and Eden that the Allies had nothing to gain if the plotters overthrew Hitler because Britain could 'trust no German at all'. It was tragic that he should have been the trusted confidential adviser to the Foreign Secretary during this period. Eden led the Foreign Office to treat the German Resistance with contempt; his subordinates agreed too readily, while the over-engaged Churchill gave the subject no real thought. There can be little doubt that as a result Europe suffered the tragedy of ten avoidable months of war with massive extra military and civilian casualties. It is a terrible responsibility.

Select Bibliography and Sources

Select Bibliography

Aloisi, Pompeo, *Mia attivita a servizio della pace*, Rome, 1946.

Avon, The Earl of, *Memoirs: Facing the Dictators*, London, 1962.

Avon, The Earl of, *Memoirs: The Reckoning*, London, 1965.

Balfour, Michael, 'Unconditional Surrender', *International Affairs*, London, October 1970.

Balfour, Michael, *Propaganda in War, 1939–45: Organisations, Policies, and Publics in Britain and Germany*, London, 1979.

Balfour, Michael and Frisby, Julian, *Helmuth von Moltke: A German of the Resistance*, London, 1972.

Bandini, Franco, in *Storia Illustrata*, Milan, 1981.

Bell, [Bishop] George, 'The Background of the Hitler Plot', *Contemporary Review*, London, 1945.

Bielenberg, Christabel, *The Past Is Myself*, London, 1968.

Birkenhead, The Earl of, *Halifax: The Life of Lord Halifax*, London 1965.

Bonomi, Ivanoe, *Diario di un anno: 2 giugno '43–10 giugno '44*, Rome, 1947.

Bowra, C. M., *Memories, 1898–1939*, London, 1966.

Bryant, Arthur, *Triumph in the West*, London, 1959.

Bullock, Alan, *Hitler: A Study in Tyranny*, London, 1952.

Butler, Euan, *Amateur Agent*, London, 1963.

Cadorna, R., *La riscossa: dal 25 luglio alla liberazione*, Milan, 1948.

Carboni, Giacomo, *L'armistizio e la difesa di Roma*, Rome, 1946.

Carlgreen, William, *Sverigis Ultrikspolitik 1939–45*, Oslo, 1983.

Carlton, David, *Anthony Eden: A Biography*, London, 1981.

Castellano, Giuseppe, *Come firmai l'armistizio di Cassibile*, Milan, 1945.

Castellano, Giuseppe, *La guerra continua*, Milan, 1963.

Castellano, Giuseppe, *Roma kaputt*, Rome, 1967.

Cavallero, Ugo, *Diario 1940–43*, Milan, 1984.

Caviglia, Enrico, *Diario (aprile 1925–marzo 1945)*, Rome, 1952.

Cecil, Viscount, *A Great Experiment: An Autobiography*, London, 1941.

Churchill, Winston S., The Second World War:

   I: *The Gathering Storm*, London, 1948.

   II: *Their Finest Hour*, London, 1949.

   III: *The Grand Alliance*, London, 1950.

   IV: *The Hinge of Fate*, London, 1951.

   V: *Closing the Ring*, London, 1952.

   VI: *Triumph and Tragedy*, London, 1954.

Ciano, Count G., see Muggeridge.

Colville, John, *The Fringes of Power: Downing Street Diaries 1939–1945*, London, 1985.

Colvin, Ian, *The Chamberlain Cabinet*, London, 1971.

Cowling, Maurice, *The Impact of Hitler: British Politics and British Policy, 1933–40*, London, 1975.

Dahlerus, Bı rger, *The Last Attempt*, London, 1947.

Dalton, Hugh, *The Fateful Years: Memoirs 1931–1945*, London, 1957.

Deakin, F. W., *The Brutal Friendship: Mussolini, Hitler and the Fall of Italian Fascism*, London, 1962.

Dell, Robert, *The Geneva Racket 1920–1939*, London, 1940.

de Luna, Giovanni, *Storia del Partito d'Azione*, Milan, 1982.

Denham, Henry, *Inside the Nazi Ring*, London, 1984.

Deutsch, Harold C., *The Conspiracy against Hitler in the Twilight War*, London, 1968.

Dilks, David (ed.), *The Diaries of Sir Alexander Cadogan 1938–1945*, London, 1971.

Dirksen, Herbert, *Moscow, Tokyo, London*, London, 1951.

Documenti Diplomatici Italiani, Rome, 1954 *et seq.*

Documents on British Foreign Policy 1919–1939, London, 1949 *et seq.*

Documents on Polish-Soviet Relations, 2 vols., London, 1961, 1970.

Documents on German Foreign Policy, series C, vols. 1 & 2, London, 1950; series D, vols. 1–11, London, 1957 *et seq.*

Documents on Foreign Relations of the United States, Washington, 1938–45.

Documents on the Conferences at Cairo and Teheran, Washington, 1961.

Documents on the Conferences at Malta and Yalta, Washington, 1955.

Duff, Sheila Grant, *The Parting of Ways*, London, 1982.

Dulles, Allen, *Germany's Underground*, London, 1947.

Dulles, Allen, *The Secret Surrender*, London, 1967.

Encounter, vols. 31, 32, 33: David Astor, John Wheeler-Bennett, Visser't Hooft, Harold Deutsch, Christopher Sykes, J. Van Roijen, Peter Calvacoressi, Harold Kurtz, London, 1969.

Feiling, Keith, *The Life of Neville Chamberlain*, London, 1946.

Flandin, Pierre-Etienne, *Politique française 1919–1940*, Paris, 1948.

Flannery, Harry W., *Assignment Berlin*, London, 1942.

François-Poncet, André, *The Fateful Years*, London, 1949.

Fuchser, L. W., *Neville Chamberlain and Appeasement*, New York, 1982.

Gamelin, General Maurice Gustav, *Servir*, vols. 2 & 3, Paris, 1946.

Garland, Albert M. and Smyth, Howard MacGaw (edd.), *Sicily and the Surrender of Italy*, Washington, 1965.

Gates, Eleanor M., *End of the Affair: The Collapse of the Anglo-French Alliance, 1939–40*, London, 1981.

Gilbert, Martin, *The Roots of Appeasement*, London, 1966.

Gilbert, Martin, *Winston S. Churchill, Volume VI, Finest Hour, 1939–1941*, London, 1983.

Gilbert, Martin and Gott, Richard *The Appeasers*, London, 1963.

Gisevius, Hans Bernd, *To the Bitter End*, London, 1948.
Grandi, Dino with De Felice, Renzo, *25 luglio – quarant anni dopo*, Bologna, 1983.
Griffiths, Richard, *Fellow Travellers of the Right*, Oxford, 1983.
Guariglia, Raffaele, *Ricordi: 1922–1944*, Naples, 1950.
Halder, Franz, *Kriegstagebuch 1939–1942*, Stuttgart, 1962–64.
Halder, Franz, *Hitler as War Lord*, London, 1950.
Harvey, John (ed.), *The Diplomatic Diaries of Oliver Harvey 1937–1940*, London, 1970.
Harvey, John (ed.), *The War Diaries of Oliver Harvey*, London, 1978.
Hassell, Ulrich von, *The Hàssell Diaries 1938–1944*, London, 1948.
Hoffmann, Peter, *History of the German Resistance 1933–45*, London, 1977.
Hollis, Christopher, *Italy in Africa*, London, 1941.
Irving, David, *Hitler's War*, London, 1977.
Irving, David, *The Trail of the Fox*, London, 1977.
Jasper, Ronald C. D., *George Bell, Bishop of Chichester*, Oxford, 1967.
John, Otto, *Falsch und zu spat, Der 20 Juli 1944*, Munich, 1984.
Jones, Thomas, *A Diary with Letters, 1931–1950*, London, 1954.
Lipski, Jozef, *Diplomat in Berlin: 1933–1939*, New York, 1968.
Lockhart, R. H. Bruce, *Comes the Reckoning*, London, 1947.
Mack Smith, Denis, *Mussolini*, London, 1981.
Macmillan, Harold, *War Diaries Jan. '43–May '45*, London, 1984.
Macmillan, Harold, *The Blast of War 1939–1945*, London, 1967.
Madge, C. and Harrisson, T., *Britain, By Mass Observation*, London, 1939.
Manvell, Roger and Fraenkel, Heinrich, *The July Plot*, London, 1964.
Marshall-Cornwall, James, *Wars and Rumours of Wars*, London, 1984.
Middlemas, Keith, *Diplomacy of Illusion: The British Government and Germany, 1937–1939*, London, 1972.
Middlemas, Keith and Barnes, John, *Baldwin: A Biography*, London, 1969.
Minney, R. J., *The Private Papers of Hore-Belisha*, London, 1960.
Mockler, Anthony, *Haile Selassie's War*, Oxford, 1984.
Monelli, Paolo, *Roma 1943*, Rome, 1946.
Montanelli, Indro and Cervi, Mario, *L'Italia dell'Asse*, Milan, 1981.
Muggeridge, Malcolm (ed.), *Ciano's Diary 1937–1938*, London, 1952.
Muggeridge, Malcolm (ed.), *Ciano's Diary 1939–1943*, London, 1947.
Muggeridge, Malcolm (ed.), *Ciano's Diplomatic Papers*, London, 1948.
Murphy, Robert, *Diplomat among Warriors*, London, 1964.
Namier, L. B., *Europe in Decay: A Study in Disintegration 1936–1940*, London, 1950.
Namier, L. B., *In The Nazi Era*, London, 1952.
Namier, L. B., *Diplomatic Prelude 1938–9*, London, 1948.
Newman, E. W. Polson, *Italy's Conquest of Abyssinia*, London, 1937.
Nicolson, Nigel (ed.), *Harold Nicolson: Diaries and Letters, vol. 2, 1939–1945*, London, 1967.
Papen, Franz von, *Memoirs*, London, 1952.

Parker, R. A. C., 'The Hoare-Laval Pact', *English Historical Review*, vol. 89, 1974, London, 1974.

Petrie, Sir Charles, *Twenty Years' Armistice – and After*, London, 1940.

Raczynski, Eduard, *In Allied London, 1962*.

Ritter, G., *The German Resistance*, London, 1958.

Roatta, Mario, *Otto milioni di baionette: L'esercito italiano in guerra dal 1940 al 1944*, Milan, 1946.

Robbins, Keith, *Munich, 1938*, London, 1968.

Roskill, Stephen, *Hankey, Man of Secrets, vol. 3, 1931–1963*, London, 1974.

Rothfels, Hans, *The German Opposition to Hitler: An Appraisal*, Hinsdale, Illinois, 1948.

Santoni, Alberto, in *Storia Illustrata*, Milan, 1981.

Santoni, Alberto, *Il vero traditore*, Milan, 1981.

Schlabrendorff, Fabian von, *Revolt against Hitler*, London, 1948.

Schmidt, Paul, *Hitler's Interpreter*, London, 1951.

Schramm, W. von, *Conspiracy amongst Generals*, London, 1956.

Seton-Watson, Christopher, 'The Anglo-Italian Gentleman's Agreement of January 1937 and its Aftermath', in *Fascist Challenge and Policy of Appeasement*, ed. Momson and Kettenacker, London, 1983.

Shirer, William L., *The Rise and Fall of the Third Reich*, New York, 1960.

Speidel, Hans, *Invasion 1944*, Berlin, 1949.

Strong, Maj-Gen. Sir Kenneth, *Intelligence at the top: The Recollections of an Intelligence Officer*, London, 1968.

Sykes, Christopher, *Troubled Loyalty: A Biography of Adam von Trott zu Solz*, London, 1968.

Taylor, A. J. P., *The Origins of the Second World War*, London, 1963.

Taylor, Telford, *Munich: The Price of Peace*, London, 1979.

Templewood, Lord, *Nine Troubled Years*, London, 1954.

Thaulero, Giustino Filippone, *Gran Bretagne e l'Italia 1943–45*, Rome, 1979.

Thompson, Geoffrey H., *Front-Line Diplomat*, London, 1959.

Toscano, Mario, *Dal 25 luglio all'8 settembre*, Florence, 1962.

Toscano, Mario, *Origini diplomatiche del Patto d'Acciao*, Florence, 1964.

Trials of the Major War Criminals, Nuremberg, Washington, 1950.

Trionfera, Renzo, *Valzer di marescialli: 8 settembre '43*, Milan, 1979.

Varsori, Antonio, 'Italy, Britain and a Separate Peace 1940–1943'. *Journal of Italian History*, vol. 1, no. 3, Florence, 1981.

Varsori, Antonio, 'Aspetti della politica Inglese', *Nuova Antologia*, Florence, 1983.

Waley, Daniel, *British Public Opinion and the Abyssinian War, 1935–6*, London, 1975.

Weizsacker, Ernst von, *Memoirs*, Chicago, 1951.

Wheeler-Bennett, J. W., *The Nemesis of Power: The German Army in Politics 1918–1945*, London, 1953.

Woodward, E. L., *British Foreign Policy in the Second World War*, London, 1970–76.

Zangrandi, Ruggero, *1943: 25 luglio–8 settembre*, Milan, 1965.
Zanussi, General Giacomo, *Guerra e catastrofe*, Milan, 1964.

UNPUBLISHED WORKS

Inskip, Sir Thomas, Diaries (lodged at Churchill College, Cambridge).
Malone, Henry, 'Adam von Trott – The Road to Conspiracy. Against Hitler.'
   D. Phil thesis, University of Texas, 1980.
McCaffery, John, 'No Pipes or Drums'.

Sources

Initials and numbers refer to papers in the Public Record Office, Kew, with the following exceptions:

1 *DBFP* refers to the printed documents on British Foreign Policy 1919 to 1939, published by Her Majesty's Stationery Office.

2 *DGFP* refers to Documents on German Foreign Policy 1918 to 1945 from the archives of the German Foreign Ministry, published by Her Majesty's Stationery Office.

3 FRUS refers to the printed documents of the US Foreign Office known as *Foreign Relations United States*, published by the US Government in Washington. There are several volumes for each year.

References in the text to Neville Chamberlain's diaries and letters come from the Chamberlain Archives, University of Birmingham. They are not listed individually except where a Chamberlain letter comes from a PRO file.

Italian Collection refers to Italian State Papers which have been photocopied and retained in the Library at St Antony's College, Oxford.

The full Cadogan diaries are at Churchill College, Cambridge. They do not contain much that is not printed in *The Diaries of Sir Alexander Cadogan 1938–1945*, edited by David Dilks. I refer to them as Cadogan Diaries.

CHAPTER ONE

1 Hollis, *Italy in Africa*; Mockler, *Haile Selassie's War*.
2 *DBFP*.
3 HMSO CMD 4827. 'Statement Relating to Defence', March 1935.
4 *DBFP*.
5 *ibid*.
6 Avon, *Facing the Dictators*.
7 *DBFP*.
8 Cab. 63/50. *DBFP*.
9 *DBFP*.
10 *ibid*.
11 Thompson, *Front-Line Diplomat*.
12 Thompson, *op. cit*. The minutes on his talks with Guarnaschelli and Vitetti at Stresa are in FO 401/35 and his memorandum printed in *DBFP* vol. 14, series 2.
13 *DBFP*.

14 Thompson *op. cit.*
15 Dell, *The Geneva Racket 1920–39.*
16 Roskill, *Hankey, Man of Secrets*, vol. 3.
17 *DBFP.*
18 *ibid.*
19 *ibid.*
20 Avon, *op. cit.*
21 *DBFP.*
22 *ibid.*
23 Interview, March 1983.
24 Mario Toscano in Sarkissian (ed.), *Studies in Diplomatic History.*
25 Templewood, *Nine Troubled Years.*
26 FO 371/19163.
27 Guariglia, *Ricordi 1922–1946.*
28 Avon, *op. cit.*
29 Guariglia, *op. cit.*
30 *DBFP*, for Maffey Report (Appendix to vol. 14, series 2).
31 Waley, *British Public Opinion and the Abyssinian Civil War, 1935–6;*
    Griffiths, *Fellow Travellers of the Right.*
32 Cab. 23/82.
33 Cab. 21/411; FO 371/19123.
34 FO 401/35.
35 *ibid.* (Committee of Five Report).
36 Aloisi, *Mia attivita a servizio della pace.*
37 Cab. 23/82; 48/38; FO 371/19155; FO 371/19159.
38 FO 371/29222.
39 Cab. 23/83; 48/35/2; FO 371/19154.
40 *ibid.*
41 FO 401/35; Cab 16/136.
42 FO 371/19157.
43 FO 371/19164; FO 371/19186.
44 FO 371/19160.
45 *ibid.*
46 *DBFP.*
47 FO 371/19165; FO 371/19164.
48 FO 371/19165; Cab. 16/136.
49 Jones, *Diary with Letters, 1931–1950.*
50 FO 371/19163.
51 FO 371/19164.
52 *ibid.*
53 Cab. 24/257; Cab. 25/282.
54 Parker in *English Historical Review*, vol. 89, 1974.
55 Cab. 24/257.
56 FO 371/19168; Cab. 24/257.
57 Cab. 23/82.
58 FO 371/19168.

59 CMD 5044, HMSO.
60 Waley, *op. cit.*
61 *DBFP.*
62 *ibid.*; Mack Smith, *Mussolini.*
63 FO 371/19168; Cab. 23/82; Cab. 23/90.
64 Cab. 23/90; *DBFP*; FO 410/13.
65 Guariglia, *op. cit.*

CHAPTER TWO

1 Cab. 23/83; Carlton, *Anthony Eden.*
2 *DBFP.*
3 *ibid.*; Cab. 23/83.
4 *DBFP.*
5 FO 371/19887.
6 Cab. 24/261; François-Poncet, *The Fateful Years.*
7 Cab. 24/261.
8 Prem 1/194.
9 FO 371/19887; Prem 1/194.
10 Prem 1/194.
11 Jones, *op. cit.*
12 FO 371/20166; FO 371/20472; Cab. 23/84; FO 371/20181.
13 Cab. 27/622.
14 FO 371/20181; Avon, *op. cit.*; Cab. 23/84.
15 Jones, *op. cit.*
16 Nicolson, *Diaries and Letters*; Griffiths, *op. cit.*
17 *DBFP.*
18 Cadogan Diaries.
19 Cab. 27/622–5. (Cabinet Committee on Foreign Policy).
20 *DBFP*; Prem 1/261.
21 *ibid.* For Gentleman's Agreement, see Seton-Watson in *Fascist Challenge and Policy of Appeasement.*
22 Harvey, *Diplomatic Diaries.*
23 The archives containing the material leading up to Eden's resignation are full. They can be found *inter alia* in FO 954/13; Cab. 23/93; Prem 1/276; Cadogan's and Harvey's diaries; Chamberlain's diaries and papers; Ciano's diaries; Grandi, *25 luglio–40 anni dopo.* The Avon papers are in FO 954, the Halifax papers in FO 800/307–28.
24 *DBFP.*
25 Prem 1/276; Avon papers.
26 Prem 1/276.
27 Harvey, *op. cit.*
28 Cadogan Diaries.
29 FO 954/13.
30 Prem 1/276.
31 Avon, *op. cit.*; Cadogan Diaries; Prem 1/276; FO 954/13.

32 Prem 1/276.
33 Cab. 32/130.
·34 Carlton, *op. cit.*

CHAPTER THREE

1 Conversation, 1984.
2 Grandi, *op. cit.*
3 Telford Taylor, *Munich: The Price of Peace.*
4 Cab. 27/623; Cadogan Diaries.
5 Cab. 27/623; *DBFP.*
6 Cab. 27/623.
7 Cadogan Diaries.
8 *DBFP.*
9 *ibid.*
10 *New York Times*, 15 May 1938; Middlemas, *Diplomacy of Illusion.*
11 *DBFP; DGFP* (series D, vol. 2, Czechoslovakia).
12 FO 800/309; *DGFP, op. cit.*
13 *DGFP. op. cit.*
14 *ibid.*
15 *DBFP.*
16 *DGFP. op. cit.*
17 *ibid.*
18 Ritter, *The German Resistance*; Wheeler-Bennett, *The Nemesis of Power*; Gisevius, *To the Bitter End*; Hassell, *The Hassell Diaries 1938–1944.*
19 *DBFP.*
20 *ibid.*
21 Ritter, *op. cit.*; Gisevius, *op. cit.*
22 *Trials of the Major War Criminals, Nuremberg.*
23 Cadogan Diaries.
24 Astor, in *Balliol Record*, 1982.
25 Prem 1/266A; Cab. 17/646; Cab. 23/95; Telford Taylor, *op. cit.*
26 FO 371/27141–5 and Prem 1/266A cover Chamberlain's trips to Berchtesgaden, Godesburg and Munich. Telford Taylor, *op. cit.*, covers these events in great detail using the British archives.
27 *DBFP.*
28 Dell, *op. cit.*
29 *DBFP.*
30 Dell, *op. cit.*
31 *DBFP.*
32 *ibid.*

CHAPTER FOUR

1 Cab. 23/95.

2 *DBFP*, Telford Taylor, *op. cit.*

3 Inskip Diary.

4 FO 371/27141; Cab. 27/264.

5 *DBFP.*

6 FO 371/27141–5; Madge and Harrison, *op. cit.*; Middlemas, *op. cit.*

7 *DBFP.*

8 Cadogan Diaries.

9 *DBFP.*

10 Middlemas, *op. cit.*; Harvey, *op. cit.*

11 *ibid.*

12 Cab. 23/95; Prem 1/226; Cab. 53/41.

13 *DBFP.*

14 Cab. 27/246; 23 September 1938.

15 Cab. 23/95; Cab. 27/646.

16 *DBFP.*

17 Cab. 27/646.

18 Telford Taylor, *op. cit.*; Schmidt, *Hitler's Interpreter.*

19 *DBFP.*

20 *ibid.*

21 *ibid.*

22 *ibid.*

23 Telford Taylor, *op. cit.*; Cadogan Diaries; Strong, *Intelligence at the Top.*

24 *DGFP*, *op. cit*; *DBFP*; Telford Taylor, *op. cit.*

25 Cab. 53/47.

26 *DBFP.*

27 Cab. 50/37.

CHAPTER FIVE

1 Madge and Harrison, *op. cit.*

2 *DBFP.*

3 Cab. 27/624; Petrie, *Twenty Years' Armistice – and After.*

4 *ibid.*

5 Cab. 27/93 for Cabinet meetings; 27/624 for secret reports on Germany (January 17 and 25); Deakin, *Brutal Friendship* and Toscano, *Origini diplomatiche del Patto d'Acciao.*

6 *DBFP*; Cab. 27/624.

7 FO 371/21665.

8 Letter from Mallet, October 1984.

9 *DGFP.*

10 *DBFP.* Cab. 27/624.

11 Middlemas, *op. cit.*; Telford Taylor, *op. cit.*

12 Telford Taylor, *op. cit.*

13 Cab. 23/98; Cab. 23/99.

14 Cadogan Diaries. Colvin, *Chamberlain's Cabinet.*

15 *DGFP.*

16 *DBFP.*
17 *ibid.*
18 Hassell, *op. cit.*; Gisevius, *op. cit.*; Ritter, *op. cit.*
19 Colvin, *op. cit.*
20 Marshall-Cornwall, *Wars and Rumours of Wars*; Astor, *op. cit.*;
   Marshall-Cornwall's statement of Schwerin's views in *DBFP.* item 269,
   3rd series, vol. 6.
21 Sykes, *Troubled Loyalty* ; Astor, *op. cit.*
22 Schlabrendorff, *Revolt against Hitler*; Gilbert, *Finest Hour*; Astor, *op.
   cit.*
23 *DBFP.*
24 Gisevius, *op. cit.*
25 *DBFP.*
26 Ritter, *op. cit.*; Gisevius, *op. cit.*
27 Dahlerus, *The Last Attempt.*
28 Dirksen, *Moscow, Tokyo, London.*
29 *ibid.*
30 *DBFP*; Prem 1/331.
31 Roberts interview, July 1984; Tennant interview, March 1985.
32 Dahlerus, *op. cit.* His evidence at Nuremberg in *Trials of the Major War
   Criminals.* The Dahlerus book on the last-minute efforts to avert war was
   exhaustively checked by the Foreign Office (File FO 371/39178). It
   proved to be almost exactly in accordance with the facts as known in
   Whitehall.
33 *DBFP.*
34 Dahlerus, *op. cit.*; FO 371/39178.
35 *DBFP*; Dahlerus, *op. cit*; FO 371/39178.
36 *DBFP*; Hassell, *op. cit.*
37 *DBFP.*
38 *ibid.*
39 'Halder's Diaries' – extract reproduced in Shirer, *The Rise and Fall of the
   Third Reich.*
40 Dahlerus, *op. cit.*

CHAPTER SIX

1 Prem 1/331; *DBFP.*
2 Cadogan Diaries.
3 Cab. 66/1.
4 *ibid.*
5 *Trials of the Major War Criminals.*
6 Cab. 66/1.
7 FO 371/23077; FO 371/23131; FO 371/23099; Cab. 66/1 contain the
   British reaction to the German invasion of Poland; FO 371/23131
   (Poland after defeat).
8 FO 371/23097; FO 371/23131.

 9 Prem 1/443.
10 FO 800/328.
11 Dahlerus, *op. cit.*
12 Charles Cruickshank in *War Monthly*, issue 75, April 1980.
13 *ibid.*
14 FO 371/22986.
15 *ibid.*
16 *DGFP*. vol. 18.
17 Interview, 1984.
18 FO 371/26542.
19 FO 800328; FO 800/322; FO 371/26542.
20 Chamberlain's letters about a negotiated peace Prem 1/443; Halifax's
    similar correspondence FO 800/328.
21 Cab. 65/13.
22 FO 800/326.
23 Hassell, *op. cit.*; Cab. 65/11; Ritter, *op. cit.*; Woodward, *op. cit.* vol. 3;
    Deutsch, *The Conspiracy against Hitler in the Twilight War.*
24 FO 800/326.
25 FO 371/24363.
26 Prem 4/100/6.
27 FRUS.
28 The War Cabinet meetings at time of Dunkirk are in Cab. 65/13.
29 Cadogan and Halifax Diaries.
30 Dalton, *The Fateful Years.*
31 FO 800/322 gives a full account of the Butler-Halifax episode. It is also
    covered by Carlgreen in *Sverigis Ultrikspolitik 1939–1945*. I am most
    grateful to Michael Bloch for providing an English translation by his
    cousin Jaske Gelbart.
32 FO 800/322.

CHAPTER SEVEN

 1 FO 371/29938.
 2 FO 371/29927.
 3 FO 371/29938.
 4 *ibid.*
 5 *ibid.*
 6 FO 371/29960.
 7 FO 371/29924.
 8 *ibid.*
 9 FO 371/29924.
10 FO 371/29936.
11 FO 371/29927.
12 FO 371/29936.
13 FO 371/29963.
14 FO 371/29946; the Caviglia denunciation is in the Italian collection at St

Antony's College, Oxford. For the Berne letters re Italian dissidents see Santoni in *Storia Illustrata*, March 1981; and Bandini in *Storia Illustrata*, October 1981. Santoni while at Reading University made an exhaustive examination of the PRO files relating to the opposition in Italy in 1941, as did Varsori.

15 FO 371/29940; Denham, *Inside the Nazi Ring*.
16 *ibid.*
17 *ibid.*
18 Interviews with Denham and Tennant 1985. S. W. Roskill cooperated with Denham in a search in the PRO about Barrow-Green's postwar mission to Italy to discover the truth about the Italian offer to sell the fleet.
19 *Storia Illustrata*, August 1981; Castellano, *Come firmai l'armistizio di Cassibile*; Santoni, *op. cit.*; FO 898/14; For Gui in Stockholm FO 371/32218.
20 Bandini, *op. cit.*; for BBC FO 898/161; Bandini's telephone conversation and letter to author, May 1985.
21 FO 371/29928.
22 FO 371/29922.
23 FO 371/33240.
24 FRUS 1943; Toscano, *Dal 25 luglio all'8 settembre*.
25 *ibid.*; Varsori, 'Italy, Britain and a Separate Peace 1940–1943', in *Journal of Italian History*, vol. 1, no. 3, 1978.
26 Woodward, *op. cit.*
27 Prem 3/242/9; FO 371/37262; McCaffery, 'No Pipes or Drums'.
28 Mockler, *op. cit.*
29 Prem 3/249/9.
30 Cab. 65/37.
31 FO 371/37260.
32 Toscano, *Dal 25* . . . , *op. cit.*
33 *ibid.*
34 Bonomi, *Diario di un anno*.
35 De Luna, *Storia del Partito d'Azione*.
36 FO 371/37260; FRUS.
37 De Luna, *op. cit.*; McCaffery, *op. cit.*
38 De Luna, *op. cit.*; McCaffery, *op. cit.*; Toscano, *Dal 25* . . . , *op. cit.*
39 *ibid.*
40 FO 371/33218.
41 Cab. 65/39.
42 FO 371/33224.
43 FO 371/37260.
44 FO 371/37264; FO 371/37265; Toscano, *Dal 25* . . . , *op. cit.*
45 FO 371/37289.
46 FO 371/37265.

CHAPTER EIGHT

1 FO 371/3726; *Corriere della Sera*, 10 October 1984.
2 Roatta, *Otto milioni di baionette.*
3 FO 371/32623.
4 FO 371/37333.
5 FO 371/37289.
6 FO 371/36283; FO 371/37289; FO 371/37282; FO 371/37799.
7 Harvey, *The War Diaries.*
8 FO 371/37264.
9 FO 371/37266; FO 371/37260.
10 FO 371/37333; McCaffery, *op. cit.*
11 Prem 3/249/5.
12 Castellano, *La guerra continua*; Garland and Smyth, *Sicily and the Surrender of Italy* gives a detailed account of the planning for Giant 2 not to be found elsewhere.
13 Garland and Smith, *op. cit.*; Castellano, *op. cit.*
14 Westphal, *Fatal Decision*; transcript of Westphal's tape is in Castellano, *Roma Kaputt.*
15 Garland and Smyth, *op. cit.*; Castellano, *op. cit.*; Cadorma, *La riscossa;* Monelli, *Rome 1943*; Carboni, *L'armistizio e la difesa di Roma*; Zangrandi, *1943: 25 luglio–8 settembre*; Zanussi, *Guerra e catastrofe*; Castellano, *Roma kaputt* and *La guerra continua*; Trionfera, *Valzer di marescialli: 8 settembre '43.*
16 Cadorna, *op. cit.*; Monelli, *op. cit.*
17 FO 371/37294.
18 *ibid.*; FO 371/37357; Macmillan, *War Diaries* and *The Blast of War.*
19 FO 371/43814. This file contains the Whitehall reaction to the Bari Convention; FO 371/37224 for the P.M.'s remarks re King.
20 Cadogan Diaries; FO 371/43837; FO 371/43814; Woodward, *op. cit.*

CHAPTER NINE

1 Flandin, *Politique française 1919-1940.*
2 Irving, *Hitler's War.*
3 *GDFP.*
4 Prem 4/100/8.
5 Woodward, *op. cit.*; Prem 4/100/8; FO 188/325.
6 Prem 4/100/8.
7 Woodward, *op. cit.*, Hoffmann, *History of the German Resistance 1933–45.*
8 Prem 4/100/8.
9 *ibid.*
10 *ibid.*
11 Interview, July 1984.

12 Prem 3/476/9; Woodward, *op. cit.*
13 Woodward, *op. cit.*; FRUS; Prem 3/476/9.
14 Letter to author 9 August 1984.
15 Interview, July 1984.
16 FO 371/34450.
17 Interview, July 1984.
18 FRUS.
19 Prem 3/197/2.
20 Dulles, *Germany's Underground*; Hassell, *op. cit.*
21 Interview, July 1984.
22 FO 371/39024; Prem 3/197/2.
23 *ibid.*
24 *ibid.*
25 *ibid.*
26 FO 371/39024.
27 Cab. 65/41.
28 FO 371/39024.
29 Prem 3/197/2.
30 *ibid.*
31 Cab. 65/46; footnote re Stalin FRUS.

CHAPTER TEN

1 Prem 3/197/2; FO 954/10.
2 Woodward, *op. cit.*
3 *op. cit.*; FRUS; Churchill, *The Second World War*, vol. 6.
4 Woodward, *op. cit.*; Prem 3/192/2.
4 Interview and letter to author.
6 Woodward, *op. cit.*
7 FO 371/38548.
8 FO 371/38560.
9 FO 371/39083.
10 Prem 3/197/3.
11 Prem 3/195/2.
12 Woodward, *op. cit.*
13 *ibid.*
14 Prem 3/197/3.
15 *ibid.*; FRUS.
16 Prem 3/3.
17 *ibid.*; 3/192/2; 3/196/6.
18 Prem 3/195/2; Prem 3/197/3.

CHAPTER ELEVEN

1 Schlabrendorff, *op. cit.*
2 Balfour and Frisby, *Helmuth von Moltke.*

3 FO 371/22109.
4 Sykes, *op. cit.*; Malone, 'Adam von Trott'.
5 Jasper, *George Bell, Bishop of Chichester*.
6 FO 371/33055.
7 Balfour and Frisby, *op. cit.*; Ritter, *op. cit.*; Bell in *Contemporary Review*, 1945.
8 FO 371/30912.
9 *ibid.*
10 t'Hooft, *Encounter*, September 1969; Rothfels, *The German Opposition to Hitler*.
11 Visser t'Hooft's visit FO 371/30912.
12 Van Roijen, *Encounter*, September 1969.
13 FO 898/412.
14 Prem 4/100/8.
15 Balfour and Frisby, *op. cit.*; conversation with Balfour, 1985.
16 Prem 3/193/6.
17 Balfour and Frisby, *op. cit.*
18 t'Hooft, *Encounter, op. cit.*
19 Dulles, *op. cit.*
20 Sykes, *op. cit.*
21 FO 371/34462.
22 FO 371/34449.
23 Sykes, *op. cit.*; Malone, *op. cit.*
24 FO 371/39137.
25 FO 371/34449.
26 FO 371/39220.
27 Dulles, *op. cit.*
28 FO 371/39065.
29 *ibid.*
30 FO 371/39080.
31 *ibid.*
32 Bowra, *Memories 1898–1939.*
33 FO 371/30912.
34 Interview with O'Neill, 1984.
35 Interview with Carleton Green, 1985.
36 Gisevius, *op. cit.*; Ritter, *op. cit.*; Schlabrendorff, *op. cit.*
37 Butler, *Amateur Agent*; Denham, *op. cit.*; interview with Tennant, 1985.
38 FO 371/39059.
39 *ibid.*
40 FO 371/39087; FRUS.
41 FRUS.
42 FO 371/39087.
43 The memorandum is in the Ecumenical Institute, Sweden. For Stockholm FO 188/460; FO 371/39087.
44 Letter to author from Rt. Hon. David Owen, MP, enclosing papers from Foreign and Commonwealth Office.

45 FO 371/39132.
46 FO 371/39087.
47 FO 371/39077.
48 Gisevius, *op. cit.*; Ritter, *op. cit.*; Schlabrendorff, *op. cit.*; FRUS;
     interview with Otto John, March 1985.

CHAPTER TWELVE

1   Irving, *Hitler's War*.
2   Bargatzky Memorandum in Hoover Library, Stanford University;
     Bargatzty articles in *Frankfurter Allgemeine*, 14 July 1984 and 2
     November 1984.
3   Speidel, *Invasion 1944*; *DGFP* ; Otto John, *Falch und Zu Spatt*; Irving,
     Trail of the Fox.
4   Gisevius, *op. cit.*; Ritter, *op. cit.*; Schlabrendorff, *op. cit.*; Speidel, *op. cit.*
5   Bargatzky Memorandum, *op. cit.*; Schlabrendorff, *op. cit.*; Schramm,
     Conspiracy amongst Generals.
6   Letter to author, October 1984.
7   FRUS; FO 371/39024.
8   Article by Hugh Cole in *Time*, 25 June 1945; Irving, *op. cit.*
9   FO 371/39062.
10 Letter Carleton Greene to author. The Eden memorandum to Churchill
     after the Bomb Plot is on FO 371/30912. PWE Directive FO 371/39077;
     Balfour, *Propaganda in War 1939–45*.
11 Letter Strauss to author, December 1984.
12 Quoted by Schlabrendorff and other German writers.
13 *ibid*.
14 Bryant, *Triumph in the West*.
15 Interview 1985.
16 Interviews October 1984.
17 Interview November 1984; Mussolini and Hassell Italian Collection, St
     Antony's College, Oxford.
18 Letter October 1984.
19 *DGFP*.
20 Cadogan Diaries.
21 Conversations with various survivors.
22 FO 954/1; FO 371/39254.
23 Letter Archduke Otto to author; FO 800/1; Prem 4/33/5.
24 FO 371/34453.
25 Letter Archduke Otto to author.
26 FO 371/39087.
27 FO 371/39088.
28 FO 371/34447.
29 Bielenberg interview.
30 FRUS.

31 *ibid.*; FO 371/39086.
32 FO 371/35178; Prem 3/197/1.
33 Cadogan Diaries.
34 Letter von Hammerstein to author.

Index

Index